TOURISTS of HISTORY

TOURISTS of HISTORY

Memory,

Kitsch, and

Consumerism

from

Oklahoma City

to

Ground Zero

MARITA STURKEN

Duke University Press   Durham and London   2007

© 2007 Duke University Press

All rights reserved

Printed in the United States of America on acid-free paper ♾

Designed by Heather Hensley

Typeset in Monotype Garamond by Newgen-Austin

Library of Congress Cataloging-in-Publication Data appear
on the last printed page of this book.

p. ii: photo by Alberto Zanella

For Dana

CONTENTS

ACKNOWLEDGMENTS

I began working on this book in 2000, long before I saw it as a book, and the intricate connections that drive its narrative took time to emerge into view. Along the way, I have been guided, prodded, challenged, and encouraged by many people, whose many conversations and suggestions have given it more depth and complexity. I could never have written this book alone, nor have I.

Among those who helped the most to shape this manuscript and to challenge me to make my arguments relevant were my two readers, George Lipsitz and Erika Doss. Erika's input has been invaluable—wise, insightful, and precise. I am very grateful for her generous advice and the carefulness with which she approached this project. My debt to George Lipsitz is so immense I feel I can never thank him enough. For his rigor, his insights, his demand that scholarship make a difference, and his extraordinary generosity, I am deeply grateful. Sarah Banet-Weiser read many of these chapters, often on short notice, and her generous and insightful input made it a more coherent book. I have also been aided immensely by the work of several research assistants, in particular Deborah Hanan, who did a fabulous job pulling together initial research for me, and Carolyn Kane, who is largely responsible for the rich group of images assembled here and who was so impressively resourceful. Courtney Hamilton did preliminary research for me what now seems like light years ago, and her work was important in helping me to shape this project. Kari Hensley was immensely helpful in the final stages.

Throughout the past six years I have given many talks on this material that provided me with immensely helpful feedback, questions that challenged me to think more deeply, queries about things that I had overlooked, and very rich conversations: at Keele University; Occidental Collage; the Norman Lear Center at the University of Southern California; the Between War and Media conference at the Maison Franco-Japonaise in Tokyo; Sweet Briar College; the University of Aberdeen; Northwestern University; the University of California, San Diego; in Japan at the Japanese American Studies Association conference, Doshisha University, the Center for Pacific and American Studies at the University of Tokyo, Kwansei Gakuin University, and Meiji University; the Clinton Institute for American Studies at the University College Dublin; Forest Lawn Museum; the International Communication Association conference; the American Studies Association annual meeting; the Society for Cinema and Media Studies conference; the Conference on Urban Trauma and the Metropolitan Imagination at Stanford University; the Institute for the Humanities at the University of Texas, Austin; the American Studies Department at California State University, Fullerton; University of Wisconsin, Madison; University of Regensberg; Martin Luther University, Halle-Wittenberg; the University of Maryland, College Park; the Cultural Studies Association; the Technologies of Memory in the Arts conference at Radboud University, Nijmegen; the Cultural Memory Group at Columbia University; the University of Pennsylvania; and the University of California, Berkeley. I am grateful to Geoffrey White and Setha Low for inviting me to speak at the American Anthropology Association and to Lisa Yoneyama, Thomas Csordas, and Rubie Watson for their thoughtful responses. I would also like to thank in particular Evan Carton, Laurie Beth Clark, Liam Kennedy, Udo Hebel, and Scott Bukatman, whose invitations to speak were part of larger conversations.

I have benefited greatly from input from and conversations with Marianne Hirsch, Leo Spitzer, Lynn Spigel, Sherry Millner, Ernie Larsen, Douglas Thomas, Ann Chisholm, Ed Linenthal, David Sloane, George Sanchez, Amy Kaplan, Lauren Berlant, Bill Brown, Amelia Jones, Toby Miller, and Alison Trope. Joanna Hefferen and John Epstein have been immensely supportive friends, as have Giovanna Di Chiro, Kara Kirk, Joanne Ross, Ella Taylor, Barbara Osborn, and John Drimmer.

Parts of chapters 4 and 5 are derived from my essay "The Aesthetics of Absence: Rebuilding Ground Zero," published in *American Ethnologist*, 31.3 (2004): 311–25, © 2004 by the American Anthropological Association. My thanks to two anonymous readers and to Virginia Dominguez for her wise input on this essay. A preliminary essay that fed into chapter 4 was published by the Social Science Research Council in *Understanding September 11* (New York: New Press, 2002). I am grateful to Craig Calhoun and Paul Price for asking me to begin thinking about these issues in the wake of 9/11. I also benefited a great deal from the conversations I had with my students at the University of Southern California that fall 2001, in particular my graduate seminar in cultural studies. The doctoral scholarship of Cynthia Willis and Jinee Lokaneeta has informed my own work. During the time I worked on this manuscript, I had the great pleasure of working with a wonderful group of people on *American Quarterly*—I learned so much through my collaborations with Raul Villa, Katherine Kinney, and Barry Shank, and during my time at *AQ* my life was made possible by the impressive work of Hillary Jenks and Michelle Commander.

At the University of Southern California, my work was supported in important ways by my colleagues; my thanks go in particular to Dean Geoffrey Cowan, Sandra Ball-Rokeach, and Larry Gross. At New York University, Ted Magder has helped to make life in New York possible, and I am grateful for ongoing conversations with Brett Gary, Sue Murray, Alex Galloway, Nick Mirzoeff, and Carlo Lamagna. My thanks to Dean Mary Brabeck and Assistant Dean Joan Malczewski for the generous funding that provided the illustrations for this book. At the Oklahoma City National Memorial, I benefited greatly from conversations with Kari Watkins, Heidi Vaughn, and Helen Stiefmiller, and in particular Jane Thomas. My thanks to Hans Butzer for sharing his insights about city renewal and the politics of memorials. For their help in securing image permissions, my thanks to Ellen Fisher at the Ad Council and Brandon Noble at Max Protetch Gallery, as well as to the many artists and designers who allowed us to reprint their images. At Duke University Press, Ken Wissoker has been a steady supporter of this book, a model of patience and savvy. Courtney Berger has guided it through the process with great skill and unflappable efficiency. Thanks to Mark Mastromarino for skillfully overseeing its production and to Judith Hoover for wrestling my prose into shape.

My parents, Robert and Marie Sturken, have been a source of steady support through the years, interested readers and consistent cheerleaders, for which I am deeply grateful. Carl and Cheryl-Anne Sturken have been generous in so many ways. My sister, Barbara Peterson, read many pages and offered lots of encouragement, and in sharing his experience of 9/11, my brother-in-law, Bill Peterson, has helped me to understand some things about survival. Kelly and Kyra Sturken, Leigh and Moira Peterson, and Maya Taylor are all inspirations in their creativity and uniqueness. Leo-Andres Polan, who arrived as this book was in press, is a source of joy and wonder.

Dana Polan is the kindest and smartest person I know. He also has a great sense of humor. My life is so enriched by his presence and his companionship. It is to him that I dedicate this book.

INTRODUCTION

Two snow globes sit on my desk. The first depicts the Oklahoma City National Memorial set against several tall buildings of downtown Oklahoma City, surrounded by snow and topped with an American flag. It is stamped with the logo of the memorial along with the slogan "On American Soil" and reads "The Spirit of This City and This Nation Will Not Be Defeated. Our Deeply Rooted Faith Sustains Us." The second is a plastic snow globe pencil holder that contains a miniature of the twin towers of the World Trade Center standing next to an oversized St. Paul's Chapel with a police car and a fire truck sitting before it. When the globe is shaken, bright moons and stars float around the towers. It is labeled, "World Trade Center 1973–2001."

Each of these objects is a souvenir, purchased at and taken away from a site of tourism. I bought the Oklahoma City National Memorial snow globe at the official gift shop of the Oklahoma City National Memorial, and I purchased the World Trade Center snow globe from a street vendor selling wares at a temporary table next to Ground Zero in lower Manhattan. Whether part of a formal or of an informal economy, each globe is an indicator of the elaborate consumer networks of mass-produced goods that exist in American culture around events of national trauma.

Both of these objects display their urban settings within insulated, bubble-like worlds. I can hold each in my hand.

FIGURE 1. World Trade Center snow globe.

They thus depict these symbolic sites as miniature worlds. The effect of the miniature is to offer a sense of containment and control over an event; the very objectness of these snow globes narrates particular stories about the Oklahoma City bombing and the destruction of the World Trade Center. Their miniature worlds are not simply small, they are also animated. When shaken, the globes come alive with the movement of snow and stars, each offering a kind of celebratory flurry that then settles back again. We look into the world of each globe as if looking from a godlike position onto a small world.[1]

Both of these snow globes are also about marking time. The Oklahoma City snow globe does not actually contain the date of the Oklahoma City bombing, which was April 19, 1995, but it is labeled as a first edition from 2002, with a limited production run of fifteen hundred pieces. It depicts a time of renewal that marks the aftermath of the bombing in which the Oklahoma City memorial is set against the rebuilt skyline of the city. The World Trade Center snow globe notes the dates of the "life span" of the building and captures it in a mystical temporal moment: the towers remain stand-

FIGURE 2. Oklahoma City National Memorial snow globe.

ing and unscathed though the emergency vehicles that signal the towers' demise are already present.[2] Snow globes are objects that, like photographs, represent a "permanent instant" in which time is arrested, yet they are also objects in which that instant is meant to be in constant replay.[3] One is encouraged to "visit" a snow globe on a regular basis, absentmindedly giving it a shake in a moment of distraction. Each globe indicates the ways these events remain in memory, in the image of Oklahoma City as a rebuilt city and of New York as frozen in the moment of crisis. A snow globe also offers a sense of time as a return: the scene always returns to the way it was before the snow flurry. The comfort of the snow globe derives in part from this expectation that it returns each time to its originary state.[4]

I see these two objects as emblems of the ways that American culture processes and engages with loss. Both are mass-produced and labeled "Made in China." Both thus form part of the elaborate global economic networks that produce objects of American patriotism (including the vast majority of small American flags, which are made in Korea and China). Each object exemplifies the complex relationship of mourning and consumerism and the economic networks that emerge around historical events, including events of trauma. Each object could also be seen as a form of kitsch. Were I creating a collection to explain the aim of this book, I would include along with these snow globes a piece of the rubble from the federal building in Oklahoma City that was distributed in informal networks, a bottle of water branded with the name of the Oklahoma City National Memorial, a mangled steel beam from the World Trade Center, a roll of duct tape, an FDNY teddy bear, a security bollard, one of the "Hoosier Hospitality" T-shirts that was sold at the execution of Timothy McVeigh, a 9/11 medallion that reads "Freedom is never free," and a design to rebuild the twin towers as two large lattice towers. Each evokes to some degree the consumerism of trauma, fear, and security and the closely woven relationship of loss to tourism and kitsch.

Tourists of History explores the complex intersection of cultural memory, tourism, consumerism, paranoia, security, and kitsch that has defined American culture over the past two decades and the ways that these cultural practices are related to the deep investment in the concept of innocence in American culture. My aim in looking at these practices and tendencies in American culture is to delve into the question of how they are directly related to the broad political acquiescence of the American public and the national tendency to see U.S. culture as somehow distanced from and unimplicated in the troubled global strife of the world. This book asks: What aspects of American culture specifically encourage a "tourist" relationship to history? How can the tourist be seen as an icon of how American culture relates to, processes, and consumes history? How is national mourning in the United States caught up in practices of consumerism? How is American memorialization repackaged as tourist practices and cultural reenactment? How does this politics of memory and emotion help to enable particular notions of innocent victimhood and a consumer culture of comfort?

Tourists of History examines these aspects of American culture at the end of the twentieth century and the beginning of the twenty-first, an era marked by two events in particular, the Oklahoma City bombing on April 19, 1995, and the terrorist attacks of September 11, 2001, which resulted in plane crashes at the Pentagon and in Shanksville, Pennsylvania, and the destruction of the World Trade Center in New York City. It is in seeing the connections between the Oklahoma City bombing and 9/11, which have both been defined as unique and exceptional events, and the interconnections of the social contexts that produced each that I hope to be able to make sense of a broader set of trends in American culture. This time period also includes the Columbine shootings, in which two students, Dylan Klebold and Eric Harris, killed twelve of their classmates and a teacher before killing themselves at their high school in Littleton, Colorado, on April 20, 1999. Importantly, the time period framed in this book both precedes and continues after these two events. The Oklahoma City bombing took place in 1995, but it was the result of a long-festering relationship between right-wing militia groups and the federal government fueled by economic changes such as the failure of family farms that had dramatically affected the Midwest and Plains states starting in the 1980s and several high-profile violent encounters between right-wing extremists and federal authorities. The terrorist attacks of 9/11 produced a frenzied consumer response to the fear of terrorism, enabling a widespread consumerism of security, yet this sense of threat had its precedence in what Barry Glassner has termed a "culture of fear" in the United States during the 1980s and 1990s.[5]

From the distant perspective of some future time, history will show how the 1990s and the early-twenty-first century are understood as a period of American history. Yet, in the midst of this time, it is hard not to see it as a particularly charged moment in American history, a time of extremist beliefs, intense polarization, dramatic economic shifts, and volatile political battles as well as a time of accelerated cultural responses, of an increased blur between the image and the material, between civic life and consumer life, and between fear and denial. It is also a historical moment when the United States has been a key player in global violence that is spiraling out of control. While the 1990s was a decade when paranoid beliefs about the U.S. government circulated among extremist groups and in mainstream politics and popular culture, the post-9/11 period is defined by a widespread fear of terrorist attack and an increased culture of security. Though they are rarely seen on a continuum, these two fears mirror one another and build on one another in important ways. Fear defines this time, and responses to fear, in particular consumer responses to fear, mark its moment in history.

The cultures of fear and paranoia that I examine in this book, which pervade all aspects of domestic life, are the driving forces behind a broad range of consumer practices of security and comfort. This comfort culture, with its attendant politics of affect, undergirds the tourism of history in

American culture. It can be found in everything from the small souvenirs that promise reassurance at sites like Ground Zero and the Oklahoma City memorial to the culture of domestic consumerism that sells soft hues and traditional wood furniture as signs of comfort, to the marketing of SUVs and Hummers as machines that will protect the American family. Cultures of comfort are complex and not easily reduced to unexamined consumerism, yet they are absolutely essential to providing a sense of reassurance that mediates the fraught, painful, and difficult world in which the United States finds itself at this moment in history. Much of the culture of comfort functions as a form of depoliticization and as a means to confront loss, grief, and fear through processes that disavow politics. This feeling of comfort is intricately related to U.S. patriotic culture. The experience of patriotism and nationalism is reassuring and comforting; it feels good to feel patriotic because it provides a sense of belonging. Consumer culture exists on a continuum with national identity and is a highly influential factor in the political agency and engagement of consumer-citizens. Thus, an American public can acquiesce to its government's aggressive political and military policies, such as the war in Iraq, when that public is constantly reassured by the comfort offered by the consumption of patriotic objects, comfort commodities, and security consumerism.

One of the primary examples of this comfort culture that I discuss throughout this book is the teddy bear. While teddy bears have a long history in American culture since the time of Theodore Roosevelt, they have emerged as particular kinds of icons in the past two decades. No context of loss seems to be complete today without teddy bears with particular insignia. This started in the beginning years of the AIDS crisis in the early 1980s, when people began to give teddy bears to people who were sick with AIDS, and the teddy bear has been increasingly deployed as a commodity of grief since that time. Over the course of the late twentieth century, teddy bears were made larger and less like actual bears, their arms sewn in permanently outstretched poses as if asking for a hug.[6] It is important to note that this recent consumerism of teddy bears is aimed not at children but at adult consumers, and it carries with it the effect of infantilization. These teddy bears are thus primarily objects that are intended to provide comfort to people, to convey the message that one can and will feel better. It is notable that after the events of 9/11, many organizations distributed teddy bears in New York City. In the first days after the attacks, when the Salvation Army organized to help people who were returning to the city after being evacuated to places like New Jersey, they greeted them with teddy bears.[7] Later, the Oklahoma City National Memorial sent six hundred teddy bears and then the state of Oklahoma sent sixty thousand stuffed animals to New York, which were distributed to children in schools affected by 9/11, family support organizations, and New York fire stations.[8]

The belief in the teddy bear as an object of comfort, for both adults and children, is thus quite strong. What is such a bear understood to offer when one gives it to someone who is traumatized or grieving? It embodies the recognition of pain and it offers, above all, the promise of empathy, companionship, and comfort. An FDNY teddy bear promises to comfort us as we confront the terrible loss of life suffered by the New York Fire Department at the World Trade Center on 9/11, and perhaps to convey the sense that we are not alone in feeling this sadness. Similarly, the feeling of comfort provided by an Oklahoma City memorial teddy bear reminds visitors of the children who died there and aims to allow visitors to leave the memorial feeling positive about the good that the bombing brought out in the people who suffered loss, rather than to come away concerned by what the bombing meant. Importantly, the teddy bear doesn't promise to make things better; it promises to make us feel better about the way things are.

Comfort culture and the consumerism of kitsch objects of emotional reassurance are deeply connected to the renewed investment in the notion of American innocence. This investment, which has a long and complex historical legacy, has emerged in particularly visible ways in relation to the contemporary culture of fear. American national identity, and the telling of American history, has been fundamentally based on a disavowal of the role played in world politics by the United States not simply as a world power, but as a nation with imperialist policies and aspirations to empire.[9] This disavowal of the United States as an empire has allowed for the nation's dominant self-image as perennially innocent. The imperialist and unilateralist ventures of the U.S. government at this moment in history (ventures that are the reason the United States is a target for terrorist retribution) are shored up in part by the capacity of Americans to see themselves as innocent and passive victims, rather than aggressors, in relation to world politics. Terrorism functions by targeting people who are not directly responsible for the wrongs being addressed, and thus by creating innocent victims. In the aftermath of both the Oklahoma City bombing and 9/11, the tragedy of the deaths of these innocent bystanders were then exploited in ways that used innocent victimhood as justification for further violence (or, in the case of

FIGURE 3. FDNY teddy bear.

Oklahoma City, for legislation that would restrict the rights of prisoners). The figure of the innocent victim is contradictory in American culture because of its implication of weakness, and this often necessitates the rewriting of victims in contexts like 9/11 into narratives of heroism.

Historically, the American public has been marshaled to support wars of aggression with the justification that it is under threat. Thus, the 1991 Gulf War was justified on the basis of the "defense" of national security, and on the eve of the U.S. invasion of Iraq, an unprovoked attack on a country that had had no involvement in the terrorist attacks on 9/11, Americans were distracted from considering the consequences of the impending war by a national preoccupation with defending the domestic home by purchasing emergency supplies, plastic sheeting, and duct tape. The popular fear of reprisal for the war became quite easily part of the justification for that war, one sold on the (false) claim that Iraq was a direct threat to the defense of the

FIGURE 4.
Oklahoma City
National Memorial
teddy bear.

United States. Innocence is a position from which such acts of aggression are easily screened out. I see this position as a kind of *tourism* of history.

TOURISM

The tourist is a figure who embodies a detached and seemingly innocent pose. In using the term "tourists of history" I am defining a particular mode through which the American public is encouraged to experience itself as the subject of history through consumerism, media images, souvenirs, popular culture, and museum and architectural reenactments, a form of tourism that has as its goal a cathartic "experience" of history.[10] I am not concerned with those contexts in which people visit sites of established historical and entertainment tourism, such as Williamsburg and Disneyland, so much as I am concerned with the *subjectivity* of the tourist of history, for whom history is an experience once or twice removed, a mediated and reenacted experience, yet an experience nevertheless. Tourists *visit* sites where they do not live, they are outsiders to the daily practices of life in tourist destinations, and they are largely unaware of the effects of how tourist economies have structured the daily lives of the people who live and work in tourist locales. Tourists typically remain distant to the sites they visit, where they are often defined as innocent outsiders, mere observers whose actions are believed to have no effect on what they see.

Tourism is a central activity in the experience of modernity, in which leisure practices are a crucial counterpart to the world of industrial and postindustrial work. In his classic study *The Tourist*, Dean MacCannell writes that the tourist is the essential identity of modern society: "Our first apprehension of modern civilization . . . emerges in the mind of the tourist," and the "best indication of the final victory of modernity over other sociocultural arrangements is not the disappearance of the nonmodern world but its artificial preservation and reconstruction in modern society."[11] In this context, native rituals are staged for tourists, and now-lost cultures are consumed by tourists in artificial settings that allow the histories of those cultures' destruction to be obscured.[12] MacCannell argues that the tourist is a primary subject position available to modern citizens.

Of course, there are many different modes of tourism today, and the actual practices of particular tourists may vary a great deal from this definition. My aim is to consider how this subjectivity of the tourist can serve as a metaphor for the ways American citizens are encouraged to situate themselves in relationship to history, and in particular to world history. The mode of the tourist, with its innocent pose and distanced position, evokes the American citizen who participates uncritically in a culture in which notions of good and evil are used to define complex conflicts and tensions. The mode of the tourist can be a easily seen in the decision to drive a Hummer because it is a "safe" vehicle and to purchase security equipment for one's home in the event of terrorist attack, while believing that those consumer decisions are disconnected from the U.S.-led war in Iraq. The mode of the tourist can also be seen in the purchasing of souvenirs at sites of loss such as Ground Zero as a means of expressing sorrow at the lives lost there, without trying to understand the contexts of volatile world politics that produced the attacks of 9/11.

The idea of a tourist is often caught up in notions of authenticity and inauthenticity. Thus, tourists visit places that are understood to be authentic in part because they see their own world as an inauthentic (modern) one; at the same time, the activity of tourism is usually regarded as an inauthentic activity, one that often must be apologized for. MacCannell writes that most critics of tourism criticize tourists not because they leave home to travel elsewhere but "for being satisfied with superficial experiences of other peoples and other places."[13] Contemporary tourism, in particular high-end tourism, is preoccupied with tourist experiences that seem to be beyond this reproach, such as exotic tourism, ecotourism, extreme tourism, war tourism, "tragic tourism," and the "dark tourism" of visiting places of death and destruction, such as former concentration camps and war sites.[14] Many forms of contemporary tourism can be said to be guided by a self-consciousness about the potential superficialities of everyday tourism. Yet, as I have stated, my aim here is not to discuss contemporary practices of tourism in this full range of engagements, but to use the traditional notion of the tourist as a metaphor to make sense of how American culture succeeds in creating a depoliticized and exceptionalist relationship to the broader issues of global history and politics.

Sites of collective trauma are seen as having a particular kind of authenticity and are often the focus of tourist activity. A site like Ground Zero in lower Manhattan, for instance, embodies competing and powerful meanings of authenticity: the authenticity of a site of violence, a place that contains the remnants of a much-photographed building, a place where the dead were not found, a place where iconic images of spectacle took place. The visits of tourists to places such as Ground Zero and the site of the Oklahoma City bombing are acts that intend to create a connection between the tourist and the site of trauma. By visiting these places, tourists can feel that they have experienced a connection to these traumatic events and have gained a trace of authenticity by extension. In the contemporary context of global consumerism, tourism can often take on the meaning of a pilgrimage. In its traditional meaning of a religious journey to a sacred site, the term "pilgrimage" implies personal transformation. And it can be said that people make pilgrimages to sites of tragedy in order to pay tribute to the dead and to feel transformed in some way in relation to that place. In such places as the Oklahoma City National Memorial and Ground Zero, the practices of sorrowful pilgrimage and tourism are intermixed and often inseparable; one can cry and take pictures, leave a personalized object, and purchase a souvenir. It hardly needs to be stated that for those who survived the tragic events at each site, the option of tourism is not available.

Tourism is also guided by media practices. Media coverage of tourist destinations is key to tourist activity, and increasingly sites of media, such as the locations where television shows and films are shot, have become tourist sites.[15] As tourists, we deploy media when we take photographs and videos in order to produce image artifacts of tourist destinations; indeed, picture taking is one of the most universal and central activities of tourism. Tourism is also defined by the activity of taking things away from the places we have visited, not only photographs but also commodities such as curios, souvenirs, and artifacts. These objects convey in turn a connection or attachment to a place.

These factors—the search for authenticity, the role of images and media, the practices of consumerism, and the distanced proximity of the tourist—are all key to my argument that American culture's relationship to memory and mourning can be defined as a tourism of history. Each enables a sense of innocence and detachment yet provides a means to feel one has been authentically close to an event, that one has experienced it in some way. In these sites of tourism, history is understood to be something that is consumed and experienced through images, memory is thought to reside in commodities such as teddy bears, and memorials are accompanied by gift shops.

My focus in this book is on aspects of cultural memory, in particular the debates about memorialization that have taken place around events of national trauma, and the ways in which memories, both individual and collective, have been circulated through the cultural responses to those events. However, I am using the term "tourists of *history*" (rather than "tourists of memory") to signify that this tourist subjectivity has a problematic relationship to the weight, burdens, and meanings of history. It is my intent to call attention to how American cultural responses to traumatic historical events enable naïve political responses to those events. They do this precisely because these cultural responses allow American history to be seen in isolation, as exceptional and unique, as if it were not part of the rest of world history and as if it were something simply to be consumed. Sites of American history, including Gettysburg, have had long histories of consumerism and commercialism.[16] This book's focus on recent sites of tourism builds on a long history in American culture in which there is an established relationship between consumerism and memory, between commercialism and national identity, and between marketing and the symbols of the past.

I use the framework of the tourism of history in order to understand how sites of loss can enable a sense of innocence and particular kinds of politically naïve responses. I am not interested in simply dismissing tourist practices and the purchasing of kitsch souvenirs as activities that are superficial and meaningless; I want to understand how certain kinds of tourist practices, broadly defined, enable people to make sense of their grief. Yet, I don't feel that the model of cultural analysis that sees such cultural practices as people "making do" with the symbols at hand tells us very much about what happens politically at such places. It may be that the purchasing and display of an Oklahoma City National Memorial teddy bear allows one to feel a connection to and sadness about those who lost their lives in the bombing and to process one's own grief. The promise of the teddy bear is that it will help to heal those most directly affected by trauma—that it will be able to make them feel better. But such a teddy bear also disables certain kinds of responses. It is not a versatile object that can be employed for a range of responses; it is a circumscribed object precisely because of the message of sentimentality and reassurance it offers. However overstated this may sound, such a teddy bear is ultimately not an innocent object.

Such seemingly innocent objects point to the underlying political implications of the tourism of history. The distanced and mediated ways that U.S. citizens engage with global terrorism and the vast discrepancies of wealth and opportunity around the world continue to create an increasingly volatile political context that will only enable more violence. Tourism is about travel that wants to imagine itself as innocent; a tourist is someone who stands outside of a culture, looking at it from a position that demands no responsibility. I examine how the practices of tourism and consumerism both allow for certain kinds of individual engagement with traumatic experience yet, at the same time, foreclose on other possible ways of understanding national politics and political engagement.

I examine tourism at sites of memory at a moment when the United States has been preoccupied with questions of memory. The period since the early 1980s has been a time of unprecedented national focus on cultural memory and nationally sanctioned remembrance. This current obsession with memory follows a period when American culture was largely disinterested in memory. While World War I produced a culture of memory in the early twentieth century, most of it regretful and concerned that such violence and destruction not be repeated, it was followed by the national sense of triumph of World War II, which subsumed any mourning of the dead into a nationalist narrative that continued through the affirmation of American consumerism in the postwar years of cold war politics. Even the social upheaval of the 1960s was rarely understood in terms of loss or memory. Yet, the fallout of the 1960s, in particular the tragic consequences of the Vietnam War, brought cultural memory into the forefront of national consciousness. With the construction of the Vietnam Veterans Memorial in 1982, it seemed as if the mourning and memory that had been held in check were suddenly released in a national embrace of remembering. Out of this emerged not only the construction of many memorials—including the Korean War Memorial, the U.S. Holocaust Museum, the Franklin Delano Roosevelt Memorial, the Oklahoma City National Memorial, and the World War II Memorial—but also an intense and highly volatile debate, replete with conspiracy theories and culture wars, about how twentieth-century American history has been officially told or mistold, remembered or forgotten.

This culture of mourning and memory has converged with the concepts of healing and closure that are central to American national identity. American mythology clings tenaciously to the belief that one can always heal, move on, and place the past in its proper context, and do so quickly. The memorial culture of the United States has thus been largely experienced as a therapeutic culture, in which particular citizens, primarily veterans and their families, have been seen as coming to terms with the past and making peace with difficult memories. This is the primary narrative generated by the Vietnam Veterans Memorial.

This belief in the concept of healing is related to the dominance of U.S. consumer practices, in which consumerism is understood to be a kind of therapy. Throughout American history, consumer culture has also played a central role in the shaping of concepts of citizenship and national identity. From its very early origins, American culture constructed itself around particular concepts of choice and individual reinvention. Indeed, recent scholarship asserts that an interest in consumerism was key in fueling even as fundamental an event as the American Revolution.[17] American consumer culture emerged with tremendous force in the late nineteenth century hand in hand with a new consumer-friendly set of values. As the historian T. J. Jackson Lears has argued, the "therapeutic ethos" of the late nineteenth century and early twentieth replaced the social mores of Protestant scarcity, thriftiness, and saving with an embrace of self-fulfillment and spending in the name of individuality, and this new ethos helped to usher in the emerging consumer society.[18] In many ways, consumer culture replaced the central role of the family and the church as the new modern American citizens imagined themselves to be less tied to the past and capable of reinvention. The American embrace of consumerism has taken hold in powerful and irreversible ways since the late nineteenth century, ways that have ultimately joined the practice of citizenship with the practice of consumerism. As I discuss in chapter 1, Lizabeth Cohen defines the postwar equation of citizenship and consumerism as the emergence of a "consumers' republic" in which consumerism, rather than social policy, is seen as the means through which to achieve social ideals.[19] In the contemporary context, government authorities speak to Americans in the language of consumerism more than the language of citizenship, inciting us every day to do our part for the national economy by spending our money, buying cars and houses, and accumulating debt on credit cards. Indeed, Americans are almost always spoken to as citizen-consumers.

Consumerism thus forms one of the primary sites of what Michael Billig calls "banal nationalism," those moments when nationalism is "flagged" at citizens, in the mundane modes of everyday practices.[20] These so-called unremarkable practices of nationalism incorporate national identity into the gestures of everyday life. Consumer culture offers banal nationalism via patriotic trinkets and commodities that incorporate national symbols and national brands. I also examine those moments when nationalism is specifically and deliberately flagged through consumerism in times not of banality but of exception. For instance, in the midst of the national crisis after 9/11, U.S. political figures, including New York mayor Rudolph Giuliani and President Bush, appealed to American citizens to help the country emerge from the crisis not by volunteering or working in their communities, but by going out to spend money. In the post-9/11 context as well, grief and loss over the tragedy of lives lost was often transposed in patriotic messages of revenge. The equation of patriotism with consumerism not only reveals the paucity of national identification in the United States, with its ready-made symbols and disconnection from history, but also demonstrates the central role that innocence plays in U.S. culture.

INNOCENCE

The self-image of the United States as innocent has been key to national identity throughout much of American history. This belief in innocence affirms the image of the United States as a country of pure intentions to which terrible things can happen, but which itself never provokes or initiates attack. This aspect of American national identity has a long and complex history and finds its very roots in the narratives that guided the emergent nation. David Noble notes that American exceptionalism is rooted in the image of the United States as a virtuous nation, distinct from and embattled by corrupt European nations. Yet, Noble points out that this notion of U.S. innocence finds its roots in many European strains of thought.[21]

Virtually every traumatic event of twentieth- and twenty-first century U.S. history, from Pearl Harbor to the Vietnam War to 9/11, has been characterized as the moment when American innocence was lost. Thus, the immediate analogies made to Pearl Harbor after 9/11 were predominantly about connecting to a previous narrative of innocence in which the United States was subject to unprovoked attack and taken unaware, as if these events were unanticipated and unforeseen. Similarly, the cold war was dependent on a belief in U.S. innocence in the face of communist threat. This investment in reaffirming innocence not only functions to mask U.S. imperialist policies, and the history of the United States as an active history of empire, but also obscures the degree to which violent conflict has been a fundamental aspect of U.S. society.

Both the Oklahoma City bombing and the Columbine shootings were occasions to affirm particular myths about the historical lack of violence in American society. These events were framed in the media as shocking because they were examples of "home-grown" violence in places that were thought to be exempt from violence (a midsize midwestern American city and a middle-class, white suburb). Oklahoma City and Littleton, Colorado, were also seen as places that were more emblematic of an ostensibly innocent American culture than cities where violence is understood as a part of the fabric of daily life. Narratives of innocence thus emerged in relation to both events, narratives that helped to perpetuate the myth that American society is not violent, despite the dominance of gun culture and the high numbers each year of deaths from gun violence; despite the violence of late twentieth-century U.S. involvement in the wars in Southeast Asia, Central America, and the Middle East; and despite the racial violence that has deeply marked U.S. history.

The comparison of the terrorist attacks of 9/11 to Pearl Harbor also evokes a "loss of innocence" narrative about being attacked on home soil. This narrative helped to affirm the jolted response after 9/11, as if the rest of the world had suddenly come into view for the American public, the anger of that world suddenly in focus. At the same time, the narrative of innocence enabled the U.S. response to avoid any discussion of what long histories of U.S. foreign policies had done to help foster a terrorist movement specifically aimed at the United States and its allies; thus the historical disavowal of American empire (in this case, U.S. policies in the Middle East) allows U.S. global interventions to be understood in a framework of benevolence rather than imperialism. This innocent narrative can be neatly summed up in the constant refrain of government officials in the days after 9/11, when they asked, "Why do they hate us?," as if such hatred were so unprovoked as to be unthinkable. This refrain allowed the Bush administration to marshal the rhetoric "They hate us because we love freedom" not only to justify its attacks on the Taliban in Afghanistan, but also to facilitate its argument for invading Iraq, a country that had not attacked us but that hated us nevertheless (that hatred now translated into threat). However simplistic this rhetoric sounds after the fact, it was profoundly effective in closing down post-9/11 debate. The media proclamations in the post-9/11 months that the attacks demanded an "end to irony" reveal that this investment in innocence is often dependent on a negation of ironic distancing or critique. In other words, innocence is something created after the fact, rather than an original condition to be recaptured. It is essential to the discourse of American innocence that it is reasserted with each national crisis, and thus by implication that it is understood to be restored and reaffirmed after each ensuing crisis.

As a narrative based on seeing violence as a force that comes from outside, the innocence narrative also cannot sustain the presence of insiders, so-called home-grown terrorists, who use guns and bombs not for self-defense but deliberately to kill innocent civilians. The existence of the militia movement and the actions of former soldier Timothy McVeigh, like the existence of the Abu Ghraib photographs that exposed the abuse of Iraqi prisoners by American soldiers in the Iraq War, disrupt the narrative of American innocence, and need to be contained. In the case of Columbine, containment took the form of blaming popular culture, which could be seen to have tainted and corrupted formerly innocent boys. In Oklahoma City, the counternarrative took the form of ascribing evil to bomb suspect McVeigh and erasing his former military past. This designation of evil did not demand explanation; it was presented as a quality that came organically from nowhere—certainly not from American culture. Both contexts smoothed over the influence of gun culture within the United States. For Abu Ghraib, the narrative of a "few bad apples" was deployed to avoid any analysis of the systemic role of the abuse and the government sanctioning of torture.

My focus in this book is on the relationship that practices of consumerism have to this maintenance of the idea of innocence, and how this sense of innocence undergirds the tourism of history in American culture. The dominant role played by the United States in global capitalism is mediated by protectionist policies and concepts that portray consumerism as an isolated rather than a global activity. A belief in the global marketplace (with its attendant neoliberalism) is accompanied by a set of narratives about the U.S. consumer as an innocent bystander to the destructive aspects of that marketplace (global sweatshops, loss of domestic jobs to outsourcing, economically driven illegal immigration). David Noble writes:

> The promise of the international marketplace is a regime of perpetual peace. A continuing irony, however, is that one must be prepared for perpetual war to achieve the goal of peace. The culture of international capitalism seems, therefore, to be deeply divided. Within this culture one is asked to accept the rational working of the natural laws of the marketplace, but one is also encouraged to develop a personality that is stronger and more aggressive than that of the leaders of the "rogue" states. One must always be ready to make the sacrifices demanded by war."[22]

Yet, the innocence-driven pose of domestic consumerism prevents the notion of sacrifice from standing in the way of post-9/11 consumerism. As I discuss in chapter 1, one of the distinguishing aspects of national discourse in the first few months after 9/11 was the entreaties by government officials for citizens not to sacrifice but to consume. Similarly, the war in Iraq was sold to Americans as a war that would demand of them no sacrifices, a fiction that has necessitated the attempted erasure of the more than three thousand American war dead, the many tens of thousands of wounded soldiers, and the actual costs to American taxpayers and to social systems.

Notions of national innocence are fragile and need constant maintenance in order to be sustained. We find that maintenance manifested in many places, including popular culture, tourism, and kitsch. Thus, the narrative of innocence is crucial to what I see as the kitschification of cultural memory in American culture.

KITSCH

The tourism of history is intimately caught up in the production and consumption of kitsch. At this moment in history, U.S. culture can be defined as a particular mix of sentimental excess and irony, a naïveté as well as a knowing wink; in such a context, kitsch thrives. As I examine throughout this book, sites of memorialization are now places where kitsch objects proliferate and offer easy formulas for grief, and teddy bear culture proliferates across many contexts. In addition, at both Oklahoma City and Ground Zero, kitsch was a key aesthetic in many of the proposed memorial and architectural designs.

The term "kitsch" emerged in the mid-nineteenth century in Germany as a description of an aesthetic that was seen as banal, trite, predictable, and in bad taste.[23] Thus, the original meanings of the term defined it as an outcome of mass culture and situated kitsch in relation to the emergent mass production of modern culture.[24] The word itself is derived from the German *verkitschen*, meaning "to cheapen"; Hermann Broch's pivotal 1933 essay on kitsch negatively referred to those who relish kitsch as "kitschmensch" or "kitsch men."[25] Kitsch is often associated with cheapness in terms of cost and production, as well as the idea that such cheap things are without any cultural refinement or taste. Mass production is a key component in this definition of kitsch, since these objects have no relationship to craftsmanship. Yet, a kitsch aesthetic is hardly restricted to cheap, mass-produced objects. Matei Calinescu notes that many objects that constitute kitsch, while they may be inexpensive, are intended to suggest richness in the form of imitation gold and silver, and that luxury goods can often be seen as kitsch in style.[26] Similarly, high-end design can often engage in a kitsch form of sentimentality.

Kitsch was thus initially associated with a set of social factors that accompanied modernity: the rise of mass culture, the sense of alienation that accompanied the shift to industrialization and urbanization, and the widespread commodification of daily life. Calinescu writes that kitsch "has a lot to do with the modern illusion that beauty can be bought and sold" and that "the desire to escape from adverse or simply dull reality is perhaps the main reason for the wide appeal of kitsch."[27] This sense of easy formulas and predictable emotional registers which form a kind of escapism is essential to most definitions of kitsch.

Debates about kitsch in the context of modernity have often focused on distinctions between high and low culture and between art and mass culture. Clement Greenberg's famous 1939 essay, "Avant-Garde and Kitsch," set up a clear contrast between kitsch and art: "Kitsch is mechanical and operates by formulas. Kitsch is vicarious experience and fake sensations. . . . Kitsch is the epitome of all that is spurious in the life of our times. Kitsch pretends to demand nothing of its customers except their money—not even their time."[28] It is not incidental to this critique of kitsch as innocent and naïve taste that kitsch is an important aesthetic for children's cultures. Thus, the cute cultures of children's aesthetics form a continuum with the cute cultures of adult kitsch.[29]

When accusations of kitsch have emerged in relation to 9/11 and Oklahoma City, they have echoed these critiques of kitsch as mass culture. The assumption is that when someone uses a mass-produced commodity such as an Oklahoma City or World Trade Center snow globe as a means of mourning, he or she is engaging in bad taste, and that this is a superficial way of responding to loss. Yet, kitsch objects, with their prescribed emotional content, are often quite spontaneously mixed with objects that are understood to be more personalized and individual. A memorial shrine at a place like Shanksville, Pennsylvania, or along the fence that surrounded the destruction of the federal building in Oklahoma City is likely to have a huge variety of objects with many different aesthetics, including teddy bears, T-shirts, Hallmark cards, handwritten notes, and flowers.

Thus, in the context of memory and loss, kitsch can often play a much more complex role than the mass-culture critique of kitsch allows for. Celeste Olalquiaga writes about melancholic kitsch and nostalgic kitsch as two distinct kinds of memory kitsch that demonstrate the needs that feed into the consumption of kitsch: "Kitsch is the attempt to repossess the experience of intensity and immediacy through an object. Since this recovery can only be partial and transitory, as the fleetingness of memories well testifies, kitsch objects may be considered failed commodities." Olalquiaga notes that kitsch is a crucial aspect of the mystical nature of the aura, as well as its destruction: "This is why kitsch may be seen as the debris of the aura: an irregular trail of glittery dust whose imminent evanescence makes it extremely tantalizing." For her, nostalgic kitsch is a form of remembrance that smoothes over the intensity of the experience of loss, selecting the "acceptable parts" of an event and consolidating them into a memory that can forget the original intensity of a traumatic experience of loss, whereas melancholic kitsch, in the form of souvenirs, sustains the sense of existential loss.[30]

The kitsch of memory thus functions in a particular way in relation to loss. Memory kitsch is deeply related to tourism. Tourist art has always had a relationship to the production of kitsch objects: Eiffel Tower key chains, Mount Rushmore spoon rests, and Tower of London dessert plates—the list is long. In his well-known essay "On Collecting Art and Culture," James Clifford maps the art–culture split in relationship to how authenticity is awarded to art and cultural objects. Tourist art is categorized, along with commodities and curios, as the lowest form of culture: "not-art" and "inauthentic."[31] Tourist art is a "fetish for the past," according to Ludwig Geisz, in which "the past is trapped within the souvenir."[32] This status of inauthenticity makes clear that tourist art is easily dismissible as the kind of cheap kitsch curio that those with taste would not purchase and display in their own homes.

These definitions of kitsch in the context of modern culture inevitably raise these kinds of issues of taste and elitism. The mass culture critiques of kitsch were, in effect, criticisms of lower-class taste, defining it as uncultured. Yet, in the contemporary context of mixing modern and postmodern styles, ironic winking and the cross-class circulation of objects, such critiques carry little meaning. Contemporary kitsch cultures defy simple hierarchies of high and low. Kitsch forms of easy emotionalism can be found in the realms of high art and architecture as easily as in cheap trinkets, and irony, which is often kitsch's antidote, can also be a part of camp's deliberate engagements with kitsch. For instance, as I discuss in chapter 5, several of the high-end architectural proposals for rebuilding Ground Zero were labeled kitsch and seemed to facilitate a kitsch relationship to both history and mourning.

In the context of postmodern culture, understanding kitsch means moving beyond simple definitions of high and low precisely because of the way that kitsch objects can move in and out of concepts of authenticity. Kitsch objects from the past can also be imbued with a kind of playful engagement with history, a kind of humorous pastiche, such as when cold war posters promoting duck-and-cover drills are recoded as home decoration. When an object of the past is labeled kitsch, it can indicate a doubled reading; that is, an object is defined as kitsch when it is seen to have an original aesthetic status that is reread as being tasteless, a lava lamp for instance, but then is recoded as valuable. Daniel Harris refers to the distancing associated with this second stage of kitsch as a "twice-removed aesthetic" that shifts toward irony.[33] Yet, the second stage of kitsch takes time. It is difficult, for instance, to think about purchasing 9/11 souvenirs in order to humorously put them on display next to souvenirs from the 1950s that have gained value because they display tastes of previous eras of popular culture. The challenge to understanding how kitsch operates today is to see the range of responses that it produces, to consider how it can encourage both a prepackaged sentimental response and a playful engagement, simultaneously and to varying degrees, with history, innocence, and irony.

It is kitsch's relationship to political culture that is most important to this book. Most kitsch conveys a kind of deliberate and highly constructed innocence, one that dictates particular kinds of sentimental responses and emotional registers. It is meant to produce predetermined and conscribed emotional responses, to encourage pathos and sympathy, not anger and outrage. People can deploy a range of practices in relation to kitsch objects, yet even when a kitsch object might be used by someone in a nonkitsch way it is rarely an incitement to historical reflection or political engagement. Kitsch does not emerge in a political vacuum; rather, it responds to particular kinds of historical events and indicates particular kinds of political acquiescence. The well-known German critiques of kitsch saw it as an element of the rise of fascism in Nazi Germany, and kitsch has often been associated with a totalitarian or fascist aesthetic. The Nazis were particularly adept at deploying kitsch to create a sense of shared national sentiment, and kitsch is a key element in superficial symbols of national unity. Greenberg wrote, "The encouragement of kitsch is merely another of the inexpensive ways in which totalitarian regimes seek to ingratiate themselves with their subjects. . . . Kitsch keeps a dictator in close contact with the 'soul' of the people."[34] During the cold war, kitsch was the dominant style of totalitarian regimes in the Soviet Union. The dissident Czech writer Milan Kundera famously wrote that it was the function of kitsch to curtain off the abject: "Kitsch is the absolute denial of shit, in both the literal and the figurative senses of the word; kitsch excludes everything from its purview which is essentially unacceptable in human existence." Kundera argues that totalitarian regimes use kitsch to sell the idea of a "brotherhood of man." In a well-known passage he states:

> Kitsch causes two tears to flow in quick succession. The first tear says: how nice to see children running on the grass!
>
> The second tear says: how nice to be moved, together with all mankind, by children running on the grass!
>
> It is the second tear that makes kitsch kitsch.
>
> The brotherhood of man on earth will be possible only on a base of kitsch.[35]

A kitsch object can thus be seen not only as embodying a particular kind of prepackaged sentiment, but as conveying the message that this sentiment is one that is universally shared. When this takes place in the context of politically charged sites of violence, the effect is inevitably one that reduces political complexity to simplified notions of tragedy. Thus, the objects produced for the Oklahoma City National Memorial, such as a teddy bear, a cute and cuddly object that is embroidered with an image of the "survivor tree" of the memorial, convey a sense of comfort. That comfort cannot speak to cause; rather, it encourages visitors to feel sadness for the loss of lives in a way that discourages any discussion of the context in which those lives were lost. What makes this object kitsch is precisely its message that this sentiment is shared and that it is adequate. Kitsch is thus a central aspect of comfort culture.

A particular turn toward kitschification has taken place within the past two decades in relation to American politics and social movements. This first became obvious in relation to the AIDS epidemic. In the 1980s and early 1990s, AIDS organizations and advocates began to produce a broad array of kitsch objects in the form of teddy bear gift items, sympathy cards, posters, and a broad array of AIDS-related merchandise, much of it sold to provide funds for nonprofit AIDS organizations. That this kitsch culture, with its preestablished codes of sentiment and symbols, was counterbalanced by a radical and biting array of AIDS art and activism was fitting. It was through kitsch that the mourning for the AIDS dead was effectively mainstreamed. It was understood in the AIDS community that this kitsch was a strategic means to raise awareness and funds, but it was not without consequences. The demand of this culture was for an innocent victim who could be integrated into the American mainstream. Daniel Harris, who wrote a well-known essay about AIDS kitsch, states:

> AIDS is vulnerable to kitsch in part because of the urgent need to render the victim innocent. In order to thwart the demonization of gay men, activists have attempted to conceal sexual practices that the public at large finds unacceptable behind a counter-iconography that has the unfortunate side effect of filling the art and writings about AIDS with implausible caricatures of the victim as a beseeching poster child.[36]

Thus, AIDS kitsch produced a childlike, innocent victim of AIDS, one stripped of sexual meaning. It also produced, hand in hand with a pop psychology ethos, a demand that AIDS patients make peace with their disease, act like saints, and adhere to a set of emotional registers that smoothed over anger and defiance within a realm of empathy and comfort.

The kitschification of AIDS signaled something that was in some ways new, a particular kind of production of kitsch that served as a means for political movements to claim their place within the nation. The merchandising of AIDS kitsch started a trend that was taken up by activists working on breast cancer, producing what is commonly referred to now as "breast cancer culture." Breast cancer fundraising and awareness campaigns have produced a merchandising culture of kitsch, beginning with ubiquitous pink ribbons and numerous teddy bears and mushrooming into a cornucopia of products such as pink ribbon candles, pins, brooches, scarves, coffee mugs, and lingerie (much of it produced by women who are themselves breast cancer survivors). The cheerful, embrace-your-survivor-status-by-purchasing-comforting-teddy-bears tone of much of the breast cancer movement was rocked by a November 2001 *Harper's* essay by Barbara Ehrenreich about her own experience with breast cancer. Ehrenreich accused this culture of "pink kitsch" of infantilizing women and encouraging them through popular psychology models to negate their own anger: "Possibly the idea is that regression to a state of childlike dependency puts one in the best frame of mind with which to endure the prolonged and toxic treatments. Or it may be that, in some versions of the prevailing gender ideology, femininity is by its nature incompatible with full adulthood—a state of arrested development. Certainly men diagnosed with prostate cancer do not receive gifts of Matchbox cars." She goes on to describe the pink ribbon culture as a cult or religion, in which "the products—teddy bears, pink-ribbon brooches, and so forth—serve as amulets and talismans, comforting the sufferer and providing visible evidence of faith."[37] Still, the marketing of breast cancer awareness has continued to expand, producing recently a Pink Ribbon Barbie, marketed by Mattel as a means to "celebrate the incredible strength, beauty and resilience of women" and for mothers to connect with their daughters.[38] Ehrenreich argues that this pink kitsch culture forecloses on what should be an orchestrated anger at the lack of research into environmental causes and what she calls the "Cancer Industrial Complex."

The kitschification of disease that is evident in AIDS and breast cancer activism forms a direct lineage to the kinds of comfort cultures that have emerged in relation to national traumas such as the Oklahoma City bombing and 9/11. These more recent kitsch cultures have profound political consequences. Hal Foster notes that in the post–cold war context, totalitarian kitsch has migrated to American culture:

> we are surrounded by "beautifying lies" of the sort noted by Kundera—a "spread of democracy" that often bolsters its opposite, a "march of freedom" that often liberates people to death, a "war on terror" that is often terroristic, and a trumpeting of "moral values" often at the cost of civil rights. . . . The blackmail that produces our "categorical agreement" operates through its tokens. For instance, in support of the "war on terror" are the decals of the World Trade Center towers draped with Stars and Stripes, the little flags that fly on truck antennas and dot business-suit

labels and the shirts, caps and statuettes dedicated to New York City firemen and police. . . . [39]

I would argue, following Foster, that kitsch is the primary aesthetic style of patriotic American culture, indeed that American political culture can be defined by and thrives on a kind of kitsch aesthetic. As Kundera writes, "No one knows [kitsch] better than politicians. Whenever a camera is in the offing, they immediately run to the nearest child, lift it in the air, kiss it on the cheek. Kitsch is the aesthetic ideal of all politicians and all political parties and movements."[40] The banality of kitsch is deeply integral to banal nationalism. In the United States, kitsch is the dominant political style of a nation that is deeply wedded to an abstract notion of populism which is distinct from the people, a sense of populism that is so kitschy that it can be easily inhabited by a president who is a member of the elite.

The kitschification of events such as the Oklahoma City bombing and 9/11 allows for, if not facilitates, the means by which these events can be exploited for particular political agendas and incorporated into a continuum of kitsch political discourse. Kitsch objects address consumers within a particular emotional register (including sympathy, sadness, comfort, and the reassurance of cuteness). On one hand, these objects skirt anger, since they are couched in terms of empathy and reassurance; on the other hand, many of them were effectively deployed in the first months after these events in declarations of vengeance. These forms of consumer culture enable a political acquiescence, in which consumers signal their "categorical agreement" through the purchase of tokens. When tokens such as teddy bears are circulated as "universal" symbols of comfort they provide a means to participate in Kundera's image of the universal second tear of emotion. The teddy bear says, We are innocent, and, by extension, the nation is innocent too. The kind of teddy-bearification of the nation that we see in the wake of the Oklahoma City bombing and 9/11 thus transposes the comfort of the teddy bear to the nation itself.

It is this relationship of sentiment to the idea of universal emotions shared by all of mankind, Kundera's second tear, that gives kitsch a broader political meaning. This form of kitsch taps into the belief in a national sentimentality, which, according to Lauren Berlant, is "a rhetoric of promise that a nation can be built across fields of social difference through channels of affective identification and empathy." She adds, "Sentimental politics generally promotes and maintains the hegemony of the national identity form, no mean feat in the face of continued widespread intercultural antagonism and economic cleavage."[41] Sentiment is the glue that holds the fragile and dispersed nation together. A kitsch image or object not only embodies a particular kind of prepackaged sentiment, but conveys the message that this sentiment is universally shared, that it is appropriate, and, importantly, that *it is enough*. When this takes place in the context of politically charged sites of violence, the effect is inevitably one that reduces political complexity to simplified notions of tragedy.

The kitschification of American political culture and of cultural memory is not uncontested, of course. As I discuss throughout this book, irony as a form of self-consciousness often works in tension with kitsch to speak to consumers and citizens in complex forms of address. Discussions of kitsch inevitably raise the question of where kitsch's boundaries lie and what it means when kitsch embodies a self-consciousness. While mass production is a key factor in contemporary kitsch, in part because of the set of iconographic codes that are easily repeatable from one object to another, handcrafted and personalized objects and images can easily be kitsch in form. In my discussions of kitsch, I show the ways kitsch forms restrict emotional registers and participate in comfort culture. This does not mean that I do not think citizen-consumers should not be comforted in the face of these sites of tragedy, but rather that we must look carefully when that comfort comes as a kind of foreclosure on political engagement.

TRAUMA AND REPETITION

Reenactment is a key feature of much kitsch. As I noted, my World Trade Center snow globe reenacts the moment of emergency and magically places the twin towers whole among objects that signal their demise. As I discuss in chapter 5, many of the proposals for rebuilding lower Manhattan engaged in various kitschy forms of reenactment of 9/11. In this book I consider the relationship between trauma and reenactment and between trauma and kitsch. Reenactment of dramatic events is a staple of popular culture in the form of television programs, documentaries, and feature films. I do not analyze those reenactments here, but rather focus on the reenactment of still photographs, tourist souvenirs, and architectural design. These often overlooked forms of reenactment are key to understanding how compulsive repetition is a response to trauma.

Theories of trauma, which are for the most part about individual psychology, are often based on a set of binary categories that define the traumatic state and its "integration." Freud believed that the compulsion to repeat was a mode through which most people would act out, rather than remember, their childhood dynamics and traumatic experiences. For Freud, patients need to work through their resistances to seeing the distinction between the present and the past in order to move beyond compulsive repetition.[42] In psychoanalysis, compulsive repetition occurs when subjects are traumatized to the extent that they repeat their moment of trauma over and over again and are unable to either narrativize it or move beyond it to make it a memory. The *work* of confronting traumatic memories is thus understood to give them representational and narrative form and to integrate them into one's life story.[43] In these theories, compulsive repetition is a state of nonintegration, a disabling form of stasis, and it is narrative integration that produces the *memory* of the traumatic event. More recent analyses of trauma demonstrate that repetition can be a central part of the processing of a narrative of trauma. In her compelling book about her own experience as a survivor of rape and assault, *Aftermath: Violence and the Remaking of a Self*, the philosopher Susan Brison writes that survivors often attempt to "master the trauma" by repeatedly telling the story of it:

> Whereas traumatic memories (especially perceptual and emotional flash-backs) feel as though they are passively endured, narratives are the result of certain obvious choices (e.g., how much to tell to whom, in what order, etc.). This is not to say that the narrator is not subject to the constraints of memory or that the story will ring true however it is told. And the telling itself may be out of control, compulsively repeated. But one can control certain aspects of the narrative and that control, repeatedly exercised, leads to greater control over the memories themselves, making them less intrusive and giving them the kind of meaning that enables them to be integrated into the rest of life.[44]

Brison argues that the construction of a narrative, and its repetition and refinement, allow for a "remaking" of the self.

Brison's argument shows the inadequacies of a binary theory that opposes repetition with the working through and narrative coherence of trauma, precisely because it is often the compulsive repetition of a narrative that allows for someone to feel some form of agency over the story of his or her own trauma. The idea of "working through" trauma, which implies the emergence of a new state of being in which the effects of trauma are properly managed, raises numerous questions and has been debated and contested across many fields of study. Given the transformative nature of the experience of trauma itself, what does it mean to "successfully" work through the memory of a traumatic experience? Is a working-through an integration or a smoothing over, a forgetting or a reckoning, erasure or recuperation?

These questions have been raised in relation to individual subjects, yet I am interested in analyzing what it means to consider these concepts in relation to how a culture, if not a nation, responds to traumatic events, analyzing the implications of cultural reenactment of trauma. I examine the forms of repetition that can be seen in architectural designs, tourist souvenirs, and the remaking of iconic images in order to consider what this reenactment produces, accomplishes, and enables.

This is a moment in history when what is enabled in the name of trauma demands examination. Twentieth-century history was dominated by the power awarded to those traumatized by the experience of world war; the past sixty years have shown the powerful ways in which survivors of historical events have been defined as primary figures of authenticity in cultures, like the United States, that often contain a pervasive sense of inauthenticity. In a culture in which authenticity is a quality that is endlessly striven for yet never achieved, the status of the trauma victim or survivor gains particular force, one that can allow for a broad range of political consequences. Over the past few decades, American culture has been preoccupied with the concept of the survivor, to the extent of producing a culture of survivor envy. Popular psychology has promoted the idea that we are all survivors to some extent, and a culture of victimhood has been prevalent in U.S. popular culture. In addition, in the context of the victims' rights movement, which I discuss in chapter 3, an embrace of victims and survivors has had broad effects in the legal system.

Both the Oklahoma City bombing and the attacks of 9/11 produced large and vocal groups of survivors and family members; in the case of 9/11, the emergence of this group was accompanied by the quick decision by the government to compensate the families and survivors with large sums of money (the families and survivors of Oklahoma City, by contrast, were not offered compensation). In both cases, the role of victims and families took on broad legal implications. Whereas in Oklahoma City, the families of the victims became involved in a legal debate by intervening into death penalty legislation, in the 9/11 context a small group of families is attempting to use the courts to intervene in the rebuilding of lower Manhattan and the memorial design. The deployment of the Oklahoma City bombing as a tool for stricter enforcement of the death penalty and the use of 9/11 as a means to justify the war in Iraq are only the most recent examples of how narratives of victimization and trauma enable a perpetuation of violence. I am concerned with the question of what gets enabled by the designation of trauma, and how the designation of survivor status awards particular kinds of cultural authority which intersect with the consumerist and kitsch context of trauma tourism.

Reenactment is a crucial factor in the cultural responses to traumatic events within this economy of survivors and consumerism. As I discuss in the chapters that follow, the famous image icons of both the Oklahoma City bombing and 9/11 have been remade again and again, until they appear to convey narratives of redemption. In Oklahoma City, the famous photograph of a firefighter holding a dead child was remade numerous times by artists around the country, in images that increasingly presented it as an image of rescue rather than death. In New York, the absence of the twin towers has promoted a constant reenactment of their twin forms in the city landscape and in the architectural imaginings of how to rebuild Ground Zero. Repetition is a means through which cultures process and make sense of traumatic events. It is caught up in kitsch and the relentless recoding of trauma into popular culture narratives, yet it is also evidence of the ways that cultures reenact, sometimes compulsively, moments of traumatic change.

Reenactments raise the question of the relationship of experience and authenticity. Experience is the category of engagement that is seen to be the most authentic, a primary mode of being that is longed for. Yet, most Americans' experience of the key events of history are mediated ones, whether the experience of watching television footage of the twin towers falling or the experience of reading a book about the survivors of the Oklahoma City bombing or watching a Hollywood film that reenacts the experience of survivors of 9/11.

In the case of highly documented events like the Oklahoma City bombing and 9/11, the vast majority of people who "witnessed" these events did so through media images, by watching television and looking at documentary photographs. Even many people who were in close physical proximity to these events watched them on television rather than in person. It is common to see the effects of these traumatic events on individuals as forming a kind of ring of intensity, echoing outward from those directly effected, such as those who escaped, who were injured, and who survived, to those who lost loved ones and those who were nearby; each step gets further away from "real" trauma. Indeed, in both these events, as attempts to memorialize began, hierarchies of grief and trauma were quickly established. In Oklahoma City there was a debate about the criteria, such as proximity to the building, that could designate someone as a survivor, and in New York there was a common tendency for people to marshal their proximity to the event when talking about it in the weeks and months afterward (when they found out, how many people they knew who were there, how close they were in terms of blocks, etc.).

This is not simply about a competition for proximity. It is more often than not a means of processing an event, of talking about it in order to make sense of one's response to it. The complexity of contemporary media events calls into question the simple equation of physical proximity to a trauma precisely because the media disperses and circulates highly charged images. Nevertheless, cultures tend to create, both officially and informally, hierarchies of grief in order to maintain it bureaucratically (in terms of insurance and compensation, for instance).

Ultimately, cultural reenactment, as well as memory kitsch, lead us to the question of how grief and loss are manifested, made visible, and incorporated into our lives and cultures in times of rupture and trauma. Judith Butler writes that the relationship of grief to vulnerability is essential to understanding the political responses to loss. She argues that close attention to grief, a "tarrying with grief," can be a means to understand the broader political implications of vulnerability:

> Is there something to be gained from grieving, from tarrying with grief, from remaining exposed to its unbearability and not endeavoring to seek a resolution for grief through violence? . . . If we stay with the sense of loss, are we left feeling only passive and powerless, as some might fear? Or are we, rather, returned to a sense of human vulnerability, to our collective responsibility for the physical lives of one another? . . . To foreclose that vulnerability, to banish it, to make ourselves secure at the expense of every other human consideration is to eradicate one of the most important resources from which we must take our bearings and find our way.[45]

It is precisely when kitsch, consumerism, and reenactment aim to smooth over the moment in which grief and loss are powerfully present that opportunities for broader cultural empathy and new ways of response are lost. Even the well-intentioned process of creating a memorial at Ground Zero to provide a place for those suffering loss has been deeply handicapped by a hurrying up of grief, an inability to "tarry" in grief, just as the turn from 9/11 to a rhetoric of vengeance was a rejection of the mode of experiencing loss and staying within it in order to feel the vulnerability it creates in us.

How to understand these kinds of experiences, from reenactment to the consumerism of grief, is one of the primary questions that cultural practices demand of us. My argument aims to move beyond the dismissal of these experiences as cheapened forms of cultural entertainment that let us off the hook, because I believe that such a critique does not allow us to make sense of how repetition and consumerism constitute certain kinds of cultural labor. For instance, one of the children whose firefighter father died on 9/11 spent the next year in kindergarten building the twin towers in blocks and then destroying them, as a means perhaps of attempting to have some power over his grief.[46] In what ways can we see the repetition of images and stories of 9/11 in the same light: as the need to reenact in order to make sense? Similarly, to dismiss the tourism that emerges around sites of mourning is to negate the ways that such tourism, even the purchasing of a souvenir, performs a kind of cultural labor that provides for empathy and connection and that demands interpretation, if for no other reason than that it will help us to understand how the memory of events such as the Oklahoma City bombing and 9/11 get deployed in the context of politics—in the context of the death penalty and the "war on terror."

This returns us to the question of innocence, since it is one of the effects of kitsch and kitsch reenactment that they produce the idea of an innocent culture, one that cannot see its own complicity in the workings of history. The consumer culture of memory helps to affirm a culture of innocent victimhood. This preoccupation with victim status is a paradoxical aspect of American culture; at a time when the United States is the sole superpower, with enormous economic and military power, a nation that is engaged in a long-term imperial political project, its culture is immersed in concepts of innocence and victimhood and a belief in the transcendent power of healing to smooth over history's burdens. The idea that the nation can heal from the wounds of history and achieve closure of some kind is the more insidious version of the belief that victims of violence can find simple closure in rituals of healing. These discourses work effectively to create a national identity that sees itself as exceptional and separated from the rest of the world.

This exceptionalism has a long history, yet it seems to be manifesting now in particularly powerful ways. American exceptionalism defines the nation not only as unique, but as exemplary. Amy Kaplan writes, "A key paradox informs the ideology of American exceptionalism: it defines America's radical difference from other nations as something that goes beyond the separateness and uniqueness of its own particular heritage and culture. Rather, its exceptional nature lies in its exemplary status as the apotheosis of the nation-form itself and as a model for the rest of the world."[47] I believe that this exceptionalism depends on a notion of U.S. innocence at home, a culture of innocence that is enabled by consumerism, fear, and kitsch. It is this culture that I examine in this book.

THE BOOK'S CHAPTERS

This book has five chapters and a conclusion, each of which addresses the issues of consumerism, memory, mourning, and kitsch in overlapping ways. In chapter 1, "Consuming Fear and Selling Comfort," I look at the interrelationship of fear, paranoia, security, and consumerism in the 1990s and the post-9/11 context, and how each helps to shore up the idea that the American citizen exists in a state of innocence. This chapter charts a trajectory from the rise of a culture of fear and of the right-wing militias in American culture in the late 1980s and 1990s to the emergence of the prison industry as an economic force in Middle America to the surge in a consumerism of security in the post-9/11 context. This chapter thus addresses the rise of a domestic military consumerism since 9/11 and the emerging aesthetic of security that governs contemporary consumerism and urban design in order to understand the interlocking roles played by fear and consumerism in American national identity.

Chapters 2 and 3 examine the twin responses to the Oklahoma City bombing: the building of the Oklahoma City National Memorial and the execution of Timothy McVeigh. In chapter 2, "Citizens and Survivors: Cultural Memory and Oklahoma City," I focus on the memorial, which opened in April 2000 and which was the result of an elaborate collaboration of survivors, families, and rescue workers. It is accompanied by a museum which tells a compelling story of the bombing, one defined by an embrace of citizenship, and which houses a gift shop of commodities about the bombing and the memorial. The memorial has been a key factor in the rise of tourism to Oklahoma City and in the urban renewal of its downtown district. In this chapter, I examine how consumerism, survivor culture, and community renewal have converged to produce particular kinds of political responses to the bombing.

Chapter 3, "The Spectacle of Death and the Spectacle of Grief: The Execution of Timothy McVeigh," is concerned with the McVeigh execution and how the media spectacle it produced constitutes a counterpart to the memorial. This chapter examines the media fascination with McVeigh and the culture of celebrity that arose around him as he was on death row and the consumerism that accompanied the execution. I consider the ways that the emphasis on families and survivors at Oklahoma City was translated into a number of legal decisions that will have an impact on the rights of prisoners for some time to come. This chapter ends with a discussion of the renewal of Oklahoma City and the role of the memorial in the city's new image.

The meaning of Oklahoma City was dramatically reconfigured in narratives of American history when the events of 9/11 took place. Chapters 4 and 5 examine the intersections of memory, tourism, and design at Ground Zero in New York. In chapter 4, "Tourism and 'Sacred Ground': The Space of Ground Zero," I look at the contested meanings at Ground Zero and how they exemplify the national response to 9/11. I see these conflicts as the result of conflicting discourses of sacredness, memory, commerce, urban design, and politics that reveal, among other things, the complex ownership, both economic and emotional, that defines the site. This chapter examines the symbolic role played by the dust from the collapse of the World Trade Center, the iconic images of 9/11, and the emergence of tourism as a central aspect of Ground Zero. Chapter 5, "Architectures of Grief and the Aesthetics of Absence," analyzes the architectural and memorial design proposals that reimagine lower Manhattan and the complex and messy debate over its rebuilding. One goal of this chapter is to clarify that seemingly rarefied areas of high culture—in this case, the elite world of celebrity architects—can also be caught up in processes of kitsch and emotional reenactment. I look at the political battles surrounding the proliferation of designs for Ground Zero and the preoccupation with the erasure of the twin towers, both in calls for their reconstruction and the tendency to redesign the site with reenactments of the towers' forms. In this context, architecture has been seen as both a redemptive response and a crass aestheticization of a place of grief. In the conclusion, I situate these issues in relation to a broader global context of consumerism and grief.

Many of the aspects of American culture that this book addresses are ongoing and constantly changing and transforming. The debate over Ground Zero shifts on a monthly basis, and the story of the Oklahoma City bombing and the city's renewal continues to be retold. Yet, the broader questions I pose in this book speak to cultural trends and tendencies that have long histories and will continue to shape American national identity in the future: What does the American dependence on kitsch consumer culture ultimately tell us about American national identity, and how does the deeply ingrained belief in American innocence shape the American worldview? It is the aim of this book to show how the meanings of consumerism, memory, and innocence help shape American national identity, and how that identity can be found in the smallest, seemingly most innocent objects, like a snow globe.

1

CONSUMING FEAR AND
SELLING COMFORT

In the first few months of 2002, the shoe and clothing
designer Kenneth Cole ran an advertising campaign
with the theme "Today Is Not a Dress Rehearsal." Cole is
known for his quirky and often politically inflected advertising campaigns. He stands out among advertisers who deploy social awareness themes in their advertising campaigns
both because he publicly contributes to charities, including
many AIDS support groups, and because he writes the ad
campaigns himself. The "Today Is Not a Dress Rehearsal"
campaign featured a series of ads in which male and female
models dressed in Kenneth Cole clothes and accessories
were posed in domestic settings amid traditional furnishings: a rustic wooden table, a worn leather couch, and so on.
Each image, with its soft hues of beige and brown, was accompanied by a different tagline: "On September 12, People
Who Don't Speak to Their Parents Forgot Why"; "On September 12, Fewer Men Spent the Night on the Couch"; "On
September 12, We Used Protection in the Bedroom, not the
Mailroom." One ad, which features a man's hand touching
a woman's hair, with wedding ring and Kenneth Cole watch
noticeably displayed ("Men's Croco Leather Strap Watch
W/Multi Function Dial $150"), reads "On September 12,
14,000 People Still Contracted HIV."

TODAY IS NOT A DRESS REHEARSAL.
—KENNETH COLE

FIGURE 5.
"On September 12,"
Kenneth Cole ad
campaign, 2002.

Kenneth Cole's "Today Is Not a Dress Rehearsal" campaign was one of the most sophisticated produced in the first months after 9/11. It spoke to the sense of crisis in the moment, and the sense of a necessary rearranging of priorities after the shock of the events of 9/11, a moment when family disputes seemed petty and worth forgetting; it also made reference to the many ongoing world crises that should not be overshadowed by 9/11, such as the AIDS epidemic. In these ways, the campaign resisted much of the exceptionalist rhetoric that defined post-9/11 discourse. Yet the ultimate intent of the Cole campaign was not simply to jolt potential consumers into putting 9/11 in perspective: it was to provide a sense of comfort in the face of fear and loss. The soft colors, muted tones, and scenes of domestic calm are selling warmth and reassurance. At the time, Cole's marketing director stated, "The world was not ready to see another typical fashion ad. Kenneth was very specific about wanting to show a relationship, warmth, humanness—moments most people would actually relate to."[1] By marketing

CHAPTER I

ON SEPTEMBER 12,
14,000 PEOPLE STILL CONTRACTED HIV...

FIGURE 6.
"On September 12,"
Kenneth Cole ad
campaign, 2002.

domestic contentment, these ads are selling the reassurance that one can be socially aware and safe.

The social message of the ads is at times offset by the occasionally jarring elements within them. In one ad, for instance, a young woman lounges on her back on a worn wooden table, eating strawberries from a bowl while a dog eats from a bowl beneath the table. A wallet with dollar bills peeking out at the edges lies next to her on the table and a Kenneth Cole leather bag is slung casually across the chair. In this context, the tagline "Today Is Not a Dress Rehearsal" reads ironically, if not comically: the image conveys not simply comfort but a sense of careless privilege. Writes Richard Stamelman, "We must recognize, as Kenneth Cole has instructed us to do, that fashion is no longer the rehearsal it once was but reality itself. Fashion now articulates, reiterates, and coincides with the reality effect put in force by September 11 itself."[2]

The selling of comfort is a primary aspect of the affirmation of innocence in American culture. While the Cole campaign represents a relatively nuanced manifestation of comfort consumerism, it can be seen in the context of the long history of the marketing of domestic comfort as a means of reassuring the national public of the cohesion of the nation. In the post-9/11 context the selling of national comfort takes on certain implications; in particular, it is a means of erasing subsequent U.S. aggression in Afghanistan and Iraq (the role of those who need comfort erases the role of the aggressors). As a country that has defined itself consistently in relation to an external danger, a country defined by fear (founded and unfounded), the United States has been shaped in many ways by discourses of security, defense, and comfort. One of the primary expressions of this national discourse has been consumerism and the marketing of products to defend the home and to provide domestic simplicity in a world of chaos and threat.

In this chapter, I examine the relationship of consumerism to comfort, innocence, and security as it has manifested in American culture during the 1990s and in the post-9/11 era. How is it that the fear of an enemy and an abstract sense of danger have shaped national identity and notions of citizenship? How have consumer practices helped to enable this discourse of security, defense, and paranoia? It is my aim to make connections between the post–cold war trends of the 1990s (in which the "search" for an enemy to define our national identity took the form of increasingly mainstream paranoid cultures and the rise of a prison state and right-wing militias) and the post-9/11 culture, defined by threat and security concerns. In both these contexts, national identity is constructed through practices of consumerism. This consumerism infuses lifestyles of comfort and security with national meaning and speaks to individual consumers (consumers seeking comfort and reassurance as much as pleasure) as part of the nation.

DEFENDING THE HOME AND HOMELAND

The United States has consistently defined itself in relation to a sense of external threat and as a state that is continuously endangered. David Campbell writes that the "boundaries of a state's identity are secured by the representation of danger integral to foreign policy."[3] He notes that U.S. foreign policy justified the invasion of Iraq in 1990 by articulating Iraq's invasion of Kuwait as a threat to the United States. Thus are imperialist policies expressed through and justified by concepts of security. William Appleman Williams writes that the definition of security in American history has often been synonymous with world control. He notes that Jefferson's doctrine "that the only way to avoid trouble with neighbors is to acquire or dominate them" is "a conception of security that has little to do with strategy and much to do with paranoid acquisitiveness."[4]

Security as acquisition has also been closely allied with the image of the United States as virtuous and pristine in relation to other nations. Campbell states, "The ability to represent things as alien, subversive, dirty, or sick has been pivotal to the articulation of danger in the American experience." Often this has been expressed as a form of paranoia: a powerful nation-state feeling continually under threat (disavowing its own power), seeing danger everywhere. This sense of danger was powerfully manifested during the cold war, when the Soviet Union was a compelling enemy against which fervent forms of patriotism were created. Yet the cold war was not exceptional; that guiding sense of danger, which preceded and has outlasted it, simply crystallized during that time.

This defining sense of danger is inseparable in the United States from a culture of consumerism. Pervading all aspects of public and civic life, consumerism was solidified in the postwar era, helping to establish what Lizabeth Cohen has called the "consumers' republic." Whereas community cohesion and action were social ideals in the eighteenth and nineteenth centuries, Cohen argues that in the consumers' republic the highest values are equated with the promises of mass consumption, both in terms of material life and in relation to freedom, democracy, and equality; in other words, consumption is the route to social ideals. Cohen states that the consumers' republic was a comforting vision which "promised the socially progressive end of economic equality without requiring the politically progressive means of redistributing wealth." The underlying message of the consumer republic is that citizens need not sacrifice as individuals in order to benefit from these social ideals. Individual consumerism, rather than social policy, was offered in the 1950s as the promise of social change and prosperity. During World War II citizens were told by the government that sacrifice (on the home front, through rationing and working for the war effort, and on the battle front) was the primary means to participate in the nation; during the postwar era, the goal was a life without sacrifice. Along with this shift, as Cohen notes, came more social inequality along racial lines, a decrease in voter participation, and increased social and political segmentation.[5]

This belief in consumption as the avenue to social change and the deep interrelationship of consumerism and citizenship has only grown more powerful since the postwar era. The news media consider measures of consumer confidence to be key indicators of the national mood, and, as I will discuss further, national crises such as 9/11 are often seen as crises of consumerism as much as crises of national strength. One could also argue that increasingly since the postwar era, marketers and advertisers, more than the government itself, speak to Americans as citizens. Indeed, government agencies and officials now deploy the style of marketers and the language of consumerism to address citizens. There is a deep alliance between the practices of consumerism and the practices of patriotism.

The home plays a very particular role in the ways that these two features of American identity—its dependence on external threat and danger and its dependence on consumerism—are realized together. Throughout U.S. history, and particularly from the postwar era onward, the home has been defined as a primary territory of defense and the nation has been articulated as individual citizens defending their privacy and their personal domain against outside enemies and government overreach. The home has also been shaped by particular practices of consumerism. As many scholars have noted, the modern home is defined by the consumption of furnishings, appliances, communications technologies, and leisure items. These consumer goods were testimony to the affluent lifestyle of the emergent middle class and symbols of American technological superiority during the cold war; more recently, they have epitomized the increased integration of work and domestic space in postindustrial economies. Thus, the postwar kitchen was seen as both testimony to the affluent lifestyle of the emergent middle class in the consumers' republic and as a symbol of U.S. technological (and, by extension, military) superiority in the cold war. Today, the integration into domestic life of communication technologies such as the Internet and cell phones has made the home a high-tech extension of work life, dissolving the boundaries between them.

Beginning in the postwar era, military research and development was reconfigured for technologies for the home. World War II military technology spawned domestic products such as the aerosol spray can, which appeared in the 1950s idealized home in such products as spray paint, hairspray, and insecticide, and the television set, which epitomized the postwar suburban home. In the late twentieth century and early twenty-first, this technological transfer has manifested most obviously in the proliferation of a consumer market for oversized vehicles, such as Hummers, that are the progeny of military transport vehicles. There is a long history of seeing this military–domestic intersection as plucky American know-how retooling military strategy for home practices. This interrelationship of military and domestic technologies helps to create a sense of fluidity between the realms of the domestic and the military in U.S. culture. Crucially, this translates into a pervasive ease with the notion of the home as a key site of national security.

In the post-9/11 era, this relationship of military security and home security has deepened dramatically. Harkening back to the 1950s' bomb shelters and civil defense, the current culture of security has taken on a new level of meaning in the context of a declared "war on terror." The home finds its counterpart in the post-9/11 context of "the homeland," with the prevailing notion that both are sites under siege. In the face of increased global insecurity and fear of terrorism, home security and homeland security have also produced an aesthetic of security that operates at many levels in American culture. David Morley has argued that the "articulation of the domestic household into the 'symbolic family' of the nation . . . can best be understood by focusing on the role of media and communication technologies."[6] One could argue that the articulation of the domestic home into the homeland of the nation is enabled in the context of post-9/11 fears by the practices of a consumerism of security. The militarization of the home is thus not only a means through which public fear of terrorism is mediated but is also a process through which the domestic household is articulated into the policies of the U.S. government. Defending the home and the desire to feel "at home" are key elements in the imperial policies of the U.S. government after 9/11. Underlying both are notions of innocence and comfort: the home that must be defended from external threat is articulated as a site of innocence, and the desire to feel at home in the United States and in the world is enabled by the idea of comfort. These form parallels with the consumerism of patriotism and kitsch in that there is comfort, if not pleasure, in the feeling of belonging that patriotism brings.

Consumerism and paranoia are both responses to disempowerment and practices enabled by notions of innocence. They underlie the act of buying a Hummer in order to feel safe in one's neighborhood while one's country is at war across the globe for, among other things, an economy dependent on the overconsumption of oil. Commodity fetishism, which endows commodities with meanings that are disconnected from their production and economic effects, enables the purchase of a Hummer to be seen as a solitary act of home defense and comfort, rather than as a politically inflected consumer decision that impacts foreign policy and the environment. The effect is circular: the fetishizing of the Hummer as a vehicle that provides individual comfort and safety helps to create the insecure environment that produces the desire to purchase the Hummer to begin with.

These aspects of consumerism and fear have reached new heights in the post-9/11 era. Yet, as I have attempted to make clear, these tendencies extend back to the postwar era and before. There are important connections as well between the fear generated in the post-9/11 era and the rise of paranoia in the relatively less threatened 1990s. Before turning to the issues raised by 9/11 consumerism, I would like to examine two elements of the culture of paranoia and fear that defined the United States in the 1990s: the right-wing militia groups that fueled the context in which the Oklahoma City bombing took place and the postindustrial shift toward a prison industry nation. These form the foundation of many of the practices that emerged in the post-9/11 context. The practices of paranoia and consumerism promote the idea that the American citizen exists in a state of innocence. They allow for U.S. national identity to be seen simultaneously as strong and naïve.

CITIZENSHIP IN THE 1990S:
PARANOIA AND THE RISE OF THE PRISON STATE

Late twentieth-century U.S. culture was marked by several defining features: the increase of highly divisive and litigious political factions that embattled the Clinton administration throughout its duration; a mainstreaming of paranoid culture in terms of a proliferation of paranoid narratives in popular culture and in both mainstream and marginal conservative political groups; the rise of talk radio as a forum for right-wing beliefs and hate speech; and the rise of right-wing militia groups promoting antigovernment violence and survival tactics. The 1980s and 1990s in the United States were defined by a pervasive culture of fear; in a time of relatively low threat, average Americans were preoccupied with potential threats to their personal security. This fear fueled the building of significant numbers of prisons to house record numbers of prisoners generated by legislation enacting mandated sentences for many crimes and long sentences for drug offenses. It was also a time of postindustrial economic shifts, with the widespread failure of the family farm, the closing of many coal mines, and loss of the industrial base of rural communities and cities in Middle America, which increased dependency on new economic trends, including the prison industry.

In the cold war era, paranoia culture had been powerfully manifested in relationship to communism; by the 1980s and 1990s, the dominant paranoia was right wing and antigovernment. This paranoia was fueled in various subcultures by a particular set of interpretations of the Constitution, including a belief in the primacy of the right to bear arms, a deep-set belief in gun culture as central to American identity, and a belief in a distinct form of "patriotism" that rejects existing government structures and takes itself to be a truer representation of American values. Ironically, the emergent racist and right-wing political doctrine appropriated many of the leftist, antiestablishment beliefs of the 1960s: that government has invaded too far into the private lives of individuals, the questioning of activities sanctioned in the name of the nation, and the critique of activities perpetrated by the U.S. government on the peoples of other nations.

One of paranoia's defining features is its assumption of a state of prior innocence and belief in the good. Notions of innocence are key to narratives of paranoia that have fueled the right-wing militia groups that proliferated in the 1990s and continue today, and that were responsible for the Oklahoma City bombing. In these narratives, the government is a ruthlessly diabolical entity that innocent citizens must defend themselves against. In many ways, this particular manifestation of U.S. paranoia is the result of the bitter shock that comes from having been naïve about structures of power. Narratives of paranoia reassure because they absolve (and hence reclaim in some fashion) that prior moment of innocence.

The Oklahoma City bombing was the central traumatic event that emerged from this set of social dynamics and its culture of the paranoid citizen. The right-wing culture that gave rise to the ideology of Timothy McVeigh, Terry Nichols, and their co-conspirators emerged from the American heartland both symbolically and geographically. This extremist culture evolved in the post-1970s as a response to the rise of identity politics and 1960s social movements, but also as an effect of difficult economic times in farming communities and the loss of an industrial base in the 1980s. It is thus a creature of postindustrialization. The increased numbers of family farm foreclosures in the 1980s and 1990s affected the Plains states both economically and symbolically, and the sense of betrayal in these communities attributed to the government and its farm policies was a key aspect in the emergence of more extremist political groups.[7] The roots of the militia groups are directly tied to the protests that took place over farm foreclosures, which were due in part to the government subsidy politics that encouraged farmers to finance their farms through substantial debt. The ideologies of the right-wing militia groups that formed at the time were thus fueled by economic disempowerment. From this emerged not only the cultural figure of the angry white male, who felt beset by the increased demands of women, racial minorities, and gay rights advocates, but also a set of subcultures that proposed radical forms of citizen resistance to the state: refusing to pay taxes, amassing arsenals of weapons and supplies to resist government response, and fantasizing about bombing federal buildings and killing federal agents.

These movements are based on racist philosophies of white supremacy and anti-Semitism, and at their core is a set of conspiratorial beliefs about a secret war being waged by the U.S. government against its citizens. The right-wing militia groups that began to thrive in the rural United States in this era included racist hate groups, both neo-Nazi groups and the Ku Klux Klan, and militia groups, many of them part of the antigovernment Patriot movement and the Freemen. Both movements deliberately borrowed patriotic names and a jingoistic rhetoric, though they defined themselves as anticitizenship. Their philosophy proposed an alternative form of patriotism, one that they presented as more authentic than the corrupted patriotism of the contemporary U.S. democracy.

The Patriot movement was fixated in particular on the Second Amendment and its definition of the right to bear arms and the fear that the government was infringing on that right. Several incidents in the 1990s affirmed this fear, including the shooting of the separatist Randy Weaver's family in Ruby Ridge, Idaho, in 1992 by federal agents, the incident that galvanized the Patriot movement, and the fifty-one-day standoff between federal agents and the Branch Davidian cult in Waco, Texas, which resulted in a shootout and fire that killed eighty-six people, including twenty-two children, on April 19, 1993. This is the incident that motivated the Oklahoma City bombers to retaliate by bombing the federal building exactly two years later. Both of these conflicts, along with the 1993 passage by Congress of the gun-control Brady Bill (named after James Brady, who was seriously injured in the assassination attempt on Ronald Reagan in 1981), were seen by these groups as evidence of the extent to which a fascist government would go to stop citizens from owning guns. While the membership in Patriot groups reached its peak in 1996 and then declined, those who monitor these groups still consider them to be a significant threat, perhaps even more so as they are less organized, with extremists acting alone rather than working in groups. In the post-9/11 context, these groups have been subject to more intensive government scrutiny and many of their leaders have been arrested. According to the Southern Poverty Law Center (SPLC), which monitors them most closely, there has been a resurgence of Patriot groups since 2002, and racist hate groups continue to grow in number.[8]

Narratives of paranoia and conspiracy are foundational to these right-wing movements. In these narratives, the true patriots are under siege and innocent citizens are being terrorized by the federal government. Their members see government forces as operating on a master plan to infringe on the rights of citizens and to wipe out antigovernment groups. These groups define government activity, and in particular the actions of federal agents, as operating according to a vast secretive and destructive plan. In this, these groups participate in typical paranoid narratives that see structure everywhere and construct master plans out of the arbitrariness of everyday life. These narratives supply motivation for events that may ultimately be meaningless. As such, they provide a particular form of comfort precisely because they posit structure and a master plan where there is usually none.

Freud identified the primary symptoms of paranoia as distrust of and hypersensitivity to other people.[9] In the traditional psychoanalytic definition, the paranoid is delusional, someone who imagines complicity and complexity, whose suspiciousness connects all events, all slights, all references to a central master narrative. The analysis of social paranoia was most famously conceived by the historian Richard Hofstadter, whose well-known essay, "The Paranoid Style in American Politics," was written at the height of the cold war. Hofstadter's concept of a *paranoid style* shifts the definition of paranoia from individual delusion to a kind of social perception. According to Hofstadter, "The distinguishing thing about the paranoid style is not that its exponents see conspiracies or plots here and there in history, but that they regard a 'vast' or 'gigantic' conspiracy as *the motive force* in historical events. History *is* a conspiracy."[10] The paranoid style views history as a master narrative. In this context, paranoia can be seen as producing a script about the way societies function, a script that understands the world in terms of connectedness and perceives it to be organized beneath the surface.[11] Hofstadter was highly critical, if not dismissive, of paranoid cultures, but a number of contemporary theorists see paranoia in a more positive light, as an indication of how citizens respond to the inadequacies of the American social fabric. These critics have posited, for instance, the potential usefulness of conspiratorial thinking as a political and theoretical position.[12]

It is thus possible to see paranoid narratives about government conspiracies as one of the strategies by which people can mediate their identification with the nation and their roles as citizens and citizen-viewers of popular culture. Paranoid citizens are those who believe that the government does not have the interests of ordinary persons at heart and is always working to deceive them; indeed, they believe that the government ultimately doesn't care whether they live or die. It could thus be argued that all U.S. citizens, rather than only members of disaffected right-wing militia groups, share to varying degrees in paranoia's questioning of how power operates, and that paranoia is a central narrative through which people mediate their identification with concepts of the nation and their roles as citizens or residents of the United States. Indeed, while paranoia about the motives of the U.S. government may be strongest on the right, it is widespread in mainstream culture. A poll taken in 1995 showed that almost one in ten Americans were convinced that the government had been involved to some extent in the Oklahoma City bombing.[13] After 9/11, polls showed widespread belief that the attacks had been orchestrated by the federal government itself.[14]

The paranoia of the citizen, which exists in these varying degrees, can be seen as the direct outcome of the daily infantilization that is a part of citizenship, as defined by Lauren Berlant:

> The infantile citizen of the United States has appeared in political writing about the nation at least since Tocqueville wrote, in *Democracy in America*, that while citizens should be encouraged to love the nation the way they do their families and their fathers, democracies can also produce a special form of tyranny that makes citizens like children, infantilized, passive, and overdependent on the "immense and tutelary power" of the state. . . . Central to the narrative mode of the pilgrimage to Washington, and so much other national fantasy, is a strong and enduring belief that the best of U.S. national subjectivity can be read in its childlike manifestations and in a polity that organizes its public sphere around a commitment to making a world that could sustain an idealized infantile-citizen.[15]

Berlant's definition of the infantile citizen is particularly useful for thinking about the culture of innocence that defines American culture. The citizen is depicted as a child, whom a paternalistic government must speak down to, who cannot take care of himself or herself. This infantilization has its flip side in a culture of anger. Paranoid citizens respond with the anger of a child who has been given little agency and few actual rights. Hofstadter has written, "Although American political life has rarely been touched by the most acute varieties of class conflict, it has served again and again as an arena for uncommonly angry minds."[16] Hofstadter wrote these words in 1963, but they resonate still.

The struggle over citizenship has been central to the conflicts of right-wing extremism. Much of the conspiracy-driven militia movement, with its various factions, such as the Freemen and the Patriots, is based on a radical critique of citizenship.[17] Members of these groups resist government activity by embracing concepts of "natural citizenship" and "common law" and refusing to participate in the defining activities of government-imposed citizenship: paying taxes; registering for gun, driver's, or marriage licenses; or voting. Much of their definition of citizenship stems from their racist philosophies, in which notions of white supremacy are used to counter the citizenship of blacks, Jews, Latinos, and various immigrant populations. Some members of these groups have gone so far as to claim to live in sovereign states rather than the United States, have used fake forms of currency to pay bills, and ascribe to the belief that there are "two types of citizens," those created by the Fourteenth Amendment and natural citizens (those born in the United States, with no obligation to follow the law).[18] Terry Nichols once wrote to a judge that he was "no longer . . . a citizen of the corrupt political corporate state of Michigan and the United States of America. . . . I am a 'non-resident alien.'"[19] Ironically, this position allies these racist right-wing militias with social movements that have taken as a political position the refusal of the community of the nation: the Black Power movement and the Nation of Islam embraced alternative nationalities with the belief that blacks and Muslims are never fully U.S. citizens, and Native Americans and U.S. colonies argue for native sovereignty against U.S. sovereignty.

Yet, while they reject citizenship in its political forms, the right-wing militia groups have been active participants in the world of consumer citizenship. A significant number of groups have made small fortunes by creating antigovernment investment scams, selling schemes to avoid taxes, marketing $250 passports in separatist nations, selling T-shirts and commodities, marketing home defense systems and survival rations, and being involved in the lucrative gun industry. When right-wing groups were focused on the Y2K concerns, which correlated with their apocalyptic philosophies, they held a series of lucrative "preparedness expos" in which merchandise and weapons were sold to great profit; the 1999 Preparedness Expo in Denver was attended by ten thousand people.[20] These "patriots for profit," as the SPLC calls them, are not the first such groups to exploit fear for profit.[21] In the 1920s, according to the SPLC, Ku Klux Klan leaders made fortunes selling memberships to millions. However, this new economy of paranoia and racism is aided in many ways by networks created by the Internet. Thus, in the 1990s militia websites marketed everything from weapons and racist

T-shirts to bumper stickers that read "Have You Cleaned Your Assault Rifle Today?" And in the early years of the twenty-first century militia websites have proliferated.[22]

Fear of surveillance and a belief in the need to defend one's home and one's privacy have helped to fuel this economy. It's worth noting that Freud defined paranoia as an aspect of narcissism and linked it to the "delusion of being noticed." He wrote that "patients of this sort complain that all their thoughts are known and their actions watched and supervised. . . . A power of this kind, watching, discovering and criticizing all our intentions, does really exist. Indeed, it exists in every one of us in normal life."[23] Certainly in the United States, which has seen an increased use of technologies of surveillance in the era of the USA PATRIOT Act, concern about government surveillance is justified. (Timothy McVeigh told a story, which he appeared to believe that the army had somehow put a microchip in his buttocks during the war which was used to monitor him.)[24] Yet, it is important to consider the broader implications of the "delusion of being noticed." For who is the citizen but someone who is rarely noticed, who is absented from the public debates and replaced by cultural figures and stereotypes—the welfare recipient, the soccer mom, the 9/11 widow, and so on—who the paranoid citizen assumes gets all the attention and all the benefits of the system? And the citizen who is most angry will struggle against this erasure by doing something to up the ante, to be noticed forever: send mail bombs, gun down schoolmates, or bomb a federal building filled with people going about their unnoticed daily lives.

Thus, the late-twentieth-century right-wing militia culture is simply an extreme manifestation of what are very common positions of national sentiment. It has also coexisted with and is not unrelated to a broader mainstream culture of fear. The sociologist Barry Glassner has written that the culture of fear in the United States in the late twentieth century was fueled by a voracious television news-making machine that capitalized on public fear to sell stories, on a political climate in which politicians used public fear to rally support, and on a consumer culture that sells products to mediate that fear.[25] He writes that in the 1990s, Americans were preoccupied, against all evidence, with fear of crime (as crime was falling), with possible plane crashes (of which there were very few), with diseases they were unlikely ever to get, and with an imagined epidemic of "road rage," while the real threats to the American way of life—poor health care, poverty, and an unregulated access to guns—went unnoticed.

This culture of fear helped to give rise to public support for increasingly Draconian prison sentences for minor offenses and drug use and for an exponential rise in the number of prison inmates. In the 1980s the average number of people imprisoned in the United States was five hundred thousand; in 2003, the number was approximately 2.1 million, of whom almost 50 percent are African American and 18 percent are Latino.[26] This increase was fueled not only by harsher drug laws and mandatory sentencing instituted in the 1980s, but by an increase in the use of prisons as forms of economic revitalization and job security in rural communities.[27] One response to the economic hardships brought by postindustrialism to small cities and towns in Middle America was to build prisons, which are considered to be a kind of "clean" industry. This prison culture has gone largely unnoticed. Built in isolated areas and small cities in states like Oklahoma and Indiana, the new prisons do not call attention to the national construction of an incarcerated society, yet the United States has become, as Joseph Hallinan writes, a "prison nation."[28] The rise of the prison nation has contributed to a reshaping of state and local economies, so that in many states more money is now spent on building and maintaining prisons than on education. Ruth Gilmore notes that while the myth that prisons create economic investments for rural communities has proliferated and provided support for the construction of large numbers of prisons in rural areas, the fiscal benefits are negligible.[29]

The prison nation is dependent on large numbers of inmates, and it is creating very hostile and potentially explosive "cities" within prisons throughout the country (with high numbers of black and Latino inmates being policed by white guards). The geographical location of these new prisons means that inmates who are largely from urban areas are incarcerated in isolated rural areas without public transportation, which makes it difficult for poor urban families to visit. The rise of a prison nation in which places of incarceration are sources of local economic pride has taken place hand in hand with a decrease, in the law and in practice, in inmates' rights. In addition, the prison population has an exploitative relationship to citizenship: prisoners are denied the right to vote and other rights of citizenship, but they are counted in the U.S. census, which translates into increased federal and state funds for their local municipalities.[30] The paradoxes of this context are many: the comfort provided by this prison society to citizens and government officials is dependent on the erasure of the citizenship rights of many prison inmates with little recourse to decent legal representation. In the post-9/11 context this prison society has reached new extremes, for instance, in the federal government's creation of offshore prison sites such as Guantánamo Bay, where inmates have no citizenship or international rights. Yet the foundations of these policies were well entrenched in U.S. prison culture before 9/11.

Crucial to this prison expansion has been the construction of supermax prisons, which place prisoners in high-tech, isolated contexts. The supermax prison is the epitome of the privatization of the prison industry and the industrialization of the prison itself, with highly structured systems of prisoner control and management. Michelle Brown writes, "Supermax classification is a managerial strategy, focused upon the redistribution of individuals on the basis of risk. The guiding principle of supermax design, consequently, centers upon isolation and exclusion, including the restriction of all communication and face-to-face contact with staff and visitors for *security* purposes." She continues:

> The growth in supermax prisons in the United States represents an important penological moment, particularly since supermax confinement is a largely American phenomenon, which other countries with similar governing structures and economic status have openly rejected. It is even more significant in the manner in which it maps contemporary patterns of global action in the post-9/11 new world order.[31]

Brown notes that the abuses at Abu Ghraib prison in Iraq, which were exposed in 2004, constituted an export of the penal practices of supermax prisons. Some of the key figures involved in the abuse had been trained in U.S. prisons. She argues that the prison-industrial complex is being exported to the war in Iraq through the prevalent use of private contractors in the war, including prison industry officials. There are complex economic interdependences of the military and prison industries in rural communities, where former military bases have been converted into prisons and where working in a prison and joining the military, as well as employment in service industries such as fast-food restaurants, are the key job opportunities for working-class Americans in a postindustrial economy. The creation of larger numbers of immigration detention centers has also fueled the economic boom of the prison industry. It is not incidental to this boom that prisons epitomize the recent trends in government outsourcing to private industries that have also characterized the war in Iraq.

Like the commodities and financial scams used to make money for the

militia groups, like the massive domestic industry of selling guns and weap-
onry, like the exploitation of stories of danger by the media, the globalized
prison industry, with its huge network of privatized support service industries, demonstrates the ways that the U.S. economy is a "fear economy,"
surviving as a form of capitalism that is fed by fear. As Joe Lockard writes,
"This fear-intensive economy elides a central truth of economic life: social
fears are a constant source of profit. Without fear and insecurity, capitalism
would not have the economic sanctions that make it profitable."[32] The fear
economy is mediated by the consumerism of comfort. The merchandizing
of arms and survival products that is key to the right-wing militia culture
and the emergence of the prison society can be seen within a framework of
paranoia and racial hatred. It can also be understood as operating within a
continuum of comfort culture: guns, home defense supplies, stockpiled ra-
tions, and prisons provide comfort in the possibility of survival and home
defense. They help to mediate the sense of disempowerment (economic, social, and racial) that fuels them. In a strange way, the personal assault rifle
and the supermax prison are not disconnected from the teddy bears that
proliferate in U.S. culture: all are intended to provide reassurance and comfort in times when the nation is understood to be under threat.

FROM THE CULTURE OF FEAR TO THE CULTURE OF TERROR

Many of the tensions in late twentieth-century American society, such as
the rise of right-wing militias and the prison industry and the intensely divisive and polarized political battles, were abruptly relegated to a more marginal status in the public arena after 9/11. The shock of 9/11 was such that
narratives of history were quickly divided into before and after, between
the era of the 1980s and 1990s and the post-9/11 context with its focus on
terrorism. Yet there are many continuities between the culture of fear and
paranoia that characterized late twentieth-century America and the fearful
preoccupation with security that marks the post-9/11 era. While the 1990s
culture of survivalism was restricted to the militia movement, it would expand in the post-9/11 context to include a much broader consumer public
with many more bourgeois and middle-class manifestations. Paranoia about
the government was the dominant narrative of extremist and mainstream
conservative groups in the 1990s; a fear of terrorism and a paranoid xeno-
phobia dominates the post-9/11 era. To say that this fear is justified is true,
of course; however, I don't want to imply that the paranoia in the 1990s was
completely unjustified about both the degree to which government agents

were empowered to invade the privacy of citizens and the way the lives of cult members were perceived by federal agents and the public at large to be of less value than others. The post-9/11 fear of violence is a response to an increase in the potential for subsequent terrorist attacks as U.S. actions and policies continue to feed violent anger toward the country throughout many parts of the world. Yet how American citizens have responded to this charged context has been influenced by the discourse of consumerism that has circulated since 9/11. Indeed, as Dana Heller notes, "9/11" has itself "attained the cultural function of a trademark."[33]

Significantly, one of the first responses to the shock of the events of 9/11 was the emergence of a belief, fueled by the media, that the national tone needed to change. In particular, in a time of fear and vulnerability it was no longer appropriate for American popular culture to be steeped in irony. This narrative revealed the degree to which irony was understood to be a symptom of a culture that was flippant about violence and its causes. Thus, it could be argued, irony in U.S. popular culture constitutes a knowing wink in a cultural context in which violence is always constructed and merely the source of disinterested shrugs. It may be that this concept of irony is particularly American, given that irony can be a key aspect of how certain cultures, such as those in Eastern Europe, have mediated repression. The American irony that was under attack immediately following 9/11 was in many ways an integral aspect of consumer culture, as American advertisers have increasingly deployed postmodern styles and ironic humor to speak to media-savvy consumers. Advertisers have thus helped to create a pervasive sense of ironic matter-of-factness in the face of postmodern ennui, contributing to the general sense that if you can't be new (and modern) and optimistic, you can at least be knowing and ironic. The dominant structures of feeling that emerged in the post-9/11 context were about fear, preparedness, and security, and these seemed to be at odds with ironic disengagement.

This concern that irony was inappropriate in a time of loss and grief also helped to fuel the turn toward sentiment and ultimately toward kitsch consumerism that characterized the response to 9/11. Irony is fundamentally about how things are not what they seem to be and a contradiction between the literal meaning of something and its intended meaning. The prescribed codes of sentiment that define kitsch culture offered simple and consumable emotional registers. It didn't matter that a post-9/11 souvenir might be kitschy in offering prescribed sentiment because emotions were so present and easily tapped into.

The post-9/11 concerns about national tone also translated into an attack on postmodernism, as if somehow postmodernism were responsible for Americans being unprepared for global terrorism. In a much-discussed essay in the *New York Times* Edward Rothstein wrote that postmodern thought produces a relativism in a time when "this destruction seems to cry out for a transcendent ethical perspective." He added, "One can only hope that finally, as the ramifications sink in, as it becomes clear how close the attack came to undermining the political, military and financial authority of the United States, the Western relativism of pomo [postmodernism] and the obsessive focus of poco [postcolonialism] will be widely seen as ethically perverse."[34] Rothstein's essay demonstrates the degree to which the sense of crisis after 9/11 produced a desire for comforting models of thought, including the reassuring philosophical frameworks that could uphold such simple binaries as evil and innocence. Postmodernism, with its constant questioning and refusal to affirm binary ways of thinking, had to be set aside, if not demonized, in a time of vulnerability.

The crisis that immediately followed 9/11 was not only political and national (if not philosophical); it was a crisis of economics and consumerism. It revealed the degree to which American culture is dependent both symbolically and economically on the activity of consumerism. In the first weeks following 9/11, consumer culture in the United States was at a standstill. The airlines did not fly any planes until September 14, and then resumed on very limited schedules, losing billions of dollars. With most Americans in a state of shock, there was little activity that fell within the framework of normality. Most obviously, television stations did not show regular programming for several days, running twenty-four-hour coverage of the crisis and losing almost $400 million in revenue.[35] Lynn Spigel writes about "the broader havoc that 9/11 wreaked on television—not just as an industry—but also as 'a whole way of life'":

> The nonstop commercial-free coverage, which lasted for a full week on major broadcast networks and cable news networks, contributed to a sense of estrangement from ordinary life, not simply because of the unexpected nature of the attack itself but also because television's normal routines—its everyday schedule and ritualized flow—had been disordered. . . . By the weekend of September 15, television news anchors began to tell us that it was their national duty to return to the "normal" everyday schedule of television entertainment, a return meant to coincide

with Washington's call for a return to normalcy (and, hopefully, normal levels of consumerism). Of course, for the television industry, resuming the normal TV schedule also meant a return to commercial breaks and, therefore, TV's very sustenance. . . . Just one week after the attacks the television networks discursively realigned commercial entertainment with the patriotic goals of the nation.[36]

The return to the television schedule was not only a return to programming, it was a return to advertising as the economic underpinning of television and also as a signifier of the comfort of routine. The reappearance of television commercials thus marked the end of the state of emergency. Advertisements signaled routine and the comfort of the mundane. This move from shock and mourning to routine consumerism, and an increased urgency about promoting consumerism, took place quite rapidly. Strangely, while taboos about irony and comedy were still in place, a belief in consumerism reemerged within a week after 9/11 without creating much controversy. For many consumers, the turn to retail apparently functioned as an expression of patriotism, if not defiance, a way to demonstrate that they had "not given in to the terrorists at all."[37]

Among the objects that Americans purchased in large numbers in the first week or two after 9/11 were American flags, which quickly sold out throughout the country; Wal-Mart sold 116,000 flags on September 11 alone.[38] In many parts of the country these flags were displayed most prominently on cars and trucks. Susan Willis writes, "Taped to the inside rear window, tattooed into the paint, or streaming from tailgate or antenna, the auto flag makes every roadway into a Fourth of July parade route."[39] Using the flag as decoration on automobiles had an ironic effect, given the role of oil politics in the crisis, yet this irony could not be acknowledged in the demand for patriotism.

These small American flags, which were ubiquitous in the first months after 9/11, are at once simple yet complex objects. One could argue that the fevered consumption of these flags, the vast majority of which are produced not in the United States but in China and Korea, was not necessarily an obvious response to the grief felt at the time. The flags emerged when people were searching for a symbol that could provide a visual signifier of their sense of solidarity with those who had been killed and a sense of their own trauma. Was their message one of solidarity and belonging? A few years later, the artist Art Spiegelman would ask, Why flags? "Why not a globe?"[40] In a certain sense, the ubiquity of the flags suggested the paucity

FIGURE 7. Street vendor near Ground Zero, September 20, 2001. AP Photo/Antonin Kratochvil.

FIGURE 8.
The street vendor Albert Drayton sells flag merchandise commemorating the terrorist attack on the World Trade Center, in midtown Manhattan, September 16, 2001. AP Photo/Amy Sancetta.

FIGURE 9. Workers sew U.S. flags on September 24, 2001, at the Shanghai Flag Factory. AP Photo/Eugene Hoshiko.

of shared symbols of unity for Americans. Even social critics such as Todd Gitlin argued at the time that Americans could embrace the flag as a symbol of belonging, that the flag could be meaningful to citizens (even educated, left-leaning ones) beyond simple, unquestioned patriotism, that, in Gitlin's words, his own act of displaying the flag was "not meant as support for the policies of George W. Bush but as an affirmation of fellowship with an injured and resolute people."[41]

The proliferation of post-9/11 flags was the beginning of a period of policing the flag's iconography. Ironic commentary on the flag, which has a long history in American art and popular culture, was already under siege by 9/11, but the kitschification of the flag took on new dimensions after 9/11. Its status as an icon of the kitsch aspects of American patriotic culture has become so overdetermined (one could argue, so fragile) that the U.S. Congress took to posturing around amendments to ban flag burning (the House passed such an amendment in June 2005 and the Senate narrowly defeated one in June 2006), despite the fact that it appears that no one is actually attempting to burn flags. Given that an ironic engagement with the flag is impossible in this climate, the flag itself has taken on new dimensions of kitsch in its proliferation in consumer products in times of crisis; it has been used to sell pizza, is worn as a T-shirt, and, in one of its most kitsch manifestations, was worn by Bono inside his jacket as he sang at the January 2002 Super Bowl halftime show while the names of the 9/11 dead scrolled behind him on the massive stage.

In the first weeks after 9/11, the consumption of flags signaled the beginning of promotion not simply of patriotism but of consumerism. One of the most revealing aspects of this shift from mourning the dead to entreaties to consumerism was the degree to which public officials very quickly began to speak to U.S. citizens specifically as consumers. For instance, Mayor Rudolph Giuliani, who was lauded in the media as a reassuring and heroic presence in New York City after the attacks and who had spoken in eloquent and compelling terms in the first week of the crisis in ways that comforted many people directly affected by the attacks, quickly turned to a kind of New York boosterism by the end of the first week. Asked how Americans could help New York in this time of crisis, Giuliani told Americans to spend money, to get on airplanes and fly to New York, to go to the theater, to buy what they could (and, by implication, could not) afford. These statements would normally be unremarkable in that they fit within an ongoing national discourse on consumerism; as statements by a public official in a time of national crisis, however, they are quite stunning. Rather than telling Americans to work together to help their neighbors, to build community, to volunteer, to contribute money to the families who had lost loved ones, or to help their own communities access their own security needs, the mayor, at the absolute height of his popularity, with the national public listening to his every word, told people to act as individuals, to spend money on themselves, to consume products and entertainment because their true mission as citizens was to bolster the economy, even if they put themselves and their savings at risk.

Just as the return to television advertising signaled a return to "normalcy," the return to consumer practices provided a sense of community with fellow citizens. One Wal-Mart store manager told the media, "The day of the attacks, we had many people who were alone come into the store because they wanted to be around other people and have someone to talk to." Writes Jennifer Scanlon, Wal-Mart "simultaneously offers itself as the necessary link between Americans and their need to keep consumer identity intact: even when the world is turned upside down, we can right it."[42] In this sense, the desire to turn to Wal-Mart as a place of connection demonstrates the degree to which consumer malls have truly replaced the village square as an expected site of congregation. Through their patriotic marketing,

Wal-Mart, McDonald's, and other brands, have succeeded in allying their corporate image with the nation. When Hurricane Katrina devastated New Orleans four years later, Wal-Mart proved to be exceptionally more reliable and better prepared than the federal government, solidifying in many ways its reputation as Wal-Mart America.

In fall 2001, the fear that tourism in New York would not rebound for a long time revealed the degree to which certain segments of the economy of New York City are particularly dependent on tourism. Indeed, New York boosterism has often taken the form of tourism as one of the few aspects of New York that allows non–New Yorker Americans to like a city that they normally disdain as arrogant and un-American. As Mike Davis wrote in November 2001, "Now folks in Iowa watch grisly television footage of the FBI raking the rubble at Fresh Kills for rotting body parts . . . and thank God that they still live on the farm, or, at least, in a gated suburb of Des Moines. However much they may admire the Churchillian pose struck by Rudolph Giuliani or the fortitude of New York's rescue workers, family vacations are not usually envisioned as exercises in 'overcoming fear.'"[43] However, as I discuss in chapter 4, the destruction in lower Manhattan would become a draw for tourists in a very short period.

In the first few weeks after 9/11, the shocked suspension of consumer spending created a crisis in itself. As early as September 19, the media became preoccupied with the story and was reporting consumer spending coming back (though, in fact, this early reporting was overblown).[44] President Bush also began speaking about consumerism on the national stage. By late September, he was sent out on a number of press events, traveling around the country to convey the message, according to the White House, "Get on board. Do your business around the country. Fly and enjoy America's great destination spots. Get down to Disney World in Florida. Take your families and enjoy life, the way we want it to be enjoyed."[45] This public relations attempt to promote the travel industry had Bush flying around the country to demonstrate that air travel was safe—a ploy that rang false given the barrage of security that surrounded him on Air Force One. (It's worth noting that Disneyland was under high security and had been considered a potential target. It has since been under much more strict security measures and has been at the forefront of exploring new forms of surveillance.)[46] In late October, after the war in Afghanistan had begun and with spending still low, the International Mass Retail Association, a lobbying group, and several House Republicans went shopping at a Target store in a photo opportunity to "lead by example." While eating a hamburger at the Crystal City, Virginia, McDonald's, Rep. John E. Peterson told reporters, "If we just hunker down in fear and don't spend normally, millions of Americans will lose their jobs." With apparently unintended irony, he added, "I had a gentleman tell me the other day, 'I bought an SUV to help the economy.' Those who can afford to kick in a little ought to do it."[47]

All the elements of Lizabeth Cohen's consumer republic are at work here: the equation of citizenship and consumerism and the selling of consumerism as the avenue to freedom, democracy, and equality. It is also the case that increasingly over the past few decades, as it has shifted from an industrial to a postindustrial base, the U.S. economy has become remarkably dependent on a high level of consumer spending. Writes the *New York Times* reporter Louis Uchitelle, "Nothing props up the economy more than consumers, and dips in their spending frighten forecasters. . . . Consumers in America spend because they feel they must spend. More than in the past, the necessities of life, real and perceived, eat up their incomes."[48] While government outlay and business investment form the other big factors in the economy, added together they come to less than half the amount of consumer spending. The post-9/11 rhetoric that people should start spending money in order to save the economy was based on an economic reality. Yet it was also in conflict with the fact that spending is often equated with optimism. Thus, the demands of the economy were directly at odds with the necessary response to a national security crisis. The historian T. J. Jackson Lears told the *Los Angeles Times* on September 29, "It is one of the real paradoxical concepts of living in a market economy and consumer culture that depends on people maintaining a state of optimism. [This] runs counter to the wartime mentality that they also need. Bush and other leaders have to promote confidence, whether or not they feel it themselves. They have to persuade the public that there is nothing to be afraid of. But there is a real danger of encouraging indifference and not maintaining a state of readiness."[49] Here again, Cohen's consumer republic is clear: one of the key features of the notion that consumerism, rather than civic engagement, is the primary means to achieve social equality is the idea that one does not and should not have to experience sacrifice in order to participate fully in the nation.

The advertising industry was particularly badly hit in the initial weeks and months, when everyday slogans that celebrated the pleasures of consumption seemed suddenly inappropriate. Many ads were quickly pulled from publications, including numerous ads that had images of the twin towers, such as a Bacardi rum ad of the twin towers rocking, and ads with now inappropriate icons, such as a Toyota ad at the Pentagon.[50] Other ads whose slogans had now become offensive were removed from pending publications, such as Coca-Cola ads that declared, "Life Tastes Good," and an American Trans Air offbeat print campaign that showed an image of a gladiator with the headline "If there's going to be a war, we'll fight it out on own turf" and a billboard with the tagline "Fly Without Being Taken."[51] Iomega Corporation, which makes computer disks, rushed to pull an ad from the September 17 *Newsweek* that featured the headline, "Tom Survived the Crash. Everybody has a story. Put it on a zip."[52] Many companies were too late to pull ads that were already in production, and the *New York Times* ran a front-page apology on September 16, stating, "The Times regrets that some references to events are outdated and that the tone of some articles and advertising is inconsistent with the gravity of the situation."

Very quickly, however, many advertisers began to devise ways of speaking to the crisis rather than pretending it had not happened. Here is perhaps an unintended consequence of a consumer republic: many of these ads succeeded in speaking to the feeling of belonging to a nation in a way that the government did not in that time of crisis. Many companies ran full-page newspaper ads that were attempts to pay tribute to those killed on 9/11 while also reaffirming their company's existence in the context of a national and economic crisis. Rushed into production, many of them appearing within a few days, these ads uniformly had a spare visual style of simple text on large white space, which evoked the gravity of the time. A number listed the names of the dead and offered condolences to the families and friends of those who died. In these ads, the corporations themselves spoke the language of the nation, evoking protection, mourning, condolence, and concern for safety.

These ads are, in effect, memorials, which speak to a mourning local and national public, yet simultaneously they are also legitimation ads intended to establish corporate citizenship and particular brands in positive terms. Those ads for companies that had been directly affected by the crisis functioned in ways similar to the many posters of missing people that circulated in New York in those first few weeks. One ad by the firm Sidley Austin Brown and Wood read, "We thank our clients and friends for your expressions of concern and support. We mourn for all who suffered loss. We continue to hope and pray for our missing colleague, Rosemary Smith, and rejoice in the safety of all of our other colleagues from our World Trade

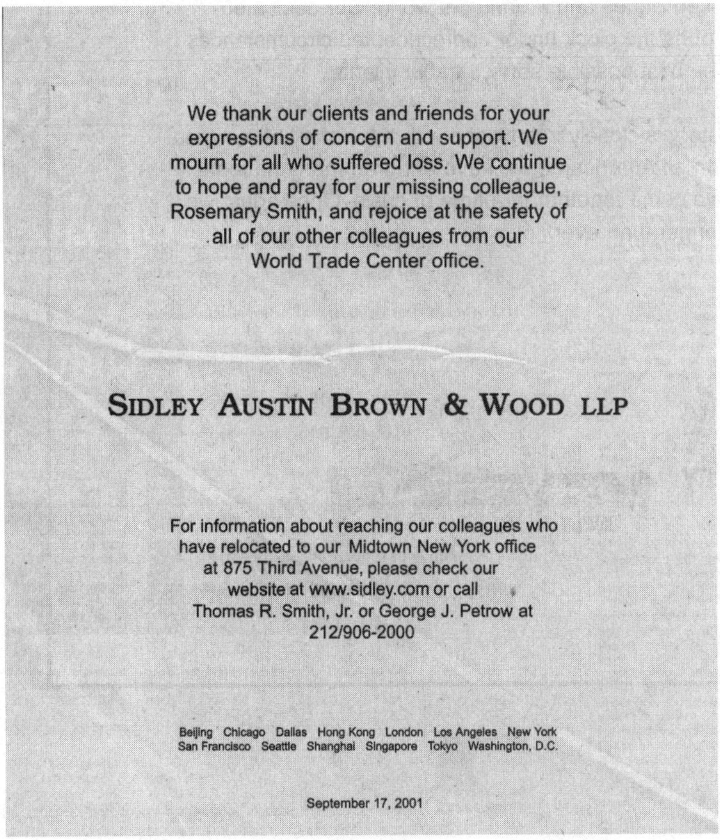

We thank our clients and friends for your
expressions of concern and support. We
mourn for all who suffered loss. We continue
to hope and pray for our missing colleague,
Rosemary Smith, and rejoice at the safety of
all of our other colleagues from our
World Trade Center office.

SIDLEY AUSTIN BROWN & WOOD LLP

For information about reaching our colleagues who
have relocated to our Midtown New York office
at 875 Third Avenue, please check our
website at www.sidley.com or call
Thomas R. Smith, Jr. or George J. Petrow at
212/906-2000

Beijing Chicago Dallas Hong Kong London Los Angeles New York
San Francisco Seattle Shanghai Singapore Tokyo Washington, D.C.

September 17, 2001

FIGURE 10. Sidley Austin Brown and Wood ad, *New York Times*, September 17, 2001.

Center office." In this ad, the mere mention of their missing colleague, her naming, retains a certain power. Morgan Stanley, which had several thousand employees in the twin towers, ran an ad signed by Chairman Philip J. Purcell: "This past Tuesday, many of us who work at The World Trade Center returned home to our loved ones. Sadly, all of us did not." These ads spoke in moving terms of loss, the loss not only of employees but of a workplace, and thus effectively manifested personalized sincerity. Companies without a direct connection to the trade center ran similar tributes, including an ad by Best Buy with small text on a large white space reading, "As you weep, we weep, As you pray, we pray, As you endure, we will endure." Such ads blur issues of corporate voice in odd ways. (Who is "we" here? Best Buy? Americans?) Ads were run by cities and governments of other countries. One of the first of these was published on September 13 in the *New York Times* by the

Oklahoma City National Memorial and the State of Oklahoma: "Oklahoma Cares," it read, adding, "You Stood With Us in Our Darkest Hour. Now We Stand With You." In this ad, an immediate connection is made between the trauma of the Oklahoma City bombing and the events of 9/11, and the support networks that the response to each implies.

The use of advertising as forms of both mourning and affirmation was also evident in several television ads that emerged in the first months after 9/11. Cantor Fitzgerald/eSpeed's offices had been on the high floors of the North Tower, the exact place where the first plane hit; they lost 658 people, more than any other company in the World Trade Center, In early 2002 they ran an ad called "Our Floors" featuring one of their surviving employees, Mike. Standing alone before the camera, he says that he was late for work that day and when he exited the subway, he says, "I remember looking up and seeing that big hole and I was thinking to myself, you know, that's our floors." He continues talking about how work was the most important thing

As you weep, we weep.
As you pray, we pray.
As you endure,
we will endure.

BEST BUY

Sam Goody • Musicland • Suncoast • Media Play • On Cue • Magnolia Hi-Fi

FIGURE 12.
Best Buy ad, *New York Times*,
September 14, 2001.

for those who survived, and the ad ends with the tagline, "To work with us, visit www.espeed.com www.cantor.com." It's a risky strategy, given the association the ad has just made of work with death. Yet the ad also aims to present work, and in particular working for this company, as life-affirming. Another advertisement used the voices of the dead to persuade viewers to make charitable contributions. The Twin Towers Fund ran a moving black-and-white ad of Timothy Stackpole, a firefighter killed on 9/11, talking in a 1998 video about how much he loves being a firefighter.

Most of the ads that emerged as a response to 9/11 deployed patriotism in order to urge consumers to spend money and to travel. This discourse of corporate consumerism, in which corporations speak to consumers as citizens, has a long history. Since the mid-nineteenth century, advertisers have used national crises as a means to sell products as American. For instance, during World War II, U.S. advertisers spoke regularly to consumers about how rationing and thriftiness as well as purchasing American goods were an important part of the war effort. After 9/11, this kind of patriotic advertising took many forms. One week after 9/11, United Airlines ran an ad that included this text:

On Monday, when you asked people how they were doing, without much thought, or much contemplation, they replied "fine" or "good."
On Monday, we passed strangers without much regard.
On Tuesday, September 11, all that changed.
On Tuesday, September 11, strangers died for each other.
On Tuesday, September 11, America was knocked to its knees.
On Tuesday, September 11, America got back up again.

K-Mart took out full-page ads with an image of the American flag and the directions, "Remove from newspaper. Place in Window. Embrace freedom." Merrill Lynch pronounced itself "Bullish on America," and Southwest Airlines promised to "Get America Flying."

Of these ads selling patriotism, the campaign of the *New York Times* was the one that most explicitly staged the events of 9/11 in the context of history. It published a series of ads starting in November 2001 that borrowed from the history of patriotic kitsch images in remaking several Norman Rockwell paintings from World War II. In one ad, a reproduction of Rockwell's well-known 1943 painting *Freedom from Fear*, a mother tucks in sleeping children while the father stands over them, holding a newspaper. In the original image, the newspaper had a headline relating to World War II, with the words "Horror" and "Bombings." In the 2001 remake, the father is holding the September 12 *New York Times*, with its large headline, "U.S. Attacked: Hijacked Jets Destroy Twin Towers and Hit Pentagon in Day of Terror." The ads make an explicit connection between Pearl Harbor and 9/11 for those who know the original Rockwell painting and borrow on the kitsch Americana of Rockwell's style. As Francis Frascina writes, the image was transformed into "a post 'September 11' digitized signifier of sentiment, family security, and the nation state under threat."[53]

The *New York Times'* use of nostalgic Norman Rockwell images was clearly an attempt to provide images of paternal comfort and reassurance: the image of a father figure connected to the world of politics via the newspaper who is a reassuring presence in a child's bedtime ritual. In the months after 9/11, marketers talked often about the comfort of familiar brands and predicted that activities that affirmed tradition and homeyness would be popular. The marketing forecasters Trend Center predicted the following indicators for post-9/11 life by October 1: "Community—people will seek out ways to socialize, including hobbies and special interest clubs. Dining—consumers will enjoy hearty comfort food rather than haute cuisine. More time will be spent with the family rather than in restaurants. Fashion—will be either defiant, with bright colors and crisp styles or subdued with darker shades."[54]

Realtors reported that numerous well-to-do families almost immediately began to redecorate in materials like soft cotton that conveyed "comfort feeling."[55] Like the Kenneth Cole ads with which I began this chapter, many advertisements reverted to images of comfortable furnishings and human contact. That comfort was being sold fit quite readily within the branding of the nation, in which national symbols are sold as forms of security and identity formation. Before 9/11, the brand of the nation was already constructed as an affirmative social space in which to construct individual identities. This enabled the connections between comfort and nationalism that proliferated in the first few post-9/11 years, with the attendant consequence that dissent or public debate became marked as the antithesis of comfort and thus "anti-American."

Many of these ads succeeded in speaking to a post-9/11 audience that was already participating in the consumption of symbols of patriotism. Yet even in a context in which kitsch patriotism was rampant, certain ads that aimed to capitalize on making connections between their products and the 9/11 crisis were subject to criticism. The humor magazine *Onion* capitalized on this with the satiric headline "Dinty Moore Breaks Long Silence on Terrorism with Full-Page Ad." In an age when consumers are particularly savvy to the construction of advertising slogans, patriotic messages are subject to the same kind of cynicism as many traditional ads. Within the advertising industry, there was debate about where the line existed between tasteful campaigns that spoke to mourning consumers and campaigns that crassly attempted to cash in on tragedy. The ad executive David Lubars told the *Los Angeles Times* that it is better to run a traditional spot "as opposed to attaching some transparent, plastic patriotism to it."[56] One General Motors campaign, "Keep American Rolling," and Ford Motors' campaign "Ford Drives America" were slammed by the *Advertising Age* columnist Bob Garfield for precisely that. General Motors' campaign promoted zero-interest financing and featured the voiceover, "On Sept. 11, the world as we knew it came to a halt. We sat glued to our television, watching events unfold that shook us to our very core. And, suddenly, the little things that had previously divided us became wholly insignificant. Now, it's time to move forward." Noting that GM was advertising a consumer incentive it would normally have been selling anyway and calling this one of several campaigns that was "beyond belief and beneath contempt," Garfield wrote that the Keep America Rolling "zero-interest sales promotion (McCann-Erickson Worldwide, Troy, Mich.) was one of the most unseemly episodes in the history of American marketing. Want to help your country? Buy a Buick. How dare they? Ford had a nearly-as-contemptible me-too version."[57] Garfield compared the opportunism of these ads to a Makita power tools ad that ran after the Oklahoma City bombing, in which the company thanked the rescuers and called attention to its donation of power equipment in the rescue effort. Similarly, when Motorola used an image in its annual report of two New York firefighters with the company's radios, it was roundly criticized. Firefighters, who were concerned that malfunctions of the radios had cost lives, called the use of the photograph a "disgrace and an offense."[58]

Marketers thus believe that it is risky for companies to flaunt their charity work in times of crisis. Kenneth Cole's "Today Is Not a Dress Rehearsal" campaign was consistent with Cole's reputation for speaking to social issues and donating proceeds to charity, but there were other companies that were accused of using 9/11 tie-ins to sell products under the guise of charity. For instance, Madden shoe company sold thirty-five thousand pairs of sneakers called The Bravest for $49.95 with the promise that proceeds would help the families of dead firefighters. Only after confronted by reporters did the company pledge 10 percent of the profits to firefighter charities. The Madden chief executive defended the company's profits of $400,000 by saying, "We have stockholders, so we walk the line between doing what is good for the stockholder and the company and doing these good deeds." He added a statement that would be laughable were it not in concert with the political spin at the time: "The most patriotic thing we can do is make money."[59]

In the first months after 9/11, the majority of ads that directly addressed the economic crisis were produced by companies that were specifically threatened, in particular, airlines, car dealers, and the travel industry. Saudi Arabia, which had been the home country of a significant number of the hijackers, ran several newspaper ads in the weeks after 9/11 that offered support and condolences.[60] When that country also produced an expensive television campaign in May 2002 which featured images of U.S. leaders, such as Colin Powell, meeting with Saudi leaders and the tag lines "The People of Saudi Arabia: Allies against Terrorism," a number of cable channels refused to run them.[61]

Significantly, many ads attempted to make connections between the economic crisis and the workers whose jobs would be the most affected if

Americans did not begin to consume as they had before. After marketing research showed that the public found employees to be credible, United Airlines produced several ads in October 2001 that placed its employees directly before a stationary camera and asked them to speak about their work.[62] In one ad, flight attendants, mechanics, and pilots, some of them visibly moved, introduce themselves and talk about their feelings about working after 9/11. One woman says that she was told to take a break after working eleven days straight, to which she responded, "I don't want to. I feel that I need to be here." Others remark, "As a company we have grown closer together," and "As long as we stick together and stay together, no one can divide us. We are United." In its visual simplicity and intimacy, the ads effectively showed that work was a strategy often used by people to deal with loss. At the same time, the ad was a reminder that a number of United Airlines employees had died on 9/11, in terrifying and brutal ways. American Airlines ran a television ad campaign in early 2002 that included a montage of images of employees walking through airports, of planes framed by sunsets, and of employees guiding planes into airport gates, with the text: "We are an airline. But we realize we are something more. We are an engine that powers the free flow of people and ideas and products and joy."

It is easy to criticize this kind of affirmation advertising that connects corporations to the nation. This deployment of national and patriotic discourses, with its ideological linkage of airline travel with idealized concepts of freedom and the "free flow of people and ideas," obscures the complexity of the role of the airline industry in the post-9/11 context. Similarly, the United Airlines campaign's use of employees performing their loyalty to the company depicts an idealized context in which issues of labor disputes, low pay, downsizing (all very present after 9/11) are unacknowledged in a mystification of labor. It is the case, of course, that while American popular culture, advertising, and government entities often present affirming images of work, U.S. government policies and industry practices have actively aided in the draining of large numbers of jobs from the American economy. Work, like innocence, is a highly mythical aspect of national narratives.[63] Yet one can have little doubt that these testimonies are genuine. When a site of work becomes a site of violence and emergency, it creates a heightened sense of purpose. Aaron Shuman and Jonathan Sterne write:

> The conceit of the United ads was that the airline discovered its workers had better things to say than anything the ad agency had scripted. So it put them on the air to tell their stories: as if United were a benevolent

FIGURE 13A, B, C.
United Airlines TV
ad, "We Are United,"
2001. Produced by
Fallon.

FIGURE 14A, B.
American Airlines
TV ad, "Way of Life,"
2002.

corporation, transparent in its motives, with the same stake in the process of business recovery as its employees. Their declarations of pride and
determination in the face of grief and loss suggested their recovery was
our own as well, customers and labor linking arms in a mission of holy
consumption to save a corporate country.[64]

It is crucial to see the way that these ads, however they glossed over the
different stakes of corporate officials and workers, are effective in making
the connection between consumerism and the nation in ways that are more
compelling than the specter of the president talking about smoking out terrorists or congressmen eating burgers at McDonald's. These ads speak to
the stakes of the dependence of the economy on consumers in terms that

make clear that those stakes are about workers keeping their jobs. These airline ads thus perform nationalism effectively. They speak to "a people" in ways that can make one can feel easily interpellated by. The ads offer comfort and reassurance to traumatized consumers, promising that the experience of flying on an airplane will return to normalcy.

These ads are also about selling security, not only the security to get on an airplane and to speak the language of consumerism, but also the security to proclaim the airline industry's survival and the promise of continued employment. In that the airlines are often understood to be national industries that represent the United States to other nations, these ads are selling both the security of the nation and the security of familiar brands. They thus form a continuum with the marketing of home security and the prevalence of a security aesthetic that has emerged full force in the post-9/11 context.

DEFENDING THE HOMELAND: THE CONSUMERISM OF SECURITY

One of the primary modes of comfort in post-9/11 consumerism is the selling of preparedness. In this context, consumer products and lifestyle modes are marketed by corporations and promoted by government agencies as a means to sell not only the idea that citizens must be prepared for adverse circumstances such as terrorist attack, but also the idea that they *can* be properly prepared for such events. The selling of preparedness is not simply selling the idea that one can prepare for particular adverse situations; it has broader implications, since it sells the comforting idea that one can . actually be prepared for the unpredictability of life and, by implication, that life is not arbitrary. In this, preparedness consumerism is deeply related to the central tenets of paranoia, which defines adversity as a "vast conspiracy" rather than something unpredictable and uncontrollable. It is thus not surprising that preparedness is a key factor in the consumer society of right-wing militias and was the key theme of the large preparedness expos before the turn of the millennium. In the case of both paranoia and preparedness consumerism, it is the comfort of structured narratives (we can be prepared for whatever comes; it is a planned conspiracy that is making this happen) that reassures.

A consumer culture fixated on preparedness and home security has emerged with particular force in the post-9/11 era, spanning everything from barrier architecture to home security products to security style. This selling of preparedness and security, which is promoted by the U.S. government as well as private corporations, has been propelled forward by the

crisis of 9/11, yet its lineage can be seen in direct relation to the preparedness culture of fear of the 1990s that fueled not only the extremist militia
groups but also the public support for mandatory sentencing that produced
the prison industry culture. Whereas in the 1990s, the culture of fear manifested in the brutal system of mass incarceration of millions of Americans,
in the post-9/11 context it can be seen in the public acquiescence not only to
the war in Iraq, but also to Bush administration policies on torture and the
incarceration of terrorism suspects at Guantánamo Bay and in secret prisons
without legal recourse or basic human rights. This political acquiescence is
directly shored up by security consumerism that offers the promise of protection and safety in times of threat and thus mediates, if not justifies, these
government policies.

The post-9/11 selling of security directly borrows from the rhetoric of
defending the home deployed by survivalist groups in the 1990s and has
explicitly created connections between the idea of the "homeland" promoted by the federal government and the home as the front line of national
turf. This slippage from the home to the homeland and back to the home
is revealing. It is now common knowledge that the war on Iraq, which has
cost American taxpayers several hundred billion dollars, has come at the expense of adequate funding to properly prevent future terrorist attacks on the
United States. The Department of Homeland Security (DHS), which was established in 2002 to oversee domestic security issues, is increasingly viewed
as inept. In the aftermath of the tragic crisis of Hurricane Katrina in September 2005, when both the Federal Emergency Management Agency (FEMA)
and the DHS (in which FEMA is now housed) were shown to be appallingly
incompetent, the public impression that the government would do little
to protect citizens from terrorism was solidified. In addition, Washington
politics has produced a context in which antiterrorism funding, funneled
through DHS, is distributed by state rather than by need, resulting in a large
per capita funding for states like Wyoming and low per capita funding for
states like New York. In June 2006, this resulted in a 40 percent cut in DHS
funding to New York City and Washington, D.C, the two cities that were
targeted on 9/11 and which remain the most likely future targets.[65] Because
of a prevalent understanding after 9/11 that the federal government would
not adequately protect New York, the city created its own counterterrorism
unit of the police department in early 2002.[66]

While the concept of a nation as a home has a long history, the use of
the term "homeland" is quite recent in the U.S. context, where historically

the idea of a homeland has more often been invoked to describe the place that immigrants have left behind. Amy Kaplan writes that emergence of the term homeland where political rhetoric has previously used terms like "civil defense," "home front," or "domestic security" marks "a transformative moment for American nationalism. For one, the usage always entails the definite article (*the* homeland), indicating its unitary meaning, as opposed to pluralistic definitions of national identity."[67] Kaplan writes that it is precisely because of this connection of the term homeland to the experiences of diaspora and exile that homeland "may evoke a sense not of stability and security but of deracination and desire."[68] Thus, she notes, the concept of homeland security "is actually about breaking down the boundaries between inside and outside, about seeing the home in a state of constant emergency" that ultimately "draws on comforting images of a deeply rooted past to legitimate modern forms of imperial power." The use of the term homeland is clearly intended to evoke a comforting image of a place of security and belonging; at the same time, it affirms the capacity of the nation to stake out terrains elsewhere, to extend its sense of belonging to other terrains.

The marketing of products that sell the militarism of domestic life to mediate fears of global insecurity effectively bridges home and homeland in its rhetoric and aesthetics. In this consumer context, corporations speak in national terms, urging citizen-consumers to assume military protocols and to surround themselves with goods that evoke security and defense. Ultimately, the integration of military technologies and lifestyle protocols into domestic life takes place at the level of aesthetics. *Style* is the key attribute through which the domestic home is articulated within the nation in the context of global terrorism.

The federal government is a key factor in this construction of the American home as the locus of security. In the post-9/11 context, the federal government has actively sold the idea through promotional campaigns that U.S. citizens and residents must be prepared for further terrorist attack and that readiness is a key feature of safety. The DHS has actively promoted preparedness by selling the idea that individual consumerism of preparedness products is about doing one's part for the nation. One of the first frenzies that erupted around this government-promoted consumerism was prompted by a mundane household product: duct tape. This silver tape (which was actually developed by the military in World War II) has always had a mystique as a household product that can fix, at least temporarily, any problem.[69] Stories have long been told of cars held together with duct tape and elaborate plumbing problems for which it was the magical adhesive. Duct tape is a sign of American bricoleur culture, in which an average Joe can fix anything as long as he has his trusty tape in hand, a symbol of an independent, can do spirit of fix-it culture.

In early 2003, duct tape emerged on the national front when the DHS began issuing high alerts in its color-coded system: red for severe, orange for high, yellow for elevated. There was increased public fear that the impending war in Iraq would result in more terrorist attacks within the United States. For many critics, the alert system is merely a way for the government to avoid liability risk—to be able to say, in the case of disaster, that government officials could not be blamed because they had warned of impending attacks (unlike with 9/11).[70] Thus the alert system has been widely regarded with suspicion, as what it means citizens should do in response is never clear (be *more* suspicious?) and because the Bush administration was accused of using the alerts to deflect public attention from negative news and to help boost presidential approval, in particular during the 2004 presidential campaign. Nevertheless, the issuing of an alert is guaranteed to get media attention. In February 2003, on the eve of the U.S. invasion of Iraq, the DHS issued a set of guidelines for average citizens to protect themselves in case of potential chemical attacks. The $1.2 million "ready campaign" was nothing if not commonsensical (with what the *New York Times* columnist Maureen Dowd called a "D'oh!" website), advising people to keep on hand water for three days, flashlights, and a battery-powered radio and to have a communication plan.[71] The campaign, which was developed with the input of focus groups put together by the Ad Council, also advised homeowners to buy plenty of plastic sheeting and duct tape to seal their homes.[72] The response to this missive was instantaneous; while late-night comedians made duct tape jokes and politicians rose quickly to state that "duct tape is not enough," millions of Americans emptied the shelves at their local home supply stores.[73] Soon, Tom Ridge, then head of the DHS, was forced to explain that people should wait for word from the government before beginning to seal their homes shut.[74]

Besides being comical, the duct tape episode was quite revealing for the ways it demonstrated the calming and reassuring effects of consumerism on national anxieties. Even when people knew that the small measures were unlikely to help much in the case of a serious attack, they purchased the duct tape anyway; sales of the adhesive rose 1,000 percent during that time.[75] Significantly, this act of consumerism helped to enable the transference of actual threat. On the eve of attacking Iraq, U.S. citizens were encouraged to use consumer products to occupy the status of the victim, in other words,

FIGURE 15. Homeland Security Director Tom Ridge unveils color-coded terrorism alert system, March 12, 2002. AP Photo/Joe Marquette.

to inhabit the position of the potentially attacked rather than the position of the attacker. This consumerism of defense successfully obscured the fact that the people who were truly threatened were in Baghdad, not in the United States.

It is one of the stated functions of the DHS to provide guidance on how to respond to potential terrorist attacks—in other words, to sell the idea and means of preparedness. The agency does this through a variety of campaigns, all of which aim to interpellate the citizen as a citizen-soldier-consumer, whose job is to protect not only the family but the home. The campaign sells the idea that readiness is the key antidote to fear with the tagline "Today America's families declare, we will not be afraid and we will be ready." On its website, www.ready.gov, the DHS explains various measures that individuals can take in case of a broad range of attacks, including biological and chemical attack, radiation from a dirty bomb, attacks with conventional bombs, and nuclear disaster, often in calmly neutral language that seems reminiscent of the procedures of civil defense in the cold war era.

In 2005, the DHS produced the "America Prepared Campaign," which featured, among other elements, the tagline "Homeland Security Starts at Home," promoting the idea that families need to create emergency plans and a "family communications plan." The campaign included a series of ads produced by the Ad Council which are based on the notion that the defending unit of American society is the family and which focus on the idea that American families need to prepare with emergency plans: "If there's an emergency, does your family have a plan?" In the print campaign, various family members pose before the camera, each with a list of instructions printed next to him or her. One father's list is "Fill up gas tank, drive home, pack minivan with emergency kit"; one young girl's is "Wait for Mommy at school," while the family dog is told "Grab chew toy, hop in back of minivan." The campaign aims at inclusiveness by showing an African American family, but its construction of the American family is revealing. These are middle-class suburban families, families who have two children and a dog, families who drive minivans. Given that the risk of terrorist attack is significantly higher in urban areas, with New York having the highest risk of being targeted, this campaign looks more like a form of reassurance to suburban America than an effective pedagogical strategy. In a city such as New York, where the vast majority of residents ride trains, subways, and buses, where huge numbers of people do not live in traditional nuclear families or with families at all, these ads would barely resonate. One final ad in the "Everyone should have a plan" campaign shows a version of a Mad Lib, those children's games used to relieve boredom on long car treks, in which a paragraph leaves certain words blank to be filled in by someone who can't see the text, thus producing an often comic effect of mismatched words. The ad reads, "If there's a(n) _____ (adjective) terrorist attack, everyone in the family should try to call _____ (phone number) to get in touch with _____ (proper name). . . . Finally, we decide if we should drive to _____ (distant location) or stay in our _____ (room in your house)." Given that Mad Libs are often used for vulgar humor, with players suggesting words to make the phrases deliberately offensive, this ad has the potential for an unintended comical effect.

Government efforts to create a populace that is prepared to respond in orderly fashion to terrorist attack reassure citizens that the government is doing everything it can to keep the country safe. Thus, the emphasis in the DHS campaigns on how individuals should respond to a crisis elides the fact that individual citizens or families can do little to affect the most important security decisions of the country, such as the securing of borders and cargo. The ready.gov campaigns take place in what is largely understood to be a security vacuum on the part of the U.S. government. Not only has the

Everyone should have a plan.

Take the first step. Talk to your family about what you would do in case of a terrorist attack or other emergency. There's no reason not to. To find out other things you can do to be prepared, visit www.ready.gov.

FIGURE 16.
Department of Homeland Security "America Prepared" campaign, 2005. Courtesy of Department of Homeland Security/Ad Council.

DHS alert system been exposed as a sham, but the news is filled with stories about the United States not properly screening cargo on boats and airplanes entering the country, while its resources are drained in the war in Iraq. In the wake of the crisis of Hurricane Katrina, the images of citizens drowning and stranded on rooftops, deserted by both federal and state governments, affirmed the popular sense of the government's incompetence. In this context, the focus on the individual home as a site for security measures makes perfect sense: if the homeland is not well defended, then the home must be defended. Ironically, the message of preparedness that is sold to citizens by the government can have the effect, not of giving the impression that the government is prepared, but of encouraging citizens to act solely as individuals. This message of self-reliance has as its counterpoint the fact that consumer-citizens are asked at the same time to subject themselves to increased governmental and consumer surveillance in the name of security. As Mark Andrejevic writes, this message of self-reliance is the

Stop at gas station, fill extra gas container, pick up Mia at school, drive home.

Email relatives, pull out emergency kit, listen to the news for official instructions, wait at home for everyone to arrive.

Walk home from school.

Wait for Dad to pick me up at school.

Wait for Mia near the toy chest in her bedroom.

Everyone should have a plan.

Take the first step. Talk to your family about what you would do in case of a terrorist attack or other emergency. There's no reason not to. To find out other things you can do to be prepared, visit www.ready.gov.

FIGURE 17.
Department of Home-
land Security "America
Prepared" campaign,
2005. Courtesy of De-
partment of Homeland
Security/Ad Council.

compensatory response to the disturbing recognition that the lumber-
ing institutions of mass society—mass armies and their hyper-extensive
equipment—aren't nimble enough to counter the flexible threat of terrorism. The work of defense has to be offloaded onto the civilian population. As the risk is generalized individual participation at every level
is required. This participation takes two forms: the interpassive one, in
which data about every transaction, every purchase, and every movement
is aggregated within the government equivalent of the total demographic
database; and the interactive form in which citizens are encouraged to
take responsibility for their role in the war on terrorism as part of their
daily lives at work, at home, and at school.[76]

As Andrejevic makes clear, the invocation to U.S. citizens to be self-reliant
and to actively participate in a consumerism of security and preparedness
also requires that consumer-citizens subject themselves willingly to a society of intense monitoring and surveillance.

The advocacy of individual action in the face of government ineptitude has manifested in many ways. Elaine Scarry uses the example of the passengers on United Flight 93, which crashed in Shanksville, Pennsylvania, and American Flight 77, which crashed into the Pentagon, to show how security functions poorly within government bureaucracy. Scarry charted the time it took the military to respond to the information that planes had been hijacked and the time it took passengers on Flight 93 to decide to act: "The military was unable to thwart the action of Flight 77 despite fifty-five minutes in which clear evidence existed that the plane might be held by terrorists and despite twenty minutes in which clear evidence existed that the plane was certainly held by terrorists. In the same amount of time— twenty-three minutes—the passengers of Flight 93 were able to gather information, deliberate, vote, and act."[77] Scarry argues that the United States needs a more egalitarian, democratic approach to national defense, one that relies on the actions of ordinary citizens. Ironically, this position is remarkably reminiscent of the rhetoric of the right-wing militias, for whom the concept of individual action is paramount. Like Scarry, they believe that collective action of value can only take place outside of government bureaucracies and structures. Unlike the position of the militias, Scarry's is a utopian view of citizens working for the public good. Yet the emergence of a citizenry concerned with security has taken place in a context of individual consumerism and in relation to the selling of the idea of the home as an individually defended space.

The home defined by preparedness consumerism is also a networked home. James Hay writes that the home defined by post-9/11 homeland security is a "smart" home that is constructed through networks: "The fashioning of the smart home as a safe and secure home has occurred amidst two intersecting developments: one toward greater responsibility at home, and another toward the proliferation of networks from the home to private/ professional providers of programs for in-home support."[78] The home that is targeted by marketers and advertisers is already constructed as a source of middle-class leisure spending, with such big-box store chains as Home Depot and Lowe's selling not only home appliances and products but the idea that the home is the source of endless projects and infinite consumer goods. This construction of the home as a primary impetus for consumerism predates 9/11, of course, and in the post-9/11 period it has expanded to include a broad array of consumer goods aimed at selling preparedness and security. Yet, despite the duct tape episode, this consumerism of security has been largely the province of the middle class and the wealthy and has defined life in the age of terror as one in which individuals with means will arm their households against threat at the expense of broader community needs. This has taken the form of an increased reliance on the consumption of high-end emergency supplies for offices and private households, the marketing of terrorism survival guide books, and the repackaging of military vehicles for domestic use. This consumerism promotes a pervasive sense that private citizens must take security into their own hands and defend themselves, echoing the defense rhetoric of the survivalist militia groups who barricaded their homes to wait for the apocalypse. The home must be constructed as a kind of bubble, immune from attack. One company, Regional Environmental Hazard Containment Corporation, has been selling inflatable plastic rooms to consumers at a cost of $3,200 to $5,000 to be used in case of chemical attack.[79]

As an industry, the selling of home (and work) security parallels the prison industry in terms of booming economic success. The Defense Department's attempt to set up an office that would trade on the futures of terrorism was closed down after it was ridiculed in the press, but trading on the uncertainty of terrorism can take place in many other forms. The selling of homeland defense has taken place in the privatizing of the military and disaster relief services through outsourcing to private companies, what Naomi Klein refers to as the Disaster Capitalism Complex; as Hay and Andrejevic note, it has also occurred through lucrative business speculation on homeland defense.[80]

The terrorist attacks of 9/11 used two key aspects of modern life, airplanes and skyscrapers, as their weapons; the consumerism of security for the home and office has focused in part on both. The fears of people who work in tall buildings have been exploited by a number of companies that are selling emergency kits with personal parachutes for corporate executives, who can imagine themselves parachuting to safety in case the buildings are targeted. The "Executive Chute" is marketed by one company as "the life preserver of the sky" and sells for $799; Safer America, a company that specializes in safety products, sells a "high rise kit" for over $1,000 which includes a protective suit, a gas mask, and an escape parachute.[81] Many experts say that such personal parachutes are unlikely to save lives and may in fact encourage people to jump into dangerous urban landscapes when leaving by fireproof staircases could be safer.[82] Yet it is easy to see where the desire to buy the emotional comfort of a parachute (long a symbol of a safety net) comes from; the most haunting images of 9/11 were those of people who jumped to their deaths, their fragile bodies falling through the air.

Similarly, tall buildings and urban buildings have been the subject of increased barrier and fortress architecture. The guarded, barricaded, and gated community has a long history in the United States. Fortress architecture emerged in marked ways in the 1980s and 1990s as a manifestation of the fear of urban crime, what Mike Davis identified as "an unprecedented tendency to merge urban design, architecture and the police apparatus into a single, comprehensive security effort."[83] In addition, the past few decades have seen a dramatic rise in the building of gated communities around the country. In the post-9/11 era, barrier architecture has proliferated in public spaces and at building entrances in cities such as New York, Chicago, and Los Angeles, primary potential targets in the case of terrorist attack. In Washington, D.C., security barriers have been erected around government buildings, and throughout the world, U.S. embassies are now barricaded like bunkers. The rebuilding of Ground Zero in lower Manhattan has resulted in the design of several heavily fortified buildings, with concrete bases and no storefronts. This image of the nation as a fortress is increasingly evident in the construction of public urban spaces and private homes as sites of defense.[84]

This new defensiveness is not limited to temporary barricades due to security concerns; it very quickly became a kind of urban aesthetic. People are accustomed to being searched when going to cultural institutions such as museums and the theater and have grown used to living in environments that are designed to resemble secure locations, with few, if any, public spaces. Many of these measures are based on antiterrorism plans developed by cities that have long histories of violence, such as Jerusalem and London; they are also pursued in an arbitrary manner that reveals the degree to which they constitute a kind of performance of security. Cultural institutions like theaters and museums began searching bags almost immediately after 9/11, even though they are not likely sites for attack; airline passengers are subjected to an elaborate array of security measures but airline and shipping cargo is not.

The marketing of security has produced not only a new array of products but a new set of design challenges and design style. It has thus helped to create an aesthetic of security that not only integrates security measures into daily life, but also gives defensiveness and militarism a kind of aesthetic coolness. In this context, a security barrier doesn't have to look like a concrete bunker, it can look like a sleek modernist bench. There has been a surge of design attention to barriers in particular as security that can be art at the same time, what the *Wall Street Journal* terms "security disguised as art."[85] Much of this design has focused on the concrete barriers that are used to prevent the entry of vehicles into buildings. The 1993 World Trade Center bombing and the 1995 Oklahoma City bombing both had high destructive impact because trucks were able to get into or next to the buildings. This has produced an industry in the construction of such devices as bollards and NoGos. Steel or concrete bollards, which now surround the vast majority of government buildings, are designed to stop a truck going fifty miles an hour. Sleek bollards are now a key feature of security design. In a particularly effective use of them, the new federal building in Oklahoma City, which sits next to the Oklahoma City National Memorial, is surrounded by bollards housed in large metal cylinders that are lit decoratively at night, in a way that echoes the lit chairs for the bombing victims that sit nearby. While Washington, D.C., has been the site of the most obvious barriers for federal buildings, there are now many projects to situate bollards around tourist sites such as the Washington Mall in ways that are less intrusive and more aesthetically pleasing.[86] Designer bollards have been created by Frederick Reeder and others to integrate into urban landscapes unobtrusively. Reeder has also designed modernist benches that can protect building entrances. His "anti-ram" bench is a thirty-five-foot slab of black granite weighing 43,000 pounds that sits before the steps of the headquarters of Fleet Bank in Boston; it looks like a work of modernist public art. Other bollards are artfully disguised as theme park elements; SecureUSA has built bollards designed as giant golf balls for a golf course near a military base and a massive gorilla bollard installed at the entrance to a theme park.[87]

Similarly, NoGos, which are designed by Rogers Marvel, are heavy concrete blocks covered in bronze and disguised as sculptural forms. NoGos are now used on the streets of lower Manhattan near the New York Stock Exchange. Writes Farhad Manjoo:

> They resemble a comic-book artist's take on a barricade, a playful and handsome gem whose actual purpose—keeping a speeding truck laden with explosives from getting anywhere near the Stock Exchange—is invisible to the public. In fact, people have found many uses for the barricades. At 2-and-a-half feet tall, a NoGo makes an ideal seat. Suited Wall

FIGURE 18. Security bollards by Frederick Reeder. Courtesy of Frederick Arlen Reeder.

Street types crowd about the NoGos at lunchtime and kids climb and stretch on them as if there were a downtown jungle gym.[88]

The desire of designers to effectively mask the function of security barriers and to give the appearance of open space in secure contexts is often in conflict with the aims of security consultants, for whom the appearance of security is as important as actual barriers. This results in "security creep," in which security experts now trump the work of architects and designers; current fears are incorporated in long-term ways into urban landscapes. Writes Manjoo, "Architecture is an art form of anticipation, the challenge of building structures that will continue to be meaningful and useful in the decades and centuries to come. Truck bombs, on the other hand, are an acutely modern phenomenon."[89]

The proliferation of high-end security design has brought with it a significant amount of ironic commentary in the design community. In 2005, the Museum of Modern Art (MOMA) produced the exhibition *Safe: Design Takes on Risk*, which combined both straightforward designs for risky environments and designs that critiqued risk culture as privileged paranoia.[90] The MOMA show demonstrated the degree to which safety concerns are incorporated into the mechanisms of daily life: fortified baby car seats, gas masks (distributed to every Israeli citizen), outfits of protective armor that can shield from physical harm and biological hazard, and earthquake survival tables. The show also revealed the degree to which designers have engaged playfully with the culture of fear. For instance, the designer Matthias Megyeri has created a line of "placebo products" that mix cuteness with defensive design. These include fences with animal shapes as spikes, "whose smiley faces, proud beaks and floppy ears allow you to inject a sense of energy into otherwise lifeless urban landscapes," jagged glass shards in whimsical shapes that can be placed on backyard walls, smiling teddy bear padlocks, and whimsical razor wire with "Mr. Smish & Madame Buttly" shapes.[91] Megyeri's design is a "comment on the growing demand for security in our modern culture, mixed with the saturation of exaggerated niceness in everything that surrounds us," according to MOMA.[92] Megyeri situates these placebo products in the context of contemporary cultures of paranoia and kitsch, but he is particularly interested in having his products operate as both an ironic commentary on contemporary security concerns and as stylish and functional designs. The fact that the rabbit icon on his security fence has one ear up and one down may be a cute gesture, but it also has a very specific security design function.[93]

Other designers in the exhibition commented on the culture of fear of those living in relatively safe locales. For instance, Anthony Dunne, Fiona Raby, and Michael Anastassiades produced the *Design for Fragile Personalities in Anxious Times Project*, which consists of several pieces of "hideaway furniture" that merge with the floor and surroundings, allowing someone to disappear within an abode. Ralph Borland's *Suited for Subversion* is a suit to protect someone participating in civil disobedience demonstrations from the blows of police batons.[94] Perhaps most revealing, the exhibition showed the complexity of the world of risk design by mixing straightforward designs with ironic commentaries on risk and essentially refusing to make many distinctions between the two. Thus, the contemporary world of design represented by the exhibition demonstrates the fluid boundaries between design for actual risks (including design for disaster relief, such as temporary housing) and designs for imagined ones. Many designs, like Megyeri's, straddle this border between straight engagement with risk and ironic commentary on risk paranoia. Kosuke Tsumura's design for *Final Home 44-Pocket Parka*, for instance, is designed as a "wearable shelter."[95] The parka is designed for the contemporary nomad (here, "final" signifies "ultimate"), with pockets

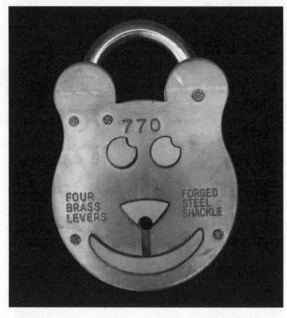

FIGURE 19.
Peter Pin, R. Bunnit, and
Didoo railings; Billy B.
Old English padlock,
2003. Sweet Dreams
Security™ series by
Matthias Megyeri.

that can be used to store food, medicine, and tools or be stuffed with in-
sulating material such as newspaper or Final Home down cushions. The
parka is accompanied by the *Final Home Bear,* a stuffed orange bear with an
emergency sign on it, which functions as a "comforting toy or insulation
when stored in the pockets of the Final Home jacket." Notably, the MOMA

catalogue description makes clear that the parka can be worn as "survival gear" by middle-class consumers, who are then encouraged to return them when they no longer need them so that they can be distributed to refugees and disaster victims. Much security design slips somewhat fluidly between these domains: the serious and the ironic, the bourgeois security market and the world of refugees and disaster victims in need of shelter, and the world of poverty that survives in part on the hand-me-down discards of middle-class consumers.

These kinds of shifting tones can also be seen increasingly in the incorporation of certain styles of militarism into middle-class consumerism, with the recoding of a military style from conservatism to coolness or, at a minimum, corporate cool. Marketing analysts have discovered that baby boomer consumers tend to like overengineered products. The trend of wearing hiking boots in urban settings and purchasing high-tech mountain gear for wearing in mild suburban winters are what the market researcher Jim Bulin calls "preparedness chic": "It's about not letting anything get in your way and, at the extreme, about intimidating others to get out of your way."[96] This correlates with the trend beginning in the 1990s of people purchasing high-end Nike running shoes as fashion items and the marketing of urban styles as outdoor wear by such chains as Urban Outfitters. Overengineering is not seen as something that needs to be apologized for by middle-class consumers; rather, it is an attribute that signifies consumer confidence and know-how. Preparedness chic is also an element in the trend that emerged during the Iraq War of recent veterans being employed to run fitness "boot camps" for urban professionals. At the Pure Power Boot Camp in New York City, former Marines and Iraq War veterans train stockbrokers, lawyers, and other professionals at 5 A.M. each weekday. When a participant skips a session, the former Marines have been known to turn up at their workplace demanding to know why. One participant, who paid close to $1,000 for six weeks of training, states, "I love the fact that they are authentic and they've actually gone through this."[97] It hardly needs to be pointed out that this kind of military consumption masks many realities of the lives of actual military personnel during this time of war.

Sports utility vehicles (SUVs) are one of the most obvious symbols of the militarization of American domestic culture and the overengineering of consumer products; while they are marketed as vehicles that can drive on rough terrain, most people are driving them in suburban and urban locales. Car manufacturers began retooling their pickup truck frames in the early 1980s

FIGURE 20. *Final Home Bear* by Kosuke Tsumura, 1994.

to make SUVs for the suburban family market, and the surge in SUV purchases, largely unforeseen by industry analysts, helped to fuel the economy in the 1990s. Statistics show that the design of SUVs, which sit high on top of truck frames, is inherently unsafe, causing higher numbers of rollovers than minivans. In his book *High and Mighty*, Keith Bradsher puts the problem of the SUV bluntly: "SUVs are the world's most dangerous vehicles because they represent a new model of personal transportation that is inherently less safe for road uses and more harmful to the environment than cars."[98]

Nevertheless, SUVs sell, according to marketers, specifically because consumers feel safe in them. Market research for the SUV was famously done by the marketing guru G. Clotaire Rapaille, a former anthropologist who specializes in luxury goods. Rapaille, who uses Jungian psychology and psychoanalysis in his work, has wowed the marketing world by analyzing what he calls the "reptilian," rather than emotional or intellectual, urges of consumers. Not surprisingly, he attributes the SUV craze to the preoccupation with fear and security in American culture, what was described in the pre-9/11 era as an "irrational" fear. Bradsher writes

> For Rapaille, the archetypes of a sport utility vehicle reflect the reptilian desire for survival. People buy SUVs, he tells auto executives, because they are trying to look as menacing as possible to allay their fears of crime and other violence. . . ."I usually say, 'If you put a machine gun on the top of them, you will sell them better,' he said. 'Even going to the supermarket, you have to be ready to fight.'"[99]

The gender politics of the SUV are revealed in the shifts of how they have been marketed. As Nicholas Mirzoeff writes, the early SUV had masculine names such as Isuzu's Trooper, whereas later models targeted at suburban women had softer names that took on "resonances of the digital frontier, with titles like the Ford Explorer and the Lincoln Navigator directly borrowing the names of the most popular web browsers. Perhaps the only honestly named SUV is the vast Chevy Suburban."[100]

The paradox of the SUV craze, according to Bradsher and others, is that the very features that consumers say make them feel safe are the ones that make the cars unsafe. Consumers told Rapaille that they felt safer higher up in the car because it's easier to see if someone is lurking behind it. They said they felt unsafe if someone could easily look in the windows of their car. Yet, it is precisely the height of SUVs and their awkward maneuverability that make them unsafe to their drivers and even more so to other drivers who might get hit by an SUV. According to Malcolm Gladwell, this means that SUV drivers treat "accidents as inevitable rather than avoidable" by choosing the passive safety of a massive vehicle over the active safety of a vehicle that handles effectively enough on the road to avoid accidents.[101]

The paradoxes of the SUV acquired new resonance in the post-9/11 era and the lead-up to the war in Iraq, when the ultimate SUV, the Hummer, took off in the consumer market. A military vehicle that was first used by the United States in the 1991 Gulf War, the Hummer skyrocketed in popularity in the post-9/11 context, selling well just as the war in Iraq was being planned and duct tape sales were off the charts. While sales of Hummers began to plateau in 2004 and have sagged since, they remain a key symbol of the post-9/11 era. The Hummer is defined by its marketers as a vehicle for

FIGURE 21. Hummer H2 ad, "Excessive. In a Rome at the height of its power sort of way."

"rugged individualists" that sells excess without guilt.[102] One of the ads for the H2 features the tag line "Excessive. In a Rome at the height of its power sort of way."

In the pre-9/11 world of 1991, when Hummers were first being tentatively marketed to a domestic market, they were targeted at Gulf War veterans, who, marketers felt, would be nostalgic for the powerful feeling of these hyper-Jeeps. Though he is not a veteran of an actual war, one of the initial consumers was, in fact, Arnold Schwarzenegger, who was famous for driving his around his Los Angeles neighborhood before such vehicles were commonplace. In many ways, Arnold himself is a signifier of the consumerism of security: faced with an uncharismatic governor and a threatening deficit, the voters of California chose him as governor in 2003 as a symbol of defiance to the inevitable pain of budget cutbacks to come. During a campaign debate he flaunted his image as a Hummer driver, at one point telling rival Arianna Huffington, "I could drive my Hummer through [your tax loopholes]."[103]

The typical Hummer owner has an annual household income of $200,000 to $300,000 and has purchased the vehicle (which carries a price tag of $40,000 to $100,000) as a second or third car.[104] The Hummer evokes power and safety, but in real-life situations of combat, such as the war in Iraq,

Humvees have actually been death traps for American soldiers. In Iraq, an inadequate number of Humvees are armored, since the war was rushed into action without adequate supplies. This caused a minor scandal in December 2004 when a soldier confronted Defense Secretary Donald Rumsfeld with a pointed question at a press conference in Iraq about the makeshift "hillbilly armor" that troops were forced to construct to protect the vehicles.[105]

The Hummer is a potent symbol of gas-guzzling denial on the part of Americans at a time when the country's insatiable desire for oil has taken it into yet another war. This has made it a favorite target of anti-SUV activists, including an arson attack on a Hummer dealership by the Earth Liberation Front, now classified as "domestic terrorism" by the FBI. The response of Hummer fans to criticism and protests is to see owning the vehicle as a form of patriotism, claiming that the H2 is "a symbol of what we all hold so dearly above all else, the fact we have the freedom of choice, the freedom of happiness, the freedom of adventure and discovery, and the ultimate freedom of expression. Those who deface a Hummer in words or deeds . . . deface the American flag and what it stands for."[106] In these words, reminiscent of Cohen's consumer republic, freedom is clearly defined as the freedom to purchase a particular kind of vehicle regardless of the political implications.

The Hummer demonstrates a triumph of the aesthetics of a domestic militaristic safety, one that affirms the U.S. imperialist ventures around the world *through style*. The marketing campaign for the H1 Hummer defines it as "a vehicle that can go almost anywhere and do almost anything. One that gives you an incredible feeling of freedom, and allows you to experience the world, and your place in it, as never before."[107] It is worth noting that it is not simply the power to trespass and invade that is being sold, but also a sense of belonging ("your place in it"). The idea of being "at home" is key to any imperialist project. This is, according to David Campbell, a "biopolitics of security":

> The SUV is the vehicle of empire, when empire is understood as the deter-ritorialized apparatus of rule that is global in scope but national and local in its effects. The SUV is a materialization of America's global security attitude, functioning as a gargantuan capsule of excess consumption in an uncertain world. . . . The SUV draws the understanding of security as sizeable enclosure into daily life, folds the foreign into the domestic, and links the inside to the outside, thereby simultaneously transgress-ing bounded domains while enacting the performative rebordering of American identity.[108]

This linkage of the world of consumer defensiveness and preparedness chic connects the nuclear family to the family of the nation. One Hummer ad, "First Day," shows a mother driving her children to school. She offers to leave her young son at the corner, but no, he insists, she can drive him to the school entrance. There, he walks through a phalanx of older kids, bullies, who clear the way for him as they turn to the Hummer and say, "Nice ride." This ad portrays the Hummer as the vehicle with which to protect the family in its movement between home and public institutions. Thus, the Hummer as nation drives its children to school with its display of techno-prowess; the nation watches its children move past the threshold into hostile territory. The military vehicle keeps the school bullies at bay, and the Hummer/nation promises to seduce school bullies (read: terrorists) into loving American consumerism. The message is that consumerism is precisely what Americans are supposed to be using as public diplomacy.

This ad points to a key aspect of the selling of SUV and Hummer security: the way they have been marketed to women as an emblem of the secure home. Susan Willis notes that during the 2004 election, the media dubbed the "security mom" a viable political type. These media portrayals, writes Willis, "conjure the plight of white suburban moms who, notwithstanding their husbands or the obvious comfort of their lives (clean, well-dressed kids, pleasant neighborhoods with well-tended playgrounds and schools, newish often large cars), still profess an overriding, deep-seated, and persistent fear for their security."[109] The security mom, Willis notes, is always depicted as white and never as concerned about the truly fearsome aspects of contemporary American society, such as rising health care and education costs and domestic gun violence.

And this returns us to the home. The home is defended because the homeland is so amorphous. Just as the paranoid narratives of the militia movement emphasized the defense of the home against invasive government forces, the militarized home, with its military vehicle in the driveway, offers the only comfort available in a time of uncertainty, when each day the policies of the U.S. government increase the risk to its citizens. Paranoia and the notion of preparedness provide similar forms of comfort. Paranoia, as Eve Kosofsky Sedgwick notes, is anticipatory. Thus, the essence of a paranoid narrative is that it succeeds in precluding the unexpected; in Sedgwick's terms, "There must be no bad surprises."[110] All negative consequences and outcomes are fantasized and anticipated in the state of paranoia in order to prevent the state of shock of (innocent) unknowing.

FIGURE 22A, B, C.
Hummer H2 ad, "First
Day/Nice Ride,"
2004. Produced by
Modernista!

Similarly, a consumerism of preparedness promises that we can be prepared. Participating in an aesthetics of militarism, consumers engage in a style that affirms the dangerous policies of an imperialist government. This consumerism sells comfort in the face of fear and the promise that we can be prepared, not simply for the violence that is inevitably to come and for the unpredictable nature of global terror, but for life itself. In this sense, paranoia and preparedness are modes of being that are as politically disabling as kitsch, since both foreclose on particular kinds of political action. The paranoid citizen is, in many ways, hampered by a sense of disempowerment that comes from seeing life as conspiracy-driven, and the consumerism of preparedness provides the sense that it is enough to protect one's home and not to be engaged in political action. Ultimately, it is comfort that is offered by each.

The prison and the shopping mall, the consumerism of preparedness and the militarization of everyday life, the selling of patriotism and the branding of the nation—these converge in contemporary American culture to maintain the notion of American innocence. The presence of the Hummer in the driveway masks the use of the Humvee in the war in Iraq, and the presence of the suburban big-box retailers allows for the erasure of the prison complex on the outskirts of town. The consumerism of comfort, whether it takes the form of kitsch or of preparedness chic, operates primarily to smooth over conflict and mask the consequences of the nation's action. It is thus a primary aspect of the tourism of history, encouraging a tourist-consumerist relationship to the contemporary crisis of security in the United States. As the citizen-consumer has replaced the citizen, the maintenance of the innocence of that citizen is contingent on the effects of U.S. foreign policy and the U.S. prison industry being rendered invisible. These aspects of American society are clearly in evidence in the context of the Oklahoma City bombing and its aftermath. In the next two chapters I turn to the meanings of that event and the ways it has both disrupted this tourism of history and been incorporated into it.

CITIZENS AND SURVIVORS

Cultural Memory and Oklahoma City

In 2003, during the beginning months of the wars in Iraq and Afghanistan, the archive of the Oklahoma City National Memorial began to send stuffed animals to children in Afghanistan and children living in a displaced persons camp in Iraq. The memorial has an extensive archive which retains, among many other things, the objects that have been left by visitors at a fence on the exterior wall of the memorial. When the archive began to accumulate too many items that were not personalized by visitors in any way, the archive manager, Jane Thomas, created a program to circulate these objects around the world. In the I Am Hope project, the staff has washed numerous stuffed animals and sent them to these children, with a multilingual tag clearly addressed to children:

> I Am Hope: When our federal building in Oklahoma City, Oklahoma, U.S.A. was bombed in April 1995, people from all around the world wanted to let us know they cared about us. This toy was left on the fence that surrounded the place where the attack happened. We do not know who left this toy, but we know it helped us feel better. We want you to have it now . . . and to know that we care. *From Oklahoma City, with love.*

In addition, the archive began to circulate many of the numerous small flags that are left on the fence to American troops serving in Afghanistan and Iraq. They travel with a tag that reads:

> A Flag from the Fence: This flag is not new. It was left on the fence at the Oklahoma City National Memorial, site of the April 19, 1995 bombing of the Alfred P. Murrah Federal Building. For the family members, survivors and rescue workers and all Oklahomans, it is a symbol of hope—the same hope that carried us through the bombings in Beirut, Khobar Towers, the bombing of the USS Cole, Kenyan and Tanzanian Embassies, and the September 11, 2001, attacks. We appreciate your efforts as you take to the field. Please carry with you this piece of "hope" from the Memorial, as we all work to make this world a better place.

One soldier stationed in Afghanistan brought the flag back with him and left it on the fence again with a note.[1]

These stuffed animals and flags can tell us many things about the complex meanings that are created when ordinary commodity objects are circulated in new contexts. What did a displaced child in Iraq, whose home had been destroyed by the U.S. invasion, understand from such an object? Did that child get comfort from this stuffed animal? At its core, the gesture is an attempt to imbue an object with a sense of traveling hope, to make a connection between two sites of violence.

Of course, one can argue that such a gesture erases many aspects of global politics in its participation in a global comfort culture. It can be seen to say, We are sorry that our attack on your country resulted in your being a refugee, but we would like to give you a stuffed animal, a teddy bear, to offer comfort. In the critique of comfort culture that I have been making in this book, I have argued that such objects, no matter how well intended, cannot be innocent. They evoke innocence, they sell innocence, and they promote it, but in their very circulation they participate in a comfort culture that simplifies and reduces, that effaces political complexity. Does the tag of earnest sentiment make these stuffed animals kitsch objects, with the prescribed emotions such objects are supposed to evoke? Or is that kitsch value negated by the affective gesture of a child who receives such a toy and uses it to feel better? When the gesture made by the Oklahoma City National Memorial archivists is seen as one made by the individuals at a site that has struggled with the consequences of violence to connect to those who are attempting to survive at another site of violence, a gesture that attempts to counter the exceptionalism of violent events, it can be deeply affecting. If we look at such a gesture in national terms, as an American teddy bear (albeit one most likely produced in Asia) that is sent to the victims of a U.S.-led war, then the meanings shift. Such an offering is also, not incidentally, a radical way for an archive to operate, given that archives normally acquire and retain objects rather than sending them out to circulate in the world. Yet this is not an ordinary archive, since it contains numerous everyday objects that were left by the general public as a means to participate in cultural memory.

The stuffed animals and flags of the Oklahoma City memorial archive evoke many aspects of the cultural memory of Oklahoma City, with their mix of consumerism and community-based emotion. One of the primary aspects of the memorial is its evocation of a community response to unanticipated violence. The bombing of the Alfred P. Murrah Federal Building on April 19, 1995, was an event of shocking impact not only on Oklahoma City but on the United States. It was shocking largely because it took place in a political context and in a part of the country in which violence of this kind was unanticipated. Edward T. Linenthal, whose insightful book *The Unfinished Bombing* is the definitive text on the memorialization of the bombing, has written that the bombing "took place in what was envisioned as America's 'heartland,' shattering the assumption that Middle America was immune to acts of mass terrorism as well as the assumption that the nation still had 'zones of safety,' such as day care centers."[2] The bombing thus disrupted particular concepts of safety and exemption from violence that reverberated well beyond its human toll. In addition, it was revealed to be the work of several "home-grown" terrorists, including Timothy McVeigh, a decorated Gulf War veteran, and Terry Nichols, also a veteran; it was later evident that they had bombed the building in retaliation for the role that federal agents had played in the massacre of the Branch Davidian cult in Waco, Texas, exactly two years prior, in which eighty-six people, including twenty-two children, had died. Thus, the bombing also demanded a recognition of terrorism as a domestic event. All of these aspects of the event converged to produce a narrative of national innocence lost.

The dead of Oklahoma City came to be perceived not only as innocent victims of arbitrary violence—people who were in the wrong place at the wrong time and who were wrongfully murdered for misguided, if not evil, intent—but as icons of a nation's lost innocence, lost not only through violence but through specifically American violence. As I noted before, this narrative of innocence is so pervasive in American political narrative and

self-identity that it is constantly reiterated in times of crisis. The lost innocence that the bombing was seen to perpetuate was a belief that ordinary
people were outside the realm of politically motivated violence, a belief that
rural areas and small Middle American cities existed somehow outside of
the world of crime, violence, and ethnic hatred that affects other American
cities. This sense of innocence was heightened by the fact that nineteen children were killed in the bombing, almost all of whom were in a day care center, ironically named America's Kids Day Care Center, which was located on
the second floor, directly above the explosion. Seen as the most innocent of
the victims, these children were the object of immense national and global
mourning, a mourning that precipitated, among other gestures, the sending
of large numbers of stuffed animals to the city and later to the memorial.
The deaths of these children brought a heightened awareness of the sense-
lessness and arbitrariness of violence (even though no such mourning had
taken place for the children, also presumably innocent, who died in Waco).

The Oklahoma City bombing has produced two primary responses: the
building of the Oklahoma City National Memorial, which was opened in
April 2000, just five years after the bombing, and the execution of Timothy
McVeigh, believed to be the man primarily responsible for the bombing, on
June 11, 2001, in Terre Haute, Indiana. The Oklahoma City National Memorial is a highly reflexive memorial, conscious of the politics of memory,
that is intensely community-based. It includes a memorial center with an
exhibition about the bombing and a gift shop that sells souvenirs that evoke
a combination of mourning, memorialization, and tourism. The memorial
and the execution have both produced memories about the bombing and
provoked debates about cultural memory, the citizen, and the process of
mourning. This process would preface the debates and conflicts that took
place in New York after 9/11 and offer a contrast to them. In this chapter I
reflect upon the response to the bombing in Oklahoma City and the local
and national meanings of the Oklahoma City National Memorial; in the following chapter, I turn to the execution as the memorial's counterpart and to
the aftermath of the memorial and execution.

ICONIC IMAGES AND REPETITION

The most famous images of the Oklahoma City bombing pair the spectacular with the intimate. Since the bombing itself was not photographed,
the initial image that circulated in television and print news shows the shell
of the smoking building, a stunningly decimated structure. The following

The headline and front page of *The Daily Oklahoman*, Thursday, April 20, 1995, reading:

THE DAILY OKLAHOMAN

MORNING OF TERROR

City Struggles With Shock of Deadly Bombing

Small Children Victims In Day-Care Center

Scores Killed In Bomb Blast; State Stunned

Terror in the Heartland

Fresh Day in City Turns Into New-Found Horror

FIGURE 23. The *Daily Oklahoman*, April 20, 1995.

morning, April 20, the *Daily Oklahoman* ran under the headline "Morning of Terror" two photographs that have since acquired iconic status. The first is an image of the federal building, once a fortified yet unexceptional bureaucratic building, as it stands in ruins. All of its normally hidden internal features—wiring, ventilation system, structural cables (its guts, essentially)—hang out. It represents a shattered body, and its image quickly came to be a symbol of national vulnerability and a wound to the body public. The image of the decimated building gains its iconic status not only for its representation of the destruction of the building itself, surrounded by the nondescript cityscape, but also for its capacity to stand in for the nation as a whole, wounded, and vulnerable.

Yet the primary image icon that emerged from the bombing is not of the building's destruction, which covered the top half of the front page (that

FIGURE 24. Photograph of Baylee Almon and the firefighter Chris Fields, by Charles Porter IV, featured on the cover of *Newsweek*, May 1, 1995.

issue of the *Daily Oklahoman* is now sold in the memorial gift shop), but the smaller image beneath it that pictures the shattering of human life. This is the photograph of the crumpled body of one-year-old Baylee Almon being cradled in the arms of the firefighter Chris Fields. This image, taken by the amateur photographer Charles Porter IV, eventually won the Pulitzer Prize and ran on the cover of *Newsweek, Time, Life,* and the *Economist*.[3] On the cover of *Newsweek*, the firefighter's helmet looms over the name of the publication itself as his figure fills the frame. The image's power derives in part from the contrast of the familiar gesture of holding a young child in one's arms with the shock of the child's lifeless form. In any tragic event, certain victims emerge as icons of all those lost, and in Oklahoma City, the children were the focus of enormous public grief and empathy. In the months after the bombing, people continued to send children's toys and drawings to the city, as if the toys and pictures could somehow provide comfort to the dead children. The photo of Baylee Almon symbolizes the shock of these children's deaths, yet its power derives from the fact that it is an image of the protective gesture of the rescue worker, whose body fills the frame as a figure of power and reassurance. Importantly, the image gained its power not only because it demonstrated the shock of violence in its impact on a small child, but also in its capacity to offer reassurance through its depiction of adults, public servants, and, by extension, the government, providing comfort in the face of such violence.

In the weeks after the bombing, this photograph was circulated widely in the media, and Aren Almon-Kok, Baylee's mother, and the firefighter Chris Fields, as well as the photographer Charles Porter were widely interviewed by the news media in reference to the photograph.[4] The image was quickly reproduced on T-shirts and small medallions and inevitably became the focus of lawsuits over its use.[5] The family and the firefighter allowed the image to be rendered into an eighteen-inch bronze statue entitled *Innocence Lost* that was used to raise funds for the Feed the Children organization; without their permission, it was used by several phone card companies, including Globalnet Communications. In this case, the company argued in stunning fashion that the image would transform the act of using the phone card into a kind of memorial, as each time people use the card, "they will be reminded of this despicable waste of life and actually hear the salutation: Thank You for supporting the Oklahoma City Disaster relief fund."[6] Almon-Kok told Edward Linenthal that the publicness of Baylee's death, which made her the focus of intense media attention, was like reliving her death in constant replay: "All of us who lost loved ones suffered terribly. But I had to look at the photograph of my child every day, in newspapers, magazines, on T-shirts and figurines. . . . I had to live her death all over again day after day."[7] She several times advocated that an image of Baylee on her first birthday, the day before she died, be used instead. (Almon-Kok's relationship to the iconization of Baylee has not been simple, though, since she herself ran a delicatessen near the memorial called Miss Baylee's Deli for a period of time and allowed herself to be featured regularly in the media, including coverage of her wedding by *People* magazine.)

Both the image of the federal building in ruins and the image of Baylee cradled in the firefighter's arms have been the subject of a number of remakes. The archive at the Oklahoma City National Memorial contains numerous remakes of the image of the building in ruins, including a model

FIGURE 25. Oklahoma City Federal Building, 1998. From The Buildings of Disaster 1998–2006 project designed by Constantin Boym. Produced by Boym Partners, Inc.

constructed by a class of high school students. In his series of metal miniatures, *Buildings of Disaster*, Constantin Boym has included a miniature of the federal building in ruins, with its characteristic stepped pile of bricks. Boym produces these souvenirs, made of nickel and a few inches tall, in editions of five hundred and sells them for $95. His miniatures of disaster have tapped into a collectable market for unusual souvenirs. His series, which attempts to be a kind of alternative history of architecture, focuses on the buildings that are associated with disasters. Thus, it is the decimated building itself that is iconic of the event, a building that would be considered truly unexceptional were it still standing. Boym's series also includes the World Trade Center, the Superdome in New Orleans, the Unabomber's cabin, and the Chernobyl reactor.

Yet it is the image of Baylee Almon that has produced the greatest array of reenactments. Many artists, both amateur and professional, felt compelled to remake the photograph in paintings and sculpture in the first years after the bombing, and to send their work to Oklahoma City and to Almon-Kok. A large number rewrite the image so that Baylee is alive, sleeping gently in Fields's arms, or, in more religious images, is being handed off to God, thus transforming its meaning into an image of salvation. A large marble

CHAPTER 2

"In Memory of... April 19, 1995"

Thenka-
Clif Doyeto

FIGURE 26. *In Memory Of...*, 1995, by Clif Doyeto. Courtesy of Clif Doyeto.

statue by the New York sculptor Miles Slater depicting the firefighter and the baby, which is part of the museum exhibition at the Memorial Center, is simply called *Rescue*. One painting by the Oklahoma Indian artist Clif Doyeto, which now hangs in the state capitol, depicts the firefighter holding a shrouded baby surrounded by other icons of the tragedy, including mourning people, the shell of the building, an American flag, a teddy bear, and the image of a rescue dog that was also popular in the media. In the version by the local artist Una Jean Carter, a line of rescue workers holding children of many different ethnicities stand before a Christ figure, with Baylee alive and smiling. While the building burns in the background, the crowd standing before Jesus depicts redemption. In a cartoon for the *Chicago Tribune* by Dick Lochner, the firefighter turns around and holds up Baylee's lifeless form to two large hands descending from heaven.

In many ways, these reenactments evoke the need to repeat an image out

FIGURE 27. *He Conquered Death*, 1995, by Una Jean Carter. Courtesy of Una Jean Carter.

FIGURE 28. Cartoon by Dick Lochner, April 1995. © Tribune Media Services, Inc. All rights reserved. Reprinted with permission.

of grief. The horror of the dead child is mediated by the comfort offered by the firefighter's presence. These reenactments were attempts to create an image of redemption and comfort from an image of trauma—to remake the image again and again until it is no longer traumatic. Oklahoma City is situated in the middle of the Bible Belt, with a large and devout Christian population; thus it is not surprising that the reworking of the trauma was facilitated by religious narratives. That these images spill over into kitsch can largely be attributed to these religious themes, in which Christian iconography is used to recode a tragic event into one of reassurance.

There were other deployments of the image that were more controversial. When Timothy McVeigh was sentenced to death, the *Arizona Republic* cartoonist Steve Benson published a cartoon that depicted the firefighter as a stand-in for "death penalty fanatics" holding the child, who says, "No more killing." Intended as a critique of the death penalty, the cartoon set off a storm of controversy and the newspaper issued an apology.[8] The image of the firefighter as a protective figure carrying a fire victim from a building had a long history prior to this image.[9] Yet, in light of the sanctification of firefighters as the iconic figures of 9/11, images that evoke this photograph of Chris Fields and Baylee keep reemerging. *Heroes*, a comic book about firefighters in 9/11 published by Marvel Comics in December 2001, featured an image of firefighters carrying a body out of Ground Zero in a pose that resembled the Oklahoma City image. The 2004 film *Ladder 49*, which depicts firefighters finding meaning after fighting a difficult blaze, was released on DVD with an image of a firefighter carrying a small figure from a blaze, one that clearly evoked the image of Baylee Almon. Baylee's iconic function thus seems to be to reestablish the image of the firefighter, to affirm his iconic role in mediating trauma. Yet when the Oklahoma City National Memorial was designed, it would not be a reenactment of the firefighter and the baby.

THE OKLAHOMA CITY NATIONAL MEMORIAL: EMPTY CHAIRS

The Oklahoma City National Memorial is, above all, a memorial to the lives of ordinary citizens. Traditionally, national memorials, which have been almost exclusively built in Washington, D.C., very rarely represent so-called ordinary citizens (those, for instance, not well known or in the military). The Franklin Delano Roosevelt Memorial, which was dedicated in 1997, has several George Segal statues that depict ordinary people listening to the radio broadcast of Roosevelt's fireside chats and standing in Depression-era bread lines, yet they are the exception in the codes of national memorialization. At the same time, the trend of the past two decades has produced at least two memorials in Washington, D.C., the Vietnam Veterans Memorial and the U.S. Holocaust Museum, that have shifted the emphasis to an honoring of survivors in ways that have radically resituated the politics of cultural memory.

Given this context, the Oklahoma City National Memorial represents both an embrace of the contemporary emphasis on survivors and their needs and a significant departure from the most common codes of national memorials in its emphasis on ordinary citizens. While the Oklahoma City memorial stands not in the weighty context of the national capital, it evokes in its very design the form and symbolism of the Washington Mall. Yet it is emphatically a memorial about Middle America, the romanticized yet often forgotten center of the country, and about the lives of the ordinary citizens in the American heartland. The presence of survivors sped this memorial into existence; no other national U.S. memorial had ever been designed and built in such a short amount of time. It is the product of an intense process of negotiation with citizens, categorized by the memorial staff as families of the dead, survivors, and those who aided in the rescue operation.[10] With 168 dead, approximately 850 survivors, and countless rescuers, those affected numbered in the thousands (the U.S. attorney's office in Oklahoma City lists twenty-three hundred people as victims and survivors, which includes families of the dead).[11] The population of Oklahoma City is under 500,000, and it is estimated that 387,000 of them knew someone who was directly affected by the bombing.[12] The rapid pace at which it was built, the participation of many people, the intense focus on the needs and desires of the survivors and families, and the role the memorial plays in the revival of the economics of Oklahoma City have converged to make this site one of the most self-conscious memorials built in the United States.

The key narrative of redemption that has emerged from the bombing is the narrative of a community coming together in a time of tragedy to create a memorial through consensus. The memorial functions in many ways as an embrace of a particular notion of community, and local concepts of community and consensus were key to its rapid construction. As the process of memorialization and rebuilding in New York has grown increasingly acrimonious, Oklahoma City looks like a more community-oriented model, and its memorial process is often depicted as evidence of the heartland's civility as opposed to the grim and combative environment of New York.

Linenthal characterizes the process of building the memorial as emblematic of increased democratization in American culture: "In Oklahoma City, the memorial process involved hundreds of people and it was consciously designed to be therapeutic: to help the community engage the traumatic impact of the bombing."[13] Yet it is also explicitly called a "national" memorial, which not only situates it in relation to narratives of American history, but also deliberately situates Oklahoma City within the nation, rather than allowing its memorialization to stand in isolation. This nationalization of the bombing was in fact almost instantaneous; many assumed that the bombing was politically motivated and that it had been the work of foreign terrorists. Indeed, early in the recovery operation to find the bodies of the dead, an American flag was attached to a grappling hook at the site so that the flag was constantly being draped over the debris.[14] The dead were thus immediately inscribed as American dead.

After the bombing, Oklahoma City very quickly became the focus of an urge to memorialize. This initially took the form of people bringing objects to leave at shrines that were created at the periphery of the space cordoned off by emergency personnel. Since the construction of the Vietnam Veterans Memorial in 1982 there has been a national focus—filtered through the media and other forms of commentary, including academic scrutiny—on the kinds of rituals that individuals participate in as a means to confront trauma and loss and to intervene into public narratives of national events. The small, individual acts of leaving objects, notes, or flowers for a person, which have been practiced outside of the national arena for many decades at cemeteries and roadside shrines, became an aspect of national culture when visitors began to leave things at the Vietnam Veterans Memorial as a means of speaking to the dead. These gestures became a central part of the media coverage and coffee-table books generated by the memorial.

In the aftermath of the bombing, the chain-link fence that was used to contain the area devastated by the bomb soon became the focus of mourning activity. People were drawn to the site from the beginning to look at the destruction and they began to leave things there: photographs, key chains, license plates, T-shirts with names written on them, and tributes to those who had died. Initially, people took small bits of the rubble as relics from the site. (Later, the rubble was distributed to state and federal agencies for display and then incorporated into a number of other memorials.)[15] This need to leave objects near the site of destruction, or to take artifacts from it, was echoed by a desire to offer memorial designs to the city. Thus, beginning less than twenty-four hours after the bombing and continuing until a

FIGURE 29. Fence at Oklahoma City National Memorial. Photo by Ann E. Clark. © 2005 Oklahoma City National Memorial Foundation.

design was chosen in June 1997, numerous designs were sent unsolicited to the city government. The need to design a memorial, like the compulsion to remake the iconic images of the bombing, appears to be a means through which people sought comfort by remaking the space itself. The desire to build a memorial is not unlike the act of leaving an object at a shrine: each is an attempt to use an object as a means to counteract loss.

There were initially many calls to rebuild the federal building as it stood, in ways that would later be reflected in the numerous proposals in New York to rebuild the twin towers as a statement of defiance.[16] Yet, in Oklahoma City this idea was quickly superseded by demands to build a memorial as soon as possible. In the flood of unsolicited proposals, offers came from the designers of well-known memorials, such as Glenda Goodacre, who designed the Vietnam Women's Memorial, and Felix de Weldon, who had designed numerous memorials, including the Marine Corps War Memorial of soldiers raising the flag at Iwo Jima. A large number of proposals from amateur designers were sent to the city and the mayor, including a significant number that were claimed to be the result of visions, implying that they were the result of some kind of divine intervention. Linenthal notes that many designs took the form of heart shapes (to indicate variations on the idea of the heartland and sympathy), teddy bears, and angels, and that often these volunteer designers were so fervent that they would call the various agencies of the city and lobby on behalf of their proposals.[17]

Many suggestions for a memorial also presented the image of Baylee Almon and the firefighter as a motif. There was such a preponderance of these suggestions that many involved in the planning for the memorial, and Baylee's mother, were concerned to make sure that these two *not* be the focus. Subsequently, a clause, informally known as the "Baylee Almon clause," was added to the competition; participants were requested "not to depict physical representation of any known person, living or dead, in their Design Entry."[18] Importantly, then, the photograph of the firefighter and child helped create a context in which figural representation was rejected, thus guaranteeing that the memorial would have an abstract design.

The democratization of the memorialization process in Oklahoma City was exemplified by the way the decision was organized. Initially, a committee of 350 people was established, which met regularly and subdivided into a huge number of smaller committees in order to make a set of decisions about the memorial process, including its mission statement. A survey of approximately seven thousand people was taken to gather a sense of what people wanted from a memorial. This is in sharp contrast to the way that the decision making proceeded in New York after 9/11, where public participation ended up largely as window dressing. The mission statement of the memorial, which was the product of much negotiation and debate among survivors, families, and rescuers over virtually every word, was finalized in what Robert Johnson, chair of the Memorial Trust, calls an "extraordinary consensus" in March 1996. It stipulated the dual intents of pedagogy and therapeutic effect—that the memorial needed to include an information center (which would include biographies of the dead and stories of survivors), the tree that had survived the blast, the names of those who died, the names of survivors, and an area for children. The process was difficult; the needs of survivors and the families of the dead were often in conflict, in some cases with family members contending that survivors should not participate in the process because they had not lost anyone.[19] Hierarchies of memorialization inevitably arose, with a sense that those who lost children has suffered more, that those who had survived had suffered less, and that those who had survived without injury even less.

The mission statement established that the memorial would encompass the area where the Murrah building had stood, most of the block across the street, and the area that had been occupied by Fifth Street in between, and that this area, in particular the ground where the building had stood, would be considered sacred ground. While the concept of sacred ground would become highly contested in the attempts to rebuild Ground Zero in New York, in part because so few of the dead were recovered, in Oklahoma City this designation was enabled by the fact that the land to be set aside for the memorial was in a relatively open urban area, rather than in the middle of a dense city. Nevertheless, the issue of sacred ground was contested in relation to the closing of Fifth Street, which was seen by some as a constant reminder of the tragedy. Oklahoma governor Frank Keating wrote to the traffic commission in 1996 that to reopen the street would be like running traffic past the Wailing Wall in Jerusalem.[20] Though people had died in the surrounding area and more than sixteen buildings affected by the blast had to be demolished, the footprint of the Murrah building was designated as the sacred ground that held the memory of the event itself.

Many of these decisions about the parameters of the memorial were made with community input. Thus, in many ways the construction of the memorial in Oklahoma City was about asserting symbolic ownership of the design by the community, rather than ceding power to the broader design community that was itself invested in such a high-profile commission. Robert Johnson, head of the Memorial Task Force, fired the professional consultant for the competition, Paul Spreiregen, after Spreiregen advised in a lengthy report that the Task Force needed to hire a jury of only design professionals to choose a memorial design. Johnson told him, "We do not universally share the same philosophical approach to the design selection process as it relates to community involvement."[21] Spreiregen responded that outside opinion was "only grudgingly tolerated" in Oklahoma City, that the history of memorials showed that the best designs had been chosen by professionals. He wrote:

There appears to be some kind of overriding concern in Oklahoma City that the memorial will somehow serve as a salve to the survivors by enabling them to deal better with their grief. By the time this memorial is completed, most of those who have been touched by this tragedy will have dealt with their trauma. The memorial will then be there for another purpose—to educate the young and old and act to reinforce a sense of community, if you will, the idea of rebirth. It is here that design excellence has its proper place—as a true sign of optimism and belief in the future for those who have survived. [22]

He may have been correct in noting that the memorial would eventually come to symbolize the rebirth of the community, but his concept of the short timeline of grief for survivors would make little sense in Oklahoma City on the ten-year anniversary of the bombing, when survivors and families could articulate how present their grief and loss remained. Yet in ways that would be prescient of the conflict over the World Trade Center memorial, this conflict of design experts and the community points to a concern by design professionals that while memorials are built in part for those grieving, grief is not the best position from which to conceive the design of a memorial that will last decades into the future. Paul Goldberger writes:

> By almost every professional standard, Spreiregen was right. Victims' families can't be expected to make a knowing judgment about what constitutes the best public memorial. Giving them control would seem to be a concession to a kind of victims' culture, elevating sentiment over any other value. In the end, however, Johnson's gamble that he could trust the families proved to be right, in large part because the mission statement set forth a program for the memorial that made the kitsch that Spreiregen feared almost impossible.[23]

Thus, ironically, it was the proliferation of kitsch remakes of the firefighter photograph and the local politics surrounding depictions of the bombing victims that ultimately dictated that the memorial would not be figurative and that had an impact on the kind of aesthetics the final design would embrace. In the end, the committee that selected the design was composed of design professionals, family members, and survivors. They announced a design competition in fall 1996 which generated tremendous interest and received 624 proposals from twenty-three countries.[24] After five finalists were put on display in April 1997, the final design, by architects Hans and Torrey Butzer and Sven Berg, was chosen in June 1997. It would eventually cost $29.1 million raised from private and public funds.

The memorial, which was dedicated on April 19, 2001, exactly five years after the bombing and almost five months before 9/11, responds to the elaborate needs laid out by the mission statement and thus operates as a series of

FIGURE 30. Memorial chairs at Oklahoma City National Memorial. © 2005 Oklahoma City National Memorial Foundation.

parts, each with different intents and aesthetics, that converge. The "Gates of Time" are two large yellow bronze monuments that stand at either end of a central reflecting pool, with the times 9:01 and 9:03 marking the frame of the event (which happened at 9:02). The "Field of Empty Chairs" consists of 168 bronze chairs, each carrying the name of a victim. The names of survivors are carved into the remnants of a damaged wall left from the building. The "Survivor Tree," an elm tree that survived the bombing, is surrounded by a terrace that looks down on the rest of the memorial. A "Rescuer's Orchard" of fruit and flowering trees stands on a terraced slope next to the survivor tree. A children's area has a tiled wall of children's messages and chalk areas for participation. The memorial forms an aesthetically careful space, in which one feels constantly guided by design elements in one's experience of it. Visitors are encouraged by the design to enter through one of the two "Gates of Time" at either end, each of which has extended ramps and staircases so that they create a transitional movement into the space. The designers stated that they wanted to "freeze the time of the bombing in space" by using the gates to create a sense of a large outdoor room. They saw the reflecting pool as a means to promote healing, with the intent that those who gaze into the water would see "the faces of those changed forever."[25] The memorial chairs stand within the footprint of the Murrah building,

FIGURE 31. Oklahoma City National Memorial at night, June 9, 2001. AP Photo/Elise Amendola.

which includes an exposed wall of the original foundation, where the names of survivors are inscribed. The designers thus see the memorial as a kind of story that visitors enter into through the gates, a space of meaning that they will then leave transformed.

The memorial design provides a negotiation between monumentality and intimacy and, as such, operates in dialogue with the history of national memorials. It references in subtle ways the spaces of the Washington Mall. While the pool may be intended by the designers to offer healing and self-reflection, it also references the reflecting pool on the mall, and the large gates evoke the Lincoln and Washington monuments. With its emphasis on the individual, the field of chairs recalls the names on the Vietnam Veterans Memorial. The memorial thus straddles a fine line between conventional and radical memorial design, a strategy necessitated perhaps by the multiple interests in its production. The need to counteract monumentality is central to the memorial's effect, since the "Gates of Time," in marking the moment of the bombing, not only frame the moment of death and loss, the moment between life and death, but could award monumentality to the bomb itself. The memorial counters this monumentality in its focus on the individual and, hence, the therapeutic.

By far the most striking aspect of the design is the field of empty chairs. Arranged in rows to indicate the nine floors of the building (though among the dead are five victims who died in surrounding buildings and on the

FIGURE 32. Memorial gates and reflecting pool at the Oklahoma City National Memorial. Photo by Ann E. Clark. © 2005 Oklahoma City National Memorial Foundation.

street) and set on the ground where the Murrah building once stood, the chairs create a separate space within the memorial itself. Each chair bears the name of one of the dead, and those that are named for children are poignantly much smaller in size. This very simple aspect of the design has a compelling and startling effect. The small chairs indicate not only vulnerability but a different kind of corporeality. They are reminders of the small chairs of elementary schools, the miniature world of toddlers (most of the children killed were very young, ranging from infants to toddlers), and the sadness evoked by the size of a child's coffin. The chairs of the memorial each have a glass base that is lit up at night, creating a field of light that is quite beautiful and powerfully evocative of the uniqueness of the individual.

The emptiness of these chairs is, quite clearly, a means of representing absence. The empty chair at the dinner table, the empty chair in the office, the empty chair on the porch—these conjure the body of the absent one. Before I first visited the memorial, I had assumed from photographs of the chairs that people would sit in them, as a kind of reflection on someone gone. Yet I have never seen anyone, except a small child, do so. This indicates that the chairs succeed in evoking presence in addition to absence, that to sit in one would actually be to sit in a chair that is already occupied in some way. Families, friends, and other visitors interact with the chairs instead by leaving objects on them (which are removed regularly by the memorial staff under a strict set of rules), sitting on the ground next to them, and gathering around them. It is an unfortunate aspect of memorial maintenance (because of problems with the grass) that the chairs are now roped off and open only to family and friends and during ceremonies. It was the intent of the designers that visitors interact with the chairs, and one cannot read the names at a distance.

Nevertheless, the memorial is seen as a place where the dead can be both found and spoken to. Families of the dead use the memorial as a means to speak to the dead, leaving them notes and speaking to others about them. One family held a wedding at the memorial, placing a photograph of their father on his chair, as a means of experiencing his participation. Often family members place on the chairs photographs of children who have been born since the bombing. Thus, the chairs provide a space where the dead are perceived to reside, even though no one is actually buried there. After much debate, the "common tissue" of unidentified remains was buried not at the memorial but on the grounds of the state capitol. The designers were adamantly opposed to remains being buried at the site, because they felt that it would "leave people with horrific images, rather than feelings of peace and hope."[26] This is in contrast to the memorial plans at Ground Zero, where there has been a strong movement to include unidentified remains at the site.

Naming is key to the memorial's effect, not only on the chairs but also on an adjacent wall of names of survivors, listed according to where they were when the blast occurred. Yet naming is a notoriously fraught aspect of memorials, one that more often than not reveals the desire to create hierarchies of the dead and that entails problems of inclusion and exclusion. For instance, Carrie Lenz, who was killed while five months pregnant, is named on her chair along with a name awarded to her never-born fetus, Michael Griffin Lenz III (Lenz was apparently killed while showing an ultrasound image of her baby to her colleagues at the Drug Enforcement Agency). This never-born child is thus tragically and ironically awarded personhood in death. Naming was also an issue in how to designate survivors. The Sur-

vivor Designation Committee of the memorial worked for months to research how survivors have historically been designated, deciding on a "zone
of danger" and a "zone of distress." Those who fit certain criteria in each
zone would thus be eligible to have their name inscribed on a wall at the
memorial or within the Memorial Center.[27] Other categories of naming raise
particular questions about how the dead are grouped and claimed. While
the Memorial Center lists the dead alphabetically, at anniversary ceremonies
their names are read by representatives of the various federal agencies that
were in the building. This has an odd effect, inscribing the dead into so-
called work families for which they themselves might have had conflicting
feelings.

The naming of the dead on the chairs, like the roll call of the dead at
ceremonies, works to provide a multiplicity of stories rather than one of a
mass of victims. It counters the monumentality of the mass violence of the
event with the intimacy of one person's presence. Linenthal has stated that
the memorial and the Memorial Center are able to focus on the stories of
individuals because, unlike in other events of mass violence, such as the Holocaust, the number of dead from the Oklahoma City bombing is compre-
hensible.[28] The naming of the dead at the memorial, like the act of leaving
a message, is a declarative act that also serves to individualize the victims.
As such, these objects and messages resist the collective subjectivity of the
victims, and the mass subjectivity of disaster in general. The bombing of the
federal building, like all events of mass injury, created an image of injury to a
mass body. The mass body of disasters, Michael Warner writes, such as natural disasters and airline disasters (and, inevitably, one could add, terrorist
acts of mass destruction), is represented as a singular entity. Those killed are
absorbed into this larger image of a collective dead, marked by death into a
singular subject. Warner writes, "Disaster is popular, as it were, because it is
a way of making mass subjectivity available, and it tells us something about
the desirability of that mass subject." Media representations are dependent
on the image of disaster, which always, according to Warner, "commands
a headline," and on creating a set of stories through which the individuals of that mass body can be typified. "Mass injury can always command
a headline; it gets classed as immediate reward news. But whatever kind of
reward makes disaster rewarding, it inevitably has to do with injury to a mass
body—an already abstracted body."[29] The acts of individualization at the
memorial—in its design, the emphasis on individuals in its museum exhibit,
and the artifacts that have been placed there—are all means to counteract

the mass subjectivity of the dead. This in turn serves to mediate the potential awesomeness of the bombing itself, reducing it from an impressive image of massive power to a collective set of stories of loss and survival.

The memorial has many ways of separating the families and survivors from other visitors at the memorial, of allowing them private grief, yet it is also a very public space that has been the intense focus of the media since it was built. There is thus a constant tension between the desire to speak publicly through a trauma and the desire to grieve without an audience. When I attended the sixth anniversary ceremony of the bombing, I was struck by the way that those attending worked to achieve personal forms of ritual and grief while under the constant eye of an enormous barrage of news cameras. Media were kept at a distance and not allowed into the space of the chairs until two hours after the ceremony began, yet what was later described by a participant as an "intimate" ceremony was relentlessly documented and commented on, receiving particular media attention that year, with its demand for public grieving and testimony, because of McVeigh's impending execution.

The highly individual nature of rituals of grief defies any simple kind of conclusion about how people negotiate loss. I was moved in watching the ceremony by an African American family that had come as a group to pay tribute to Casandra Booker, who died at the age of twenty-five while applying for social security cards for two of her four children. They each wore T-shirts with her photograph and the words "In Memory of Casandra Booker," and then below the image the words "My Mother," "My Aunt," "My Sister-in-Law." These shirts were so carefully constructed and so emphatic in their statement of the personal nature of loss (*my* mother). T-shirts are a contemporary means of making political statements and proclaiming allegiances (whether to brand names or to causes); they are one of the primary means for an individual to make a declaration. Numerous families wear T-shirts with images of those lost to the memorial ceremonies. These shirts provided a forum for the media (some of whom photographed and interviewed this family) but were also a testimony to the personal connection to an absent loved one, actually wearing his or her image on one's body and inhabiting it, so to speak.

One of the primary ways that individuals are encouraged to interact at the memorial is through the fence that is now placed on an outside wall at its entrance. This was the same fence where people initially left objects. The designers had envisioned three small sections of fence in the children's area that would encourage a similar activity, arguing that the fence itself was not as important as "what the fence allows to happen." Yet several family members were concerned that this fence, which had been so important to them in those first years, would be lost, even though a few felt it was an "immature" form of memorial.[30] When the memorial was completed, the fence was transported by volunteers to an outside wall, where it is both separate from and part of an entry into the memorial. The material on the fence is only a fraction of the massive inventory of objects that the memorial has acquired and which are part of its archive.

In its incorporation into the memorial design, the fence remains a primary site where people come to leave objects and messages. There are much-considered rules concerning this activity and these objects, which reflect the overall thoughtfulness and intensity of the memorial's intended rituals. Objects that are left on the fence are allowed to stay for a maximum of thirty days. The memorial staff then removes them if they are not related to a particular victim or agency and according to issues of space and durability. The memorial staff will not place something at the fence if someone sends it in; it must be placed there in person. Rules are different for the chairs, where items are left for seventy-two hours after an anniversary ceremony, and otherwise removed and discarded after twenty-four hours (though the staff will, on request, move an object then to the fence). This policy was the result of an extended debate among families, survivors, and rescue workers because many survivors and rescuers thought that it would look tacky to have objects left on the chairs.[31]

The Memorial Center, which opened in February 2001, now houses a massive and growing collection of materials in its archive. According to the archivist Jane Thomas, once people realized that their collection was "more than 3,000 teddy bears," they began to send in other materials: photographs, documents, artwork, and personal material from families; trial materials; and documents, such as surveys, from the process of writing the mission statement of the memorial. The archive has six areas of collection: the history of the site; the incident itself, including rescue and recovery; responses to the event, including media coverage; the investigation and trial; spinoffs, such as new regulations and laws that resulted; and memorialization.[32] It now houses over eight hundred thousand pieces, including documents related to the McVeigh and Nichols trials, seventy thousand photographs, newspaper articles, and over one hundred thousand objects, such as cards, letters, quilts, art objects, uniforms, memorial designs, the personal effects of some victims, reporters' notes, shattered glass from the building, and items from the building such as the playhouse from the day care center's play yard.[33]

This extraordinary attention to detail, the rapid accumulation of this huge collection, and the self-consciousness with which the memorial has come together through endless discussion, debate, and consensus make it a deeply reflexive place in which visitors are constantly offered interpretations of the memorial and a set of guidelines on their experience. One could even argue that this makes the Memorial Center and the memorial itself postmodern, in that the experience of both is mediated by their own presentations; for instance, the Memorial Center exhibition has a long section devoted to the design and building of the memorial and the intentions of its design. This reflexivity operates in concert with what I see as a kind of *organized spontaneity* that comprises individuals' interactions with the memorial at the fence and chairs. People know before they come to the memorial what acts are connected to the fence, or they can see these codes immediately. These individual assertions of personal and cultural memory at the site are almost instantly contained within it, ascribed a timeline and a name. For instance, a message of graffiti, which was spontaneously scrawled on the wall of the former *Journal-Record* building (which now houses the Memorial Center) during the rescue operation, reads in large, angry letters, "Team 5, 4–19–95, We search for the truth. We seek justice. The courts require it. The victims cry for it. And GOD demands it!" It is accompanied by a plaque that explains, "A rescue worker originally painted the message on this wall during search and recovery efforts in April 1995."

This organized spontaneity connects the Oklahoma City Memorial to the Vietnam Veterans Memorial, where, for instance, an initial spontaneous leaving of objects became quickly codified so that any objects that are left are now immediately put in plastic bags, tagged, and removed daily by the National Park Service (NPS) to an archive. While this kind of activity was not initially anticipated by the Vietnam Memorial's design, it was an expected activity in Oklahoma City and was the focus of concerned debate on how best to facilitate and maintain it. Like many of the objects left at the Vietnam Memorial that are cryptic and secretive, refusing to tell their stories (a pack of cigarettes, a shot of whisky, and hats with obscure insignia), the artifacts at the Oklahoma memorial tend to be only partially declarative.[34] Some objects are quite explicit in their intended meaning; others are less obvious. The memorial staff found several black hats on the fence, which they later found out were left for a victim who liked to wear black hats; they also found a fishing pole, which was left for a young child whose grandfather had said he wanted to take him fishing when he was older.[35] There has been a trend in leaving license plates and key chains with the names of other places, which is presumably about marking geographical distance and the journey to the memorial, as if to say, I came the distance from there to see the memorial. This would seem to indicate the memorial's meaning as a destination and the site of pilgrimages.

The memorial design thus encourages many different kinds of responses, encompassing as it does a broad range of spaces, each with particular intent. Visitors are encouraged to be active in responding to the memorial, by leaving objects on the fence or drawing things in the children's area. People often depart from the proscribed codes in interacting with the memorial, for instance, dipping their hands into the water in order to leave handprints on the bronze gates. The memorial is open all the time and is a place that people often wander through at night. It is staffed constantly by volunteers, many of whom are survivors. Many family members and survivors work as docents for the Memorial Center and are frequent visitors to it. It has what is often referred to as a fervent volunteer culture, with seventy-five volunteers working every week.

The memorial is thus integrated into the community of Oklahoma City in complex ways that are about integrating a difficult past into the everyday. This intense community involvement is a factor in the relationship of the memorial to the National Park Service, which is in charge of the rangers and brochures at the site. According to the memorial's executive director, Kari Watkins, the Memorial Foundation restructured its relationship to the NPS in 2005. The NPS, says Watkins, expected the local community to recede as it has at other, similar sites, but the community in Oklahoma City is too invested to fully hand over the site.[36] Thus, as in the design of the memorial, the local community has consistently made clear, both emotionally and financially, its ownership of this national site. This incorporation of the memorial into the city has been facilitated by the sense of community and local pride that is a part of the memorial, and its pedagogical mission, one that is fervently expressed and dedicatedly carried out, and that centers in many ways on an embrace of citizenship and civic life.

THE CITIZEN AND THE EVERYDAY

Charles Griswold has called memorials a "species of pedagogy," in that they construct narratives about the past and how it should be understood.[37] However, most memorials are essentially ineffective as forms of political pedagogy. They pay tribute to the dead, but they cannot speak in more than very simple terms to the complexity of history. The Memorial Center reveals the tension between memorialization and pedagogy. The memorial's ostensible pedagogical mission is most evident in the institutions that are housed in the former *Journal Record* building that sits on the site: the Memorial Center, which houses an exhibition about the bombing, and the Memorial Institute for the Prevention of Terrorism, a nonprofit organization created by Congress in 1998 that facilitates research on the causes and effects of terrorism, with a particular focus on the work of first responders.[38] The Memorial Center tells a narrative of the bombing and its aftermath in ten chapters, using an array of explanatory texts, artifacts, videos, and interactive exhibits. The exhibition is intended to take visitors through a timeline of these events, beginning with the activities of the city in the early morning of April 19, 1995, before the blast, and ending with the design and construction of the memorial. Like other aspects of the memorial, it is very carefully designed and conscientiously attentive to the needs of survivors and families who visit there. Indeed, the voices of survivors are the central guiding narrative of the exhibit.

While the Memorial Center is clearly effective for many survivors, it is most obviously aimed at those who did not experience the bombing. The Center's pedagogical intent of explaining the meanings of the bombing and the ways that people in Oklahoma City responded to it is aimed at the unknowing, those who, one could say, have no personal memory of the bombing. Yet, the Memorial Center is not simply an exhibit that tells the story of the bombing and its aftermath; it attempts to create an experience of it. As such, it uses forms of reenactment with the intent that such forms will create empathy, if not a shocked concern, among the center's visitors.

The Memorial Center begins by placing visitors in an experiential relationship to the event. Relatively soon in the exhibit, groups of up to twenty-five visitors are asked to enter a room that is set up to replicate the hearing room at the Water Resources building, which once stood across the street from the Murrah building. The door is shut behind them, and as they stand in the room, an audiotape begins to play. This is a recording of the hearing that began at exactly 9:00 A.M. on April 19, and which is the only recording of any kind of the bomb blast itself. The mundane activities of the hearing are heard for two minutes, and then are interrupted by an enormous boom. At this point, the lights go out and visitors can hear the sounds of people screaming and yelling about getting out of the building (two people were killed in the Water Resources building). At that moment, a wall with photographs of the 168 bombing victims lights up, and the door opens onto the next exhibition room, where the first media images of the bombing are replayed over and over on a television monitor.

This reenactment intends in many ways to produce a cathartic response in museum visitors. The first time I went to the Memorial Center, I was shaken by this experience and found it chilling to hear the voices of people who were scared and shocked in the first few seconds after the bomb's explosion. The reenactment comes precariously close to a kind of theme park reenactment, yet with the intent to shock visitors out of their experience as distanced viewers and into an experience of trauma. The reenactment places visitors in the position of residents of Oklahoma City before the bombing, for whom the bombing arrives as a shock that disrupts a "day like any other." Thus, even though visitors enter the Memorial Center and this room knowing that the bombing took place, the reenactment experience is an attempt to place them in the position of the unexpecting, one could say innocent, public for whom it was, on April 19, 1995, a shocking event. As such this reenactment bears some similarities to the entrance to the exhibition at the U.S. Holocaust Museum in Washington, D.C. There, visitors must take an elevator to the beginning of the exhibit, where they are shown a video of the arrival of U.S. soldiers at the death camps, replaying, in effect, the moment that the general public became aware of the shocking reality of the camps.

This kind of theme park reenactment has become less exceptional in museum contexts. At the Imperial War Museum in London, for instance, museum visitors can enter a kind of diorama with sound and light that reenacts the experience of an air raid shelter and bombed street during the London Blitz, and "The Trench" exhibit, in which viewers walk through a re-created trench from World War I that uses lighting, sound, and smell to re-create the experience of trench warfare. Reenactment is now a primary strategy in museum exhibitions, in particular science exhibitions, that are attempting to incorporate interactive and sensory media into their educational forms in order to appeal to viewers who have been schooled on Disneyland modes of entertainment. However, the experience at Oklahoma City stands out for two reasons: it is not optional (it is difficult though possible to continue on through the exhibition without going through it) and it is a deliberate attempt to have visitors experience a trauma.

What kind of experience is this? Cultural codes would award it more authority, perhaps, than the experience of watching a television movie about

FIGURE 33. Photographs of victims of the Oklahoma City bombing in the hearing room at the Memorial Center, where an audiotape of the bombing is played. AP Photo/Laura Rauch.

the Oklahoma City bombing (of which there have been none). The audiotape is a documentary recording, unrehearsed and spontaneous. Yet its replaying is intended to produce a secondary experience of trauma in visitors, to give them a visceral experience of witnessing, via sound, the moment that those on tape are traumatized.

One of the potential pitfalls of such a reenactment is its capacity to award monumentality to the bomb itself, to become a witnessing to the explosion rather than to the loss it produced. These elements of reenactment are also reflected in the design of the memorial, with its emphasis on the time of the bomb's blast. The two monumental gates that frame the memorial pool mark, or one could say reenact, the minute before (9:01) and after (9:03) the bomb. This timing intends to mark the moment of transition, from life to death, from the prebomb moment to life after the bomb. Yet the size of these gates also acts as a kind of counterpoint to the intimacy of the chairs that stand next to them, which signify the individuals who died. In a certain sense, these gates evoke the size of the bomb itself, its monumentality.

Indeed, the next room in the Memorial Center plays the first few minutes of television coverage, shot from a helicopter circling the smoking Murrah building, in which the reporters seem to be in awe of the power wrought by the bomb. The cameras are too distant to see anyone being pulled from the rubble, and in the aerial shot, it is the body of the building itself that appears wounded. The reporters' voices are excited as they exclaim, "Holy Cow! About a third of the building has been blown away!" Representations of the bombing thus create risky terrain at the memorial and in its exhibit, precisely because they can slip easily into a kind of gee-whiz fascination with the force of the bomb. The inclusion of a room that was destroyed by the blast also comes perilously close to playing to a fascination with the forces of the blast. One of the many objects on display is the mangled axle of the rental truck that was used to carry the bomb and which was essential to the identification of the suspects. This has been referred to by Executive Director Kari Watkins as the "prize possession" of the collection because it was so important to the investigation into the bombing; on display in a glass case, its mangled frame evokes the power of the bomb.

The primary focus of the exhibition, however, is the value of ordinary life. Throughout the exhibit, descriptions of the event itself are counteracted with a fervent embrace of the importance and meaning of everyday life. The exhibit begins, for instance, with a section called "A Day Like Any Other," displaying photos, audio recordings, and texts about the ordinary life in Oklahoma City in the early morning before the bombing: people getting up, making breakfast, going to work, taking their children to school and day care, firefighters and others reporting to work, a prayer breakfast at the local convention center, and so on. The effect is not only a kind of nostalgia for the noneventfulness of life before the bombing, but also a very explicit valorization of ordinary lives and people, the people who are living their lives in anonymity, just trying to raise their kids, make a living, and do something meaningful, however small. This narrative presents the innocence prior to the event: these were lives lived in innocence of what was to happen. As the exhibit continues, this valorization of the everyday is central to the effect of the many objects on display from the bombing: broken coffee mugs, children's shoes, briefcases, and eyeglasses, all carefully arranged in rubble to evoke how they looked when found. Some of these objects, such as a briefcase, are identified as belonging to specific victims. The ordinariness of these artifacts takes on a tragic poignancy, as if each were an emblem of the prior innocence that they embodied before they came to signify tragedy. Damaged and dusty, their forms torn and fragmented by the explosion, these artifacts stand in for the bodies of the injured and dead.

The embrace of the everyday in the exhibit is integral to its defiant upholding of the category of citizenship. The exhibition thus responds to the fact that those who bombed the Murrah building were not only targeting the federal government but also engaging in a critique of citizenship. The right-wing militia movements, such as the Patriots and the Freemen, with whom McVeigh and Nichols were in sympathy, are deeply antigovernment and base their philosophies in part on a critique of U.S. citizenship as a false category of belonging; they have created alternative forms of citizenship for themselves. While the complexity of this critique is not explained in the exhibit, apparently because of a fear that any explanation of their actions would rationalize them, the exhibit is also clearly responding to their intent by emphasizing again and again the importance of being active citizens and government workers. It thus presents an explicit narrative about the importance of the individual in civic life and in the functioning of democracy. This is related to the way that the memorial places an emphasis on the role of government agencies in the Murrah building and defines "families" of workers. In fact, the building housed nineteen government agencies (the only nongovernmental agency was the America's Kids Day Care Center), including the Social Security Administration, the Secret Service, the Department of Health and Human Services, the Departments of Labor and Agriculture, and the two targets of the bomb, the Bureau of Alcohol, Tobacco and Firearms (ATF) and the Drug Enforcement Agency (DEA).[39] It did not, ironically, house the FBI, which right-wing militias wanted most to injure. The highest numbers of casualties were in the Social Security Administration, the day care center, and the Federal Employees Credit Union, which were on the lower floors (ATF and DEA were on the top floor). The location of the bomb thus ensured that it would kill many more civilians and low-level government workers than the agents who are the most responsible for dealing with right-wing militias. This geography reveals many aspects of the structure of the working lives of many Americans, not only federal employees, for whom child care and work environments are combined in ways that increasingly are potentially dangerous to children.

The narrative of the Oklahoma City Memorial Center focuses on citizens going about their everyday lives, aided by the federal government, as a means of affirming the social structure. The exhibit talks of government workers, who "work, in essence, for us," and states, "By 9 A.M., the Murrah building is a hub of activity—ordinary people performing everyday activities." Of the couple who were at the hearing at the Water Resources Board, the script reads, "The Wikles are typical of the countless people who conduct business everyday in freely accessible government buildings throughout the United States." Again and again, the story of the bombing reminds visitors that these ordinary people were participating in the experience of citizenship. The Social Security Administration is a compelling example. In this mundane federal office, several older couples were killed while inquiring about benefits, and several families were killed together while applying for benefits for their newborn children—attempting, in effect, to award them citizenship. (Teresa Alexander, a nurse and mother of three, died while applying for a card for her son; Casandra Booker, mother of four, died while applying for cards for her twins; in one family, two children, ages three months and three years, and their grandmother were killed, while their mother, Daina Bradley, had to have her leg amputated in order to be rescued at the site.) All told, forty people, including many staff members, were killed in the Social Security office.

The ironies presented by this tragic example are multiple. Social Security, a government program that grew out of the devastation of the Depression, represents the government as economic protection, ensuring not only the future status (for these children) as workers and taxpayers but also as retirees. A Social Security number constructs a particular kind of citizen: hardworking, taxpaying, and rule-obeying, precisely the kind of citizen that right-wing militias want to resist. Visiting this office would be understood in any other context as a boring, irritating, and necessary task in negotiating government bureaucracy. Yet the bomb rendered these simple activities of citizenship eventful, meaningful, and visible. It accomplished precisely the opposite of its intended message. In the terms of the memorial, it made the everyday life of the citizen seem heroic.

An emphasis on the role played by rescue workers, large numbers of whom were on the scene very quickly, is also central to the exhibit's presentation of civic duty. Again, an embrace of the ordinary is used to construct stories of heroism, of people who risked their lives to save others in what were chaotic, dangerous, and confusing circumstances. One nurse, Rebecca Anderson, died from falling debris after attending to the injured; her story as an "angel of mercy" receives particular attention. The many very compelling stories of rescue workers are used to affirm government forces at work, the efficiency of the unified incident command. This testifies to the particular role that disaster plays in shoring up belief in the government, the nation, and the system.

The Memorial Center's emphasis on the ordinary is also evident in the "Gallery of Honor," which contains photographs of those who died, along with objects brought by their families. Many of these are conventional objects of mourning, with religious symbols; others speak to the potential of the insignificant and the small to create effect: next to one child's photograph are Lion King figures, next to another's are characters from *Sesame Street*; a can of hairspray signifies one woman, a lipstick another. Here, the Oklahoma City Memorial bears many similarities to the AIDS memorial quilt, with its use of mundane images and objects to conjure a life.[40] Each poses the question, How do you remember a life?, and in so doing reminds us of the charged meaning of the seemingly insignificant.

The exhibition of the Memorial Center is marked by stories of fate. For instance, it tells the story of one worker who attributes her survival to the fact that she was searching through a file cabinet instead of sitting at her desk, and the story of a woman who sat down at a meeting with eight other women, all of whom simply disappeared before her. In other ways, the stories of survivors (many of which visitors can choose to view on interactive monitors) both defy and fulfill expectations of survivor discourse.[41] While many survivors talk about how they see life differently now and are grateful to the community of rescuers, friends, and families that have sustained them, others are angry, saying that memorialization is not and can never be enough. Many talk of being depressed, one of panic attacks at seeing a Ryder truck (the rental truck that held the bomb). One woman states, "The terrorists ruined my whole life and that of my family. My husband is now my ex-husband after a 27-year marriage." Another recounts her problems with disability and lack of a job and medical insurance: "Although the memorial has been wonderful, I have fallen through the cracks and I am very unhappy." A chapter of the exhibit about the first year after the bomb focuses on often frank testimony of the difficulties of the everyday in the wake of disaster and the limits of closure and healing. As one survivor states, "I have learned that you cannot let anyone tell you 'get over it.'" It is a testimony to the Memorial Center that it includes this range of responses and allows these tensions and conflicts to be on display. At the same time, these stories of fate allow the narrative of the memorial to remain at the level of individual triumph over victimization rather than to frame such stories within the context of larger issues of social and political agency.

So many aspects of the Oklahoma City National Memorial make it stand out as a form of remembrance: the rapidity with which it was built; the elaborate participation of survivors, rescuers, and families; the relentless and ongoing documentation of what the bombing meant and what the memorial means; its complex self-referentiality and interpretive mode; and its role in the revitalization of Oklahoma City. In the self-referential narratives of the Memorial Center, it is understood that experiences are mediated and layered. While the exhibit freely borrows footage of the media coverage of the event, it also attempts to unpack that coverage, presenting, for instance, reporters' notebooks of that day as artifacts. The memorial speaks both in its design and its exhibit about the importance of healing, yet it also acknowledges the impossibility of such a narrative, the incompleteness of these processes. In its emphatic creation of multiple spaces for participation, from the fence to various places where visitors and children are asked to write statements and make drawings in response to the exhibit, the memorial's design and exhibit are highly conscious in their encouragement of many narratives of cultural memory over a single, dominant narrative. This gesture, so earnest and thoughtful, can also be seen as a means of containing those narratives and packaging them for consumption.

Yet in its often self-congratulatory tone and emphasis on sentiment, the memorial exhibition also presents a story that inevitably depoliticizes the bombing. The focus on discourses of citizenship does not allow for any discussion of the failure of the government in the complex set of events that led to the bombing. As Erika Doss writes, "Focused on the 'comfort' of survivors and on cultural tourism, the Oklahoma City National Memorial represents a lost opportunity to engage in critically and historically informed public conversations about dissent, violence, authority, loss and grief in America."[42] This is the inevitable consequence of the Memorial Center's location at the charged site of the bombing. The sense that the memorial itself is the site where the dead are honored and mourned produces a discourse of sacredness that cannot allow any discussion about why the bombing took place, what motivated it, and what it says about American society. This is precisely the limitation of memorial pedagogy. This emphasis on sentiment, in the form of comfort, over analysis is only heightened by the integral part played by consumerism in the memorial experience.

TOURISM AND RENEWAL

It is not incidental to the experience of the Oklahoma City National Memorial that it sits in the middle of a typical downtown area of a midsize American city. Like the downtowns of many other small cities that were decimated in the second half of the twentieth century by the movement of populations and businesses to the suburbs, the center of Oklahoma City was, at the time of the bombing, an often deserted space, with a small number of office buildings and hotels. Oklahoma City represents a typical story of urban decline, in which the postwar period brought suburbanization and freeways that drained the downtown of its focus. In the 1960s, the city hired the architectural firm of I. M. Pei to create a plan for urban redevelopment; Pei responded in a typical mode of design at the time, which was to clear whole blocks of storefronts for massive projects like a convention center and a massive shopping center modeled on the Doge's Palace in Venice.[43] Ironically, this kind of urban design was quite similar to the design that produced the World Trade Center in New York by razing a whole business district in the late 1960s. The shopping center was never built, and the oil industry bust of the 1980s and 1990s and the savings and loan crisis, which drained available funds for renewal projects, all contributed to a depressed downtown, filled with empty office space, at the time of the bombing. Yet in 1993, two years before the bombing, the voters had approved, by a slim margin, a sales tax that ultimately would provide $350 million for urban renewal, which was later augmented by $1.5 billion in public and private investment coming into downtown. (It's a local joke that the tax was so successful in changing the city's economy that no one will admit now to having voted against it.) Not far from the memorial, the formerly industrial Bricktown district was renovated to become a downtown draw, with restaurants, clubs, and a canal. A new federal building opened next to the memorial in March 2004, and two stadiums, a performing arts center, and a new library have all been built in the ten years since the bombing.[44] The city is thus in the midst of an economic renewal that has taken place hand in hand with the memorial's emergence as a destination site.

When it was constructed, the memorial stood apart aesthetically from the rest of the downtown area, creating a kind of aesthetic shock when one came upon it in the middle of the run-down area. Since 2004, the landscape of the downtown area has changed so much, partly because of the memorial's influence, that it no longer appears distinct so much as in a continuum with the surrounding architecture. The new federal building, which sits at an angle to the Memorial Center and which was designed by the Chicago firm Ross Barney and Jankowski Architects, appears to flow architecturally from the memorial. The memorial designers Hans and Torrey Butzer had designed that corner of the lot around the memorial in anticipation of the federal building eventually being built, and the new building manages to have a modern and airy quality. The federal building is a model of hidden security features, with narrow yet stylishly modern windows and surrounded by steel bollards that are designed to be lit at night and that appear more decorative than barrier architecture. The emergence of bollards as a form of security design was precipitated by the bombing of the World Trade Center in 1993 and the Oklahoma City bombing; in both cases, trucks containing bombs were driven right up to and under the buildings, ensuring loss of life. The new federal building both incorporates this new context of security design and attempts to present an open sense of space.

With a renovated river park and what is thought to be a very successful use of public funds for urban revitalization, Oklahoma City is now looked to as a model for urban renewal for other midsize cities.[45] Hans Butzer and other architects are now working on various private development projects for mixed-use renewal in the downtown area, with the anticipation that populations will move back into downtown from the large suburban sprawl around the city, in a final stage of postindustrial urban shift.

The memorial plays a particular role in this urban renewal. It is, by far, the most well-known aspect of Oklahoma City. At its dedication, and at each anniversary of the bombing, the memorial is the focus of intense national attention, which escalated at the time of McVeigh's execution in June 2001. At its tenth anniversary in April 2005, the ceremony received all-day coverage on CNN and was the focus of massive media attention. Reporters covering issues of 9/11 routinely return to Oklahoma City to make comparisons between the two sites. The memorial is the site of national and international pilgrimages. In a part of the country largely without landmarks, it has marked a site as significant and meaningful. Hundreds of thousands of people visit it each year, many of whom are driving across country on Interstate 40 (which passes right by downtown Oklahoma City) and stop by on their way. The renewed tourism of downtown Oklahoma City is thus deeply connected to, if not largely attributable to, the memorial. Executive Director Kari Watkins states, "The memorial is the heart of the city and has been a strong catalyst for the renewal of downtown Oklahoma City. Is it a destination spot? Absolutely, and we are glad that it is."[46]

On the eve of the memorial's tenth anniversary, the staff commissioned several market research surveys about the image of the memorial and its visitors in anticipation of launching an eventually successful fundraising campaign called Second Decade (which raised $17 million). These studies revealed that the vast majority of people who visited the memorial were not from the surrounding area; indeed, the attendance of local residents was quite low. They also revealed that for a very high percentage of visitors, the

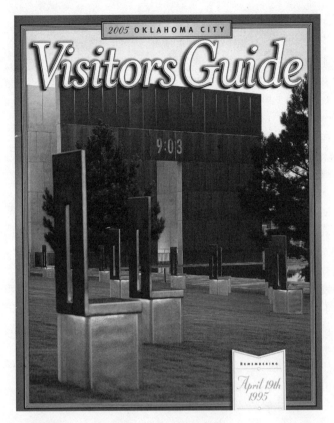

FIGURE 34. 2005 Visitors Guide to Oklahoma City.

memorial was the primary reason for their visit to Oklahoma City.[47] The memorial responded to these studies by instituting sponsored free days at the museum, which brought in many local residents.[48]

The role of the memorial in putting Oklahoma City on the map of a national and international consciousness has not happened without ambivalence about the role that the memorial should play in the city's image. The memory of the bombing is, as Oklahoma State Senator Cal Hobson once said, "a hell of a way to have economic development."[49] The city would rather promote its urban renewal projects as key elements in revitalizing the city, and the memorial staff has worked hard for the city to acknowledge its importance to local tourism. In 2005, the city put the memorial on the front page of its visitors guide, affirming its centrality to the city's positive image. Increasingly, conventions at Oklahoma City incorporate the memorial into their programs. In April 2006, the Building Owners and Managers Association held a conference that incorporated a panel including Watkins and FBI agents from the Institute for the Prevention of Terrorism and a visit to the memorial, given that building management is now dominated by security.[50]

It is often stated by officials in Oklahoma City that the city was almost invisible in the national consciousness before the bombing. "Prior to '95, we didn't really suffer from a bad image," Steve Collier, executive director of the Oklahoma City Convention and Visitors Bureau, told the *New York Times* during the media onslaught of the McVeigh execution. "Surveys told us that we didn't have an image. The negatives dated back into our history: 'The Grapes of Wrath,' the Dust Bowl."[51] This act of violence provided Oklahoma City with a national identity and accomplished what many disasters often do: it reaffirmed the ability of a community to provide comfort and reassurance, and it allowed ordinary people to do heroic things. This is key to what Linenthal calls the "progressive" narrative of the bombing, a narrative of local pride and community affirmation. As Governor Frank Keating noted in 2001, "To be known as a community where something bad happened, but to be known as a community where people showed the world how to respond to that bad—that is extraordinary."[52]

The memorial's relationship to tourism is related to this affirmation of community and raises important questions about the consumption of mourning and the kitschification of grief. One of the key features of the memorial is its gift shop, which occupies a prominent space in the Memorial Center and is integral to the memorial's broader meaning. The memorial is funded and maintained by a trust, which works in cooperation with the National Park Service. It receives no government appropriations, and is thus dependent on an endowment, membership and admission fees, and sales from its gift shop. The revenues from admission to the museum and sales from the gift shop constitute the majority of the memorial's income, generating $1.3 million in 2004, whereas endowment earnings and grants totaled only $500,000.[53]

The merchandise at the gift shop presents a set of contradictory narratives about the memorial which reveal its conflicting roles as a place of mourning, a site of civic pride, and a tourist destination. The shop sells tasteful drawings of the memorial, remembrance plaques, postcards, T-shirts, books about the memorial and survivors, and videotapes of media coverage of the event. It also sells a broad range of souvenir merchandise that is meant to be used and worn by tourists; these spill over quickly into kitsch: memorial logo notepads, bumper stickers with the slogan "On American Soil," coffee

FIGURE 35. Merchandise from the Oklahoma City National Memorial gift shop.

mugs and glasses, teddy bears with the memorial insignia, running shorts with the museum logo, a Decade of Hope adult windbreaker, bottled water branded with the memorial logo, and the snow globe that I discussed in the introduction to this book.

The ubiquity of the teddy bears at Oklahoma City, while part of a larger national trend of giving teddy bears to the grieving, brought this trend to unusual proportions. Ever since the beginning years of the AIDS crisis, when people began to give teddy bears to those sick with AIDS, the teddy bear has been deployed as a commodity of grief, one that often operates as a kitsch object of easy sentiment. In Oklahoma City, at the first memorial service after the bombing, teddy bears sent by the governor of Illinois were distributed to the mourners, and news photographs featured the rather startling image of city officials standing somberly at the service while holding teddy bears. (It is impossible to imagine, by comparison, a group of European officials standing at a memorial ceremony while holding teddy bears.) After these images circulated in the media, the city was inundated with thousands of teddy bears, so many that they had to search for people to give them to.[54] Many proposals for teddy bear memorials were also sent to the city. While

FIGURE 36. Bottled water from the Oklahoma City National Memorial gift shop.

teddy bears have proliferated at other sites of mourning, and are featured in New York as FDNY teddy bears, they had a particularly official role in Oklahoma City. The ubiquity of teddy bears as a response to the bombing and as integral to the Oklahoma City memorial reflects the increased energy devoted to a consumer comfort culture more broadly in the United States. It also demonstrates a particular kind of ease with teddy bears as symbols of reassurance, circulating as easily through the world of adults as of children. Immediately after the bombing, the *Boston Globe* cartoonist Dan Wasserman depicted a teddy bear apparently so saddened by the news of the bombing that it shields its eyes. Wasserman donated the cartoon to relief efforts, which helped to raise over $65,000.[55] In the aftermath of the bombing, Wasserman's cartoon evoked the dead children, perhaps the image of a child's toy mourning the child's absence. Yet as the years have passed and teddy bears have proliferated, the image looks increasingly like

FIGURE 37. President Clinton and Hillary Rodham Clinton at a prayer service in Oklahoma City, April 1995. Photo © Wally McNamee, Corbis.

the teddy bear of the nation itself, sadly shielding its eyes. One of the key aspects of the predominance of teddy bears at Oklahoma City, and later in New York after 9/11, is the belief so clearly invoked in their power to comfort: these bears are seen to have almost magical powers of reassurance and the ability to comfort not only in the face of immense loss, but also across cultural and geographic borders. One of the most striking aspects of the I Am Hope project, which sends teddy bears and other stuffed animals to children whose lives have been damaged by the wars in Afghanistan and Iraq, is the belief embedded into the project that this will make a difference, that these teddy bears will make people feel better. In other cultures, stuffed animals might seem superfluous when medicine and food are needed, yet in American culture, they have acquired the status of necessities.

The kitsch elements of the merchandise at the memorial gift shop raise a broader set of questions about the increased dependence of nonprofit organizations on merchandising in the absence of foundation funding. It makes sense to consider how this set of consumer products compares to the merchandising that exists around other memorials. The Vietnam Veterans Memorial generated a number of posters and T-shirts (and the Frederick Hart statue of three men that accompanies the memorial was made into posters, T-shirts, a Franklin Mint miniature, and a plastic model kit). The AIDS quilt,

FIGURE 38. Cartoon by Dan Wasserman, April 1995. © Tribune Media Services, Inc. All rights reserved. Reprinted with permission.

which also depends in part on the selling of merchandise as a source of funding, sells coffee-table books, coffee mugs, tote bags, T-shirts, and AIDS quilt teddy bears. The U.S. Holocaust Museum sells a small set of memorial items but concentrates largely on selling books that interpret the Holocaust as a historical event.[56] It is inconceivable that the Holocaust Museum would sell T-shirts or running shorts emblazoned with the museum's logo or, for that matter, that someone would purchase them and wear them while exercising. New York City has been inundated with memorial souvenirs, which cover a range of styles. For the most part, these participate in the informal economy of cheap souvenirs and are not sold as part of an official organization. It remains to be seen what the planned gift shop at the proposed museum at Ground Zero will sell, but it seems likely that what is now an informal economy of souvenirs will become more official.

The tourist economy in Oklahoma City points to the multiple functions of the Oklahoma City Memorial. It is not simply a memorial to the dead or a tribute to survivors and rescue workers. It is also a fervent declaration of civic life, American identity, and local pride. Thus, the memorial logo, which depicts the survivor tree, displays the slogan "On American Soil." The slogan simultaneously evokes the shock of the bombing (How could this have happened on American soil?), the importance of the land in the midst of farm country, and a defiant attempt to reclaim the land of the memorial from the image of the decimated federal building. The very existence of the memorial is thus often coded as an act of defiance; the memorial logo does not memorialize the dead but speaks a message of triumph rather than defeat in the face of hatred and violence.

It is also the case that the selling of merchandise at the memorial is continuous with its message about the inviolability of citizenship. The message of citizenship is also one of consumer-citizenship. Going to the gift shop is an inclusive part of the visit, just as it is at other national memorials and at national parks. Visitors are supposed to consume at the memorial. The gift shop provides the counteractivity to leaving an object at the fence or by the memorial chairs; it provides the means for visitors to take something away from the memorial as a memento. That these objects might include clothing to be worn on a summer vacation, or teddy bears that are similar to travel souvenirs, seems to be unremarkable for most of the tourists who visit the site.

Yet the consumption of kitsch memorial objects does matter. Just as I have argued that the Oklahoma City snow globe presents a contained view of the complexity of the bombing, many of the objects at the gift shop present a simplified and prepackaged set of emotions through which to respond to the tragedy of the bombing. Thus, one could argue that the memorial teddy bear allows one to feel sad for what happened and to feel comforted, and then to move on. It may be a simple act to purchase such an object, but it is ultimately not an inconsequential one. This is precisely because that feeling of comfort, which is similar to the feeling of sadness and affirmation of community that is so powerfully conveyed by the exhibition, allows us as visitors to leave the memorial feeling positive about the good that the bombing brought out in the people who suffered loss, rather than to come away concerned at what the bombing means. This discourse of healing at the memorial and in its museum and gift shop merchandise thus forecloses on its educational mission. One of the key features of kitsch is that it invokes the idea of universal emotion, that the emotion conveyed by a kitsch object is shared by all of mankind. A kitsch object not only embodies a particular kind of prepackaged sentiment; it also conveys the message that this sentiment is universally shared, and that it is enough. Thus, the marketing of memorial kitsch in Oklahoma City helps to further narratives of innocence—by implication, national innocence.

The contradictions of combining mourning with consumerism are not lost on the designers and the memorial staff, who are constantly engaged in processes of self-examination. As the memorial moves into its second decade, the staff are hyperconscious of its changing meaning. As the memorial becomes integrated into the downtown area, its meaning is affirmed yet also evolves. It no longer has the same sense of urgency. Paid admission to the museum has declined, as has the number of visitors to the memorial, from a high of 575,000 in 2001 to 283,000 in 2005. Yet since 9/11, many aspects of the memorial seem increasingly prescient. Watkins notes that after 9/11, staff held an all-day session to discuss the changed meaning of the memorial and ended up reaffirming their original mission of "remembrance and education." One of the key aspects of that educational mission is the Memorial Institute for the Prevention of Terrorism, which sponsors research on terrorism with a particular emphasis on training first responders. The Institute was the result of a desire by those involved in creating the memorial to have a "living memorial" that would have social impact. While its work is allied to the memorial project, its research functions autonomously and is thus not implicated within the restricted context of mourning found at the memorial. In addition, the Memorial Center has a large educational program with outreach to schools, sends out materials from the archive in "Hope Trunks," and has designed a program about preventing violence.

As the memorial archive has continued to grow, it has also fostered several projects that aim to create outreach as well as to deal with the problem of accumulating too many artifacts. The archivists initially thought that donations to the archive would taper off or plateau, but they have continued to arrive, with more materials coming in from rescue workers in recent years.[57] Because it was established with the idea of being the central archive about the bombing, a one-stop archive, it has acquired most of the records of the trials on the bombings. It also continues to accumulate a large number of objects from the fence, some of which are circulated in the I Am Hope projects.

In many ways, the memorial process in Oklahoma City stands in sharp contrast to the acrimonious debate that has taken place so far in New York City over the memorialization of 9/11. In Oklahoma City, the memorial design process foregrounded community involvement at all costs and has a system of checks and balances in the form of numerous community standing committees, such as the conscience committee and the archive committee. In addition, the memorial process was guided by a particular ethic about keeping political involvement out of the process.[58] The process that created the memorial set the tone for how it would function once established, as a community-defined organization. States Watkins, "We have lots of stakeholders, lots of investors in this place, and we have to involve them in major decisions. This memorial belongs to the world now."[59]

This emphasis on community is part of what has allowed the Oklahoma City memorial to exist as a combination of elements and tones, to incorporate a set of contradictions into its various elements. With its spare narrative and elegant design, the memorial is a kind of modernist antikitsch. It aims, as its designers have said, to allow the narrative of remembrance to be open. It stands in contrast to the Memorial Center and the gift shop, which participate in forms of remembrance that fall easily into prepackaged sentiment and kitsch. Yet what shines through in both contexts is an earnest belief in and ethos about the primacy of community engagement and consensus, one that allows these different elements and approaches to coexist. At times, this earnestness seems to spill over into a production of innocence; at others, it produces an honesty about irresolution.

The memorial was not the only outcome of the Oklahoma City bombing. The bombing also produced several high-profile trials, an execution, and changes in federal law. The meaning of the memorial has been caught up in the ongoing legal proceedings about the bombing, as some of the families of the victims and survivors were actively involved in the legal process, and the execution of McVeigh was also caught up in consumerism, the media, and survivor discourse. It is to this and the tenth anniversary of the bombing that I turn in the next chapter.

THE SPECTACLE OF DEATH AND THE SPECTACLE OF GRIEF

The Execution of Timothy McVeigh

On June 10, 2001, every action by Timothy McVeigh was part of a countdown of "execution protocol." At 4 A.M., McVeigh was moved in a van to a holding cell in the "death house," a windowless building in the middle of the federal prison in Terre Haute, Indiana. There he was confined to a room nine feet by fourteen feet, where he was allowed to bring a small amount of reading material and to watch a black-and-white television set. At noon, he was given his last meal, which consisted of his choice of two pints of mint chocolate chip ice cream. At 4 A.M. the next day, his lawyers paid him a last visit, at which time the executioners, Bureau of Prison staff members from outside Terre Haute who had volunteered for the job, entered the death chamber. At 6:30, twenty-four witnesses—journalists, selected survivors and family members, and federal officials—were escorted into the witness boxes outfitted with one-way glass, and McVeigh was led into the chamber and strapped onto a gurney. He stared directly into a camera that was sending a live image to a federal facility in Oklahoma City, where several hundred people were watching. The warden asked McVeigh if he had any last words and, receiving no reply, read the charges against him. The officials pronounced that they were ready for the execution, and at 7:10 several chemicals in succession were released into McVeigh's veins until he stopped breathing several minutes later.[1]

At the same time, in a field across from the federal penitentiary, thousands of onlookers and media personnel stood waiting for word that McVeigh had died. Unable to witness the proceedings themselves, they waited for the warden and the witnesses to narrate McVeigh's final moments, to tell them if he had spoken, and to explain what any expressions on his face had meant to them. Among those holding vigil outside the prison were numerous death penalty protestors. Many in attendance at the execution, however, were there to affirm the death penalty process and to celebrate McVeigh's death. Among those in the crowd were souvenir vendors selling T-shirts declaring "Die Die Die!" and buttons declaring "McVeigh Must Pay." The execution had become a tourist event, for which some people had taken off work and traveled to Terre Haute (essentially, to make a pilgrimage there) in order to stand several hundred yards from a prison where a thirty-three-year-old man was being put to death for setting off a bomb that had killed 168 people. Most of the survivors and family members from Oklahoma City chose either to stay home, to go to the memorial instead (which was also surrounded by media), or to watch the execution via closed-circuit TV in Oklahoma City.

The execution of Timothy McVeigh evokes many aspects of the tourism of history. The discourse surrounding the death penalty is one of obfuscation and provincialism. Despite the fact that the reasons given for the continued practice of the death penalty, such as deterrence, have been consistently proven to be ineffective, the United States remains the sole developed nation that continues to execute sigificant numbers of prisoners each year. Despite the fact that increasing numbers of cases of innocent prisoners on death row have been revealed each year, and that there is solid evidence that the death penalty is awarded unequally to blacks and Latinos and those who have insufficient legal counsel, the death penalty retains a significant (if falling) amount of support among the American public. The execution of these prisoners is a form of spectacle, one that is intended to be consumed—by witnesses, by politicians, by the American public, by the nation. Thus, the meaning of an execution is never private; rather, it is a public pronouncement of the right of the state to take the life of a citizen. The continued practice of the death penalty in the United States contributes to the production of national innocence and the culture of comfort. It allows the state to affirm its power and it takes place within a discourse of comfort, in particular the questionable justification that executions provide comfort to the victims' families. As a gesture to the idea that death provides closure, and thus that the execution of a murderer will provide healing for those who have suffered loss, executions provide a false sense of the ability to contain violence.

The execution of Timothy McVeigh formed part of the twinned response to the Oklahoma City bombing; the Oklahoma City National Memorial is the other. While the memorial is a fervent response to the tragedy of the bombing, an attempt to demonstrate the consequences of violence, it will always be allied with McVeigh's execution in Terre Haute six years later and the legal legacy it produced. The bombing, the memorial, and the execution placed these two cities, formerly unnoticed in the national arena, in central roles in defining American culture and history. Both the bombing and the execution are events of violence, one committed by an individual steeped in antigovernment fervor and paranoia, the other the dispassionate and sanctioned violence of the state.

In the media event that took place around the trial and execution, the families and survivors of the Oklahoma City bombing were active, grieving participants in the legal process, and the memorial was heavily featured as an image that justified the demonization of McVeigh. In the years after the bombing, the families and survivors were relentlessly interviewed in the media and became quite adept at telling their stories. Many of them grew resentful of the intrusiveness of reporters and the insensitivity of the constant "How do you feel?" questions.[2] Yet several admitted, in particular when media coverage reached new heights with McVeigh's execution, that they were using the press attention as a means of keeping alive the memory of their loved ones.[3] McVeigh's trial and execution were thus not only a legal process but a site of mourning, where certain family members and survivors were encouraged to participate not as witnesses but as mourners, and to perform their grief in the legal process.

In this chapter, I examine the processes by which McVeigh was constructed in the media and how his trial and execution became the site of a public performance of grief and victimhood as enacted by the Oklahoma City families and survivors. I situate this in relationship to the tenth anniversary of the bombing, and the interrelationship between the execution and the memorial. This is a story of spectacle, the spectacle of death and the spectacle of grief, and how each impacted the legal meanings of memory and loss.

From the moment he was discovered by the FBI to be sitting in a jail cell not far from Oklahoma City a few days after the bombing of the Murrah Federal Building, after being arrested for driving without a license plate or registration, Timothy McVeigh was constructed by the media as a figure of evil. The photo opportunity that took place when U.S. marshals walked him from the jail to a waiting vehicle showed a man with military-style close-cropped hair in a jail jumpsuit, stony-faced, walking among a group of grim-looking officials and surrounded by an angry crowd. Lou Michel and Dan Herbeck, the authors of the controversial book about McVeigh, *American Terrorist*, write:

> FBI officials would later deny that the Perry jail walkout was designed as a media event, or that anyone called the news agencies to give them the location of the photo opportunity. They would deny accusations that they delayed the prisoner move until all the top media outlets could get there. . . . But there were plenty of cameras in place when McVeigh, still wearing the bright orange jail jumpsuit, left the courthouse for the flight to Oklahoma City.[4]

Michel's and Herbeck's book, which was released a few months before the execution, was a central means through which McVeigh himself constructed his celebrity. The authors interviewed McVeigh at length, and the book often speaks as though looking through his eyes: "As the cameras whirred around him, though, McVeigh was still preoccupied with the potential for a Jack Ruby–like strike on his life. Squinting into the bright afternoon sun, he scanned all the local buildings for snipers, moving his eyes slowly from left to right and then up and down in a z pattern he had learned in the Army." The controversy over the book can be attributed to this kind of inside-the-head prose style. The book was roundly condemned by people in Oklahoma City, and the authors themselves were portrayed as naïve at best for giving McVeigh a voice in the public. The book makes a deliberate attempt to connect to the memory of the bombing, featuring an image of the memorial on the back cover and an appendix of the names of the victims. But victims in Oklahoma City understood *American Terrorist* as giving McVeigh a platform from which to speak, and after the authors offered to contribute part of the proceeds from the book to the memorial, Robert Johnson, then the memorial's director, turned them down. In addition, the Oklahoma legislature passed a resolution in spring 2001 condemning the book.

FIGURE 39. Timothy McVeigh being led from the Noble County Courthouse, Perry, Oklahoma, April 21, 1995. AP Photo/David Longstreath.

The book attempts to tell McVeigh's story in a neutral journalistic style and to juxtapose his interpretation of events with those of others, yet in its psychobiographical style, it undercuts this neutrality. It is almost certain that McVeigh lied consistently to these reporters, in particular about the participation of others in the bombing. Indeed, on the very issue of his arbitrary arrest by the police, McVeigh's version of events seems quite specious. When he was pulled over by an Oklahoma State trooper for driving without a license plate, he had many things in his car that would render him a suspect: a gun, right-wing pamphlets, and the T-shirt he was wearing, which had a quote from Thomas Jefferson that was favored by militias: "The tree of liberty must be refreshed from time to time with the blood of patriots and tyrants." (This T-shirt is now illustrated like a relic in the book.) In McVeigh's self-aggrandizing version of the story, he himself actually planned for this arrest, in fact orchestrated it—a version that is inconsistent with his subsequent actions.

The media coverage in the last six months of McVeigh's life was overwhelming, with major newspapers running at least one story a day on him and his impending execution. He was constructed in this coverage in all the codes of celebrity: speculation about his thoughts and desires, fascination with those who had access to him, front-page tabloid articles about his darkest secrets, and, as the execution neared, a blow-by-blow account of his movements, a relentless preoccupation with his last meal, diagrams of the spaces he inhabited, and many hours of live coverage charting every second of the execution process itself. McVeigh, as Neal Gabler writes, received the kind of glamour treatment from *Newsweek* magazine that was usually only accorded movie stars. The cover photo of McVeigh staring off dreamily into space, his lips resolute but also soft, was pure Hurrell, the romantic photographer of Hollywood's golden age. . . . The interview inside was pure *Photoplay*: gushy, reverent, excited. McVeigh looked, wrote *Newsweek*, "a lot more like a typical Gen-Xer than a deranged loner, much less a terrorist. His handshake was firm and he looked visitors right in the eye. He appeared a little nervous, maybe, but good-humored and self-aware. Normal."[5]

This attention to detail is part of the apparatus of the death penalty procedure, which is intended to protect the interests of the state, yet it also serves to heighten the morbid fascination of the public. The execution demonstrated how the enactment of the death penalty can be a celebrity-making machine. It continued even after his death, with detailed coverage of the transportation of his body from the prison. (As a war veteran, McVeigh was actually eligible for a military funeral, though his family did not request one. After he speculated about the possibility of demanding one, Congress passed a law to prevent him from doing so).[6]

McVeigh was an active agent in his own media coverage. Though he had refused to speak at his trial, he confessed his crime to his lawyers and, after his conviction, confessed it to various reporters. He corresponded for several years with reporters, responding to their questions and providing his own commentary on their stories. He even began to send them holiday cards and what he called "social" letters. In a group of letters that he wrote to the Oklahoma City reporter Phil Bacharach that were published in *Esquire* magazine, he teases Bacharach, chats about his favorite television shows (*The Simpsons* and *King of the Hill* at various points) and the movies he's watched on TV, and argues various political points.[7]

As a citizen of the prison system, McVeigh had at various times been without amenities such as television, although television is used routinely in prison as a form of behavioral and crowd control. But he wrote these letters while at the U.S. Penitentiary Administrative Maximum, or supermax, federal prison in Florence, Colorado. This $60 million 450-unit prison has been called the "Alcatraz of the Southwest"; it houses some of the most famous of those convicted to life imprisonment for terrorist crimes, including the Unabomber Theodore Kaczynski, the World Trade Center bomber Ramzi Ahmed Yousef, and Terry Nichols. Supermax prisons are designed to implement brutal policies of isolation. In many of the sections, lights are left on twenty-four hours a day and prisoners are allowed to leave their small cells only one hour a day. McVeigh clearly used his correspondence with the media to relieve boredom, and he often described aspects of prison life to these reporters, including his brief encounters with Kaczynski, whose cell was nearby. When the prisoners in what was known as "Bomber Row" were taken outside for their one hour of exercise, they could speak to each other by shouting from one exercise area to the next.[8] One of the strangest outcomes of these encounters is the letter written by Kaczynski to the authors of *American Terrorist*, in which he discusses McVeigh's likeability and intelligence, and states matter-of-factly that the bombing was a "bad action because it was unnecessarily inhumane."[9]

The primary aspect of life in an isolated context such as death row is boredom. Indeed, many argued that McVeigh should have been given a sentence of life without the possibility of parole rather than a death sentence because then he would have had to spend the rest of his life contemplating what he had done. As designed, the prison system is about *doing time*, a routine that never varies, a relentless boredom—a kind of anticelebrity. Time is meant to be a weight and a burden in this context. In high-profile cases, the death penalty serves to speed up time, an acceleration that creates drama out of the tedious prison routine and gives each minute special meaning.

As the media focus on McVeigh increased, Attorney General John Ashcroft took the unprecedented step of restricting reporters' access to him, banning all radio and television interviews with him. Yet even after Ashcroft's move, McVeigh wrote a letter to Fox News relating that he had considered killing former attorney general Janet Reno, which then made the headlines.[10] The press in turn treated his every statement and letter as a major story. In many of these stories, McVeigh's letters were photographed and presented like objects of historical weight, as if his handwriting itself could reveal something about what his actions had meant. Perhaps the oddest of the allegiances that McVeigh created with the press was with the well-known author Gore Vidal. In 1998, the *Los Angeles Times* reporter Richard Serrano sent McVeigh an essay written by Vidal in which he claimed that the Bill of Rights was being "steadily eroded" by the federal government; afterward he and Vidal began corresponding directly.[11] Vidal made several statements to the press about the correspondence, calling McVeigh "intelligent" and, most famously and insensitively, telling the *Daily Oklahoman* that "the boy has a sense of justice."[12] Though he did not follow through, Vidal agreed initially to be one of McVeigh's personal witnesses at the execution, which he planned to write about for *Vanity Fair*. Vidal's interest in McVeigh is reminiscent of the relationships of other well-known writers with death row inmates, including Norman Mailer's friendship with Gary Gilmore, which prompted his book *The Executioner's Song*, and Truman Capote's relationship with Perry Smith, chronicled in *In Cold Blood*. In each case, these writers were ultimately understood to have romanticized these criminals.

McVeigh's ability to get his voice into the media in the last few years of his life, which was in contrast to his silence during his trial, was understood by the families and survivors of the Oklahoma City bombing to be an explicit and direct infliction of pain upon them. Just as the media was focused on McVeigh in the months before the execution, it was also focused on the families and survivors, who were interviewed constantly as a counterpoint to what he said. The families' anger was heightened by McVeigh's referral, in *American Terrorist*, to the deaths of the nineteen children in Oklahoma City as "collateral damage."[13] Thus, McVeigh's ability to get his words into the media became a constant source of pain to many people in Oklahoma City. They also resented his access to the press and that he had leisure time enough to conduct such correspondence. There was also a strange intimacy in their statements, in which they would often call him "Tim," as if he were someone they knew well. It seemed increasingly that the desire of many families and survivors to see him die was really a desire to have him simply be silenced.

At the same time, many of those in Oklahoma City fed the media frenzy by demanding over and over again in public statements that he apologize for his actions, so that they too appeared to be invested in his every word. In the end, one of the narratives that consistently emerged from the reporters who interviewed McVeigh, which was equally galling to those who saw him as the embodiment of evil, was how affable and ordinary he seemed, and that he had been, until relatively recently, a model citizen. In response to a question from Fox News about his "collateral damage" remark, he said, "Collateral damage? As an American news junkie, a military man, and a Gulf War veteran, where do they think I learned that?" Indeed, he was apparently a "model prisoner" in the system that put him to death.[14]

THE SPECTACLE OF EXECUTION

The media spectacle that surrounded McVeigh was fueled by the spectacle of his execution. For the most part, the American public finds it easy to ignore executions, which become news only at various points in the cycle of electoral politics. For instance, George W. Bush presided over more than 130 executions during his relatively brief tenure as governor of Texas, but very few of them, with the exception of the execution of Karla Faye Tucker (because she was both a woman and a repentant born-again Christian), were noticed. Many death penalty opponents believe that the spectacle of executions is important in fighting against them; indeed, it is argued that if executions were televised, public opinion would turn quickly against them.[15] This is difficult to predict, however, since the history of executions has shown that they have often operated as public forms of entertainment and voyeurism that have tended to bring out the sadism rather than the humanity in their audiences.[16]

McVeigh's execution was one of the most public in American history and single-handedly raised very troubling issues about the investment of Middle America in both the prison industry and the death penalty. As an unrepentant killer who had professed his guilt (not in the courtroom but in the media), and as a white man whose well-qualified defense team was financed by the state, McVeigh was often referred to as the "poster boy" for arguments for the death penalty.[17] Many of the arguments made against the unfairness of the death penalty (that it is disproportionately imposed on black and Latino defendants and those who have killed white victims, that it ignores the fact that many poor defendants have inadequate legal counsel, that it is conceivable that the state has killed many innocent people) did not apply to McVeigh. Many people who are ambivalent about the death penalty took the stand that if anyone deserved it, he did. These views were only somewhat tempered by the fact that McVeigh himself made the decision several times to stop appealing his sentence, and stated in the media that he was ready to die.

Just as the bombing put Oklahoma City on the map of national consciousness, the execution put unprecedented focus on previously unrecognized Terre Haute, Indiana. Like Oklahoma City, a college football town, Terre Haute was best known for its relationship to sports, in this case, as the former home of the basketball player Larry Bird. As a small city with a large prison, Terre Haute is typical of the rise of the prison industry and its integration into the economies of the Midwest as farming and industrial economies have turned to a prison economy. As I discussed in chapter 1, prisons are seen as a central source of income and economic survival for the rural areas and small towns that were decimated by farm closures, the closing of coal mines, and the loss of industrial jobs, economic changes that also gave rise to the militia movement during the 1980s and 1990s.[18] The execution served as an occasion for the city of Terre Haute to affirm itself in relation to the prison and to its citizens by, for instance, holding town meetings in preparation, closing schools for the day, and providing services such as special buses for disabled protesters.[19] Thus, this high-profile execution, the first by the federal government in decades, was an occasion for this small city to signal its pride in housing a federal prison, one that had only recently been outfitted with a "death chamber."

The spectacle of the execution began many months prior, during the time that McVeigh was feeding stories to reporters, when many people began to make plans to attend the execution, not only family members and survivors from Oklahoma City but many others who were either pro– or anti–death penalty. This created what the *Wall Street Journal* called a "carnival air," in which commodities were sold and events planned.[20] Only a small number of people would witness the execution in person, but these onlookers were going to Terre Haute to stand outside the prison during the execution. Early on, buttons and t-shirts started appearing on eBay with pro-execution slogans; one read "Hoosier Hospitality—Terre Haute, May 16, 2001, Final Justice," referring to the Indiana state nickname; another had a media image of McVeigh with the words "Terre Haute Extra Hangin' Times"; and yet another, "Stop the Killing, Let McVeigh Live."[21]

Judith Anderson, the mayor of Terre Haute, told the *New York Times* that while the town had no control over what people sold at the site, "We're just asking that it be in very good taste."[22] It is a revealing statement in its recognition of the inevitable relationship between consumerism and executions. Is it possible to think that an item *sold at an execution* could ever constitute "good taste"? The mayor, who seemed to have a propensity for making tactless comments, also told reporters that the prison had wanted to execute the death row inmate Juan Raul Garza first, since the prison had never performed an execution, but Garza's case was stayed by President Clinton. "I know they were hoping for a dry run," she stated. "They wanted Garza, because there would not have been much media for that." She added, "I think we might have one of the highest number of militia groups in the Midwest!" The groups had told her, "'He killed innocent children; we weren't with him for the trial, and we're not with him now.'"[23]

The carnival spectacle of the execution exposes the fact that executions are sites of consumption, whether in the form of trinkets or media images.

FIGURE 40. Supporters of the death penalty near the U.S. Penitentiary, Terre Haute, Indiana, June 10, 2001. AP Photo/M. Spencer Green.

FIGURE 41. Items for sale at the Body Art Ink tattoo shop in Terre Haute, Indiana, June 9, 2001. AP Photo/M. Spencer Green.

Yet the crowds gathered to "celebrate" the execution with their handmade signs and buttons were also emblematic of another aspect of American society: the catharsis of anger in the act of vengeance. The anger at McVeigh was not merely the anger of those who had been directly hurt by the bombing, but a more general, potentially national anger, one that could produce T-shirts that read "Die Die Die!" In a certain sense, vengeance is a counterpart to consumerism in the tourism of history. Vengeance offers the simple narrative that the score can be evened, that violence can resolve violence, that executions can provide the comfort of resolution.

The spectacle of McVeigh's execution was muted by the fact that its May 16 scheduled date was delayed by the discovery of thousands of pages of FBI documents that had not been previously disclosed. By the time Attorney General Ashcroft declared that the execution would go forward as planned on June 11, there was already, even among those opposed to the execution, a collective weariness with its omnipresence in the news, and many fewer people participated in the local media spectacle than would have originally because they could not make last-minute travel plans. The television news still carried the event relentlessly live from the outskirts of the prison, but the confusion over the delay, the meaning of the missing files, and the government's desire to just get on with it had tempered the tone of the event. At the same time, the delay exposed the apparatus of the spectacle of the execution, as all of the potential onlookers, including people who were taking time off from work to be there, had to change their travel plans, and local businesses were stuck with food that they had prepared for the expected crowds.[24]

The intense media focus on the McVeigh execution masks the fact that most U.S. executions take place with little publicity and few protests. Yet executions are in general highly visible in political discourse in the United States. The Oklahoma City bombing was greeted almost instantaneously by a call from President Clinton and Attorney General Reno for the death penalty for those responsible. The death penalty was understood to be an appropriate means of affirming the strength of the state. It is also, revealingly, seen as providing comfort to those grieving. In *When the State Kills*, Austin Sarat writes:

At a time when citizens are skeptical that government activism is appropriate or effective, the death penalty provides one arena in which the state can redeem itself by taking action with clear and popular results. This helps explain why the immediate response to the bombing in Okla-

FIGURE 42. Journalists at the federal prison in Terre Haute, Indiana, June 11, 2001. AP Photo/ *Tribune Star*, Jim Avelis.

homa City was the promise that someone would be sentenced to death, and it also helps explain the energy behind the recently successful efforts to limit habeas corpus and speed up the time from death sentences to state killings. A state unable to execute those it condemns to die would seem too impotent to carry out almost any policy whatsoever.[25]

As I noted earlier, the United States stands alone among developed nations in its embrace of the death penalty. The death penalty is outlawed in the European Union, where executions have not taken place since the 1960s, and the numbers of executions in the United States puts the country in the same statistical category as China and Saudi Arabia. European nations were particularly vocal in their condemnation of McVeigh's execution at a point when Euro-American relations were beginning an all-time low, with the second Bush administration having already made several policy decisions that were very unpopular with European allies (these relationships would only worsen two years later with the war in Iraq). The death penalty is often held up as a prime example of American hypocrisy because of the contrast between the U.S. discourse on human rights and the country's investment in a "barbaric" practice that has been proven to be unjust. As a headline in the British newspaper the *Independent* observed, execution is defined in Europe as "the American way of death."[26]

The role the execution plays in American ideology in affirming the power of the state, if not the very functioning of government, necessitates that executions be public in some way, even though the law restricts them from public view. As Michel Foucault famously wrote in *Discipline and Punish*, historically the spectacle of the public execution, in which people were hanged, tortured, and brutalized before crowds of onlookers, functioned to affirm the power of the state through spectacle; in the modern state, beginning in the late eighteenth century, punishment is hidden from public view and power is affirmed through its invisibility and inevitability. "In the ceremonies of the public execution, the main character was the people, whose real and immediate presence was required for the performance. . . . Not only must people know, they must see with their own eyes. Because they must be made to be afraid; but also because they must be the witnesses, the guarantors, of the punishment, and because they must to a certain extent take part in it."[27] Jinee Lokaneeta argues that the fact that McVeigh's execution took place behind closed doors did not make it any less spectacular: "Even though citizens cannot watch the spectacle of executions as they did in the past, they can be made to imagine them through the representation of the execution. . . . The spectacular nature of McVeigh's execution was substantiated by the fact that the victims' families and survivors as well as the media were present at the event despite there being nothing to see."[28]

This aspect of spectacle is crucially tied to the role of witnesses in an execution. In most U.S. states, a person cannot be legally executed without the presence of members of the public.[29] The public debate over techniques of execution, which has resulted in the rise of lethal injection and a rejection of the electric chair (after a few notorious cases of malfunction), is, Sarat argues, much more the result of public concern about the pain, "real or imagined," *suffered by witnesses* than the pain of the condemned.[30] It is also the case that those who witness executions in private are then asked to recount their experience before the media in order to affirm their role as surrogates for the public view. Those reporters and family members who witness an execution either in person or via closed-circuit television are asked to recount what they saw for the media. Hence, even though executions are withheld from public view and have become increasingly sanitized and medicalized (with the presence of doctors, the use of medical equipment such as needles, and the mandating of autopsies), they remain in the public eye. The absence of photographic images of executions (though some exist and others circulate in popular culture) only renders greater the value of the imagined scene.[31]

There is a significant debate among death penalty opponents about whether the televised image of an execution would serve to increase or decrease support for the death penalty. As concerns about whether or not lethal injection is painful have increasingly been raised, lawsuits claiming it to be cruel and unusual punishment have proliferated. Importantly, these debates cannot be separated from broader issues of comfort culture, since the underlying discourse here is not whether the state should take a life but whether the state can do so in a way that is not painful or distressing *to witnesses*. The debate over lethal injection raises the specter of the witnesses, since alternative methods that would be easier on inmates would be more gruesome (including jerking movements) for witnesses to see. As the *New York Times* notes, "At the core of the issue is a debate about which matters more, the comfort of prisoners or that of the people who watch them die."[32]

The issues raised by the witnessing of executions converged in new ways with the McVeigh execution because of the large numbers of victims and survivors. In this context, the political clout of the Oklahoma City families and survivors has been significant. A group of them successfully lobbied Congress in 1996, only one year after the bombing, for the passage of the Anti-Terrorism and Effective Death Penalty Act, which limits the rights of death row inmates to appeal (a law that, it must be said, is likely to succeed in the execution of wrongly accused black, Latinos, and indigent inmates). The group began their campaign after one family member heard the story of a death row inmate who was appealing his case again after seventeen years of appeals. The group lobbied Washington wearing buttons that read, "17 Years Is Long Enough." The story of their lobbying mission is proudly featured in the exhibition of the Oklahoma City memorial. The potential contradictions of this position are evident in the logo that they adopted: "Oklahoma City Bombing Victim Death Penalty Appeals Reform Committee—Friends Forever."

Some of the families and survivors also successfully appealed to the courts and to Attorney General Ashcroft to give them unusual powers of witnessing at the trial. Two special acts of Congress were signed into law by President Clinton: the Victims Rights Clarification Act permitted victims who testified at the trial to watch the trial on days when they were not testifying, and a second act allowed them to watch the proceedings on closed-circuit television in Oklahoma City.[33] Thus, while Judge Richard Matsch, who presided over McVeigh's trial in Denver, Colorado, barred television cameras from the courtroom, he allowed for a closed-circuit television feed of the proceedings to be sent to Oklahoma City for families and survivors to watch. Similarly, Ashcroft made the extraordinary move of allowing a closed-circuit image of the execution to be sent to a prison in Oklahoma City for those survivors and family members who chose to watch it (ten people from Oklahoma City were chosen by lottery to witness the execution in person in Terre Haute).

The desire of some of the families and survivors to actually witness the death of the man who killed their loved ones raises the question of the relationship of the citizen to executions. What is the intended role of the citizen in an execution? It is not, as the law dictates, to *not* watch. After all, the primary argument for the existence of the death penalty is deterrence. Even though this deterrence has proven time and again to be ineffective, public sentiment for the death penalty is based both on vengeance and on the notion that it scares potential criminals. In this logic, the invisible execution must be publicly acknowledged. It could be argued, of course, that it is precisely the role of the citizen to watch, to *consume*, the execution as a national event. This accounts in part for why the calls by public officials, including Ashcroft, for people to ignore the execution and for the media to restrict coverage of it appeared so hypocritical, given the spoken investment in the state in the symbolism of the event.

In refusing twice to continue to appeal his death sentence (a move that essentially trumped the lobbying by survivors and families to restrict his right to appeal) and in giving interviews and writing letters to the media, McVeigh was clearly attempting to ascribe himself agency in the process by which he would die. That move was taken quite personally by the survivors and families in Oklahoma City. The tortured relationship of the survivors, families, and rescue workers to the fate of Timothy McVeigh raised the specter of vengeance, and its role in the legal process. Many of the survivors were explicit in their desire to imagine McVeigh suffering. Sarat writes, "The voice of vengeance demands that the pain inflicted in the crime will equal the pain experienced in punishment." Survivor Arlene Blanchard stated that McVeigh should be put in solitary confinement for life or simply hanged from a tree: "I know that it sounds uncivilized, but I want him to experience just a little of the pain and torture that he has put us through." William Baay, a rescue worker, told the newspaper, "I don't think that conventional methods should be used. They should amputate his legs with no anesthesia [this is a reference presumably to survivor Daina Bradley, whose leg was amputated at the scene with no anesthesia] . . . and then set him over a bunch of bamboo shoots and let them grow up into him until he's dead."[34] Of course, the execution itself did little to fulfill these fantasies of pain and suffering.

The extraordinary role that the survivors and families played in the trial, sentencing, and execution of McVeigh is evidence of the increased power of crime victims in the criminal legal process. The survivors and family members testified in large numbers at the trial and at the sentencing phase. There is, Sarat writes, an important legal and moral distinction between vengeance, which is personal and emotional, and retribution, which involves reason. The victims' rights movement has been highly successful in what Sarat and others term the return of revenge in the legal process. This is based on the belief that victims can achieve healing through witnessing the suffering of the criminal, that they can gain "social equilibrium" only if they become agents in the punishment of those who have wounded them. The primary way this has been institutionalized in the courts has been through the use of "victim impact statements" in the penalty phase of trials. This reconstitutes the legal process as one that can and must serve as a form of public healing and, Sarat notes, transforms "courts into sites for the rituals of grieving."[35]

The victims' rights movement aims to recast public sympathy in the criminal process. Martha Minow writes, "In an effort to shift the focus to the defendant's responsibility for the victim's suffering, the victims' rights movement counters the efforts of criminal justice reformers to arouse sympathy for the defendant."[36] The movement is also propelled by belief in the healing quality of public testimony. The incitement to public grief is encouraged not only by politicians, because it allows them to play the role of the protective and indignant leader, but also by the media, which capitalizes on the voyeurism of millions of viewers for whom public grief forms a compelling spectacle. This emphasis on public grieving has also functioned to further a public fascination with the relationship of victims to criminals in a way that inevitably feeds into the celebrity of the criminal.

The dominant presence of victim testimony in trials was evident in the 2006 trial of Zacarias Moussaoui, who was sentenced in May 2006 to life imprisonment for his role as a relatively minor player in the terrorist attacks of 9/11. Moussaoui now resides in the federal supermax prison in Florence, Colorado, where it was promised he would "rot" for the rest of his life.[37] In contrast to the McVeigh trial, the jury in the Moussaoui trial refused to award the death sentence, although by a slim margin. The sentencing phase of the trial became an occasion for the prosecution to bring many family members of 9/11 victims before the jury to talk of their pain, and for them to show graphic and detailed images of the victims of the destruction of the World Trade Center. Prosecutors played 911 phone calls from inside the World Trade Center and the cockpit voice recorder from United Airlines Flight 93. The "victim impact project" of the trial, according to the *Washington Post*, "cast prosecutors and FBI agents in the unusual role of therapists and grief counselors."[38] This performance of victimhood transforms courtrooms into sites of public grief. As in Oklahoma City, the families of the 9/11 victims have very diverse opinions on the death penalty, with many making public statements of revenge and many arguing against the death penalty as a solution.

In the case of Oklahoma City, the tortured relationship of the survivors and families to McVeigh provided constant fodder for media stories, and the execution was accompanied by numerous stories about exactly what families and survivors did that day.[39] The demand for the public testimony of pain and grief, which forms the basis of 12-step programs, is also based on the belief that it is somehow morally wrong for those who have suffered to heal in private, away from public view. Many people in Oklahoma City were clearly tired of the media coverage by the time of the execution; for others the media served as a cathartic means to talk about and remember their loved ones. Finally, however, only 232 of the one thousand people who had signed up to watch the execution attended it, out of twenty-three hundred eligible survivors and family members.[40] The number of survivors and family members who have been involved in these processes has always been small, as in New York, but their words and actions are often taken to stand for all of the hundreds who lost loved ones in or were injured by the bombing.[41]

The publicity about the numbers of survivors and family members who wanted to witness the execution obscured the fact that many of them either chose not to watch or took a stand against the death penalty, many of them on the basis of their Catholic beliefs. This created a difficult debate in Oklahoma City.[42] In the months before the execution, many death penalty opponents held vigils in Oklahoma City outside government offices and were arrested there. Their movement was fueled by the fact that a local police chemist whose testimony helped to convict numerous prisoners and resulted in eleven executions was suspected of having misrepresented the analysis in many cases, including one in which a man had been freed after fifteen years in prison.[43] One of the primary figures in this debate is Bud

Welch, whose twenty-three-year-old daughter, Julie, was killed while working as a Spanish translator in the Social Security office. Welch not only befriended McVeigh's father, Bill McVeigh, after the bombing (because he feels empathy for McVeigh's loss of his son), but he also became a spokesperson for and member of the board of directors for the national organization Murder Victims Families for Reconciliation, which advocates against the death penalty. It is safe to say that Welch, who grew up on a dairy farm and ran a gas station in Oklahoma, has been transformed by the death of his daughter, and in his response has emerged as a figure of conscience. In the speech that he has given many times around the country, Welch talks about meeting Bill McVeigh and Tim's sister, Jennifer, finding commonality with them, and weeping with them. He claims that the death penalty is "about revenge and hate. And revenge and hate is why Julie and 167 others are dead today. That was McVeigh and Nichol's revenge and hate for the federal government, for Waco, for Ruby Ridge. . . . It won't help me any when Tim is killed. . . . I think Gandhi put it very well about the Old Testament—'An eye for an eye leaves the whole world blind.'"[44]

In its emphasis on the last words and movements of the prisoner, an execution is a theatrical event with many acts. In the case of McVeigh's execution, so much emphasis had been placed on speculation about his last words that his decision not to speak carried tremendous weight. Many attempts were made to read meaning into his facial expressions in the execution chamber. The reporters who were witnesses for the most part described McVeigh's face as expressionless; some of the family members in Oklahoma City read his face as an unrepentant expression of hostility and evil. This was clearly aided by the fact that the prison had made the decision to place the camera for the closed-circuit feed not next to the witness gallery but directly over the gurney to which McVeigh was strapped, so that he was staring directly into the camera both before and after he died. As one family member, Paul Howell, whose daughter was killed in the bombing, angrily told reporters, "We didn't get anything from his face."[45]

McVeigh's final refusal to speak was his last tactical move to give the impression that he was in control of his own death. He also attempted to establish his own agency in the final statement that he released to the press through prison officials, which consisted simply of his handwritten version of William Ernest Henley's 1875 poem "Invictus," which famously ends, "I am the master of my fate. I am the captain of my soul." The *New York Times* columnist Frank Rich writes:

FIGURE 43. *New York Post* headline, June 11, 2001. AP Photo/Kathy
Willens.

He was indeed the master of his fate in the perverse ways that mattered to
him. He is eternally famous. He publicized his anti-government absolut-
ism and repeatedly exposed the ineptitude of his Waco nemesis, the F.B.I.
He sowed enough doubts about the government's account of his crime
that a USA Today/CNN/Gallup Poll on the eve of his execution found
that two-thirds of the country believed that he had successfully withheld
the names of accomplices.[46]

The media coverage had run full circle when McVeigh's choice of "Invictus"
was analyzed by a number of publications, including the high-brow *Times
Literary Supplement*, which attempted to establish how he had misinterpreted
the poem.[47]

McVeigh's act of terrorism was one of several factors that set into motion
a shift in membership in right-wing militias throughout the United States.[48]

Member numbers peaked in 1996, but they then began to decline. The FBI, in a shift that many, including McVeigh, attributed to the Waco disaster and the Oklahoma City bombing, changed its tactics to less violent ones, and a standoff with the Freemen in Montana in 1996 ended with a nonviolent surrender. The antigovernment Patriot movement was split by the bombing, in particular because of the deaths of the children, and some cooperated with the FBI to identify their most extreme elements. In the post-9/11 context, members of these groups have been subjected to increased surveillance and a number of leaders have been arrested. Yet the Southern Poverty Law Center (SPLC), which monitors right-wing extremism, states that membership in these organizations has been on the rise since 2003, and that racist neo-Nazi groups continue to gain strength. In addition, the SPLC states that the dispersal of groups when their charismatic leaders are jailed often means that more violence can occur from rogue members.[49] McVeigh's death continues to fuel conspiracies about the participation of others in the bombing, usually referred to as "others unknown," the belief that McVeigh was merely a patsy, and the belief that the government was complicit in the deaths.[50]

Yet McVeigh's death also seems likely to forgo closure precisely because he is a more effective target of rage as a presence rather than as an absence. Bud Welch tells the story of a woman whose husband was murdered, and who supported the death penalty until her husband's murderer was put to death. Then she found that she was unable to channel her rage anywhere and that this inability to vent her anger made her fall apart. He concludes that the death penalty can actually prevent rather than enable healing. The Cartoonist Jim Lange effectively portrays the false promise of closure in the form of a teddy bear, caught in a door that refuses to close.

The demonization of public figures like Timothy McVeigh has the effect of foreclosing on any consideration of their motives and beliefs: they are dismissed as irrational, insane, and inhuman, their words not only suspect but actually dangerous in and of themselves. This was evident in McVeigh's case with the attorney general's unprecedented order to bar him from television and audio interviews (though not contact with print journalists), a move that effectively gave McVeigh's words more power. A similar move was evident in the Bush administration's request in fall 2001 that U.S. news networks refrain from broadcasting Osama bin Laden's speeches in response to the bombing in Afghanistan. The administration did not simply stop at its assertion that these speeches might have coded messages for further potential terrorist actions; they made clear that they felt that any broadcast of bin

FIGURE 44. *Closure*, by Jim Lange. © April 16, 2004, *The Oklahoman*.

Laden's words was inflammatory—that these words were so powerful that they had the capacity to incite violence. This is quite remarkable given that, as some reporters have noted, such an attempt at censorship was never made of Saddam Hussein during the Gulf War or, for that matter, Adolf Hitler during World War II. This overinvestment in the words of such a figure renders them all-powerful in their abstraction.

This fear of the power of words is clear in the exhibition at the Memorial Center in Oklahoma City. The exhibition tells the story of the bombing, its investigation, and the trials of McVeigh and Nichols in detail, and includes a very brief examination of domestic and international terrorism before 2000. Yet it studiously avoids discussing the reasons why right-wing militias exist and what their existence says about American ideology. The exhibit discusses terrorism in highly tentative ways. One can go through the exhibition without ever understanding the ideas that motivated McVeigh and Nichols and the basis of those ideas. In turning McVeigh into a cardboard figure of evil, the exhibit forecloses on a broader understanding of how he was an angry all-American boy, a completely home-grown product, a product of the U.S. military as well as extremist beliefs. Like the debate over McVeigh's public statements to the media, the exhibit displays a fear that any discussion of these beliefs will give them a voice and a platform, that it would in fact constitute an endorsement of them. This overdetermination of the power of the words of a public figure is the central disabling aspect of the process of demonization.

This is in marked contrast to the public image of Terry Nichols, McVeigh's co-conspirator, who was tried in federal court for the deaths of eight federal agents, and then again in Oklahoma for the deaths of civilians. (McVeigh had been tried only in federal court for the lives of the eight federal agents.) The Oklahoma State attorney was criticized for trying Nichols at great expense a second time in the state because he had already received a life sentence in federal court; many people in Oklahoma City felt that the second trial was unnecessary and a waste of money.[51] Yet the victims' rights position prevailed, as some family members argued that it was important that Nichols be tried specifically for the deaths of their loved ones. In a legal move that reflects a great deal about the political context, the charges of this trial cited the victims as 160 civilians and the five-month fetus that Carrie Lenz was carrying at the time of her death, her never-born child thus awarded personhood not only through his naming on her memorial chair, but also in the legal system. Nichols was sentenced to 161 consecutive life terms on August 19, 2004, after a trial in McAlester, Oklahoma, that was remarkable for its lack of press attention. At his conviction, the family members told the press that this was the only time that anyone had been held accountable legally for the majority of the deaths of the bombing.[52] Nichols, who had converted to Christianity in prison, apologized for his role in the bombing at his sentencing, as he had in 1998. In a strange twist on the discourse of healing, he offered to correspond with survivors and families "to assist in their healing process."[53] John Taylor, whose daughter had been killed in the bombing, bitterly told the media, "I'll save the stamp."[54]

CULTURAL MEMORY AND OKLAHOMA CITY

In April 2005, there were many ceremonies to mark the ten-year anniversary of the Oklahoma City bombing. Former President Clinton and Vice President Cheney attended an elaborate memorial ceremony which was covered by a record number of media.[55] Yet the stories that emerged at the time were disruptive of any simple notions of closure. The *Chicago Tribune* observed that while $40 million was donated to the city in the aftermath of the bombing, more than sixty families had been thrown into poverty, many of them because of losing a family member with a job.[56] Numerous rescue workers have been diagnosed with posttraumatic stress disorder (PTSD) and have lost their jobs and families. Some of these workers, for whom PTSD symptoms emerged most pronounced several years after the bombing, responded to their stress by drinking, compulsive gambling, and petty fraud.[57] In March 2004, when the new federal building was opened across the street from the memorial, despite its high-security design, a number of employees in the Department of Housing and Urban Development who were survivors of the bombing refused to work in the building; they were allowed to work in an office a few blocks away.[58] One of the most compelling signs of the long-term effects of the bombing is the fact that many survivors continue to find shards of glass slowly exiting their bodies.[59] (Aren Almon-Kok, the mother of Baylee Almon, the one-year-old who was photographed in the arms of a firefighter, has become the national spokesperson for the Protecting People First Foundation, which advocates for protection against flying glass.)[60]

The meaning of the Oklahoma City National Memorial is caught up in a twinned relationship with the execution, paired with it throughout history. In a cartoon for the *Los Angeles Times*, Michael Ramirez depicted this relationship in disturbing terms, with an image of an execution chair sitting among the chairs at the memorial. The memorial and the execution both arrest time, the memorial in marking in its design the exact moment of the bomb, and the execution in its emphasis on the exact moment of death. The memorial and execution also form two polar approaches in the discourse of healing. In the language of the state and the law the execution promises to provide retribution and closure, yet in its incitement to revenge can potentially promote further cycles of violence. In its self-conscious engagement with the complexities of mourning and its acknowledgment of the lack of closure in loss, the memorial is a tribute to a community's response to loss. In both contexts, the practice of consumerism is offered as a means for people to process grief and to feel comforted by the illusion of closure. Thus, the consumption of the execution as tourism and media spectacle and the consumption of the memorial share many parallels. Both offer the promise of resolution that they cannot fulfill.

The Oklahoma City bombing is also inevitably paired in its historical meaning with the terrorist attacks of 9/11. This has extended far beyond an abstract symbolism; it has involved an extended exchange between the people of Oklahoma City and those in New York. Not only did the Oklahoma

FIGURE 45. Cartoon by Michael Ramirez, 2001. Distributed by Copley News Service.

City memorial run a full-page ad in the *New York Times* reading, "You Stood With Us in Our Darkest Hour, Now, We Stand With You," but the memorial also sent six hundred teddy bears to New York, and the city sent sixty thousand in what they called the Hope Bears project.[61] Survivors and families in Oklahoma City traveled to New York after 9/11 to aid in consoling families. The Oklahoma City memorial produced a traveling exhibition in 2002 entitled "A Shared Experience: 04.19.95–09.11.01," in which the shared aspects of the two events were explored and similar objects from each displayed. On the ten-year anniversary, there were FDNY and NYPD officers in attendance in Oklahoma City.

Yet, in other ways, the events are quite distinct in how they have been defined in American culture. The 9/11 attacks overshadowed Oklahoma City as a defining event of terrorism in U.S. history. Because of their magnitude, the fact that they were perpetrated by Islamic fundamentalists who were easily coded as "others," and the political context (and the administration in power) in which they took place, they were responded to as acts of war rather than criminal acts. The overwhelming response to 9/11 also resulted in substantial compensation payments to victims' families. (After quickly approving a $7 billion package of compensation for victims of 9/11, Congress refused several times in 2002 and 2003 to reopen the question of compensation for victims of previous terrorist attacks.)[62] The issue of compensation is complex, and in New York it has been an inevitably convoluted and contested process. Compensation discourse is not unrelated to the victims' rights movement, in that it is based on the notion that loss can be compensated.

On this issue of compensation, the contrast between Oklahoma City and New York is stunning. There was never any discussion of federal compensation for those affected by the bombing, which, given that the victims died in a federal building, is rather remarkable. The rush to fund compensation for 9/11 took place, of course, in the midst of a national and economic crisis and was largely motivated by a desire to shield the failing airline industries from massive lawsuits. Yet the absence of any debate about compensation in Oklahoma City is revealing. Many families went bankrupt after the bombings and suffered economic hardship. When the 9/11 package was approved, it created understandable resentment in Oklahoma City. Even the federal funding for the memorial came in the form of low-interest loans rather than direct funding. The memorial's director Kari Watkins believes that the absence of federal compensation was important to the rebuilding of the community and that the compensation money has had a negative effect on the process in New York: "We never expected the feds to bail us out."[63]

People representing the Oklahoma City memorial have visited their counterparts in New York often, and representatives of the memorial and rebuilding process in New York have visited Oklahoma City several times. Yet in their statements about how the places are so different, and in essentially ignoring the advice they were given there, those in New York seemed to have learned little from the experience of memorialization in Oklahoma City. This is indicative of the way that an exceptionalist narrative dictates the memory of 9/11 in New York City, and the issue of how to rebuild lower Manhattan. The exceptionalist narrative, which stated that the events in New York were the worst terrorist attack and the most symbolic of this moment in U.S. history, dictated a certain kind of erasure of Oklahoma City. That erasure has been unfortunate, because the debate in New York City could be better informed by the experience of Oklahoma City. With this in mind, I turn, in the next two chapters, to the fraught debate over the memorialization of 9/11 in New York.

4

TOURISM AND "SACRED GROUND"

The Space of Ground Zero

On October 14, 2001, weeks after it had become clear that there were no survivors left to be pulled from the rubble at Ground Zero in New York, and with the recognition that the bodies of many of those who had died would never be recovered, the City of New York decided to distribute the dust. Mayor Giuliani set up a procedure through which the families of the dead received an urn of the dust from the site for a memorial ceremony. The dust (which was otherwise being hauled from the site to the Fresh Kills landfill on Staten Island) was gathered into fifty-five-gallon drums, covered by American flags, blessed by a chaplain at Ground Zero, and given a police escort to One Police Plaza.[1] Officials wearing white gloves scooped the dust into four thousand small urns, each engraved with 9–11–01 and wrapped in a blue velvet bag.[2] By this ritual, the dust was transformed into a substance that was understood to be sacramental and ceremonial (handled with white gloves), moved from drums (indicating refuse) to urns (indicating individuals, ashes, the remains of life), yet that was also official (accompanied by police escort) and national (covered by flags).

This attempt to make the dust sacred, to turn it into a relic, reveals many aspects of the construction of meaning at Ground Zero in the years since 9/11. While analyses of

FIGURE 46. Urn filled with dust from Ground Zero, presented to relatives of the victims, October 28, 2001. AP Photo/Robert Mecea.

9/11 have tended to focus on the role of spectacle in the event, as the years have gone by it is the material refuse of 9/11 that, at least in New York City, has been most fraught with conflict and contested meanings. The dust is simultaneously ashes, refuse, evidence, and a fatal contaminant. Its status remains ambiguous and troubling. As late as 2006, certain family members of the dead continue to advocate that it be returned to Ground Zero from Fresh Kills. And starting in 2005, several young (and previously healthy) people who had been rescue workers at Ground Zero or employees who fled the area died of respiratory disease that was attributed directly to their exposure to the dust at Ground Zero. They are most likely the first of many survivors of 9/11, rescue workers, and janitors who worked in the cleanup whose lives will be shortened by the time they spent at Ground Zero.[3] It is perhaps in the dust of Ground Zero that the meanings of this site are most complexly embodied.

It could be said that Ground Zero was created in the moment on September 11, 2001, when the World Trade Center collapsed, shockingly, in a cloud of dust and debris that, as some witnesses said, "chased" down the streets of lower Manhattan in New York. Within a few hours, the media had found the name, and it stuck.[4] Ground Zero is a name pulled from history, its origins inextricably tied to the destruction caused by nuclear bombs; it began as a term used by scientists for a bomb's point of detonation, thus defining a bomb's central site of destruction. The term implies nuclear obliteration, yet it also, ironically, conveys a starting point, a tabula rasa. For instance, the architect Michael Sorkin's book about rebuilding New York is titled *Starting from Zero*.[5] And, as Amy Kaplan writes, "We often use 'ground zero' colloquially to convey the sense of starting from scratch, a clean slate, the bottom line," a meaning that, she says, resonates with the "often-heard claim that the world was radically altered by 9/11, that the world will never be the same."[6]

As a term, "ground zero" defines New York as the focal point of 9/11, inscribing the space within a narrative of exceptionalism in which New York is the most important and unique aspect of 9/11. The exceptionalism that defines the events as the worst American experience with terror had an instant effect on how the Oklahoma City bombing was viewed, almost immediately redefining it as 9/11's smaller and less significant precursor. (In fact, the term ground zero was used quite often in Oklahoma City to identify the place where the bomb had wreaked the most damage.) The term also effectively erases the other events of 9/11, including the crash of American Airlines 77 at the Pentagon, which killed 189 people, and the crash of Flight 93 in Shanksville, Pennsylvania, which killed forty people. The idea of ground zero as a blank slate or as the targeted center of the bombing thus sets into motion a set of narratives about 9/11, both the narrative of lower Manhattan as the symbolic center of the event and the narrative that 9/11 was a moment in which the United States lost its innocence. Both enable a very particular narrative of exceptionalism, one that proclaims the events of 9/11 to be unique in the history of violent acts. This sense of historical exceptionalism hovers behind the nomenclature of lower Manhattan as Ground Zero—not only in disavowal of the original meaning of the term but also in the belief, widely circulated and deployed politically, that history itself was transformed on 9/11.

Yet what is Ground Zero as a place or a destination? It is, of course, a temporary name. Presumably, when the site is fully rebuilt, it will officially be called something else, the new World Trade Center perhaps. As a place that is defined as existing in between two places (the World Trade Center and its replacement), Ground Zero is more a concept than a place. It is an ephemeral space, yet one charged with meaning.

In the years since September 2001, Ground Zero has become a site of destruction and reconstruction, of intense emotional and political investments, a highly overdetermined space. It is a place inscribed by local, national, and global meanings, a neighborhood, a commercial district, a tourist destination, a place of protest, and a site of memory and mourning. The narratives that have been layered on Ground Zero reveal the complex convergence of political agendas and grief in this space, as if, somehow, the production of new spatial meanings will provide a means to contain the past, deal with the grief, and make sense of the violent events that took place there. The narratives and meanings produced at Ground Zero matter at the local level precisely because they have impacted in profound ways the redesign of an enormous area of a densely populated city and because they reveal the problematic relationship between urban design and commercial interests that govern a metropolis such as New York. These meanings and narratives matter at a national level when they are deployed in the service of national agendas, within a broader global context in which images of the United States are exported with political consequences. Ground Zero is a site where practices of memory and mourning have been in active tension with representational practices and debates over aesthetics: a place, one could say, defined and redefined by a tyranny of meaning.

Ground Zero is also a space defined by and experienced through media technologies, a place constantly mediated through images, a place "visited" via websites and by tourists, a place filled with photographs that is itself relentlessly photographed. The Lower Manhattan Development Corporation, which is in charge of rebuilding the site, had a webcam up for a few years so that viewers could monitor its changing landscape. It is the case that the space of Ground Zero was, from the moment of its naming, already defined through mediatization. The collapse of the World Trade Center towers was witnessed by an extraordinary number of viewers, by those standing on the rooftops and streets of Manhattan, Brooklyn, and New Jersey, by millions of television viewers throughout the United States, and by many millions of television viewers worldwide. September 11 is thus often seen as an event of the image, in which some new register of the spectacular was "achieved."

The intense networks of media that defined the events of 9/11 demonstrate the increased fluidity between public and private media, as cell phone conversations and answering machine messages left by those who were trapped in the towers or on hijacked airplanes and the so-called amateur images of home video and still cameras were incorporated into the ongoing network and cable news coverage. This blurring of public and private paralleled an intermixing of old and new media (in boundary crossings that inevitably made those distinctions seem inadequate). In the age of digital technology, it is often imagined that the ether space of virtual media is just out there, without much of a technological infrastructure. Yet when the towers fell, they took with them the primary antennas for network broadcasting in the region and key wireless transmitters for cell phone transmission in lower Manhattan, forcing many telecommunications companies to switch to antennas and transmitters on top of the Empire State Building.[7] This was an antenna of an older era of media, which was exalted for beaming broadcast signals in the 1970s west to New Jersey and beyond.[8] This mix of old and new media continues; while television images are central to the cultural memory of 9/11, it has in many ways been defined by a plethora of still photographs, both amateur and professional.

In this chapter, I look at the meanings that have been generated about Ground Zero through the frameworks of spectacle, dust, photographs, sacred ground, and consumerism. I am interested in examining how the reconfiguration of Ground Zero as a site of cultural memory production has produced particular narratives of redemption that participate in the production of innocence and the political acquiescence of the tourism of history. My focus is thus on the discussions and debates that have taken place around Ground Zero and the overabundance of meanings that have been generated about this site. Ground Zero has been transformed from a site of destruction and loss into a battleground, over which the families of the dead, politicians, real estate developers, and designers claim ownership. It is the primary place that defines 9/11 in the United States. When people want to make a statement about 9/11, Ground Zero provides them a meaningful site at which to do so. A discourse of sacredness, one derived from its status as a place where many died, is in conflict with a discourse of urban economics and urban renewal. At the same time, the symbolism of Ground Zero and the lost World Trade Center towers has been deployed as the justification for a series of wars and destructive policies of the U.S. government. In this sense, an examination of the meanings of Ground Zero can tell us a lot about how national meanings converge with local politics in a place that many people, for many different reasons, feel belongs to them.

FIGURE 47. Iconic image of towers exploding, *Newsweek* extra edition, September 2001.

SPECTACLE AND MOURNING

It is impossible to consider the meanings projected upon Ground Zero without first considering the role played by images, and in particular spectacular images, in its making. The space of Ground Zero is haunted by the images that were produced on the day of September 11, images that have been described by so many as "cinematic." The spectacle was heightened by the timing of the impacts of the two planes, so that a huge number of people on the streets in New York and throughout the world on television were watching the North Tower burning when the second plane hit. As the *Newsweek* cover makes clear, the image of the South Tower exploding, which was captured by many cameras, became an emblem for the event, inscribed here with the time it happened, as if the instant image demands a time stamp. The cover isolates the second tower, allowing it to cover the magazine's logo while the North Tower, already filled with smoke, is hidden behind. It is in many ways

CHAPTER 4

FIGURE 48. Tower 1 falling, September 11, 2001. Photo by Steve McCurry/ Magnum Photos.

a simple image, a familiar one, of pyrotechnics and distanced, spectacular violence.

The television image of the two towers exploding had been prophetically imagined in flight simulator computer games, one of which, Microsoft Flight Simulator 2000, included at the time a joke about flying the plane into the Empire State Building.[9] The image of the towers falling, captured by the cameras of many people standing on rooftops throughout the city, is a more haunting image, less familiar and shockingly unreal. The towers fell inward, like a planned demolition, but the cloud of dust that they produced, which flooded lower Manhattan, was dramatically otherworldly. When the towers fell, and the space of lower Manhattan was transformed from the World Trade Center into Ground Zero, the spectacle of the event was replaced by a vast pile of debris, a massive ruin that was, at least initially, off-limits to cameras.

It is now common among theorists and commentators to characterize the terrorist attacks of 9/11 as acts intended to produce not so much death as an image. As Slavoj Žižek has written, "We can perceive the collapse of the WTC towers as the climactic conclusion of twentieth-century art's 'passion for the Real'—the 'terrorists' themselves did not do it primarily to provoke real material damage but *for the spectacular effect of it*."[10] Žižek's glib pronouncement, which defines the complex politics of this event within a reductionist framework (they did it to create the image), nevertheless points to the image as a central aspect of 9/11's exceptionalist discourse. Yes, it is said in this exceptionalist narrative, other violent historical events have killed more people, have destroyed cities more completely, have been more devastating politically, yet none has reached this level of spectacle, none was seen live by so many millions of people, none looked like this. Yet the essence of spectacle is an erasure: the awe-inspiring image of the explosion masks the bodies that are incinerated within it.

One of the consequences of this emphasis on the spectacle of 9/11 is the equation of terrorism with spectacle. The collective Retort, for instance, argued that in the attacks of 9/11, the United States experienced a kind of "image defeat" and was wounded at the level of spectacle: "A state that lives more and more in and through a regime of the image does not know what to do when, for a moment, it dies by the same lights."[11] Yet terrorism is often at its most effective and devastating when it operates beneath the image, underground. Julian Stallabrass notes the paradoxes of "vanguard Islamic revolutionaries" who "deny themselves all that capitalist spectacle has to offer, and harden themselves against mundane sentiment and appetite, yet who still hold to the effectiveness of the image, and propagate images of their acts through websites." Their aim, though, according to Stallabrass, is not to produce spectacle so much as to produce "bodily fear (not the sublime of air shows), to blanket a city with the smell of fire and blood, to bring to a people sunk in spectacle the ineluctability of arbitrary death. The July 2003 London underground bombings were not meant primarily to create images, but to spread the terror of living burial among the city's populace."[12]

In the aftermath of 9/11, the images of spectacle were countered by a proliferation of images and street-level mourning throughout the city. The striking, clean images of the towers exploding were mediated by a profusion of posters for the missing and snapshot images, a proliferation of photographs in a vernacular intervention into the street life of the city. Just as in Oklahoma City, small and spontaneous memorials sprang up immediately around the city, in Union Square, and at numerous fire stations. These

FIGURE 49. Union Square memorial, September 17, 2001. © Lorie Novak, www.lorienovak.

shrines, which included photographs, candles, and messages written to the dead and missing, as well as numerous images of the now-lost twin towers, clearly indicated that in times of loss, the act of leaving an object at a meaningful site is a cathartic one. Leaving flowers, writing collective messages, and lighting candles were declarative acts that aimed to individualize the dead. Whereas the images of spectacle produced an image of a collective loss, of a "mass body," these rituals sought to speak of the dead as individuals. As such, these objects and messages attempted to resist the transformation of the individual identities of the victims into a collective subjectivity, and thus to resist the mass subjectivity of disaster. It can also be said that many of the spontaneous shrines were participating in long-established codes of mourning that were already highly ritualized.

Many of the shrines were dismantled by the city after about a week, yet the photographic images of them continued to circulate. Like the memorial fence at Oklahoma City, these shrines were places where people who were not in New York at the time of 9/11 felt that they could connect to the event and offer condolences by leaving objects coded with mourning: photographs, teddy bears, messages, and FDNY hats. As months passed, many of these materials were put on display in major thoroughfares in the city, such as Penn Station and Grand Central Station. As the site of Ground Zero became more established, the large shrine at St. Paul's Chapel, a church that

FIGURE 50. Shrine in New York, September 2001. Photo by Alberto Zanella.

sits right next to Ground Zero and was used by rescue workers during the recovery period, has remained the primary place where people leave objects, messages, and tributes and come to look at them. It is testimony to the way the ritual of leaving objects functions that many people, apparently without ironic intent, left objects, including many New York T-shirts, at a spontaneous shrine created at the mural of the New York skyline at the New York New York Casino in Las Vegas (where there is now a more permanent display).[13] The need to connect to a space that signified New York, even in a highly constructed, kitsch way, made such a gesture seem appropriate and meaningful.

These spontaneous rituals of mourning in the first few weeks after 9/11 were quickly incorporated into the media spectacle of 9/11 as the media operated to shape the public aspects of mourning. For instance, newspapers such as the *New York Times* and the *New York Post* aimed to "own" the event, as did CNN and other television news networks. Rituals of mourning that took place in public spaces throughout the city were all immediately mediatized and packaged as they were reported on, often by reporters who were themselves traumatized participants of the events. Within this media context, many people, in New York and throughout the country, began their days in the months after 9/11 reading and often weeping over the "Portraits of Grief" in the *New York Times*, in which the lives of the individuals who had been confirmed dead were described in highly individualized and often whimsical fashion. As an attempt to individualize the dead out of the mass body produced by the towers' destruction, these often idiosyncratic obituaries also had the effect of democratizing the normally exclusive pages of the *New York Times*' obituary section for several months. Nancy Miller reads a complexity in the portraits, of moments when family members were exhausted about talking about the lives of the dead, of lives that were highly structured by long commutes to work, of the unfulfilled aspects of lives that the portraits determinedly depicted as fulfilled (in a mode quite common to obituaries). She writes that she could not "identify with these lives from which all traces of unhappiness were banished," even as she feels compelled to keep collecting the portraits.[14] As forms of public grieving, the portraits also indicated the need to name the dead that emerges in the wake of mass death, which often takes the form of inscribing names on a memorial or in the common practice of reading the names of the dead in commemorative ceremonies. Naming and describing the unique quirks of those lost serve to pull these individuals out of an abstract image of mass death and to render them different, unlike any others.

DUST

The towers of the World Trade Center were made of steel, concrete, asbestos, wood, plastic, and glass; they were filled with desks, computers, tables, and paper, yet they crumbled into dust. In one of the most noted lines of the documentary *9/11*, one of the firefighters says, "You have two 110-story office buildings. You don't find a desk, you don't find a chair, you don't find a computer. The biggest piece of telephone I found was a keypad and it was this big. The building collapsed to dust. How are we supposed to find anybody in this stuff? There's nothing left of the building."[15] There was an unbelievability in the transformation of such formidable buildings into particles of dust. How could so many material objects be reduced so quickly to dust? How could those buildings, those objects—those people—suddenly be gone?

The dust dominated the images of the immediate aftermath of the towers' collapse. It was infinitely photographable, producing haunting images of a cityscape coated in dust as if it were a few inches of snow, transforming the outline of debris into strange, layered shapes. In one well-known image by the photographer Susan Meiselas, a realist statue of a businessman sitting on a bench, *Double Check*, that had been created by the well-known figurative

FIGURE 51. Dust covering Seward Johnson Jr. sculpture, *Double Check*, in lower Manhattan, September 11, 2001. Photo by Susan Meiselas/Magnum Photos.

sculptor J. Seward Johnson in 1982, is blanketed in dust and debris, as if he were a businessman frozen in time. The owner of Chelsea Jeans, a clothing store that eventually closed down a year later for lack of business, kept preserved a window in which the rows of pants were coated with the dust; an image of a tea set covered in the dust was featured in the *New York Times*; the mayor refused to clean the shoes he wore on his first trip to Ground Zero; people wrote messages in the dust, which were then photographed by the *New York Times*.[16] People's experience of the trauma of that day was gauged in terms of their proximity to the dust—those who wandered the streets coated in it, those who went home with it on their clothing, in their hair, on their faces, who breathed it.

The dust from the collapse of the World Trade Center acquired many meanings in the months after 9/11. It was initially a shocking substance—something uncanny yet strangely familiar. Some of it was recognizable: papers, remnants of the ordinary business of life before that day, now transformed; balance sheets from financial firms, previously objects of mundane business transactions, were transformed into historical objects and collectable items, materials conveying poignancy and loss. It is easy to remember years later that in the first few days after 9/11 there was an urgency to find survivors in the rubble, an ultimately doomed mission. What is often forgotten is that the city also had an urgent need to clean up the streets of lower

CHAPTER 4

FIGURE 52. Chelsea Jeans Memorial, 2001. Photo by G. Paul Burnett. © *The New York Times*/Redux Pictures.

FIGURE 53. Tea set in 9/11 debris, 2001. Photo by Edward Keating. © *The New York Times*/Redux Pictures.

FIGURE 54. Dust-covered snow globe near Ground Zero, September 24, 2001. AP Photo/Eugene Richards.

Manhattan near the New York Stock Exchange so that it could reopen the following Monday. Even as the shock of what had happened was still being registered, the city deployed an army of sanitation trucks to scour away the dust. Thus dust was initially understood as a substance that had to be cleaned away so that life could continue and as an impediment to moving forward. It was also quickly experienced as a form of contamination, clogging people's lungs and later producing what became known as the "World Trade cough," now understood to be a symptom of debilitating and potentially fatal respiratory disease.

Soon, though, the dust was imbued with new meanings. Once it became clear that very few people had survived the cataclysmic collapse of the two buildings, the dust was defined not simply as the refuse of the towers' collapse, but as the material remains of the bodies of the dead (ultimately, only 1,592, or 58 percent, of the 2,749 people killed were identified). Processes of grief often involve a need for a material trace of the dead. In the long history in which people have mourned in the absence of remains, there have been rituals that substitute objects (empty coffins, flags, photographs, headstones) as touchstones, material artifacts that can provide some kind of corporeal presence to mediate the absence of the dead. At Ground Zero, this need transformed the dust into a new kind of substance, one freighted with significance, which resulted, as I have noted, in its being blessed and placed in

FIGURE 55. New York police sift through refuse at Fresh Kills landfill, October 24, 2001. AP Photo/Beth A. Keiser.

urns for the families who wanted it. As Patricia Yaeger writes, this revealed the "impulse to convert this detritus into something hallowed and new." [17]

Yaeger writes that the detritus of the World Trade Center towers was disturbing precisely because its status was unclear: Is it rubble or body part? As such, it can be seen as a polluting substance, in Mary Douglas's anthropological terms. [18] It coated surfaces with specks of life, death, body, paper, and building. The dust needed to be scrubbed away precisely because of its liminal status—as both refuse and body. And it was removed, intensely and efficiently, along with the larger chunks of building debris, to the Fresh Kills landfill. There, body parts were still sought after, but the debris had already been transformed through its location into the category of rubbish.

The multiple meanings placed upon the dust at Ground Zero are indicators of the ways that various discourses have come into conflict there, including those of sacredness, commerce, and urban design. The desire to see the dust as a means to render present the dead is deeply connected to concepts of sacredness at the site. The recoding of the dust is also implicated in the controversy on the role that Fresh Kills landfill has played in the meanings generated at Ground Zero, and how those meanings have intersected with the definition of science that has emerged in the process of DNA identification. Fresh Kills had been closed in early 2001, with a plan under way to turn it into a park, when the city reopened it after 9/11 and sent all of the debris there, except the steel girders of the towers.[19] Although a huge effort was made to locate any remaining body parts that might have been sent to the landfill, there is lingering concern that the landfill is a repository for the remains and ashes of the dead.

Thus, even after it was relegated to the dump, the dust of Ground Zero continued to haunt precisely because its status was not trash. Dust is not, as Carolyn Steedman argues, about refuse or rubble so much as it is about a cyclical materiality. It is a reminder of continuity, a vestige of what was that continues to exist. The dust in the archive, she argues, evokes the material presence of the past—a "not-going-awayness" and an imperishability of substance: "This is what Dust is about; this is what Dust *is*. . . . It is not about rubbish, not about the discarded; it is not about a surplus, left over from something else: *it is not about Waste*. Indeed, Dust is the opposite thing to Waste, or at least, the opposite principle to Waste. It is about circularity, the impossibility of things disappearing, or going away, or being gone. Nothing *can be* destroyed."[20] In Steedman's terms, dust symbolizes the cyclical nature of material existence, both the reduction of material objects to dust and the gathering of particles into new forms. Attempts to preserve the dust are interventions into this cycle of materiality; as such, they are attempts to arrest the moment of crisis.

It may be that the meaning of the dust as a toxic substance will be its most enduring signification. As survivors of 9/11 and rescue workers who worked at Ground Zero continue to get sick, and continue to die, with estimates as high as 70 percent of rescue workers and first responders with some form of lung disease, the sense that the dust was poisonous grows.[21] This is evident not only in the emerging public debate about these deaths, and in the statements of those who are ill, but in the transformed status of remnants of the dust. In August 2006, the New-York Historical Society put on display the clothing and dust that had been preserved from the Chelsea Jeans store near Ground Zero. When the store's owner went out of business a year after 9/11, he donated the encased storefront of clothing covered in dust to the Historical Society. As the clothing was installed at the Historical Society, it was treated not only as a "historic and possibly sacred" substance but also, primarily, as dangerous and toxic, attended to by a crew wearing hazard suits working in a sealed bubble.[22] The senior conservator of the Society told the *New York Times*, "It's strange to be so carefully preserving something that is so destructive." Thus, while the dust is still seen to be a remnant of the dead, its status as the toxic mix of pulverized offices, computers, glass, and equipment has transformed it into a polluting substance, otherworldly and dangerous, something not to be breathed or touched.

THE PILE AND THE PHOTOGRAPH

While the dust was scoured from lower Manhattan, the massive amount of debris left at the site of the World Trade Center transformed it into a construction and engineering puzzle, which construction companies and crews had to undertake to "unbuild" in a huge excavating task. In the nine months from September 2001 to May 2002, Ground Zero was a demolition site, divided into four quadrants, each of which was the province of a different construction company. The whole project was overseen by a formerly obscure department of New York City, the Department of Design and Construction.

In his book *American Ground: Unbuilding the World Trade Center*, William Langewiesche writes that "at the heart of it, under the skeletal walls rising to 150 feet above the street, the debris spread across seventeen acres in smoldering mounds. It was dangerous ground, of course. Workers at the site called it simply, 'the pile.'"[23] Langewiesche's book, which received significant attention as the only firsthand account of the recovery operation, describes the ways that the various groups involved in that operation—the firefighters, the police, and the construction workers and engineers—fought constantly over the meaning of the pile and how it should be treated. The firefighters were angry at the construction workers, who, they felt, used their enormous machines callously, as if the ground were not littered with the dead. The construction crews, for their part, were angry at the firefighters because they perceived them to be treating their dead differently from the civilians who died there. Langewiesche writes:

> There was resentment by the police, who had lost plenty of their own people, and by the construction crews, who took it upon themselves to remember the far greater number of civilian dead. These tensions flared especially over the differing treatment of human remains—on the one extreme, the elaborate flag-draped ceremonials that the firemen accorded their own dead, and on the other, the jaded "bag 'em and tag 'em" approach that they took to civilians. . . . It was a surprisingly ganglike view, and it encouraged a gang mentality among others on the pile.[24]

FIGURE 56. Ground Zero, October 3, 2001. AP Photo/L. M. Otero.

Langewiesche's depiction of firefighters as less than heroic became the source of tremendous controversy. His book was embraced as a relief from the emotionalism of Ground Zero hero worship and condemned as an account that renders individual firefighters invisible next to heroic engineers. The book's (now qualified) charge that firefighters participated in looting produced a particularly volatile debate because the sanctification of the firefighters has been so powerful. Yet it could also be argued that *American Ground* was inevitably controversial precisely because it defines Ground Zero in unsentimental terms as an engineering problem—the problem of hauling away massive amounts of debris, steel beams, concrete slabs, and crushed vehicles and of rebuilding infrastructure—rather than as a sacred site. While Langewiesche's book criticizes the firefighters, it sanctifies the Department of Design and Construction employees and the construction workers at the site. They too have since undergone a change of image, as post-9/11 investigations revealed numerous connections to the New York mafia, and one company head was banned from the site.[25]

Very few people were given access to the pile, and it remained both a dangerous and, to a certain extent, secretive place about which stories were told. People did peer over the temporary barriers around it, though, staring and taking photographs, and even being photographed themselves.[26] The transformation of the site from a recovery and demolition operation into a site for observation, tourism, and reconstruction was marked by a ceremony (of which there have been many) at Ground Zero on May 31, 2002. On that day, flanked by rows of firefighters and police officers, the recovery workers took out an empty stretcher, intended to symbolize the unidentified dead, followed by a flatbed truck carrying the last steel beam of the twin towers' debris covered with an American flag.[27] As the beam of the now-destroyed building was attended to in a funereal ritual normally reserved for the dead, the ceremony effectively demonstrated the ways that the building itself, and its remains, continue to stand in for the dead.

The dust defined the materiality of the pile at Ground Zero, yet the defining medium of the street-level response in the aftermath of the towers' destruction was the still photograph. As I have mentioned, the emergence of photographs was almost immediate, as the city was quickly plastered with flyers for those who were missing. These missing posters, made in desperation by friends and family members, were posted near hospitals and rescue centers and on the streets of lower Manhattan, rapidly filling up the visual landscape at eye level. Each of these images began as one of hope, imbued with the belief that the person would be found, would be *recognized*. Yet within a week of the towers' fall, it became clear that there would be very few survivors, and the missing posters were transformed into images that marked, if not catalogued, the dead. The posters remained within the cityscape, tenaciously clinging to buildings and signposts, becoming increasingly faded and torn, their deterioration a kind of evocation of grief. The images on these missing posters powerfully evoked a kind of prior innocence: people smiling in vacation photos and at family gatherings, testimony to a time "before," when such a context, such an event, was unimaginable. The temporal rupture of these images demonstrated in many ways the power of the still image to convey a mortality and finality. The identifying text, at once forensic as it noted particular physical characteristics ("eyes: blue"; "eagle tattoo on right arm") and personal in its plea ("Have you seen John?"), was transformed from the language of identification into one of fate: "1 World Trade Center, Marsh 97th Floor"; "Cantor Fitzgerald"; "Last seen on 102nd Floor of One World Trade Center."

The photographs in these posters were freighted with new meaning. As Marianne Hirsch writes, "Violently yanked out of one context and inserted into a totally incongruous one, they exemplify what Roland Barthes describes as the retrospective irony of looking at photographs—the viewers possess the deadly knowledge that the subject of the image will not know."[28]

FIGURE 57. Missing poster, outside Bellevue Hospital, October 2001. Photo © Lorie Novak, www.lorienovak.com.

This "deadly knowledge" is not simply about the fate of those imaged, but the transformation of the photograph itself—the image's change in status from casual snapshot to talisman to a trace that marks the absence of the dead. These photographs of people alive and naïve about events to come also acted as counterimages to the iconic images that came to define 9/11, not only the images of spectacle but also the haunting images of people falling and jumping to their deaths.[29] Later posters responded to the increased surety that those lost were dead by speaking directly to the victims rather than to other witnesses, saying "Please come home" and "We are thinking of you," a gesture that evokes a kind of memorial "conversation with the dead" that is quite similar to the messages left at memorials and sewn into the panels of the AIDS Memorial Quilt, among other objects.[30] Photographing posters in Hudson River Park near the site of Ground Zero, the photographer Lorie Novak writes of these images, "Placed near the site as public

FIGURE 58. Grand Central Station memorial wall, October 24, 2001.
Photo © Lorie Novak, www.lorienovak.com.

memorials, the photographs also become portals to speak to the dead."[31]
Novak photographed one poster for Nichola Thorpe on which someone had
written "Found—Rest in Peace," yet which they left on the wall at Grand
Central Station (fig. 58). The poster was thus transformed into a message for
the lost one and as a memorial to her, now no longer missing.

As they were transformed into memorials, the missing posters were
themselves eulogized. Increasingly tattered and worn by weather, they were
photographed as they clung to buildings, and in some places, such as train
stations and hospitals, were assembled on display. For some observers, it
was precisely their worn quality that imbued them with the most poignant
meaning, as if they eloquently pictured a loss of hope yet a tenacity to keep
going.[32] Eventually, many of the posters were assembled into an exhibition,
Missing: Last Seen at the World Trade Center, September 11, 2001, which traveled

around the United States the following year, and many posters are now a part of various archives about 9/11, thus, to a certain extent, completing their transformation from objects of searching and hope to historical objects of mourning.[33] At St. Vincent's Hospital in Greenwich Village, an entire wall of posters was preserved under plastic and remained facing the street for many years afterward.

It is striking that still photographs seem to have played a dominant role in the response to 9/11, far more than the television images. Unlike the television images which defined the media spectacle, the photograph seems to aid in mediating and negotiating a sense of loss. In the first months after 9/11, in addition to the proliferation of photojournalism, there was a frenzy of amateur picture taking in New York and an obsession with looking at images.[34] September 11 has been referred to as one of the most photographed events in history, producing an "iconomania" of images.[35] Initially, the site of Ground Zero was considered to be taboo for photographing; as Hirsch writes, police told people to "show respect" by putting their cameras away.[36] This was not only because the site was considered both a crime site and a site of emergency where the dead were still missing, but also because it was in an unprecedented state of tension and high alert. In the moment of crisis, photography was thus initially seen as a suspect activity. At the same time, a moral discourse emerged in which photographs were seen to be inappropriate, if not touristic, signifying a superficial response to the site. Handmade posters near the barrier of Ground Zero told people to put their cameras away. One poster admonished, "I wonder if you really see what is here or if you're so concerned with getting that perfect shot that you've forgotten this is a tragedy site, not a tourist attraction."[37]

Nevertheless, even in the early weeks, rescue workers and volunteers were photographing at the site, and there was a proliferation of amateur images throughout the city. By December, there were several photographic exhibitions that were quickly installed in open storefronts, where anyone could bring their snapshots and videotape, the most popular of which was the exhibit *Here Is New York*, which was later released as a book and which by December had sold inexpensive copies of over thirty thousand images.[38] These shows were hugely popular with both tourists and New Yorkers. They conveyed both local and global meanings, raising the specter of the exceptionalism of the event. Kari Andén-Papadopoulus writes that the organizers of *Here Is New York*, ultimately self-conscious about the New York–centric aspects of its exhibition, began encouraging contributions of images from

a democracy of photographs

FIGURE 59. Cover of *Here Is New York*, 2001.

around the world. While it is clear that the exhibit could easily, as Andén-Papadopoulus charges, fall into a "myopic focus" that could echo "the official self-glorifying rhetoric of the U.S. in the wake of the attack," it is also the case that the exhibit began initially as a response to local needs and the use of photography as a means of processing the local response to 9/11.[39] It is notable that the *Here Is New York* project explicitly identified itself as a "democracy of photographs" and used tactics, such as scanning the images, printing them all the same size, and hanging them from lines in the gallery, that demanded a distinction from the proliferation of spectacular media images.

It thus seems as if the urge to take photographs and to look at the images of disaster was a means of assimilating the event. As Diana Taylor writes, "We, the backgrounded participants in this drama, were nonetheless *there*. In photography, some of us found an act of unity of sorts: we were all focused on the same thing, we were all framing what we saw from our position. . . . It was a way of doing something when it *seemed* that nothing could be done."[40] Photographs can serve to inspire awe and voyeurism through the spectacular, but they can also make catastrophe feel containable. Much of the effect of these exhibitions was a sense of the visceral role the images could play, a catharsis not only in seeing gritty snapshot images of the events of that day, which seemed to have a more raw and spontaneous quality than the news images, but also close-up images of Ground Zero, a place still off-limits.

While missing posters and snapshots proliferated an array of amateur images throughout the city, certain photographs emerged quite rapidly as image icons of 9/11. Just as the children were the iconic figures of Oklahoma City, the firefighters emerged as the iconic figures of 9/11, and their deaths were the focus of enormous public grieving. As figures the firefighters embodied not only a sense of reassurance, in what was understood as their straightforward masculinity, the guys that one could count on, but also the immensity of their sacrifice, put simply by many people as "They had entered the buildings as people fled them." The sanctification of the firefighters had the effect of erasing the selfless and heroic acts by many people that day, including minimum-wage security guards and civilians. That this simple and one-dimensional image of heroism would later be debunked, as the complexity of actual lives came more into focus, was inevitable, yet to a certain degree the sanctification of the firefighter in 9/11 has remained strong.[41]

It is thus not surprising that one of the most lauded images to have been created of 9/11 was a photograph of firefighters. This image, taken by Thomas E. Franklin of *The Record* newspaper of Bergen County, New Jersey, shows three firefighters looking upward as they raise a flag at Ground Zero, as enormous piles of debris tower over them. The Franklin image won the Pulitzer Prize and has been widely disseminated, appearing on a huge variety of merchandise, both official and unofficial. It circulated through a broad array of cultural formats, ending up being reenacted at sports events and, among other places, as a display honoring firefighters at Madame Tussaud's Wax Museum and as a snow globe. A three-foot-high bronze version of it was made by the Utah artist Stan Watts, who donated it to Engine 325 and Ladder 163 firehouse in Woodside, Queens.[42] There is thus a direct lineage from the image of the firefighter Chris Fields cradling Baylee Almon in Oklahoma City to the image of the firefighters of 9/11. Just as people sent in children's toys addressed simply to Oklahoma City in the months after the bombing, those who "felt the need to do something" sent in statues, teddy bears, letters, food, flags, and other objects to the New York Fire Department, which by July 2002 had run out of space for them.[43]

As has been widely noted, the Franklin image did not emerge in isolation but is itself a reference to one of the most famous images of American history, of American soldiers raising the U.S. flag on Iwo Jima during World

FIGURE 60. Photo by Thomas Franklin, 2001. Reprinted with permission from North Jersey Media Group.

War II. Indeed, in many ways the gesture of three firefighters raising the flag at Ground Zero was *already a reenactment* of the Iwo Jima photograph, a reenactment by both the firefighters and the photographer.[44] The original image, which also won a Pulitzer Prize and was later immortalized in bronze in the Marine Corps War Memorial, is so central to American concepts of triumph and sacrifice that it is consistently the source of remakes; it proliferated on wartime enlistment posters, was reenacted in Hollywood films, was made into a postage stamp, and has been endless fodder for cartoons.[45] It is an image whose iconicity has had an extraordinary longevity. In 2006, the story of the flag raising became the basis for a film directed by Clint Eastwood, *Flags of Our Fathers*, which was based on a book about the lives of the men depicted in the photograph. Numerous cartoons referencing Ground Zero as Iwo Jima proliferated after 9/11.[46] For instance, on September 13, the cartoonist John Deering of the *Arkansas Democrat-Gazette* produced a

FIGURE 61. Original prizewinning photograph at Iwo Jima, February 23, 1945. AP Photo/Joe Rosenthal.

drawing of the firefighters and police in the pose of Iwo Jima, raising a flag at Ground Zero, and a reenactment of the raising of the flag was part of the half-time celebration at the 2002 Super Bowl.

Those images that gain iconic status establish a set of codes by which subsequent images are defined: they create an iconography for depicting certain kinds of events. This is particularly the case with images that tap into concepts of national identity. There is thus a tendency on the behalf of photographers to attempt to create (and the public to embrace) pictures that fit into familiar codes and narratives of sacrifice and heroism. In the well-documented story of how the firefighters took the flag from a boat at a nearby marina and raised it on the afternoon of September 11, just as the adjacent Building 7 of the World Trade Center was about to collapse, Franklin took the photograph on the fly with the firefighters unaware that they were being photographed. As the image worked its way through the publication process, it was instantly understood to be iconic and to refer to the Iwo Jima flag raising.[47]

The firefighters who raised the flag in the famous image saw it as an indicator of hope at a moment of despair when, as one put it, "everyone needed

FIGURE 62. Marine Corps War Memorial in Arlington, Virginia, 2006. AP Photo/Pablo Martinez Monsivais.

FIGURE 63. Cartoon by John Deering, Arkansas *Democrat-Gazette*, 2001. © Creators Syndicate. Reprinted with permission.

FIGURE 64. Sticker in honor of FDNY firefighters featuring Franklin photograph.

a shot in the arm."[48] The hope of the gesture was quite quickly transformed into a discourse of revenge in which the photograph has largely been interpreted as one of defiance. As Franklin himself has said, "The hook with this picture is the symbolism, bravery, and valor. They (the three firefighters) are saying 'screw you' to whoever did this."[49]

One of the primary meanings that has emerged in the sanctification of the firefighters in the post-9/11 context is their reinscription as soldiers. It is now known that many firefighters were sent to their deaths through faulty communication and misguided, if understandable, decisions and that they did not have to die in such numbers. Yet narratives of heroism serve to make their deaths seem less futile. The remaking of the Franklin image was thus about fusing the firefighters into a narrative of U.S. military victory, a remarkable feat given that it is an image of an event in which the United States was attacked and hundreds of firefighters died; it was also about remaking the image of 9/11 from one of catastrophe and loss into one that could be deployed as a military response. As Andén-Papadopoulous writes, "We can-

CHAPTER 4

FIGURE 65. Commemorative 9/11 coin featuring Franklin photograph.

not understand the power and popular resonance of Franklin's photo of the three firefighters . . . if we don't take account of its aesthetic devices—and the ways these devices feed the official self-glorifying rhetoric of the U.S. in the wake of the attack."[50] The popularity of the Franklin image is thus an indicator of how the remaking of the Iwo Jima image is not simply about a repetition of image codes; it is about how images themselves help to facilitate particular ideological responses to loss.

Like the image of the firefighter cradling the dead child that came to symbolize the tragedy of the Oklahoma City bombing, the image of the three firefighters raising the flag has become the source of tensions, controversy, and contradictions. The *Bergen Record*, which owns the rights to the image, initially set up a charity organization for all revenue generated by the image, in collaboration with the three firefighters, yet the arrangement became acrimonious over decisions on what uses to approve and financial arrangements. The firefighters were more concerned that money be raised than that aesthetic judgments dictate the image's use. Jennifer Borg, the

FIGURE 66. President George W. Bush in the Oval Office, March 11, 2002, with postage stamp based on the Franklin photograph of three firefighters at Ground Zero, from left: Billy Eisengrein, George Johnson, and Dan McWilliams. AP Photo/Kenneth Lambert.

Record's attorney, states, "They wanted to put the image on things that we, as a newspaper, didn't agree with. . . . 'How can you deny a family from getting money because you won't license it on snow globes, just because you don't think that's appropriate? Who cares about appropriateness? We're going to too many funerals.' But as a newspaper we are safeguarding the images, journalistically, through its context."[51] The image was made into a postage stamp, to great fanfare, in March 2002, which is reported to have raised over $10 million to assist emergency workers and their families, but the money has been mired in the bureaucratic red tape of the Federal Emergency Management Agency.

These contradictions are made even clearer in relation to the fetishization of the flag depicted in the image. Initially the flag was signed by officials and sent from New York to Afghanistan, where it was raised at Kandahar airport. As Susan Willis writes, "Passed from the hands of the firefighters to those of the Marines, the flag designates a shift in America's interests away from a host of domestic needs left pending after 9/11, and towards a politics aimed at military operations overseas, whose repercussion on the domestic is, then, the militarization of the homefront under the guise of Homeland Security."[52] In many ways, the circulation of this iconic flag is not dissimilar to the American flags that were left at the Oklahoma City memorial and which were recirculated when the memorial sent them to soldiers in Afghanistan (at least one of whom brought his back to the memorial upon his return). In these instances, the "banal" nationalism of the flag loses its banality, and it is the very circulation of the flag that creates meaning, both the gestures of connection that the passing on of the flag produces (in the context of Oklahoma City memorial flags, which circulated with a message of "hope") and the larger implications of what it means when flags travel in non-U.S. contexts.

Through a series of incidents in which the original owners of the flag asked to borrow it back, it became clear that the original flag had been lost or stolen and replaced somewhere along the way of its symbolic journey.[53] The owners have created a website, findtheflag.com, which they hope will prompt someone to return the flag so that it can be donated to the Smithsonian. Thus, the flag itself, understood as a potential commodity, has come to symbolize the contradictory world of post-9/11 formal and informal commerce.

The remakes of the photograph have also, perhaps inevitably, been the subject of a debate over representation. In January 2002, the photograph became the model for a planned memorial to the firefighters in which the sculptor changed the three white firefighters into a racially diverse group: one white, one Latino, and one black. At the time, those involved felt that this racial diversity would be a way to memorialize all of the people who had died and would operate as a metaphoric statement rather than a literal one. Yet at a moment when the firefighters in the photograph, like their Iwo Jima predecessors, were the subject of media attention precisely because they were depicted in the image, such a transposition was impossible. The outcry was immediate, and firefighter organizations rejected the planned sculpture as "political correctness run amok."[54] This demonstrates the limits of figurative representation in an era of heightened sensitivity about difference; in other words, contemporary codes of representation do not allow a figurative statue to be without racial meaning. This conflict echoes the response to the Frederick Hart statue that was erected next to the Vietnam Veterans Memorial in Washington, about which numerous people have speculated on the racial identity of the three soldiers, and whose presence made the female veterans feel left out.[55] If all the firefighters in the statue are white, as they were in the photograph, then the memorial exposes the reality of the New York City Fire Department, which is that it is, despite many attempts to integrate it, 94 percent white in a city that is less than 50 percent white.[56] If they are transformed into a racially diverse group, they represent a politically correct ideal, a belief that the fire department could be a different kind of club, but then the statue would ultimately not be representative of the fire department as it stands or the firefighters who died.

The photograph of the three firefighters takes place at Ground Zero, but its focus is on the renewal signified by the firefighters and the patriotic significance of the flag raising. Images of Ground Zero are, like the site itself, weighted with meaning that, like the flag from the Franklin photograph, can be exported with specific political intent. Shortly after 9/11, the photographer Joel Meyerowitz, who spent years photographing the World Trade Center towers from the roof of his studio farther uptown, was granted access to photograph the site during the months in which the debris was cleared. Meyerowitz was angered to learn that the police department was preventing people from photographing at the site: "I was going to go in there and make an archive of everything that happened at Ground Zero. . . . I wanted to communicate what it felt like to be there as well as what it looked like: to show the incredible intricacy and visceral power of the site."[57] Meyerowitz's photographs are stunning images. In them, the massive piles of debris are rendered beautiful under the bright spotlights of the demolition crews. While he photographed many of the recovery operation personnel, who are often formally posed before the camera, it is the chaotic, jagged debris of the buildings that is rendered most startlingly in the images, at once abstract and awesome. He writes, "It's hard to come to terms with the awful beauty of a place like this. After all, the site—thick with grief and death—was dangerous, noisy, poisonous, and costly almost beyond measure. And yet the demolition at Ground Zero was also a spectacle with a cast of thousands, lit by a master lighter and played out on a stage of immense proportions."[58]

Meyerowitz works with a large-format camera, and the images are printed large, thirty by forty inches, so that they have a lush, luminescent quality. It is precisely because of this classical style that Lawrence Weschler juxtaposed them with classical paintings by Renaissance and Romantic painters in his book *Everything That Rises*.[59] Meyerowitz has had a number of exhibitions of the photographs; he published a large number of them in a massive coffee-table book, *Aftermath: World Trade Center Archive*, in 2006, and the book has quite a number of fold-out images which emphasize the immensity of the scale of the debris.

The detail created by Meyerowitz's large-format camera is instrumental

FIGURE 67. Ground Zero, 2001. Photo © Joel Meyerowitz. Courtesy of Edwynn Houk Gallery.

in creating the lush, awe-inspiring aspect of the photographs. At the same time, this detail has forensic implications and functions as what Meyerowitz emphatically calls a photographic archive:

> I want the archive to be useful to whoever would make their way into it. Engineers come to my studio to sit with the archive. They see procedures, tactics, the systems in place to get rid of all this stuff. They see the pressures the materials suffered. Lawyers come in droves because of all the lawsuits pending. They look at the pictures asking how many people are wearing their masks and how many aren't. Workers and other participants in the cleanup have said to me, "You know, I was there every day for nine months and I look at these pictures and am amazed at how much I've forgotten already."[60]

Clearly Meyerowitz's images are not simply works that document what happened in the clearing of Ground Zero. They are aesthetic objects, with an artistic visual power. As such, they have an effect that is both intimate and spectacular, what Liam Kennedy has termed "an epic quality and scale" that lends an aura and weightiness to them.[61] It is likely for these reasons that twenty-eight of the Meyerowitz images (including images of the pile and of rescue personnel at Ground Zero) were selected by the U.S. State Department in 2002 for an exhibition that traveled around the world for two years, to targeted areas in North Africa and the Middle East, such as Dar es Salaam, Istanbul, Kuwait, and Islamabad, as well as numerous sites in South America, Asia, and Europe, as a form of cultural diplomacy.

The easy deployment of Meyerowitz's images as public diplomacy, in which they were exhibited with quotes from President Bush, Secretary of State Colin Powell, and former New York mayor Rudolph Giuliani, raises questions about how their aesthetics function. As Kennedy points out, Meyerowitz's emphasis on the role of the images as an archive was also a means to downplay their acknowledged beauty, yet it was precisely their visual beauty that made them potential cultural messengers of the Bush administration's attempt to justify its response to 9/11, the war in Iraq. The rhetoric of the texts in the exhibition makes this connection clear. The statement from Assistant Secretary of State Patricia Harrison is "The exhibition will convey to foreign audiences the physical and human dimensions of the recovery effort, images that are less well known overseas than those of the destruction of September 11. Joel Meyerowitz captures the resilience and the spirit of Americans and of freedom-loving people everywhere."[62]

The exhibition contextualizes these photographs as a means to convey a generalized image of suffering and resilience, one that is intended to humanize Americans who were increasingly the source of anger from outside the United States. State Department officials attempted to make connections at many exhibition sites between the imagery of Ground Zero and local events, with uneven results. At the National Museum in Nairobi, the exhibit was placed next to an exhibit by local photographers of the bombing of the U.S. embassy in 1998, yet the size of Meyerowitz's images overpowered the local images. In Bangladesh, the exhibition was the site of protests.[63]

The Meyerowitz photographs are a compelling example of how attempts to find redemption in disaster and to find meaning in death and destruction can be easily deployed for particular political purpose. When used as cultural diplomacy, with the explicit attempt to create a better image of the United States throughout the world, these photographs are vulnerable to the charge that, as Kennedy puts it, they affirm an exceptionalism about 9/11: "that the United States is the epicenter of the culture of humanity."[64] This exceptionalist narrative was intricately a part of the discourse of sacredness that emerged at Ground Zero.

As the realization took hold soon after September 11 that there were many bodies that would never be recovered, the ground on which the towers had stood was declared by many to be "hallowed" or "sacred." The concept of sacred ground enabled many things at the site and has been a particularly powerful and limiting designation both at Ground Zero and in national politics.

What does it mean when sites of violence are declared sacred? The term *sacred* has a religious meaning, and it has been the case that many religious figures have performed ceremonies at Ground Zero. In fact, it is remarkable how quickly the site became Christianized, not only through the presence of priests who performed services for those working in the recovery operation, many of whom are Catholic, but also through the preservation of a cross constructed of two steel beams found in the rubble, called "miraculous" by rescue workers, which was left standing at the site after the recovery operation was completed.[65] Yet the concept of sacred ground at Ground Zero comes not from the blessings of priests, but from the loss of life that took place there. Traditionally in American culture, ground has been considered sacred when blood has been spilled on it. When Abraham Lincoln famously conferred on the cemetery at Gettysburg the status of sacred ground, he did so in the name not only of the men who had died there but also of those who fought and lived: "But, in a larger sense, we can not dedicate—we can not consecrate—we can not hallow—this ground. The brave men, living and dead, who struggled here, have consecrated it, far above our poor power to add or detract."

Not all battlefields are considered sacred, nor all places of violent death. Gettysburg was an exception both because at the time it was understood to be an important turning point in the Civil War and because the intense violence there resulted in great numbers of dead. The concept of sacredness at Gettysburg was from the beginning—and in Lincoln's speech this was quite explicit—related to the nation. It was the nation, "conceived in Liberty," that was under threat, and the work that Lincoln proposed for those who were present to hear him speak was that of ensuring that the "government of the people, by the people, for the people, shall not perish from the earth." When death is transformed into sacrifice and made sacred, it is almost always deployed with such political intent.

Thus, in American culture, the concept of a sacred place has been almost exclusively secular and national rather than religious. American battlefields have most often been experienced, according to Edward Linenthal, as "sacred patriotic spaces" visited by "those who seek environmental intimacy in order to experience patriotic inspiration."[66] The connections made between Gettysburg and Ground Zero, which have included numerous readings of the Gettysburg Address at anniversary ceremonies at the site, explicitly confer patriotic meaning on the site, a move that situates the 9/11 dead (regardless of the fact that many were not U.S. citizens) within the history of the sacrifice of soldiers who have died for the nation.

The status of Ground Zero as sacred ground is highly contested, precisely because of the potential limitations and broad effects such symbolic meaning has. A site of sacred ground is charged with meaning. It implies not daily life but worship, contemplation, and a suspension of ordinary activities. In a sacred space, all activities have meaning, all are transformed into rituals. Sacred ground cannot be, for instance, a neighborhood, which is defined by the ongoing everydayness of life, work, commerce, and public interaction. Indeed, one could argue that it is precisely a kind of mundane everydayness and routine that defines the familiar sense of a neighborhood. Thus, notions of Ground Zero as sacred ground are antithetical to the stakes held by residents and workers in lower Manhattan and has been a constant source of concern for them. As Setha Low writes, the relationship of the residents of lower Manhattan to their neighborhood was dramatically disrupted; not only were the physical markers of familiar space destroyed, but there was also a huge change in the composition of who actually lives there. For residents, retrieval of a sense of the quotidian is crucial, something that is explicitly in contrast to prevailing notions of sacredness. Nevertheless, even though the residents' contention that they "do not want to live in a graveyard" has provided a powerful intervention in the debate about how lower Manhattan should be transformed, their needs have been largely ignored and usurped by the demands of families and politicians, who have designated an increasingly large segment of the space as sacred and off-limits to daily life.[67]

The inscription of sacred ground at Ground Zero has been so emphatic that it seems necessary to note that places of violence and loss of life do not automatically produce feelings of sacredness. In cities where violence is a factor of everyday life, such as Jerusalem, there is often an insistence on life going forward rather than inscribing a multiplicity of spaces of loss. In the wake of certain disasters, such as the Chicago fire of 1871 and the 1906 San Francisco earthquake, Kevin Rosario argues, a desire to think in terms of optimism and looking forward predominated.[68] Kenneth Foote writes that the process of sanctification of a site involves several shifts: the site is bounded from the surrounding environment, carefully maintained for long periods of time, undergoes a change of ownership (most often from private to public), attracts continued ritual commemoration, and often attracts additional (sometimes even unrelated) memorials and monuments. Foote contrasts this process of sanctification with the process of rectification, whereby a site is "put right and used again," and the process of obliteration, in which all traces of the violence are erased.[69] The spectacular aspects of 9/11 have created a sense of specialness, yet there are many examples throughout history of cities that have been destroyed in which very small areas have been designated as sacred places for mourning while the cities have been renewed and rebuilt. In addition, as Foote notes, there are numerous sites within the United States that have been scenes of famous violence, such as mass murders, that remain unmarked and unsanctified.

There are important consequences to the amount of space at Ground Zero that has been designated as sacred in relation to the space that is being reclaimed for everyday life. The destruction of the World Trade Center was massive. The collapse destroyed an entire area of the city, not simply the seven buildings of the trade center itself, but other buildings in the immediate area. The towers fell inward, yet their debris covered a wide area, and people were killed not only in the towers, but in the surrounding few blocks.[70]

Within this wider area, certain spaces are now considered to be more symbolic than others. Primary among these are the footprints of the two towers. Early on in the design process, in July 2002, Governor Pataki promised the families of the dead that he would not allow buildings to be built on the footprints of the towers.[71] From the beginning the many different design proposals for the site treated those footprints, which are each two hundred feet on each side and about one acre in size, as sanctified locations. The master plan for the site by the architect Daniel Libeskind and the memorial design, *Reflecting Absence*, by Michael Arad fully inscribe this hierarchy of space, with the footprints designated solemn and unique spaces, voids in a public plaza.

The importance placed on the two footprints of the towers is deeply ironic when one considers how the World Trade Center complex was experienced when it stood. Built by the Port Authority of New York and New Jersey in 1970 by the architect Minoru Yamasaki, the twin towers had long been considered not only examples of banal modernism, but ineffective examples of urban design, what the architecture critic Paul Goldberger calls an "antiurban" design.[72] The complex was notable for all the myriad ways that it did not integrate into the surrounding neighborhood. The primary experiences that individuals had of the complex were twofold: the experience of being up in the towers themselves, looking down upon the city, and that of being in the underground complex of shops and public transportation on which the two towers sat. Michel de Certeau once referred to the view from the World Trade Center as a god's-eye view of the city, one that fulfilled "a lust to be a viewpoint and nothing more."[73] He contrasted this view to the many meaningful acts that take place at street level, the "speech acts" of pedestrians that make meaning of the city's landscape. Within the trade center complex, there was no level of the street, or speech act, that mattered. The plaza of the twin towers was notorious as a badly designed area, neither conducive to public gathering nor even, for most people, the primary entry point to the towers. Most people entered the towers from the underground complex that was connected to the subways and PATH (Port Authority Trans-Hudson) trains to New Jersey; thus, in a sense, the underground mall was the street of the complex. It is fairly safe to say that the foundations, or footprints, of the buildings were truly unremarkable while the towers stood. Indeed, in terms of their actual structure, the towers never had actual footprints on the ground. They reached upward to the sky from the underground mall into which they were integrated, and while there are remnants of the columns of the tower's structures, they were never integral to the experience of the site underground. To look at Ground Zero is to see the footprint of that underground complex.

Given that the concept of the footprint is unlikely to have emerged from people's personal experience with the World Trade Center complex prior to its destruction, one must ask how it has acquired such important symbolic meaning. The idea of a building's footprint evokes a sense that a structure is anchored in the ground. It is also anthropomorphic, as it implies that the building left a trace, like a human footprint, on the ground. This concept was used in the design of the Oklahoma City National Memorial to designate the part of the memorial that pays tribute to the individuals who died there. The bronze chairs of the memorial stand in rows within the area where the federal building once stood, and the foundation of the destroyed building was left exposed at the edges of this part of the site. Hence, the Oklahoma City memorial deliberately renders the land where the building stood and where people died a more meaningful place to mourn the dead than the surrounding area. This is a relatively small area of the memorial. In New York, it constitutes a large area in the middle of a densely packed city.

The emphasis on the footprints of the two towers demonstrates a desire to situate the towers' absence within a recognizable tradition of memorial sites. The idea that a destroyed structure leaves a footprint evokes the site-specific concept of ruins in modernity. In the case of Ground Zero, one could surmise that the desire to reimagine the towers as having left a footprint is a desire to imagine that the towers *left an imprint* on the ground. Their erasure from the skyline was so shocking and complete that there have been constant attempts to reassert them into the empty sky. The desire for the buildings to have had a footprint could thus be seen as a kind of struggle with their absence.

Ironically, the rebuilding of the footprints in the designs for lower Manhattan means that they will have to be re-created from remnants of columns that remain at the site.[74] This creates tremendous conflicts with the challenge of rebuilding infrastructure in an urban environment in which the city is often as complex underground as above. Like the families and survivors of the Oklahoma City bombing, the families of 9/11, who have cohered into several different groups, including the Coalition of 9/11 Families, have been awarded a certain moral authority in the debates about how the area will be rebuilt, in deference to the fact that many of them will never recover the bodies of their family members who died there. This moral authority has affected, more than anything else, the sanctification of the footprints, and the families organized several protests at the site to demand that infrastructure not be built under the footprints.[75] As I discuss further in chapter 5, the design of the memorial creates voids in the site of the footprints, yet this raises the uncomfortable prospect that the space underneath the memorial will hold ordinary infrastructure, such as subway lines and parking for the buses that are expected to be delivering tourists to see the memorial. This prompted some family members to declare (and the governor to promise) that the footprints are sacred "from bedrock to infinity," and to demand that there be no commercial development housed beneath them.[76] This designation of the area under the footprints as sacred space necessarily raises a set of uncomfortable questions about the symbolic materials of the site. Where will the dirt for this symbolic place come from? The dust and debris that filled it are now gone. Clearly, the dirt will not come from the Fresh Kills landfill. (Actually, soil excavated from the site to make way for the construction of the World Trade Center was used as landfill to create nearby

Battery Park City.) In other words, the reconstruction necessary to re-create the footprints would seem to render their status as a sacred space deeply ironic. In the debate over the International Freedom Center in 2005, the sacred space of Ground Zero seemed to be enlarged, to include not only the footprints but a full "quadrant" of six and a half acres bounded by Fulton, Greenwich, Liberty, and West streets. In addition, there have been several hair-splitting debates about whether or not their reconstruction will be able to fit exactly into the space where the tower structures stood, raising the anxiety that the remembrance of the event will be distorted if the replication of the footprints is not exactly the same as the space where the towers stood. Several members of the jury and some family members were outraged to find out that the dimensions of the memorial may not exactly replicate the footprints; one told the *New York Times*, "To do any less, I think, would not be telling the story. People who come years from now will have no idea what the original dimensions were."[77] Plans for a transportation center at Ground Zero now include a plan to put the tower column bases under glass so that they can be seen by the public, awarding them a kind of relic status.[78]

It is also the case that the mediatization of Ground Zero has facilitated this fetishizing of the footprints. Numerous design renderings of the site have overlaid images of the footprints onto aerial images of the hole at Ground Zero, in which no footprints are actually visible, in an attempt to imagine them there. The effect of such graphics is to embody the footprints in a way that counters the fact that they do not exist. The footprints have been constantly reimagined via computer images onto the remaining empty space in such a way that they appear to be imprinted on the ground.

Thus, though the desire to see the footprints as sacred is part of a modern intent to designate concrete meanings to a part of the site of Ground Zero, they will be inevitably re-created as they never were. The desire to render them sacred, and to imagine them as the place where those who died still remain, is not unlike the desire to preserve the dust. Each provides a frame-work for thinking about the destruction of the towers in tangible, com-forting forms. Through this reinscription and reconstruction of space, the arbitrary aspects of who lived, died, and suffered that day are placed within a framework of symbolic space as ordered meaning. This concept of sacred-ness has been so powerful at Ground Zero, in ways that have garnered po-litical heft and made the footprints symbolically inviolable, that within one year it became impossible for alternative visions of the site to be considered. As time passes, this choice may ultimately seem like the most crucial and most short-sighted decision made about how to rebuild Ground Zero. As Philip Nobel writes, the choice evokes the ghostly presence of the twin towers' original architect Minoru Yamasaki: "The designation of the footprints as holy ground has had a devastating effect on the planning possibilities at Ground Zero, but the two enormous squares also made a very awkward site for the memorial they were fated to contain. Their sanctification was Yamasaki's revenge. . . . His critics were forced to genuflect to his meaningless geometry."[79] In this process, the footprints of the buildings are asked to give the vanished dead a home, a place where they are imagined to be, where one can imagine visiting them, to make them present in the absence of their remains. And it is, above all, the absence of remains that haunts this site.

RUBBLE, RELICS, AND REMAINS

The space of Ground Zero emerged in the years after 9/11 as a paradoxical site, one that was seen as profoundly empty yet filled with massive amounts of material, a site that refused, ultimately, to yield what was wanted from it, in particular the remains of the dead. As the site was scoured clean in the nine months of its "unbuilding" and its remnants were removed to Fresh Kills, there was a plethora of objects that were retained from the site and given the status of relics. The problem of preservation was also one of scale. The jagged shards that hovered over the ruins of Ground Zero, which were photographed by Meyerowitz, looked like fragments of a gothic cathedral— a strange reminder of the gothic references of the "skin" of the towers' construction. A few weeks after 9/11, Metropolitan Museum Director Philippe de Montebello suggested that the jagged fragment should be kept for a memorial.[80] For de Montebello, this fragment was not only an icon of survival, but "already, in its own way, a masterpiece"—not only, one suspects, because it has created the haunting image of a modern ruin, but because it looked like a modern work of art. These shards were enormous, up to eight stories high, and much larger than any memorial design could accommodate. Nevertheless, for several years, many advocated for their return to the site and were angered that they were not featured in the proposals for the memorial design.[81] It is worth noting that throughout history ruins have often been incorporated into memorial sites to evoke the destructive power of hatred. Some of the most effective memorials of World War II, for instance, use the shell of a building, a ruin arrested in its deterioration, to convey the shock of violence and act as a cautionary in the present. The Atomic Dome at the Hiroshima Peace Memorial Park, Coventry Cathedral in England, and the Kaiser Wilhelm Memorial Church in Berlin, among others, incorporate ruined structures to evoke a sense of the destructive forces that changed the meaning of those places.

The steel beams of the twin towers became a source of fascination in the aftermath of 9/11. Several of the beams were featured in the news media as sources of potential information for the investigation into how the towers fell. Others were retained by the Port Authority as potential objects for display, as historical artifacts. Several of them have circulated in exhibitions about 9/11, and one is prominently displayed in the controversial National Museum of American History exhibition, *The Price of Freedom: Americans at War*, which uses it to anchor an exhibition affirming U.S. wars of expansion as operating in the name of freedom.[82]

The majority of the steel beams that were part of the rubble were shipped off to faraway places where they would be melted down and reused. Langewiesche's book ends with a scene in which the steel beams from the towers are loaded into a beat-up foreign tanker that will take them to China and India, where they will be melted as scrap:

> The ship was rusty and badly maintained. Its deck machinery looked like it had been broken for years. . . . The steel tumbled down with a roar, and sent shudders through the ship . . . lying haphazardly where it had fallen, already in foreign hands, and destined for furnaces on the far side of the globe. It was a strangely appropriate fate for these buildings. Unmade or remade, whether as appliances or cars or simple rebar, they would eventually find their way into every corner of the world.[83]

Langewiesche's unsentimental portrayal of the building's material as anonymous scrap, though global in its effect, was a deliberate attempt to show the antisymbolic materiality of the building's refuse. Yet the potential symbolism of the tower's beams was not lost in the political attempts to exploit 9/11 for the war in Iraq. A single beam from the South Tower was shipped with much fanfare to Louisiana, where it was melted down to form the bow of the USS *New York*, a massive troop transport ship. In his public remarks, Governor Pataki made clear the political agenda in doing so: "We're very proud that the twisted steel from the WTC towers will soon be used to forge an even stronger defense. The USS *New York* will soon be defending freedom and combating terrorism around the globe."[84]

While it was a project of "unbuilding," the clearing of the site of Ground Zero was also one of preservation. Huge numbers of 9/11 objects now exist in official collections in places like the New-York Historical Society and in many personal collections.[85] The Port Authority retained approximately seven hundred artifacts from the site, which are housed in a hangar at JFK Airport.[86] Many of these remnants, which include crushed police cars, fire trucks, and part of the television antenna from the top of the South Tower, are slated to be part of a permanent exhibit in a memorial center at the site, like the objects on display at the Oklahoma City National Memorial. A number of traveling exhibitions of the objects of 9/11 have taken place in the years since (in addition to a large number of exhibitions in general about 9/11): the National Museum of American History had a touring exhibition, *September 11: Bearing Witness to History*, and the New York State Museum organized a traveling exhibition, *Recovery: The World Trade Center Recovery Operation at Fresh Kills*, which includes over fifty objects.

In addition, quite paradoxically, the city handed out a large number of artifacts from Ground Zero to municipalities and organizations around the country for some of the many small memorials to 9/11 that have sprung up in unlikely places. The most popular item for these memorials was the steel from the trade center, used for memorials in Louisiana, Texas, Pennsylvania, Arizona, Florida, and elsewhere. Thus, though most of the steel was sold for scrap, some of it was recoded as sacred material. Said one architect who worked on the Texas 9/11 memorial, "They are so mangled . . . it's electrifying to touch them. It brings home the horror of the day."[87] The shifting status from refuse to sacred object is steeped in irony. The steel beams, which seem easily recoded into objects that embody the disaster and which are barely acknowledged in the many proposals for the memorial at Ground Zero, were handed out essentially for memorial consumption to local governments throughout the country. The use of a steel beam for a memorial at the site of the former World Trade Center could potentially carry the same kind of power that sites like Coventry do, as a preservation of ruins that speak to a particular moment of loss. Yet, transported elsewhere and transformed into memorials, the beams seem precariously close to kitsch status.

Nevertheless, it is clear that objects acquire a particularly charged set of meanings in the aftermath of disasters such as this. What is the experience of looking at a mangled object that has survived the collapse of a building? Like the photographs of the missing, these objects seem to evoke a fragile connection to a prior time, a time before, a time innocent of what was to come. An artifact is also an emblem of fragility and vulnerability: a mangled column, a crumpled police car, or a crushed file cabinet not only evokes the force with which the buildings fell but also stands in for the human bodies that did not withstand the fall. Thus, the objects are imbued with the tragic meaning of bodies lost. They are objects of melancholia and displacement that seem to evoke the immensity of the event within their crushed forms.

In this context, in which symbolism is somewhat arbitrarily awarded, the specter of the Fresh Kills landfill disrupts any simple categorization. Like the dust, which was selectively sanctified, the refuse and rubble of the twin towers has been subjected to painful and fraught compartmentalization. After the refuse was hauled to Fresh Kills from lower Manhattan, it was screened, scoured, and raked in order for workers to search for more human remains and to sort out any objects of value or worth keeping. It was thus inevitable that Fresh Kills, where the murky status of refuse, dust, debris, and human remains is troubled, would emerge as the countersite to Ground Zero. A huge number of objects were retrieved there and catalogued for potential retrieval by those who once owned them. Eight thousand photographs that were found in the rubble were scanned and placed on a website where families and survivors could view them.[88] In February 2004, a minor scandal erupted when it was claimed that FBI agents, who had run the recovery operation at Fresh Kills, had taken objects from the site, including a Tiffany globe that ended up on a secretary's desk in Minneapolis.[89] Later it was revealed that numerous objects from Ground Zero and the Pentagon had made their way into the personal collections not only of FBI agents, but also former FBI director Robert S. Mueller and former Defense Secretary Donald Rumsfeld, who has a shard of metal from the jetliner that hit the Pentagon.[90] The source of much consternation, these personal collections were not very different from those assembled by lesser-known citizens who had access to these charged sites, including rescue workers at the pile and others who gathered objects from lower Manhattan before it was cordoned off. Each revealed a desire to have a connection to an event through the objects that embody it and that have a temporal trace of that moment.

The liminal status of Fresh Kills as both a garbage dump and the site where valuable artifacts and human remains were recovered has created anxiety about its relationship to the sanctified Ground Zero.[91] The New York Department of City Planning has initiated plans to turn the twenty-two hundred acres of Fresh Kills into a public park and memorial, which would include two large earthworks the length and width of the twin towers and a memorial at the mound on the landfill that is known as 9/11.[92]

This prompted some families to organize a group, WTC Families for Proper Burial, in support of removing the dust from the mound and burying it at Ground Zero. This group sued in federal court in August 2005 to order the city to move the dust back to lower Manhattan.[93]

The absence of remains defines these discussions. The cataclysmic destruction of the towers produced a context in which the desire for remains has reached extraordinary heights. This takes place in a larger context in which violent events of history have intersected with the emergence of new forms of forensic science. Federal funding of $80 million for the trade center investigation was used in a massive effort to identify the almost twenty thousand remains that were found at Ground Zero and Fresh Kills.[94] When the operation was suspended in April 2005, only 1,592 of those who died had been identified, and in the final two years of labor, only 111 more were identified. The DNA identification process was closely followed in the media, which wrote stories of the anonymous scientists methodically pursuing their grim labor in refrigerated trailers and out of the limelight. The belief that all remains could be identified was powerful, shored up by a belief that science could provide the key to positive confirmation of the dead.

Ground Zero continues to be haunted by the fact that many who died there have not been recovered or identified. In spring 2006, as crews began to dismantle the contaminated former Deutsches Bank building, which stands next to Ground Zero, they found additional very small remains, part of a skull, and a set of plastic airplane wings.[95] This prompted calls for the Defense Department to send in its special Joint POW/MIA Accountability Command, which specializes in identifying remains of missing soldiers.[96] Many of these bone fragments were tiny, the "size of a pinkie nail," yet some relatives were quoted in the media as hoping that these would identify their loved ones. "The discovery is a 'double-edged sword,'" Monica Gabrielle was quoted as saying, "where you think, 'How egregious,' and 'Perhaps something of Rich will be found.' Neither is a comforting thought, not five years later."[97] In fall 2006, after small fragments were found in an abandoned manhole nearby, the city initiated a long-term search of a broader area.[98] Each time, these revelations have produced renewed calls by family groups to bring in specialist teams to search more thoroughly. It is precisely the discourse of science that allows such tiny fragments to stand in for the body and, in a certain sense, to verify that such a person existed, and was there. Constance Penley has argued that in contexts of loss, empirical knowledge and material remains help to facilitate mourning:

This desire to know, no matter how shot through with fantasmatic thinking—disavowal, guilt, projection, overidentification, and all the rest—is a desire whose reality and efficacy must be acknowledged. The families of MIAs, of accident and murder victims, even the relatives of those killed by Jeffrey Dalmer want to know, demand to know, in exact and excruciating detail, how their loved ones died. Over and over, they say that they cannot go on, cannot resume their own lives until they know. Tell us anyway, they say, no matter how horrible; knowing is infinitely better than not knowing. Knowing, then, allows mourning to proceed.[99]

The search for remains, the fervent belief that scientific method can identify those remains, and the demand that the search continue for the tiniest traces of those lost—in Penley's formulation, one can see these demands as a search for a narrative, not only for proof that someone died at the World Trade Center, but the belief that those traces will tell the story of how someone died.

The issue of this lack of remains is so charged at the site that it seems impossible to consider it within the broader context of human violence in the modern era, when the history of human warfare and, more recently, of terrorism has produced a huge number of contexts in which remains have not been recovered. This discourse of science is so powerful in relation to 9/11 that the unidentified remains have been sealed and will be housed at the World Trade Center memorial, in the hopes that future scientific developments will allow them to be identified at some point.[100] By comparison, when this issue arose at the Oklahoma City memorial, the designers successfully resisted the placement of remains at the memorial itself precisely because they understood how the presence of remains would change the public space of the memorial.

This belief in the power of forensics for identification, for the surety of identity, recalls the posters of the missing, which held out the hope that those small details, a scar or birthmark, would allow someone to be found, his or her uniqueness reaffirmed. There is a poignancy in the belief that science can affirm not only the presence but the absence of someone. Twentieth-century history demonstrated the way the missing have haunted conflicts and been deployed for political ends. The MIAs of the Vietnam War, for instance, were the source of numerous fantasies about the existence of living POWs in the years after the fall of Saigon and fostered the emergence of an entire culture devoted to stories about their existence and, later, the hunt for their remains. The absence of their remains was repeatedly deployed in political contexts until the late 1990s to prevent the U.S. government from resuming international relations with Vietnam. Similarly, while the absence of many remains at Ground Zero is a haunting reminder of the degree of destruction that took place there, it is also a means by which the space will be constantly defined as a site that has refused to yield the dead, where those remains still need to be found.

TOURIST DESTINATION

The transformation of the space of Ground Zero from a site of emergency to one of recovery to one of tourism took place within a relatively short period. Indeed, it could be argued that because of the vast numbers of images of the World Trade Center collapse, the site was the focus of consumption from its inception. Initially, as I have noted, lower Manhattan was a restricted area, blocked off from view, in which looking was discouraged. Yet even one week later, people, many of them in the role of tourists, headed downtown to try to get a look.[101] By December, the police patrolling the boundaries of the area had become more accommodating to the crowds because, as one told me, "people have the right to look." As early as November, the site of Ground Zero was being called "the city's hottest attraction," even though officials in the tourist industry, though desperate to revive tourism in the city, were reluctant to acknowledge the trend.[102] On December 30, a viewing ramp, commissioned by the city and designed by four well-known architects (David Rockwell, the team of Elizabeth Diller and Ricardo Scofidio, and Kevin Kennon), was opened by St. Paul's Chapel and tickets were distributed to accommodate the large crowds who came to see the view.[103] By the spring, the *New York Times* and other publications were running travel features on where to eat downtown after visiting Ground Zero, effectively constructing the site as a tourist destination. Indeed, in March 2002, the *Los Angeles Times* characterized the act of dining out in lower Manhattan in symbolic terms: "Going out to dine in the shadow of ground zero would be unthinkable if it weren't an act of defiance in the face of terrorism and a vote of support for the beleaguered neighborhood."[104] The transformation from a site of emergency to a site of tourism and commerce was ironically commented on in a *Doonesbury* strip (fig. 68). In late fall, American Express ran an ad campaign about downtown Manhattan businesses, showing people opening their stores and restaurants, with the words, "Their electricity has come back. Their phone service has come back. Now it's your turn." When

FIGURE 68. *Doonesbury* cartoon © 2001 G. B. Trudeau. Reprinted with permission of Universal Press Syndicate. All rights reserved.

it reopened in spring 2003, the Millenium Hilton Hotel, right across from the site, became a draw for tourists.[105]

It is important to note that the transformation of Ground Zero from a place of emergency to a place of tourism is not in conflict with the desire to see it as sacred ground. Like those diners who felt they were supporting the neighborhood, many of the tourists at Ground Zero, particularly in the first months, were acting both as tourists and as mourners. Tourist locations, like sacred sites, are places people make pilgrimages to. Standing on the viewing platform that first year, most people responded in ways that evoked both mourning and tourism: they stood looking in shock, they cried, and they took photographs of what they saw. Ironically, however, Ground Zero is a uniquely unphotogenic space. Tourists patrol its perimeter with cameras in hand, yet it is rendered in photographs as a kind of banal space of emptiness—a void, but in some senses a meaningless one. This may be one reason why photographs and postcards of the World Trade Center, rather than images of Ground Zero, are sold there.

The mixture of tourism and mourning was a part of the response to 9/11 from the start. Within a week, as World Trade Center postcards were rapidly sold, it was reported that New Yorkers themselves were buying souvenirs of the city and purchasing large amounts of patriotic merchandise.[106] There was also an immediate commerce of World Trade Center artifacts and trinkets on eBay, which then came under criticism and created a charity auction to compensate.[107] The deep hole at Ground Zero is surrounded by an open fence that allows viewers to look throughout the site along its perimeter. In response to the large numbers of people visiting the site, the Port Authority set up a photographic display about the history of the area that also includes a timeline of the day of September 11 and over the years has presented vari-

FIGURE 69. Tourists at Ground Zero, August 2006.

ous exhibitions of photographs along the periphery. This frames Ground
Zero as a pedagogical exhibition and thus allows it to be seen as an exhibit
itself, rather than as a construction site; it also compensates for the fact that
the site has little to show that can conjure up its intense meaning. Tens of
thousands of people go to observe Ground Zero every day. People can now
ride through Ground Zero on the PATH trains, which resumed operation in
November 2003.[108] This commuter train to New Jersey, which existed long
before the building of the World Trade Center and always operated at the
lowest level of the site, below even the subway, was thus transformed into a
strange combination of both determined business-as-usual commuter transport and a kind of monorail tour through Ground Zero.

The emergence of Ground Zero as a tourist site also redefines lower
Manhattan through paradigms of tourism. Lower Manhattan is not new to
tourism, most obviously because the twin towers were themselves a tourist
destination, though almost exclusively for tourists taking the elevators to
the observation deck on the North Tower. The post-9/11 tourism of Ground
Zero is markedly at street level and involves a much less formalized commercialism. It is now a place where trinkets, souvenirs, and commodities
are sold. The proliferation of commodities includes FDNY hats and T-shirts,

FIGURE 70. Souvenirs for sale at Ground Zero, 2003.

NYPD dolls, and glass replicas of the twin towers, the vast majority "made in China."

The tourism at Ground Zero integrates into the informal street economy of New York City. New York City has a complex system of licenses in operation, which enable a broad, legal economy of street vending. Because these licenses are limited (though, in a policy that acts as a strange acknowledgment of the difficult lives led by U.S. veterans, veterans are exempt from acquiring licenses), there is also a vast network of illegal street vendors, most of whom are part of broad international and immigrant networks. It is one of the ironies of postindustrial and global economies that the majority of patriotic American merchandise, such as small flags and "I Love New York" stickers, are produced outside the United States, in China and Korea.

This economic network responded rapidly to the events of 9/11, apparently fully aware that certain kinds of objects, such as models of the towers, had instantly become desirable. Souvenir distributors in New York produced new designs about 9/11 as early as September 12 that were then faxed to their manufacturers in Korea and China, who churned out new merchandise in four days. Once air traffic resumed, the souvenirs were shipped in, and pins, decals, and buttons with the flag, the twin towers, and the Statue of Liberty began appearing on street corners within a week.[109]

The intermixing of patriotic merchandise with the 9/11 merchandise sold at Ground Zero has the effect of constantly reinscribing the space as one of national meaning. While it is now a commonplace to see the site in national terms because the attacks aimed to injure the United States, the fact remains that several hundred people who were killed there were not American citizens. Nevertheless, the presence of patriotic merchandise at Ground Zero helps to mediate potential criticism of the level of kitsch in many of these souvenirs and the questionable practice of selling merchandise at a site of mourning. In their ethnography of the vendors and consumers at Ground Zero during 2002, Molly Hurley and James Trimarco found a range of responses from consumers about the appropriateness of selling memorabilia at the site, dominated by a concern that, whatever the motives of consumers to acquire a memento, no one should make a profit from violence.[110] Hurley and Trimarco note that the police patrol the area with a certain code about what kinds of objects should be sold and who should sell them. Street vendors are much more likely to be subject to the wrath of police officers than of consumers, even though local stores that sell similar merchandise have not been targeted.[111] The City of New York has also sent out a number of cease and desist letters to entities, including eBay, for their "blatant attempts to profit from mass murder."[112] Here, as in Oklahoma City, the question of what constitutes a "proper" object of remembrance and a memorial commodity is particularly fraught, and one that will certainly factor into the construction of a memorial museum (potentially with a gift shop) at Ground Zero. While these souvenirs circulate through many informal economic networks, they are also part of a much broader consumer economy related to 9/11, an economy that includes a huge number of books, from journalistic accounts to academic analyses, and a plethora of objects, both high and low end, that imagine and reimagine the two towers. It also includes high-end objects like Christopher Radko's expensive designer 9/11 Christmas tree ornament, which was marketed in the first years after 9/11 and which was sold as a memory ornament.[113]

Inevitably, these souvenirs, like the World Trade Center snow globe I discuss at the beginning of this book, raise questions of the role of kitsch and reenactment in the cultural memory of traumatic events. It is the case that 9/11 has generated an extraordinary number of kitsch objects. As the *Salon* writer Heather Havrilesky wrote on the first-year anniversary, "Sifting through the consumer fallout from 9/11 can incite the kind of cultural vertigo heretofore only achieved by spending several hours in a Graceland giftshop."[114] As I have noted, kitsch operates not only to produce a set of

FIGURE 71. 9/11 pin commemorating 343 firefighters, 23 police officers, and 37 Port Authority police officers.

FIGURE 72. 9/11 commemorative coins.

prescribed and contained emotions, but also to provide simplistic notions of comfort that facilitate political acquiescence. Daniel Harris writes in an essay on "The Kitschification of Sept. 11":

> Does an event as catastrophic as this one require the rhetoric of kitsch to make it less horrendous? Do we need the overkill of ribbons and commemorative quilts, haloed seraphim perched on top of the burning towers and teddy bears in firefighter helmets waving flags, in order to forget the final minutes of bond traders, restaurant workers and secretaries screaming in elevators filling with smoke, standing in the frames of broken windows on the 90th floor waiting for help and staggering down the stairwells covered in third degree burns? . . . Through kitsch we avert our eyes from tragedy.[115]

Harris points to the many ways kitsch can smooth over tragedy and in which kitsch objects constitute a kind of erasure of the effects of violence. The souvenirs at Ground Zero, like many of the objects sold at the gift shop of the Oklahoma City National Memorial, can engage with history only in very limited ways. They are objects that focus on loss and memory through narratives of redemption that inevitably collapse history into simple narratives. The focus of such objects is invariably not the *why* of such events or the complexities of history so much as it is about producing feelings of comfort. Just as the vast majority of the objects sold at Oklahoma City are about affirming the redemptive aspects of the city's response to the bombing and emphasizing how the community responded to it, many of the objects that circulate at Ground Zero offer a kitsch rendition of redemption, with images of angel figures surrounding the twin towers and an affirmation of rescue workers. This is evident in my snow globe, in which the police car and fire truck stand next to the two magically still-standing towers; the power of the scene imagined in the globe is the affirmation and comfort offered by the emergency vehicles signifying a protective response, one that in the fantastic world of the snow globe has kept the towers standing. This emphasis on redemption is a key element in the deployment of such events for political gain.

The purchasing of souvenirs at Ground Zero is in many ways the shadow activity to the shrines that sprang up in New York in the days after 9/11. The shrines indicated a need that people felt to leave objects in a ritualistic fashion. The souvenir economy provides a different relationship to objects at Ground Zero. Instead of leaving an object, visitors take an object away. As an object purchased at the site, a souvenir offers a trace of that place, a veneer of authenticity. Even if it is purchased at the airport, a keychain with the Eiffel Tower offers up a connection to Paris. The souvenirs sold at Ground Zero, and to an only slightly lesser extent around Manhattan, are thus a means of marking place, of creating connections to this highly over-determined and intensely symbolic site.

The fervent tourism at Ground Zero, which has not appeared to lessen as time has passed, is a primary example of what I am calling the tourism of history. By necessity as a site of mourning, Ground Zero is stripped of its larger political meaning and situation within global politics. As a tourist destination, it is a unique site, an exceptional one, in which the terrorist at-tacks that created it can only be defined as having come from out of the blue. As I discuss in chapter 5, any attempt to situate 9/11 within broader histori-cal contexts at the site of Ground Zero, which the canceled International Freedom Center attempted to do, would inevitably clash with the inscrip-tion of the site as one of unique and immense loss. The souvenir culture at Ground Zero functions as a means to provide connection to the site, to testify to a visitor's pilgrimage there, and to provide comfort—the comfort of kitsch, and the comfort that commerce continues. The paradoxes of this comfort are many: while the souvenir culture of Ground Zero helps to pro-duce a narrative of innocence, in which the United States and New York were sites of unsuspecting and unprovoked attack, the concept of heroism that attempts to inscribe firefighters with quasi-military status must resist such qualities of innocence.

These souvenirs also participate in a kind of reenactment, a stasis in which the moment of the towers' fall is imagined to not yet have taken place. In the constant reinscription of the twin towers, these objects project a fantastic time, in which the towers still stand yet are charged with the meaning of their loss, their presence reenacted. In the next chapter, I examine the archi-tectural design proposals for rebuilding lower Manhattan and constructing a memorial at Ground Zero, and the forms of reenactment and kitsch that have emerged in these designs that reimagine Ground Zero.

5

ARCHITECTURES OF GRIEF AND THE
AESTHETICS OF ABSENCE

In September 2002, the *New York Times* ran series of design proposals for how to rebuild lower Manhattan, at that point an empty pit after the debris of the two collapsed towers of the World Trade Center had been cleared. Among them was a proposal for an office building complex by Peter Eisenman, a well-known New York architect and the designer of the Holocaust memorial in Berlin, which opened in 2005. In his proposal, Eisenman designed a set of buildings which he saw as "building, memorial, and landscape" at once, high-rise office structures clustered around the footprints of the World Trade Center.[1] While they have straight forms on the interior, the buildings are clad with crumpled façades designed to look as if they are in a state of perpetual collapse. From an overview perspective the buildings appear to be an exploded structure; from the street, their façades seem to be collapsing downward in rapid motion (fig. 73).

Eisenman's design was quite clearly a reenactment of the towers falling, one of the most traumatic moments of 9/11. The *New York Times* described it this way: "The buildings would echo the devastation wrought on 9/11 and offer a striking memorial to the fallen towers; at the same time they would provide three million square feet of new office

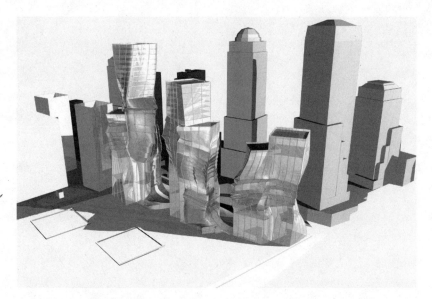

FIGURE 73. *New York Times Magazine* WTC proposal, New York, N.Y., 2002, by Peter Eisenman. Rendered aerial view from northeast. Courtesy of Eisenman Architects.

space."[2] The apparent lack of irony in the presentation of the building was notable. While the *New York Times* downplayed his reenactment strategy, Eisenman himself characterized the building as "a certain beauty coming a moment before a disaster."[3] As a form of compulsive reenactment, the design is quite compelling: one can see the buildings falling again and again within its forms, a constant reminder of the shock of that moment. The design is a kind of mournful remembrance of the destruction of the towers. Yet as a proposal for rebuilding lower Manhattan, it bordered on the absurd. Could one imagine that such a complex could ever be built, and that businesses would rent space within it? Could one imagine a world in which such a design would seem appropriate as a means of rebuilding a devastated urban area? This design is so strangely out of proportion to the pain that surrounded Ground Zero one year later that it can only be read as an indicator of grief, unprocessed, inchoate, in a continual state of reenactment.

The *New York Times* proposals came from a group of architects, calling themselves the Downtown Study Group, who had begun meeting to discuss architectural responses to the official planning process.[4] Solicited by the *Times* architecture critic Herbert Muschamp for the newspaper, the designs aimed to use innovative architectural design to rethink the space of lower

FIGURE 74. *New York* magazine WTC proposal, New York, N.Y., 2002, by Peter Eisenman. Rendered aerial view from southeast. Courtesy of Eisenman Architects.

Manhattan and now largely seen to be "wounded." Eisenman had another similar design featured in *New York* magazine (fig. 74), which also presented a group of proposals the following week.[5] In further display of the collapsing buildings design along with the many other hundreds of proposals for rebuilding Ground Zero, the question of its potential insensitivity was never raised, as if architecture and the grief at Ground Zero inhabited separate universes. We can see, however, that in both realms a shared sense of loss fixed on the absences of the twin towers.

In this chapter I examine the architectural and design debates that have taken place in New York in the years since 9/11 about how to rebuild lower Manhattan and to create a 9/11 memorial, and how they demonstrate both the compulsive repetition of grief and the reinscription of Ground Zero within a tourism of history. This is a context of volatile conflict, high emotional stakes, and competing and incommensurate discourses, which the dissonance of Eisenman's design exemplifies. The destruction of the two towers prompted not only an outpouring of grief and an almost immediate discussion of memorialization; it also put into motion a very public and fraught debate about the role of architecture and design in the rebuilding of the city and the construction of a memorial. Ground Zero has factored in deep and complex ways in the architectural community's imagination; the debate over how to rebuild lower Manhattan has produced both a revitalization of the public discussion of architecture and, ultimately, a situation in which the aims of architecture and design have been defeated by the politics of economics and emotion.[6] Throughout this public debate, the shadow of the twin towers has loomed over efforts to reconceptualize the landscape. Ground Zero is not only the site of architectural imaginings; it is a place in which the story of 9/11 appears to be in a state of constant replay, whether in architectural design or in the constant reinscription of the space as a site that can be rebuilt only in reference to 9/11.

MISSING TWINS

After the destruction of the World Trade Center, the extraordinary outpouring of grief for the twin towers worked to personify them in emotional ways that would have been unimaginable while they stood. This nostalgia often took the form of imagining the two towers as "two brothers" embracing or representing the abstract forms of the towers in figurative terms. This was a common theme in the children's drawings after 9/11 and in many of the memorizations of them in shrines. Thus, amid the posters for the missing, there also circulated a number of mournful posters that read, "Missing: My Two Lovely Twins, Age 28."[7] Much of this personification and nostalgia was directly tied to the fact that the towers were two almost identical buildings. Of course, many other buildings were destroyed on 9/11, including the other five, shorter buildings of the World Trade Center complex, but it was the twinning of the two towers (in addition to their size) that seemed to prompt whatever affection they received while they still stood. As Paul Goldberger notes, the towers created a kind of visual interaction, a back and forth, prompting viewers to look from one to the next and back: "One would have been deadly dull, and three would have been a cluster. Two identical towers, set 130 feet apart, corner to corner, could play off against each other, their masses not as inert as they looked, since each shape was engaged with the other."[8] This twinning effect was also part of what made the terrorist attacks on New York so devastating: not one plane but two, not one building collapsing but two, with the second moment of impact acting as an indicator of the uniqueness of the event. (This twin effect also enables the erasure in 9/11 history of the planes that struck in Pennsylvania and at the Pentagon.) Two years after 9/11, the *New Yorker* would publish a cover in

FIGURE 75. Child's drawing of twin towers, 2001. © de.MO 2001.

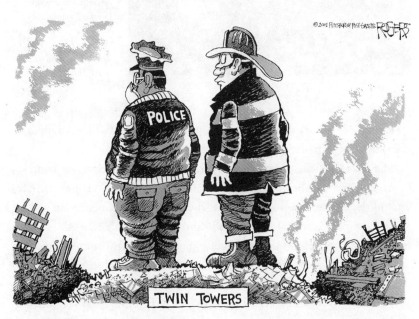

FIGURE 76. Twin Towers, 2001. Cartoon by Rob Rogers. © The *Pittsburgh Post-Gazette*/Distributed by United Feature Syndicate, Inc.

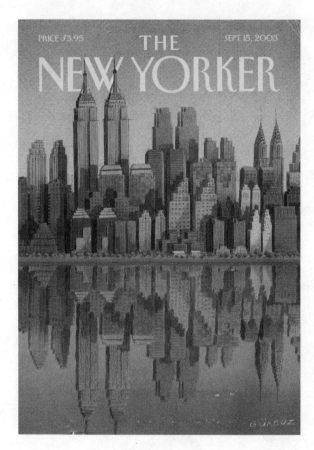

FIGURE 77.
September 15, 2003,
New Yorker cover. Il-
lustration by Gürbüz
Dogan Eksioglu.
Reprinted by permis-
sion of *The New Yorker*,
Condé Nast Publica-
tions, Inc.

which the New York skyline was imagined as multiple twinned buildings, each standing in pairs, in wistful tribute.

The erasure of the towers thus posed a dilemma in the various contexts in which they had been inscribed. While people placed images of them around the city, attempting to reinsert them into the skyline, and images of them continue to circulate at Ground Zero and around New York, the film industry immediately scrambled to erase them from forthcoming films. Several fall 2001 releases, such as *Zoolander* and *Serendipity*, and several television shows that had featured them in their credit sequences, such as *Friends*, digitally eliminated the towers from those scenes. When the late PBS commentator Louis Rukeyser removed them from his financial newsletter in October 2001, he was taken to task by readers: "Would you remove the photograph from the mantel of a loved one you lost?"[9] The act of erasure which was seen initially as a way to be accurate and to prevent further grief was thus

FIGURE 78. Brooklyn Heights promenade, October 2001. Photo ©
Lorie Novak, www.lorienovak.com.

understood to be an insult to the memory of the towers. The initial idea that
guided many of these immediate attempts to eliminate images of the towers
was that it would be traumatic for television and movie audiences to see the
towers as they had stood, which is in complete contradiction to the fact that
at the same time New Yorkers and others were rapidly buying World Trade
Center postcards.[10]

The longing for the twin towers also took the form of mourning a re-
constructed skyline and conceiving of the skyline as "wounded" in some
way. This rhetoric had the effect of envisioning the skyline as a kind of
organic entity, a body with a missing limb. Diana Taylor writes, "The loss of
the Towers triggered a phantom limb phenomenon: the more people recognized the lack, the more they felt the presence of the absence."[11] One of the
first organized memorials to 9/11 took place in March 2002, when a group

FIGURE 79. *Tribute in Light*, 2002, by John Bennett, Gustavo Bonevardi, Julian LeVerdiere, Paul Marantz, Paul Myoda, and Richard Nash-Gould. Courtesy of Max Protetch Gallery.

of artists created *Tribute in Light*, in which two blue streams of light reached from near Ground Zero into the night sky. *Tribute in Light* was intended to pay tribute to the dead. But one could not help feeling that it was really the loss of the towers that the light memorial mourned. Just like the towers, it was designed to be seen from a distance, and its scale succeeded in overpowering the surrounding buildings. The artists who created the memorial, Paul Myoda and Julian LaVerdiere, originally called the project "Phantom Towers." One of them remarked, "Those towers are like ghost limbs, we can feel them even though they're not there anymore."[12] *Tribute in Light* has been repeated on each anniversary of 9/11 and has continued to evoke the haunting of the towers. If seen from a distance as one approaches New York, it can seem like a ghostly shadow of the past.

CHAPTER 5

This idea of the towers as present rather than absent, as a limb felt though not seen, or a ghost presence is evident in much of the art produced in the aftermath of 9/11. In the many artistic reimaginings of Ground Zero, the towers remain a constant refrain, constantly reemerging in the space as if they cannot be erased from people's artistic imaginations as they had from the skyline. In other words, their constant reassertion in designs indicates a desire, whether articulated or not, to reiterate the psychic presence they retain. Immediately after 9/11, Art Spiegelman created a cover for the *New Yorker* in which the towers were barely visible as black shadows on black, an image haunting in its somber familiarity, the towers always there though barely seen.[13] Evoking absence, artist Hans Haacke created 110 white poster-size sheets out of which a silhouette of the two towers had been cut, and pasted them over existing posters (whose space rental had expired) around New York City.[14]

More surprising, in July 2002, when the *New Yorker* magazine asked a group of artists to reimagine the space, the artists produced a series of ironic, oddly humorous, ambivalent, and whimsical proposals that almost all replicated the towers in some form.[15] Despite its intention to use humor and cynicism to intervene in the hypersentimentalization of the site, this project became an exercise in reimagining twin structures, two buildings, figures of two. Nancy Rubins inverted the towers with a proposal for two 110-story underground structures, and Spiegelman proposed 110 one-story buildings. Vitaly Komar and Alex Melamid, who are well known for their avant-garde work on issues of aesthetics and taste, produced a comical pro-posal for a farm on lower Manhattan, with the Cortland Street subway sta-tion surrounded by cows and fields. The two silos of the farm are unmistak-able references to the two towers, hovering over the bucolic rendition like a shadow of the past. Tony Oursler created two scaffoldings in the shape of the two towers that would hold video screens onto which the video coverage of 9/11 would be replayed in a continuous loop. He suggested that the foot-age be run for a period of time and then buried, so that it would "consume itself."

The idea that the towers should be mourned as lost buildings is so taken for granted in the debate over how to rethink Ground Zero that few have attempted to question it. This means that lower Manhattan is constantly conceived as a space of absence, not only where the dead are lost but as a place that will always seem to be lacking the towers no matter what is built in their place (and whatever is built will always be seen as having been built *in*

TWO HOLES CARVED INTO THE EARTH, THE SAME SIZE +SHAPE AS THE WORLD TRADE CENTER.

FIGURE 80. From the *New Yorker* series "After the Towers." Proposal by Nancy Rubins. Courtesy of Nancy Rubins. Originally printed in the *New Yorker*, July 15, 2002.

their place). Some of this mourning of the towers has evolved into campaigns, many of them quite fervent, to rebuild the towers as they stood. Polls taken from residents in May and July 2002 showed that a significant number of New Yorkers wanted the towers to be rebuilt.[16] In November 2002, one group, the World Trade Center Restoration Movement, placed a billboard downtown proclaiming "Rebuild the Towers . . . Bigger and Better Than Before."[17] They later handed out stickers that read "Yes I'd work on the 110th floor!"[18] These groups often deploy jingoistic rhetoric to make their case, claiming, as Team Twin Towers does, that to "build anything shorter or smaller than the Twin Towers is tantamount to kneeling to terrorism. No terrorist organization has the right to dictate building heights or what a skyline should look like."[19]

FIGURE 81. From the *New Yorker* series "After the Towers," by Komar and Melamid. Courtesy of Alexander Melamid. Originally printed in the *New Yorker*, July 15, 2002.

The idea of rebuilding the towers is thus seen largely as a defiance to terrorism and the public support for rebuilding the towers was largely based on notions of symbolism rather than practicality. One can see this fervent embrace of the towers, two buildings that went mostly unloved while standing, as a kind of displacement, a mourning not for the buildings themselves but for what they represented: an earlier, more innocent time of unabashed urban skyscrapers and their dramatic push to the sky. In many ways, the towers embodied not arrogance so much as the innocence of banality. The desire to rebuild or reimagine the towers is not exclusive to amateur designers; it has been a key aspect of the architectural debates about how to rebuild Ground Zero.

FIGURE 82. From the *New Yorker* series "After the Towers." Proposal by Tony Oursler. Courtesy of Tony Oursler and Metro Pictures. Photographs by Evan Fairbanks/Magnum Photo. Originally printed in the *New Yorker*, July 15, 2002.

THE ARCHITECTURE OF MEMORY

Though few would initially admit it, especially in the first year after 9/11, the fact that a large area in a major metropolitan city was destroyed created an *opportunity* for architectural design and urban planning. The site of Ground Zero has been the object of an extraordinary number of architectural proposals and memorial designs that began almost from the moment the towers were destroyed. Much of the vision of rebuilding lower Manhattan takes place in an exceptionalist mode, rarely taking into account the ways other cities have been rebuilt.[20] The design community seemed to feel immediately compelled to use design as a means to mediate grief, reconceiving the space in a huge variety of cityscapes, as a large open public space of green, as clusters of office towers, as the rebuilt twin towers, and as a memorial park. Within two weeks of the towers' destruction, the *New York Times* interviewed many prominent architects about how and whether the space should be rebuilt. Almost all advocated for rebuilding the area with tall skyscrapers that, in the words of Bernard Tschumi, dean of Columbia's School of Architecture, would be "bigger and better." The urge seemed to be to advocate for symbols of strength in what had been a moment of defeat. The architect Robert A. M. Sterne said, "The skyscraper is our greatest achievement architecturally speaking, and we must have a new skyscraping World Trade Center." In that early moment, only the architects Elizabeth Diller and Ricardo Scofidio were willing to speak ironically: "Let's not build something that would mend the skyline, it is more powerful to leave it void. We believe it would be tragic to erase the erasure."[21]

This widespread embrace of the skyscraper reveals many of the paradoxes of the urban environment in which Ground Zero sits. New York is one of many modern cities that are defined by their skyline. As paired buildings that dwarfed all other buildings in the skyline, the World Trade Center towers were the ultimate declaration of the power of skyscrapers. From the beginning the towers were a sign of the way powerful economic interests in New York produce urban projects that often have little to do with urban planning or economic need. The Port Authority, which is under the jurisdiction of the governors of New York and New Jersey and which was created to oversee the ports and shared transportation systems of the area, was never intended to be an entity involved in real estate. It also operates outside of the jurisdiction of New York City. Indeed, one of the stunning facts that came to light after the towers fell was that they had never been subject to New York City building codes (though this did not mean that their building codes had been substandard). When the Port Authority decided to build the World Trade Center, it used its political muscle to obliterate a large area of lower Manhattan that was known as Radio Row, where a huge number of electronic stores were thriving. The myth perpetrated by those building the towers, which included the financier David Rockefeller, was that the area torn down to make way for the trade center was seedy, but many historians have pointed out that it was a thriving business district that employed large numbers of people.[22] Despite local protests, the Port Authority succeeded in demolishing the neighborhood. While they had done so previously in neighborhoods like Bay Ridge in Brooklyn to build the Verrazano-Narrows Bridge, which spans the entrance to New York Harbor, their project of building the World Trade Center was not justified by transportation needs. It was, most critics agree, a project of hubris, one that was not even justified by economic need for office space. Indeed, for most of its history, the Port Authority and the City of New York were some of the primary tenants in the World Trade Center, since the towers had produced a glut of offices in the area.[23]

Skyscrapers are immensely symbolic structures. Paul Goldberger notes that, despite their symbolic value, skyscrapers don't make economic sense above eighty stories because the infrastructure needed to build higher floors increases the building's expense beyond the point of profit. Indeed, the future of skyscrapers in the United States seemed to be, at least before 9/11, primarily in moderately sized buildings of fifty to at most seventy stories (as opposed to Asia, where very tall buildings continue to be built).[24] In addition, the urban needs of lower Manhattan in 2001 were markedly different from those in the 1960s. The World Trade Center represented an earlier, industrial model of urban planning, which called for businesses in the transportation and financial industries to be densely located near each other in order to compete. (Initial plans for the complex envisioned the towers being filled not only with businesses related to international trade but also businesses related to the port.)

By 2001, enabled by new technologies and postindustrialization and prompted by the 1993 bombing of the World Trade Center to have their records held off-site, downtown's financial companies had regionalized to New Jersey, Connecticut, and New York counties north of the city, and office space in lower Manhattan had a high percentage of vacancies. As office spaces have been converted to residential spaces, for which there is an enormous need in Manhattan, the space needs of the area have changed. After 9/11, most urban planners and architects saw lower Manhattan as a place where a mixed-use design—residential, business, commercial, and cultural—should be built in conjunction with a designated memorial. However, in the fraught context of New York politics, the possibility of design professionals gaining authority was unlikely. Indeed, the architecture critic Ada Louise Huxtable wrote a prescient essay in the *Wall Street Journal* just one week after 9/11 in which she predicted that the rebuilding process would be stymied by the structure of New York and national politics: "One can almost predict what the New York process will be. This city can show its compassion, and its resolve, as it is doing now, but it is also a city incapable of the large, appropriate gesture in the public interest if it costs too much."

Huxtable imagined an earnest process in which municipal groups would announce a competition, followed by a "fuss in the press," and finally a compromise, ending in "a properly pious, meaningless gesture that everyone can buy without loss of face or obvious shame."[25]

As the messy process of rebuilding continues, it is clear that architects and designers will ultimately have very little say in the reimagination of lower Manhattan, not simply because of the complex ownership of the site and the byzantine political context that defines where it stood, but also because it is so overdetermined symbolically at a local and national level. In this context, the erection of a symbolically tall skyscraper simply cannot be questioned and a memorial design must be affirming of codes of heroism. The needs and desires of residents are at odds with those of the families, who have gained increasing power, and the demands of the real estate developer Larry Silverstein, who acquired the lease for the World Trade Center six weeks before it fell, have clashed with the Port Authority, which owns the land. The dominance of commercial interests at the site, working in tandem with the Lower Manhattan Development Corporation (LMDC), which was established in fall 2001 by New York Governor George Pataki (which, some have noted, is a political agency with clout and structure like the Port Authority itself), has produced what is increasingly viewed as a travesty of vision.[26] As the process has grown increasingly tortured, the Port Authority has taken on more and more power, in a replication of its ruling hand in building the original World Trade Center. The architect Michael Sorkin writes that the process of redesigning lower Manhattan has been one of betrayal that, under the guise of openness, has failed the public. He argues that the process "has been corrupted by a meagerness of vision and a vanishing and over-aestheticized sense of loss."[27]

The design community's original response to 9/11 was highly charged and active, producing hundreds of designs. This surge of architectural response was met initially by skepticism. The idea of architecture as renewal was seen to be in conflict with the sense of Ground Zero as a sacred site of loss. As high-profile architects began to produce proposals, both spontaneous and commissioned, they were accused by a few critics of turning Ground Zero into an architectural beauty contest. The role of architects in reimagining lower Manhattan has been paralleled by a populist rethinking of the area, which has taken place not only in grassroots campaigns but also through various news outlets, such as CNN, which created public forums for people to submit their own designs. The debate about the site thus became framed for a period of time as one of elitism versus populism and of aesthetics versus mourning. In a 2002 debate with the architect Daniel Libeskind, Leon Wieseltier of the *New Republic* declared, "There is something a little grotesque in the interpretation of ground zero as a lucky break for art. Lower Manhattan must not be transformed into a vast mausoleum, obviously, but neither must it be transformed into a theme park for advanced architectural taste."[28] Wieseltier's views are echoed in many of the statements that have been made by the families of the dead, for whom any aestheticization of the site is counter to its sacred status as the final burial place of their loved ones. This anxiety about the role of aesthetics has a long history. The debate over rebuilding Ground Zero is a reminder that, in moments of trauma, aesthetics almost always are understood as antithetical to processes of grief.

In New York, an aversion to aesthetics was voiced not only by organizations that represented the families of the dead, but also by a constituency that felt that the "high" art of architecture would use design for the ego fulfillment of "starchitects" while ignoring the business needs in the area. The *New York Post* ran several inflammatory headlines about the architectural debates ("The Wrong Stuff—Keep World Architects Away from Ground Zero"), and its reporters repeatedly attacked the New York architectural circle for its embrace of world-renowned architects. Situating itself as the newspaper that represents the working man and underdog (as opposed to the *New York Times* and its ostensibly cultured readership), the *Post* advocated for the local "hacks" who had designed the majority of New York's mostly nondistinct office buildings.[29] The stakes of high and low, and local and outsider, were clearly put into play.

Nevertheless, it is evident that the longing of architects and nonarchitects alike to redesign Ground Zero was not simply motivated by commercial interests or by a desire for narratives of redemption; it was also about the need to see design as a response to loss. In January 2002, the Max Protetch Gallery held a show, *The New World Trade Center*, of quickly conceived proposals for Ground Zero produced by a number of architects that Protetch had asked to reimagine the space downtown.[30] As the architecture critic Philip Nobel writes, so soon after 9/11, at a time when reports of the dead were still coming from Ground Zero, the flippant tone of many of the entries rang with dissonance. "To scan the offerings from this grand, eclectic assembly of poobahs, insurgents, and unknowns . . . was to witness the fracturing of architecture as a profession and the limits of architecture as a communication medium." He asks, "Was it—could it ever be—too early for form?"[31]

FIGURE 83. *The Twin Twins* by Asymptote (Hani Rashid and Lisa Anne Couture), 2002. Courtesy of Max Protetch Gallery.

The proposals in the Protetch exhibition ran the gamut from fanciful imaginings of strangely organic-shaped towers wrapped together over the site, to green proposals for the landscape. Yet in its reimagining of the space the exhibition revealed the ways that architectural design was also functioning as an attempt to create renewal out of death and destruction, to virtually fill up the empty space of Ground Zero and to imagine it whole. Many of these proposals functioned as homages to the twin towers, as if the space could not be imagined without them. Hani Rashad and Lise Anne Couture (Asymptote) created two undulating towers that would emit sun and light into the tower structures and include "sky gardens." Lars Spuybroek of NOX created a honeycombed structure of interlocking towers that mimicked the structure of wool threads dipped in water. Carlos Brillembourg repeats the form of the two towers, but like many architects, he felt the need to open up the spaces of the towers, here by hollowing out their cores and adding 40 percent more window space. He also proposed that the complex include subsidized housing for artists and writers. While most of the proposals were somewhat monumental in their ambitions, many of them proposing either large buildings or large voids symbolizing absence, the Tokyo architect Shigeru Ban submitted to the show a small model, called *A Departure from the Ego*, of which he wrote, "I designed this temporary World Trade Center Memorial immediately after September 11, without being asked by anyone.

FIGURE 84. *Oblique World Trade Center* by NOX (Lars Spuybroek), 2002.
Courtesy of Max Protetch Gallery.

Maybe I was motivated because of my experience of building the 'Paper Church' after the Kobe earthquake of 1995."[32]

In the years since the 2002 Protetch show, thousands of proposals for how to rebuild Ground Zero have circulated, from amateurs and professional architects, in informal and official competitions.[33] A series of open forums set up by the LMDC, which were largely criticized as public relations vehicles in a process in which public sentiment was ultimately ignored, nevertheless did help to establish a context in which it seemed appropriate for anyone who felt a stake in the rethinking of Ground Zero to offer a design. Media entities like CNN hosted websites on which anyone could post a design, and numerous other sites sprang up with designs for the space. In the first two years, the LMDC received over four thousand unsolicited designs.[34] As I have noted, both *New York* magazine and the *New York Times* commissioned design proposals from well-known architects in what were

FIGURE 85. *A New Gateway for the City* by Carlos Brillem-bourg, 2002. Courtesy of Max Protetch Gallery.

FIGURE 86. *A Departure from the Ego* by Shigeru Ban, 2002. Courtesy of Max Protetch Gallery.

acts of quasi-ownership, as if these publications were the city itself.[35] The *New York Times* project, which was organized by its well-known architecture critic Herbert Muschamp, was distinguished by its lauding of architectural celebrity. It can thus be said that the destruction of the towers inspired an enormous amount of energy about urban renewal and design in ways that were very similar to the role that design played in the renewal of Oklahoma City. In both contexts, design created a sense that an urban area could be rethought and could project a renewed image of the city. In Oklahoma City, that energy helped fuel an aesthetic and economic renewal in the downtown area as a whole. In New York, that energy has thus far been stymied by the economic and emotional investments in the site. Nevertheless, in New York, as the media followed the various design proposals and contexts, architecture became part of a public discussion in unusual ways.

In this highly charged context in which design was both invested with enormous stakes and the source of anxious concern, the LMDC ran two competitions for the design of a master plan for the site.[36] The first, in which the firm Beyer Blinder Belle was asked to produce six designs for the site, brought a storm of protest when the mundane designs were unveiled in July 2002. Called "six cookie-cutter losers" by Huxtable, the designs were actually the first indication that the demand by the developer Larry Silverstein to rebuild the exact amount of office space that the towers had housed, with the essential acquiescence of the city and the Port Authority to his position, would mean that any design would have to cram a crowd of bulky office towers into the site.[37] Faced with such a negative public response, the LMDC went back to the drawing board and invited proposals from a group of well-known architects, which culminated in the unveiling of five different designs, which went on display at the Wintergarden in the World Financial Center next to Ground Zero to great fanfare in December 2002. Two finalists emerged from this contest, Daniel Libeskind and the THINK Project (led by Rafael Viñoly and including Shigeru Ban and others), and in February 2003, Libeskind was selected by Governor Pataki as the master planner of the site.[38] The fierce competition for the Ground Zero master plan was a high-profile and increasingly nasty public campaign, in which the two finalists, Viñoly and Libeskind, took to name-calling in public, Viñoly referring to Libeskind's design as a "wailing wall" and Libeskind fatally labeling THINK's design, which consisted of two steel grids in the shape of the towers, "two skeletons in the sky."[39]

This competition and the ensuing rancor it produced have been much

FIGURE 87. Proposal for master site plan by THINK, 2002. THINK (Shigeru Ban, Frederic Schwartz, Ken Smith, Rafael Viñoly); contributors: William Morrish, David Rockwell, Janet Marie Smith; engineers: Arup, Büro Happold, Jörg Schlaich. Courtesy of Frederic Schwartz.

written about, with many New York publications following each stage of the process with fascination. Yet it has been little noted in this relentless analysis that one of the most striking features about the majority of these proposals, from high-end to amateur, is the way they have reenacted both the presence of the twin towers and the events of 9/11. There has been very little questioning (and almost none initially) of the constant reemphasis of the footprints and the reassertion of the twin towers in these designs. The discourse of sacredness has inscribed the footprints of the towers with a particularly charged meaning, and in relation to that the repetition of the towers in these designs, either as absence or presence, is remarkable. This underscores the way this reenactment has functioned as a kind of mourning and a compulsive repetition, one that has constituted both stasis, with architectural imaginings caught in the moment of trauma, but also mourning. As such, these architectural reenactments perform the same kind of cultural labor as the remakes of the image icons of Oklahoma City and 9/11, in which each remake attempts to construct narratives of redemption out of images of loss.

These initial design tendencies of reenactment can be seen in the Protetch exhibition, which, just a few months after 9/11, was dominated by designs that were memorial in their aesthetic. Asymptote's hollowed-out tower shapes are intended to "commemorate the vastness of what was lost by duplicating and reduplicating the Twin Towers' former presence," and Carlos Brillembourg's hollowed-out towers echo the twin towers in mournful ways.[40] Others presented designs that would function as a memorial on the anniversary of 9/11, a concept that would emerge later in the master plan. For instance, Hariri and Hariri proposed eleven "weeping towers," which on each anniversary would "transmit a mist from their skin, allowing the architecture to participate in the event."[41]

Even as the years have passed, and many more proposals have been put forth for lower Manhattan, the twin towers have remained a central haunting absence. Some designs make reference to the towers by envisioning the space as a void or a site that should be filled with green parks and left unbuilt.[42] Other proposals have echoed the shape and form of the twin towers as if the architectural debate about the negative aspects of their design had never happened. Still others, like the Peter Eisenman proposal, compulsively reenact the events of 9/11. That many of these designs were seriously discussed and were given the cultural imprimatur of such publications as the *New York Times*, even though many of them were not only feasibly impossible but strangely inappropriate, is an indicator of a particular kind of disconnect between design imagination and the fraught emotional terrain of Ground Zero. This would seem to affirm the way these proposals were a kind of cultural processing of the loss of 9/11.

For instance, in the second LMDC competition, which was presented to the public in December 2002, the British architect Norman Foster produced two "kissing towers" that he described as "two towers that kiss and touch and become one."[43] Foster's plan, which consists of two towers angling together and apart, held observation decks and "sky parks." The design was oddly reminiscent of the numerous children's drawings that had proliferated throughout the city, in which the towers had been imagined as brothers embracing each other. Other proposals, such as the one by Richard Meier and associates, including Eisenman, proposed a lattice-shaped building of interlocking towers that would incorporate shadow twin towers by extending two long piers into the Hudson River the size and shape of the former towers, as if to permanently install their shadow.[44] It hardly needs to be said that while conceptually this may be an interesting way to memorialize the towers, it is an ineffectual way to rethink the rebuilding of an urban district. The THINK project design offered two lattice structures of steel in the shape and outline of the two towers, into which would be inserted several cul-

FIGURE 88. Proposal for master site plan by Norman Foster, 2002. © Foster and Partners.

FIGURE 89. Proposal for master site plan by Richard Meier and Partners Architects LLP, Eisenman Architects, Gwathmey Siegel and Associates, Steven Holl Architects. Courtesy of Richard Meier and Partners Architects LLP, Eisenman Architects, Gwathmey Siegel and Associates, Steven Holl Architects.

tural and conference centers. Toward the top of the structures, an elongated shape connected the two buildings. To many, this shape looked uncannily like the image of an airplane hitting the towers; the architecture critic Suzanne Stephens wrote, "At the approximate place where the planes hit, an abstracted twisted element literally ties the two buildings together. But as a symbolic connection to 9/11, it struck many as too gruesome a marker, and references to it were quickly downplayed."[45]

It was ultimately these references to 9/11 that doomed the THINK project, even more than the strange impracticalities of its design, which make it hard to believe that it was almost selected. Why would constructing a lattice structure in the shape of the twin towers be an effective way to rebuild lower Manhattan? Governor Pataki was quoted as saying that he would never agree to build "those skeletons." As Goldberger writes, the THINK designers

> did not even attempt to design office buildings; they simply left the eastern and northern sections of the site free for commercial development. The only thing they cared about designing, it seemed, was the commemorative structure, which overwhelmed all else. It not only occupied the footprints, it occupied the sky, and the architects wanted it to be seen not only as a memorial but as a symbol of the public realm. The message was that civic and public uses overrode private uses. The issue of office space, that had so dominated the dialogue about the program, was neutralized by THINK gesture.[46]

This gesture toward the public was laudable, yet it remains the case that the THINK design was an uncanny reenactment not only of the twin towers but also of the catastrophic events of 9/11. In many ways, it exemplifies the degree to which architecture has had a tortured relationship to memory in its attempt to address how lower Manhattan should be rebuilt.

It is tempting to interpret the constant reimagining and reenactment of the twin towers as a form of disavowal. Norman Foster explained his proposal's reenactment of the towers as a kind of unconscious response: "It wasn't a conscious decision to emulate the Twin Towers; at first we designed something completely different."[47] To think of these designs as a form of compulsive repetition is, of course, to indicate that they constitute a kind of overwhelming grief, one that must be couched in terms of architectural criteria rather than be acknowledged. One could speculate that the grief evident in the constant desire to reimagine Ground Zero not as renewed but as a site of memory is also, for the architectural community, about a disavowal of the role of the buildings themselves in the tragedy of 9/11. While no one believes that buildings can be built to withstand the effects of being hit by jetliners filled with fuel, it is nevertheless the case that the twin towers, like most other skyscrapers, were inherently unsafe for the people who worked in them. Thus, to reimagine the twin towers is to disavow so much: the fact that it was as much the buildings that killed people as the planes that destroyed them (many more people died from the buildings' collapse

FIGURE 90. *Ground Zero*, 2003, by Ellsworth Kelly. Collage on newsprint. Courtesy of Whitney Museum.

than from the impact of the planes), that they were symbols of architectural achievement at the expense of those who worked inside them. It is to disavow the most harrowing images of that day, that of people falling and jumping to their deaths because they were trapped by the buildings themselves. The mourning of the loss of the buildings thus acts to screen out the deaths of those who died there.[48]

Many of these architectural proposals thus form a kind of high-culture tourism of history, in which designs use form to negate public space and render the city a series of abstract shapes that bear little resemblance to the lived spaces of architecture. Yet, at the same time, these designs are evidence of difficult, if not tortured, attempts to grapple with memory. There were many other proposals that rejected the skyscraper as too dangerous and emphasized the horizontal, and other proposals that envisioned the site as an open and green space in a part of the city that has few parks. For instance, in November 2001, Michael Sorkin Studio developed a comprehensive plan for lower Manhattan that put major streets underground and envisioned the area as interlocking spaces of green. In 2003, the artist Ellsworth Kelly proposed creating a large square green space over Ground Zero. He did this by pasting a green square on an aerial photograph of the site that was in the *New York Times*.

The dominance of architectural reenactment in these early designs shows the difficulty of reimagining the space anew. Indeed, reenactment of what took place the day of September 11 is a key element in the original master plan by Daniel Libeskind. As the rebuilding process has become increasingly fraught and divisive, Libeskind's master plan grows more and more invisible, yet it is worth reexamining his original plan, since its aesthetic demonstrates the way that reenactment and memory have dictated visions of the site. Libeskind can be said to have won the design competition precisely because of his ability to negotiate this terrain fraught with aesthetics and mourning and because of his appeal to populism. In sharp contrast to the five other proposals with which he competed, Libeskind presented his proposal not as a reconstruction of lower Manhattan so much as a memorialization of the site. In fact, his proposal is titled *Memory Foundations*. He initially kept part of the slurry wall of the pit of Ground Zero exposed in his design, to pay tribute not only to the "bathtub structure" of the foundation of the trade center, which keeps the water of the Hudson River at bay, but also to the experience of Ground Zero itself. Fully cognizant of the demand for symbolism that existed at the time, he imagined a set of buildings that ascended along a spiral, culminating in a tall and slender skyscraper that would be 1,776 feet tall, and was intended to echo the Statue of Liberty across New York Harbor. Governor Pataki, who chose the Libeskind design over the recommendation of the panel he had appointed to make the decision, quickly dubbed the building the Freedom Tower. As the London newspaper the *Guardian* noted, Libeskind adeptly played "the patriot card" in winning the competition.[49]

Libeskind's triumph was to present himself not as an architect, but as a mourning citizen, and this presentation resonated not only with the families of the dead but with the public at large. In the presentation of his design, he was the sole architect in the competition who wrote biographically. Born in Poland, he grew up mostly in New York, and at the time of the competition had lived for fifteen years in Berlin. (He moved back to New York upon winning the competition.) He presented himself as an intensely patriotic New Yorker: "I arrived by ship to New York as a teenager, an immigrant

like millions of others before me, my first sign was the Statue of Liberty and the amazing skyline of Manhattan. I have never forgotten that sight or what it stands for. That is what this project is about." It is important to note that while Libeskind has knowingly deployed the narrative of the immigrant to great effect, his is one particular immigrant narrative that serves to screen over other such stories.[50] He is the grateful refugee, the immigrant who has even greater patriotism than those who preceded him. His charismatic immigrant persona thus overpowers other immigrant stories that have circulated around 9/11—of undocumented restaurant workers at Windows on the World, whose families in Mexico did not even know the name of the place they worked, or the eager young first-generations who worked as traders in the scrappy low-level financial firms that were placed on the higher floors of the towers.

Libeskind, who has a larger-than-life quality, thus evokes a set of his-

torical meanings as a culture figure: a Jewish refugee, a patriot immigrant,
and, not least, as the architect of the Jewish Museum in Berlin, one of the
primary interpreters of Jewish history and cultural memory. Libeskind's
presence in the process of rebuilding Manhattan has thus been coded as
redemptive. By all accounts, his capacity to sway crowds and to make emotional connections in his discussion of architecture with nonarchitects is
unusual among architects, most of whom are not known for their skills in
winning over the public. Libeskind has been praised as magnetic and charismatic and criticized as sentimental and self-promoting. Martin Pedersen
writes, "Part poet, part politician, part used car salesman, part visionary,
part cheerleader, he speaks brilliantly off the cuff. . . . It's magnetic. I have
never seen an architect with this sort of stage presence."[51] In his book *Breaking Ground*, Libeskind speaks in highly emotional terms about Ground Zero,
about the "soul" of the site residing in its bedrock, and about the ways the
families responded emotionally to his work.[52]

　　　　　　　　　　　　　　　　　　　　　　　　　　　　　　　CHAPTER 5

Libeskind's style is thus a highly populist one in which he speaks of architecture that appeals directly to a public rather than requiring learned interpretation: "Architecture is about creating a multi-layered fabric of the city. . . . It's not about prescribed things you should know about. People discover things on their own, discover architecture on more than one level."[53] This is ironic given that at the Jewish Museum in Berlin there are numerous plaques that suggest to visitors how to respond to particular spaces. Yet there is no denying that Libeskind's personal style appeals to broad audiences and exudes a populist feel.

His plan for Ground Zero is not the first time that Libeskind has used memory as a guiding means for design. As he states, "I have been trying [in my work] to redefine the relationship between architecture and memory."[54] And indeed, this is precisely the same strategy he deployed in designing his now-famous building for the Jewish Museum. As Noah Isenberg has written, Libeskind often described the Jewish Museum (as he did the site in New York) as a building about his own biography, and the museum, which is a compelling edifice, has often been seen to be more of a memorial than a museum.[55] In many ways, Libeskind's plan for Ground Zero resonated with families and much of the media precisely because what people wanted at that point, just a little over a year after 9/11, was not an architectural plan, but a memorial. Thus, when a memorial design was added to Libeskind's plan, which was itself already a kind of memorial design, it inevitably produced a site overdetermined by memory.

In his philosophy of architecture and memory, Libeskind deploys a "narrative architecture" that is intended to tell stories, what Martin Filler calls an updated *architecture parlante* of "buildings whose forms 'speak' of their function."[56] Libeskind has stated, "To describe memory onto a building as the postmodernists tried to do is only a banality. Architecture is a communicative art, it tells a story. But so many buildings tell a story of a solipsistic kind. They are autistic, they tell a story only of their own making. But I believe architecture should tell stories about other things, that go beyond themselves."[57]

Memory Foundations narrates a memory of the day of September 11. It initially included "The Park of Heroes," demarcating the space where firefighters entered the buildings, and a "Wedge of Light," a triangular plaza where the sun was supposed to reach from 8:46 to 10:28 a.m. each year on September 11, each an explicit restaging of 9/11. In designating the footprints of the towers as voids in the space, an element that is reiterated in Michael Arad's design for the memorial at Ground Zero, *Reflecting Absence*, Libeskind used an aesthetic of absence to reiterate the presence of the two towers. This concept of the void has been a central element of Libeskind's architectural style. It is used quite extensively in his design for the Jewish Museum in ways that invited the criticism that it transforms the museum into a space of Holocaust loss rather than one of the broader history of the Jews. Some critics have seen the emphasis on the void in Libeskind's work as a preoccupation with death, calling it "nearly necrophiliac."[58] Libeskind himself often characterizes his own work as driven by his experience of being the child of Holocaust survivors:

> As an immigrant, whose youth was often displaced, I've sought to create a different architecture, one that reflects an understanding of history after world catastrophes. I find myself drawn to explore what I call the void—the presence of an overwhelming emptiness created when a community is wiped out, or individual freedom is stamped out; when the continuity of life is so brutally disrupted that the structure of life is forever torqued and transformed.[59]

Libeskind's propensity for reenactment is also tied up in the elements of his work that critics have seen as kitsch. In *Memory Foundations*, the reenactment of the events of 9/11 is essential to the patriotic elements of the design, elements that were characterized by many as Libeskind's "wrapping himself in the flag." From its tower at 1,776 feet to its rhetoric of freedom and equation with the Constitution, Libeskind's original master plan used narrative to inscribe the space of Ground Zero within the nation. Indeed, one could argue that the design is a patriotic memorial design masquerading as architecture. Previously a supporter of Libeskind's design, the *New York Times* critic Herbert Muschamp wrote a now-famous critique of it before the final decision was made, accusing it of being "astonishingly tasteless" and "an emotionally manipulative exercise in visual codes." Muschamp went further to state, "A concrete pit is equated with the Constitution. A skyscraper tops off at 1,776 feet. . . . A promenade of heroes confers quasi-military status on uniformed personnel. Even in peacetime that design would appear demagogic." Muschamp's critique was an extreme version of the kinds of criticisms made of Libeskind by members of the architectural community, in which he is the subject of polarized views and by whom he is often accused of being too sentimental. As Muschamp wrote, "Had the competition been intended to capture the fractured state of shock felt soon after 9/11, this plan would probably deserve first place. But why, after all, should a large piece of

FIGURE 93. New version of "Wedge of Light" in the Daniel Libeskind master plan, 2006. Courtesy of Lower Manhattan Development Corporation. Reproduced with permission.

FIGURE 94. Libeskind master plan, seen with Statue of Liberty, 2002. Courtesy of Lower Manhattan Development Corporation. Reproduced with permission.

Manhattan be permanently dedicated to an artistic representation of enemy assault? It is an astonishingly tasteless idea. It has produced a predictably kitsch result."[60] Muschamp, who would retire from the *Times* soon after this conflict, had come under criticism for his role in recruiting high-profile architects to produce designs for his own newspaper. His criticism here was stinging.[61]

It is the case that Libeskind's popularity at least initially with the public had to do with the easy emotionalism and kitsch elements of his design and in the design's rejection of irony. Libeskind has long proclaimed himself to be a critic of "fashionable irony."[62] Had it been built as intended, his memorial plan would have operated as an element in what is often described as the "Spielberg style" of history, in which simplistic symbols are deployed to evoke empathetic responses in viewers. As Hal Foster wrote at the time, "The real pessimists glimpse a Trauma Theme Park in the making, with Libeskind a contemporary cross between Claude Lanzmann and Walt Disney, the perfect maestro for an age when historical tragedy can become urban spectacle."[63] In many ways, the reenactment of Libeskind's design shares a sense of suspended time with the snow globe souvenir from Ground Zero, which I describe at the beginning of this book. In my souvenir, the twin towers are still standing, together, whole, and untouched, though they are surrounded by police cars and fire trucks that make clear the sense of emergency. This reenactment, like *Memory Foundations*, reproduces again and again that sense of emergency.

In the years since he was lauded as the master architect for Ground Zero, Libeskind has been increasingly marginalized, and key narrative elements of his design have been trimmed or eliminated, to the point where the *New York Times* began referring to him as the "incredible shrinking Daniel Libeskind."[64] Once the darling of the New York media for his empathetic public persona, Libeskind was increasingly the source of media derision. When his original symbolic "wedge of light" was shown to be unworkable because of the presence of the Millenium Hilton Hotel, it was jokingly referred to as the "wedge of shade" and the "wedge of lies." As Philip Nobel has written, Libeskind's penchant for metaphor, which was initially what made him so popular, would ultimately help to erode his credibility in the media.[65]

It's worth noting that Santiago Calatrava, whose design for the PATH and subway transportation center at Ground Zero has been the subject of unqualified praise, also deploys numerous elements of memorial reenactment in his design. Calatrava's design was chosen by the Port Authority in a limited competition, without much semblance to any public forum. It was thus little discussed in public until it was unveiled. The design is dramatic, with the building's roof creating a soaring effect of two wings reaching into the sky. The roof is designed to open to the sky on the anniversary of 9/11, in a ploy not dissimilar to Libeskind's "Wedge of Light." Calatrava has also not shied away from patriotic symbolism; the building will have on display a large American flag that was pulled from the rubble at Ground Zero, and Calatrava has stated, "The building itself embodies the idea of the 11th of September."[66] Yet Calatrava's building, which could easily be accused of re-enactment, seems to have avoided accusations of kitsch precisely because its dominant style is classic modernism—its embrace of cathedral-like spaces and sleek modern form overpower these national references. In part because it is a Port Authority project, and thus shielded, as the World Trade Center towers were, from intense public scrutiny, the immense cost of the building has drawn little attention. Suzanne Stephens notes that the estimated price tag of $2.2 billion is more than the estimated cost of the Freedom Tower: "Some wonder what time reality pulls into the station."[67] In a *Wall Street Journal* editorial, Debra Burlingame, a board member of the World Trade Center Memorial Foundation whose brother died as one of the pilots of the plane that hit the Pentagon and who has been a critic of the plans for Ground Zero, wrote, "Some $2 billion of that is federal money, which means that the entire country is supporting the 'awe-inspiring' makeover of a terminal that will serve a mere 40,000 commuters (a number so embarrassing the Port Authority upped it to 80,000 by including round trips). The chief executive of a construction firm involved in the building illustrates the absurdity of what insiders call a 'vanity project' by pointing out that $2.2 billion is enough to build a metropolitan airport."[68] Yet the PATH system services New Jersey commuters, and the PATH's renovation when the World Trade Center was built was always used as the concession to the fact that the Port Authority is owned by New Jersey as well as New York. Finally, it is perhaps most in relation to the debacle of the Freedom Tower that the Calatrava building has been so embraced, as it promises to be more open and uplifting than the overly symbolic and heavily defended Freedom Tower.

THE FREEDOM TOWER AND THE MALL

Libeskind is often depicted as the aesthetic visionary who is at war with the crass commercial interests of real estate developers, and nowhere was this more evident than in relation to his design for the Freedom Tower, which,

FIGURE 95. World Trade Center Transportation Hub, designed by Santiago Calatrava SA. Courtesy of the Port Authority of New York and New Jersey.

it became quickly obvious, the developer Larry Silverstein intended his own architect, David Childs, to design. The conflict between Childs and Libeskind has been the fodder for much attention, followed avidly by reporters for the *New York Post* and the *New York Times*, chronicled in a 2004 PBS *Frontline* documentary "Sacred Ground," and detailed by the architecture critics Paul Goldberger and Philip Nobel.[69] The product of conflicts of ownership and power, and weighted with symbolism, the Freedom Tower has since emerged as the icon for how the rebuilding of Ground Zero is producing not a vision of renewal but a misguided, overbuilt, security-driven vision of urban design.

The Freedom Tower has been called many unfortunate names in architecture circles, from the "mongrel tower" to the "franken tower." Clearly, its design indicates a failure of architectural vision; it is also the case that the building was so overburdened with political and national meaning that it was fated from the start. It is likely to stand as a unique symbol of the post-9/11 era, in which jingoism and security became the dominant national discourses. From the beginning, when Libeskind proposed that it stand 1,776 feet and Governor Pataki named it the Freedom Tower, this building has been presented as an act of defiance, as the building that would render patriotic the New York skyline and assuage the fear that the attacks of 9/11

FIGURE 96. Freedom Tower, aerial view, 2006. Architect: Skidmore, Owings and Merrill LLP. © Skidmore, Owings and Merrill LLP/dbox.

had emasculated the nation. Demands to use the symbolism of skyscrapers to rebuild Manhattan, to counter what the *New York Post* in typical fashion called "urban planning by Atta," have formed a neat parallel to the deployment of a revenge rhetoric of 9/11 by the Bush administration to justify wars in Afghanistan and Iraq.[70] The cornerstone of the Freedom Tower was laid with great fanfare on July 4, 2004, and then as work on the site stagnated and proceeded in fits and starts, was quietly taken away and put in storage.[71]

The criteria for rebuilding lower Manhattan increasingly have had little to do with urban planning and residential needs, but have been driven by real estate greed and the need to construct symbols of U.S. technological, economic, and, by extension, military power.[72] That this building will itself be a target has been a given from the beginning. When Pataki announced the new design, in which the lowest two hundred feet of the building will be a concrete bunker, he proclaimed that it would "restore and reclaim our skyline" as a "symbol of America," and David Childs defiantly called it the "safest building in the world." In a feeble attempt to allay concerns about security, Pataki added, "If one of those giant corporations that Larry [Silverstein] lures to the Freedom Tower occupied the top floors and wants to hire one of my kids, I'd be honored to have them working there and be confident about their safety."[73] Nevertheless, the erection of a patriotically symbolic building will inevitably invite fears of a reprisal. One could argue, of course, that the best way to build a secure building at Ground Zero is to build something smaller and without a symbolic name. Ultimately, the Freedom Tower will most likely end up being a symbol not of U.S. power, but of its fear, deeply embodying the new aesthetic of security. As the *New York Times* architecture critic Nicolai Ouroussoff writes:

> Somber, oppressive and clumsily conceived, the project suggests a monument to a society that has turned its back on any notion of cultural openness. . . . If this is a potentially fascinating work of architecture, it is, sadly, fascinating in the way that Albert Speer's architectural nightmares were fascinating: as expressions of the values of a particular time and era. The Freedom Tower embodies, in its way, a world shaped by fear.[74]

The design of the Freedom Tower thus presents in a microcosm how violence and history converge in a cyclical fashion: if a tower is built to defy history, then it will be a symbol to be targeted.

The tower has been redesigned numerous times. In spring 2005, the design was sent back for revision by the New York Police Department because of fears about security, and what reemerged was essentially a skyscraper sitting on a huge concrete bunker on which, instead of a spire, sits a single antenna. The Freedom Tower thus has come to resemble a fortified version of one of the twin towers. In an eerie replication of the World Trade Center towers, the federal government and the Port Authority will, of necessity, be the primary tenants.[75] Since government agencies will be paying premium rents rather than the reduced rates the Port Authority paid in the twin towers, this arrangement will make it, in the words of the *Washington Post*, "the most highly subsidized symbolic skyscraper in the nation."[76] This has caused considerable distress for government workers whose memories of 9/11 make them reluctant to work in the building, in ways that are eerily reminiscent of the workers who refused to work in the new federal building in Oklahoma City.[77] As late as March 2006, the *Daily News* wrote an editorial advocating "Lose the Freedom Tower," calling it "today's hot potato, tomorrow's white elephant. . . . The claim that the spire stretching 1,776 feet into the air will demonstrate American resilience and values rings more hollow with each passing day."[78] Similarly, John Heilemann wrote in *New York* magazine, "Outside the governor's office, there's universal agreement that the tower—vast, expensive, iconic, incendiary (it's the architectural equivalent of a bright-red flag being waved at a charging bull), and thus possibly unrentable—is the biggest obstacle to the rebuilding of ground zero."[79] Subsequently, the design team proposed to encase the nearly two-hundred-foot-high concrete base within glass prisms.[80] In spring 2006, the Port Authority and Larry Silverstein reached an agreement to have the Authority take over the construction of the tower, thus in a certain sense coming full circle back to the original governing structure of the World Trade Center.

The Freedom Tower is likely to emerge not as an icon of the freedom-embracing post-9/11 society but as an icon of a defended, security-obsessed, barricaded urban space. With its concrete solid base, it will not have street-level activity or storefronts. Similarly, the first building completed at the site, the building of 7 World Trade Center, has no storefronts and a well-fortified single entrance that is offset from the street. Seven World Trade Center, which was designed by David Childs and built quickly by Silverstein with little public input, features many aspects of new security design, not only its well-barricaded base but also wider staircases and a solid concrete core around its central elevators. Because it fell late on the day of September 11 and thus had been fully evacuated, demolition and construction proceeded without the recovery effort of searching for remains. Since it opened in spring 2006, it has found tenants slowly. Via Group, the advertising agency that Silverstein Properties hired to promote the new tower, designed a campaign that showed the views from the highest floors of the forty-story building with the tagline "To leaders with vision: Your office is ready." Via executives felt it was strategic to sell the idea of working in the building not for its cheaper rents, but as a visionary investment in the future of Ground Zero.[81]

While much of the design of security, as I discussed in chapter 1, has become sophisticated in masking design, the dominance of security experts in the implementation of design often means that it is precisely the appearance of security that is being sought, a kind of "security creep." Buildings like the

Freedom Tower, which are designed to be set back from the street, can thus be impediments to the reactivation of street life that designers had longed for in the wake of the towers' destruction. Writes Farhad Manjoo, "The building's concrete base is surrounded by a large plaza topped with trees, steps and a fountain. If you're working in downtown New York one day 10 years from now, the steps might be a nice place to stop and have a burrito. On the other hand, you can see in this picture the cause of architects' fears. The plaza is surrounded by a line of vehicle-blocking posts that resemble tombstones, and you've got to climb a mountain of stairs to get to the building, barricaded against the street."[82]

Three additional building designs for the site by three prominent architects—Norman Foster, Richard Rogers, and Fumihiko Maki—were unveiled with much fanfare for the fifth anniversary of 9/11 in September 2006. The three structures, which are designed to line the periphery of the planned memorial in ways that are at least reminiscent of Libeskind's original master plan of a spiral of buildings and which are each quite distinct from the other in style, were greeted by architecture critics as the culmination of a dysfunctional process. Ouroussoff quickly proclaimed them to be "towers for forgetting" that "rise above the mediocrity we have come to expect from a planning process driven by political opportunism, backdoor deal-making and commercial greed" yet which "illustrate how low our expectations have sunk."[83] Huxtable notes that "whatever the pious rhetoric, their proximity to sacred ground, and the care with which the reality is skirted, they are machines for making money, just as the Twin Towers were, with only some rearrangement of the square footage. . . . They do not so much reach for the sky as drop down from it on a designated parcel."[84] The architects presented their works as icons of transparency, and Foster asserted that the slanted roof of his design was tipping its hat toward the memorial (which provoked Huxtable to ask in print, "Is he serious?"). Hampered by the demand that they create enormous amounts of office space, so that the amount of space of the World Trade Center towers will be replicated at the site, the buildings appear quite bulky. Each is designed to have several stories of retail in each tower, so that they may resemble urban shopping malls. The difference from most urban shopping malls, however, is that consumers will look down from their shopping onto the memorial voids below.

This image of several stories of shops overlooking the memorial points to the endless contradictions at work in the competing discourses of Ground Zero: mourning, memory, sacredness, commerce, security, and nation. In

FIGURE 97. World Trade Center site with buildings designed by Norman Foster, Fumihiko Maki, and Richard Rogers, September 2006. Image: SPI, dbox. Courtesy of Silverstein Properties.

particular, concerns about how to reintroduce retail shops in the highly overdetermined site of Ground Zero also promises to be in conflict with the sanctification of the site. The underground mall of the World Trade Center was one of the most successful shopping malls in the United States, in part because of the large numbers of commuters who came through the mall in addition to the tens of thousands of workers from the towers. In addition, the trade center mall was a central shopping area for local residents, especially those in Battery Park City, which is adjacent to the area and for whom the loss of the Borders bookstore was particularly difficult. Yet the need for commercial retail development is in potential conflict with both the notion of sacredness that has marked the site and with the heightened sense of security. Indeed, when the need to attract commercial interests in a rebuilt Ground Zero was initially discussed, it was made distinctly clear that the Target Corporation would not be welcome to open a store there.[85] Other retailers, including Wal-Mart, are in discussion with developers, but the sense of sacred ground extends well beyond the designated area for the memorial, below ground as well as above. The question of how this concept of sacredness will spill over into the surrounding area remains unresolved, in particular since the sense of sacredness encompasses all sixteen acres for many who feel ownership of it. "Are they going to have Victoria's Secret selling underwear?" one family member asked the *New York Times*. "Who knows? . . . How hypocritical will it be for us to have a totally 9/11-related memorial quadrant and directly across Greenwich Street you have shops facing it which, overtly by the signage, are inappropriate?"[86] As negotiations over the site have proceeded, and the concepts of sacredness and drive for commerce have clashed, there has emerged an increasingly distinct division between the eight acres of commercial area and the eight acres of the memorial and its companion museum. The felt need to memorialize at the site was so immediate that it overshadows all of these attempts at redevelopment, and it is perhaps at those liminal and threshold spaces between the memorial and the retail and commercial district that these tensions will reside.

THE RUSH TO MEMORIALIZATION

That Libeskind's master plan, *Memory Foundations*, was more of a memorial than an urban plan was itself a response to the overwhelming desire, shared by designers, families, and politicians, to see Ground Zero largely in terms of memorialization rather than renewal. In fact, the urge to speak about a memorial in New York was almost instantaneous; by the next day, even as the number and names of the dead remained unknown, memorials were being suggested. In some ways, immediate discussion of a memorial allowed people to begin to construct narratives of redemption and to feel as if the horrid event itself was over—containable, already a memory. It is the case, of course, that the World Trade Center memorial will be a tourist destination, as Ground Zero is now, and estimates are that five million people will visit it each year. The process of building a memorial is thus not only caught up in debates over sacred ground and ownership of the space, but also in its economic future as a place of tourists and tourist commerce.

Like the process of creating an architectural plan for the area, the process of creating a memorial was fueled by political interests and the debate about meaning of the site. The memorial competition was organized by the LMDC less than two years after 9/11, a time frame that is considerably short in the history of memorialization. While the process in Oklahoma City took place in an equally short time and was equally fueled by the concerns of families and survivors, the memorialization process in New York demonstrates the broad differences between these two contexts. The process of constructing a memorial in Oklahoma City was one of hard-won consensus, in which high stakes were placed on reaching agreement and creating a smooth process. In New York, the different factions have found their place, so to speak, in opposition to each other rather than by working together. While members of the LMDC and the memorial committee went to Oklahoma City and met with the museum officials and families there, they returned to New York in large part convinced that the example of New York, in particular because of the issues of redevelopment and ownership, was quite different.[87] The contrasts of the two contexts is remarkable. For instance, in Oklahoma City, the ardent emphasis on community involvement at the beginning, despite its difficulties, meant that the process was less easily derailed. The Oklahoma City memorial designer Hans Butzer argues that this allowed the process to survive differing opinions: "Some people hated the design. But the community input gave the process integrity and moral authority, and it held firm. Once the design is selected, it should not be changed. Tweaked, yes, but not changed. It undermines the whole process."[88]

While the desire to build a memorial at Ground Zero can be seen in terms of the broader context of the turn toward memorialization in the United States over the past twenty-five years, it also intersects with a changing history of memorialization in New York City. Many argue that New York has throughout much of its history disavowed memory. James Sanders writes that New York has always "abhorred the very idea of memorials" and, in contrast to Washington, D.C., has largely built monumental structures that were functional. "In New York, as nowhere else, the monumental instinct was put to work and made to pay—and thus seamlessly integrated with the commercial energy and vitality of the rest of the city."[89]

Yet over the past two decades the landscape of lower Manhattan has become the site of a broad range of memorials, including the Vietnam Veterans Memorial in Battery Park, the Irish Hunger Memorial in Battery Park City, which opened in July 2002, and a planned memorial at the African Burial Ground in Tribeca. In addition, the World Trade Center had already housed a memorial for those killed in the 1993 bombing there, of which a small fragment has been recovered. Since March 2002, the damaged sculpture *The Sphere* by Fritz Koenig, which once stood in the plaza of the World Trade Center and was unearthed from the wreckage, has stood in Battery Park as a temporary memorial.[90] This seeming proliferation of memorials prompted the *Newsday* columnist Jimmy Breslin to quip that while uptown had a Museum Mile, downtown now had a "Misery Mile."[91]

It is also the case that lower Manhattan is filled with a variety of public sculpture and was, especially in the 1980s, the site of numerous temporary artworks in its undeveloped spaces. Devin Zuber contrasts the fractious space of Ground Zero with several lyrical artworks that engaged the landscape of the city. For instance, Agnes Denes created *Wheatfield: A Confrontation* in 1982 on two acres of land that were slotted for development in lower Manhattan. In view of the towers, she planted two fields that grew into golden wheat that were then harvested, the work ending to the sorrow of local residents. Denes intended the field to act as a political intervention, to question the status quo by contrasting the beauty and practicality of the wheat field in relation to the buildings of metal and glass behind it.[92] In 2004, Christo and Jeanne-Claude's Central Park project *The Gates* was seen by many as a public engagement with the space of the city that stood in sharp contrast to the memorial debate. Christo and Jeanne-Claude filled the park with saffron-colored banners hanging from gates along miles of walkways, offering, Zuber argues, fitting templates for how a memorial at Ground Zero could provide poignant content without being overtly political.

There are many other memorials that have been built to commemorate those who died on 9/11. (Groundbreaking also took place in June 2006 for a downscaled Columbine memorial in Littleton, Colorado.) There has been a proliferation of memorials around the country made from relics from Ground Zero, including the "Rolling Memorial," a tractor-trailer covered with the names of the 9/11 dead.[93] Many of these memorials throughout the country incorporate the steel beams of the twin towers in some fashion as well as other rubble from Ground Zero. Groundbreaking took place on June 15, 2006, for the memorial near the Pentagon, which will have 184 cantilevered benches, one for each person who died, shaded by eighty maple trees, and which will be 165 feet from where American Airlines Flight 77 hit the Pentagon.[94] The House approved $5 million for a memorial at the site in Shanksville, Pennsylvania, where Flight 93 crashed. Both designs have minimalist aesthetics and both were immediately and predictably the source of debate, as critics charged that the crescent-shaped group of red maple trees in the Shanksville memorial was a sign of sympathy for Islamic terrorists and that the Pentagon memorial enshrines loss at the expense of honor.[95] The Pentagon is not a place that is normally conducive to tourism, and while Shanksville has emerged as a place of tourism, it is overshadowed by New York precisely because of its remote location. Around the New York area, memorials have been created or are planned on Staten Island, in Westchester County, Hoboken, Jersey City, and several other locations.[96] There are also many other memorial forms: a 9/11 quilt, a grove of trees in Massachusetts with one tree for each person on the flights that left from Boston, benches, murals, land and hospital wings named after those who died, and innumerable shrines that still exist in New York fire stations. In many ways, this proliferation of memorials is more likely to fulfill existing needs for mourning than any singular memorial could.

In addition, as Kenneth Foote notes, places that acquire the status of sacred ground often attract additional memorials to them. Thus, the surrounding area around Ground Zero is likely to be peopled with numerous memorials over the next decade, in ways that seem appropriate to the contrasting views of how 9/11 should be remembered. The first ones include a memorial in the American Express building of the World Financial Center to the eleven American Express employees who died, which includes a pool into which single drops of water continuously fall, creating concentric circles, and a fifty-six-foot-long bronze relief wall dedicated to the firefighters, which was opened in June 2006 alongside Engine Company 10 and Ladder Company 10 on Liberty Street across from Ground Zero. In a kind of neoclassical figurative style, the bronze wall depicts the burning towers and the firefighters working at the scene. It was funded by a local law firm and has inscribed on it the names of the firefighters who died at Ground Zero as well as the name of one of the law firm's partners, Glenn Winuk, a volunteer firefighter on Long Island, who rushed to the trade center after evacuating his own building and died there.[97]

It could be argued that the proliferation of literal and figurative memorials such as this could alleviate some of the pressure on the World Trade Center memorial to appeal to all constituencies. Yet the Ground Zero memorial will be not only the largest memorial built, but the most fought over and the most burdened with symbolic weight. When the LMDC announced the memorial competition in spring 2003, a proliferation of ideas about memorials had already circulated on websites, in proposals sent to the LMDC, and as part of various architectural designs. The New York curator Anita Contini, who was hired by the LMDC to oversee memorial and cultural facilities at

FIGURE 98. Firefighter memorial at Engine 10, across from Ground Zero, 2006.

the site, remarked, "It's almost as if the world has to do this for their own therapy—like when something happens to someone in your neighborhood, you show up with food, and now, the whole world is making offerings."[98] In ways similar to the surge in design interest in rebuilding the site, designing a memorial seems to provide a catharsis for amateurs and professionals to process what happened on 9/11. Not the least among those who advocated for a large memorial was Rudolph Giuliani, who in his outgoing speech as mayor asked that the site of Ground Zero be left undeveloped and become the site of a "soaring, monumental, beautiful memorial."[99]

The memorial competition was an open contest in which 5,201 entries were submitted from around the world, making it the largest architectural competition in history. In November 2003, the LMDC placed eight finalists on display in lower Manhattan, where they were subject to public debate and significant criticism. Most observers felt that the eight proposals were unexceptional, minimalist, and timid designs that looked more appropriate for a corporate plaza than a memorial. Most designs resorted to conventional uses of water (to broadly signify renewal) and large modern forms, and all rejected figuration. The contestants had been given guidelines that asked them to recognize the 2,979 dead as individuals, to provide space for contemplation, to create a separate space for families and a place for unidentified remains, and to make visible the towers' footprints. They were encouraged to "convey historic authenticity" by including "surviving original elements," though none of the finalists did. There were numerous calls for the competition to be scrapped and started over and for the city to abandon its pose of populism and to commission a design from a well-known architect. For instance, the *New York Times* art critic Michael Kimmelman wrote a polemic for elitism as a condemnation of the finalists' designs, asking, "Does anybody today care that the pope did not hold an open competition for the Sistine ceiling?"[100] Kimmelman advocated that the city commission a design from a well-known architect. For others, the primary concern was the dominance of modernist minimalism in the designs, which were perceived as a rejection of figural representation and attributed widely to the presence of the architect Maya Lin, the designer of the Vietnam Veterans Memorial, on the jury.[101] While the jury had a contingent of political appointees and representatives from the victims' families, it also had many artists and curators. Lin was hardly the sole representative of modernist aesthetics, though she was the best known outside of art circles.[102] Ironically, this debate echoed practically word for word the debates that took place over Lin's now iconic memorial, which resulted in the construction of two representational memorials in addition to her minimalist wall of names.[103]

As in that earlier debate, the dominance of modernist tendencies in the designs was understood as a rejection of codes of heroism and an antimonument style.[104] For instance, Dennis Smith, a former firefighter who wrote a book on the recovery effort, wrote that in the finalists' designs, "the universal elements—air, water, earth and light—are celebrated. Nature is celebrated. Nowhere is there a representation of a human being."[105] Yet, if anything, the debate over the Vietnam Veterans Memorial demonstrated vividly the problematic aspects of figural representation as a means to mourn the dead, since each figural statue raised issues of exclusion. As I have noted, this problem was made clear again in the controversy of the statue that was designed to replicate the now-famous photograph of three firefighters erecting a flag at Ground Zero. Because the statue attempted to be racially inclusive in response to the politics of identity that dictate contemporary representation, it was accused of distorting the truth, which was that the three firefighters were white.

Inevitably, this debate reenacts traditional concepts of high and low cul-

FIGURE 99. Proposal for 9/11 memorial by Desmond Hui. Courtesy of Desmond Hui.

ture and taste, in which high art is equated with modernism and figural representation with the masses. Reportedly, the jurors were astonished by what they considered to be the "tastelessness" of some of the entries, all of which were posted on the LMDC website and some of which were subject to public derision.[106] These designs included an oversized question mark, a large egg, shapes that conjured airplanes hitting buildings, and a glowing apple on top of a spire.[107] In the design by Desmond Hui, two airplanes are imagined as "two doves" returning to an ark, "carrying the memory of those on board as well as those in the twin towers," with the names of the victims inscribed on glass in the footprints of the towers and also on the seats of the planes themselves.[108] The kitsch elements in these designs demonstrate a kind of depoliticization of the story of 9/11. In these forms of kitsch reenactment, the story of jetliners hitting buildings, the use of simplistic symbols of hearts and angels, and the deployment of jingoistic signs define 9/11 in isolation from history, as a story of a tragedy that just happened. Yet some of these designs, such as Hui's, deploy reenactment in ways that actually engage more directly with the story of what happened that day than minimal modernism. All of the designs raise the issue of the relationship of memorials to pedagogy, and what message, beyond that of mourning loss, memorials are supposed to tell. It is the case that memorials are in general not particularly effective sites for pedagogy about why par-

FIGURE 100. Aerial view of *Reflecting Absence* by Michael Arad and Peter Walker, 2004. Courtesy of Lower Manhattan Development Corporation. Reproduced with permission.

ticular tragedies have taken place, since they are focused on mourning the dead. The most successful memorials are those that create a space that allow for a variety of responses to loss, and that happens most often in the absence of figurative representation.

The final memorial design, *Reflecting Absence*, by Michael Arad (who was then asked by the jury to collaborate with Peter Walker), consists of an open plaza of trees into which two "voids" with reflecting pools will dip down into the space of the towers' footprints.[109] In the original design, visitors walk down ramps along the edges of the pools, each of which has cascading water falling down into the voids. The ramps lead to underground galleries where the names of the victims of 9/11 are inscribed, which were perceived by Arad as spaces of calm and solitude. Originally, one room was designed to contain a large boxlike container where the unidentified remains would be interred, as a kind of cenotaph. The original plan proposed an elevated

FIGURE 101. Underground galleries in original proposal for *Reflecting Absence* by Michael Arad and Peter Walker, 2004. Courtesy of Lower Manhattan Development Corporation. Reproduced with permission.

plaza that, Suzanne Stephens notes, "would make it psychologically more inaccessible to the general public." She adds that "the site of the plaza with two voids reminded many of the large and maligned windswept one that existed there before." Stephens goes on to note that the underground galleries "look like an underground parking garage."[110] The design came in for more biting criticism from the *New York Post*, which took to referring to the voids as "giant storm drains."[111]

The void is a primary aesthetic of Arad's memorial design. This gives it a certain kind of coldness, which was interpreted by many to be a corporate or minimalist aesthetic.[112] Although *Reflecting Absence* is not minimalist with a radical intent, it is imbued with a modernist aesthetic of emptiness. While it is designed as a memorial to the people who died, its aesthetic of absence also seems, like that of so many of the designs that have circulated, an evocation of the towers. Much of the criticism of the design has fixed on this quality, calling it "void of honor, truth, emotion and dignity."[113] One widow wrote to the *New York Times*, "'Reflecting Absence' is an appropriate name for this design. It truly represents absence—the absence of any reminder of what it is supposed to memorialize!"[114] The "voids" that demarcate the footprints of the towers in the memorial design replay the presence/absence of the twin towers. One could argue that the desire to rebuild the towers and the designation of void spaces where the towers once stood are essentially the same.

It was perhaps inevitable that the chosen memorial design would satisfy few of the needs expressed over Ground Zero. As James Young, one of the jurists, remarked, "We chose to recall the terrible absence left behind by the building's footprints, the hopeful renewal of life as found in the groves of trees, and the individual lives of the victims, many of whom died trying to save the lives of others. In the end, none of us believed that any single memorial could ever adequately express the overwhelming sense of loss experienced by the city and by the victims' families that day."[115] Since it won the competition, the Arad design has been so transformed from its original intentions that it may ultimately retain little of the designer's intent, to the point where the *New York Times* architecture critic Nicolai Ouroussoff proclaimed its "death by committee."[116] Arad was initially asked by the jury to collaborate with the architect Peter Walker to aid in adding trees to the open plazas of the design. At the time, it was noted by many architecture critics that the memorial completely ignores the Libeskind master plan in eliminating its cultural building and also ignoring important structural aspects of the site that were already planned.[117] Libeskind, who has since denied that he was opposed to the memorial, reportedly announced at the time to the LMDC, "I will fight this! I am the people's architect!"[118] Arad has in turn been the subject of increasingly unfavorable media attention, culminating in a devastating portrayal in *New York* magazine that revealed that he was barely on speaking terms with any of the collaborating architects and was so volatile that he had been barred from important meetings.[119]

Yet the primary battles that have emerged over the memorial design are not between designers but between the forces that are vying for emotional ownership of the memory of the site and its political meaning: the LMDC, the Memorial Foundation, a small but increasingly vocal group of families, the firefighters, and the Port Authority. This has resulted in a context in which design criteria and aesthetics have been awarded increasingly less value in relation to security concerns, cost estimates, and certain families' desires to treat the site as the burial ground of those lost.

One of the key issues in dispute was the role of the underground galleries. After initially approving the design, some family members began to feel that putting the names underground was negatively symbolic and dangerous in terms of security, and formed the Put It Above Ground Campaign that gathered thousands of signatures. Sally Regenhard, who founded the Skyscraper Safety Campaign after her firefighter son was killed at the trade center, told the Associated Press, "This is a disaster waiting to happen. Putting something like this below the ground is a very, very bad idea."[120] One family member, Rosaleen Tallon, spent several weeks in March 2006 maintaining a nighttime vigil at Ground Zero (with a small band of regulars who hang out there, including, strangely, former subway vigilante Bernard Goetz), to protest the memorial's design and the fact that most of it was underground.[121] At various protests Tallon stated, "The symbolism of going down is wrong here, my brother was going up to rescue people."[122] A small group of family members formed the Take Back the Memorial alliance, which has intensely followed each development in relation to Ground Zero.

Soon the public prominence of these family members, whose number of active members is quite small, began to change their image from one demanding sympathy to one of meddling and obstruction. *New York* magazine began to call them "the Grief Police."[123] Throughout 2005 and 2006, the family groups and the Memorial Foundation were often increasingly at odds; the Coalition of 9/11 Families petitioned in court in March 2006 to stop construction of the memorial, specifically to prevent the pouring of concrete over the footprint of the North Tower, which they claim is still the site of remains of hundreds of victims.[124] A group of downtown business and community groups then filed a brief in the suit claiming that the Coalition would "bring the rebuilding process to a grinding halt" and "leave lower Manhattan with an unhealed wound at its center for years to come." One resident stated, "I don't think there's any great love for the final memorial design, but we in the community really just want to get on with it."[125] Two of the jurors who had originally chosen the design, James Young and Michael Van Valkenburgh, were prompted to write a *New York Times* editorial in which they stated, "This is not an underground memorial. . . . It is stitched into the fabric of the city and streets around it, allowing visitors to peer into the depths of destruction from street level. After they descend they can look up to the heavens through veils of falling water."[126]

The battles over the memorial imploded in May 2006, when the firm contracted to construct the memorial came in with an estimate close to $1 billion.[127] The mayor and governor immediately announced that they both intended to cap the cost of the memorial and its accompanying museum at $500 million, itself already an astronomical cost, and outrage that the project was so out of control proliferated. The *New York Times* editorialized, "The only thing that a $1 billion memorial would memorialize is a complete collapse of political and private leadership in Lower Manhattan."[128]

The memorial was then redesigned in a process overseen by Frank J. Shiame, a construction executive, who, after consulting all the parties involved, presented five options to the governor and the mayor to choose from. This would seem to be an extreme version of the committee approach to design that is perhaps an inevitable outcome of the overdetermination of the space of Ground Zero, where ultimately the politicians are acting as architects.[129] The redesign moves the names above ground, eliminating the underground galleries and leaving the voids and waterfalls in place, and creating space above and below ground for a memorial museum. The elimination of the underground galleries, a primary feature of Arad's concept of contemplative spaces, constituted a kind of evisceration of his design's intent, rendering it almost unrecognizable. As Ouroussoff writes, the redesign was "less a design than an exercise in value engineering . . . a list of names around twin reflecting pools linked to a vast underground museum—a remarkable banality after two years of intense thinking."[130] In 2006, TBWA/Chiat/Day was hired to create a fundraising campaign for the memorial, which deliberately chose not to focus on the images of 9/11. Instead, the campaign shows scenes of everyday life with the question, "Where were you when it happened?" Given the negative publicity over the memorial's cost, the campaign has an uphill battle; its primary tagline is "It's time." It thus attempts to tap into the sense that donations to the memorial might help the process move forward and get unstuck.[131]

These family groups have also loudly and persistently been critics of the plan for naming in the memorial. The fact that the question of how to name the dead sparked volatile debate is not usual in the building of memorials. It is in the stakes of naming that the collective and individual meanings of memorials converge, and how memorials name individuals (which they have only recently done) constitutes the primary statement about the events they remember. In Oklahoma City, the dead are each individually named on bronze chairs and arranged according to where they died. At the Vietnam Veterans Memorial, the names are listed chronologically for when people

FIGURE 102. Plaza parapet of revised design of *Reflecting Absence*, 2006. Rendering by Squared Design Lab. Courtesy of Lower Manhattan Development Corporation. Reproduced with permission.

died, rather than alphabetically as initially proposed.[132] It was Arad's original intent to arrange the names "in no particular order" around the pools, which he later revised to an arrangement of "meaningful adjacencies" that would establish echo relationships between workers and family members, but would be clear only to those who knew them. From the very beginning, though, the firefighters demanded that their names be listed separately and designated by insignia. Others argued that the dead should be listed according to location and the places where they worked, and many family members are refusing to support the memorial until their plan for the names is accepted.[133] In December 2006 a compromise agreement was reached in which Arad's concept of "meaningful adjacencies" was reconfigured so that the names will be grouped according to where someone died, the company they worked for, or the plane they were on. In addition, firefighters and police officers would be grouped by company or precinct. While visitors who know the connections between, for instance, fellow workers, will see many of these groupings, company names and the ages of the dead will not be listed. Many family members were not mollified by this arrangement, and some of them launched an ad campaign in January 2007 to protest.

This raises a set of questions which were central to the debate: Would those who died have wanted to be named in death in relation to the companies where they worked? What of those who were temporary workers, those who hated their jobs? In a certain sense, this explains the fervor with which the firefighter's union has demanded that the firefighters be designated in death by their jobs, because it is the firefighter status that has given their deaths meaning. At the memorial services at the Oklahoma City National Memorial, the names of the dead are read according to the agency they worked for. After ten years, this has a strange ring to it, as if the federal government insisted on reclaiming the dead again and again. Moreover, the World Trade Center memorial is designated to include 2,979 names, of all of the dead who died on 9/11, including those at the Pentagon and on Flight 93 (excluding, of course, the hijackers themselves).

Naming is central to how people make meaning and individualize the dead at memorials, yet naming is always fraught with conflict. For instance, there were disputes about whose names were included on the Vietnam Veterans Memorial (including whether some of the dead had been killed in the proper war zone), and a debate has emerged over how to name those who have died since 9/11 of causes related to it. Naming in a memorial is one means to counter the reality that society awards more value to some lives than others. A name says very little about people's life, their hopes, or the people who loved them. It can, however, function as a reminder of the particular individuality of those lost. In contrast, the media coverage of 9/11 has established a hierarchy of the dead, privileging the stories of public servants, such as firefighters, over office workers, of policemen over security guards, and the stories of those with economic capital over those without, of traders over janitors. In the federal compensation to families, there were huge discrepancies in the valuing of life since the values of economic capital (through equations of potential earning power) rather than need were the basis for compensation. The compensation debate also raised a comparison to the victims of other incidents, such as the Oklahoma City bombing, who were not compensated for their loss.

The dominance of a small yet very vocal group of families in this debate is heightened by their designation of Ground Zero as the site where their loved ones are located. Despite the fact that the site was cleared in the first year, as I discussed in chapter 4, remains continue to be found in the area. Thus, the issue of remains haunts Ground Zero. In this sense, Fresh Kills landfill is the painful countersite to Ground Zero; several family groups are still advocating that the dust at Fresh Kills be removed and placed at Ground Zero, as if it were somehow feasible to separate it from the rubble. In October 2005, those families went to court to convince a judge to "scoop up" the debris at Fresh Kills and return it to the World Trade Center site,

FIGURE 103. Sign at Ground Zero. Photo © Paul Colangelo/Corbis, 2003.

prompting the *New York Post* to call them the "kin who can't let go."[134] The specter of Fresh Kills, of the unretrieved dead, haunts this memorial design, and has produced an awkward hybrid intended to satisfy the needs of both families and tourists.

These demands, which have essentially usurped the strategies of designers, have ultimately produced a context in which the space and scale have been asked to provide significance. Like the height of the Freedom Tower, which is intended not only to provide national symbolism but to speak strength through its immensity, the vast area awarded to the memorial, with its large voids in the footprints, inscribes a great deal of the potential public space as inaccessible, void. It's worth noting that by comparison, some of the most effective memorials and tributes to loss have been small and contained (the area covered by the Vietnam Veterans Memorial's tribute to over fifty-seven thousand dead is tiny compared to the 9/11 memorial design). And, like the Freedom Tower, the memorial will be a site of intense security. The Port Authority and the state have promised to install the latest high-tech equipment there. The site will be patrolled by armed guards and outfitted with "smart cameras" that will try to match faces with databases of known terrorists. The memorial spaces of contemplation will thus exist within a security aesthetic. In April 2006, public concerns about security at the site were increased when a memo by Governor Pataki's senior advisor for counterterrorism, James K. Kallstrom, to LMDC was leaked to the press. In it, Kallstrom noted that it is precisely those aspects of the design that "encourage and engender public interaction" that "constitute vulnerabilities from a security perspective."[135]

The evisceration of the memorial design, and the accompanying shift in emphasis to the thirty-thousand-square-foot Memorial Museum, makes clear that the real focus of visitors at the site will be the museum rather than any contemplative memorial space. The huge voids of the design, encompassing the two footprints as well as the space around them, blandly listing names alongside the pools, and the increased security context of the site dictate that it will be a place ruled by memory, in which design innovation is absent. This triumph of explanatory exhibition over contemplative spaces that are potentially open for interpretation represents a particular kind of narrowing of the meaning at Ground Zero.

MUSEUMS OF MEMORY

The initial master plan for Ground Zero incorporated several cultural institutions at the site, including dance theaters and exhibition spaces, as a means of reconceiving it as both a commercial and a cultural site. Over the years that the design and memorial were chosen, two museums were planned for the site: the World Trade Center Memorial Museum, which will be integrated with the *Reflecting Absence* design and which will use artifacts to tell the story of what happened in New York on 9/11, and the International Freedom Center, which was intended to address issues of freedom more broadly throughout world history and which, amid much controversy, was canceled by Governor Pataki in September 2005. These two museum plans reflect the desire to see the site as a place where pedagogy can take place, and like the memorial center at Oklahoma City, both raise questions about how pedagogy can take place at sites of loss.

Nothing makes the difficulties of this more clear than the controversy that took place over the planned International Freedom Center. The Freedom Center was planned as a museum to the concept of freedom throughout world history, with the naïve belief that Ground Zero could be not only the site of mourning but also a site of pedagogy about world events. But the plans to create a museum to the abstract concept of freedom were as misguided as building a Freedom Tower there. Despite its intentions to situate 9/11 in a broader context, the center raised thorny issues of attempting to teach at a site charged so intensely with mourning. Predictably, the center provoked ire from the well-organized family groups, who staged a number of protests at the site. The protests were sparked by an editorial in the *Wall Street Journal*, "The Great Ground Zero Heist," written by Debra Burlingame. Claiming that the center would be an anti-American diatribe about Abu Ghraib, with an appointed board including a "Who's Who of the human rights, Guantanamo obsessed world," including the financier George Soros and the Columbia professor Eric Foner, Burlingame wrote that dispensing this history "over the ashes of Ground Zero is like creating a Museum of Tolerance over the sunken graves of the USS Arizona." [136] In addition, families protested the inclusion of the Drawing Center, which was originally intended to be housed in the cultural building, because it was not "9/11-related"; subsequently, Governor Pataki capitalized on the controversy by criticizing an exhibit the center had previously held that contained controversial images of 9/11. The *New York Times* stepped into the fray with an editorial advocating keeping "Ground Zero Free," which received a large number of chastising letters from readers. [137] When the center was canceled, the *New York Post* declared "Good Riddance" and claimed credit for itself in the banning of the "America-haters." [138]

That the cancellation of the Freedom Center was censorious was clear, though anyone with knowledge of the history of memorial museums could have guessed the outcome. When Pataki declared in June 2005, "We will not tolerate anything on that site that denigrates America, denigrates New York or freedom, or denigrates the sacrifice and courage that the heroes showed on Sept. 11," he raised the specter that even commercial interests would find themselves under attack from the increasingly politically powerful group of family members who had garnered moral authority at the site. The *New York Times* reporter David Dunlap speculated, "It is not too far-fetched to imagine Borders returning to the trade center, where it once had a large, well-regarded bookstore. Would it be at liberty to sell DVD's of 'Fahrenheit 9/11' or books by the historian Eric Foner?" [139]

One of the ironies of the debate over the Freedom Center was that many of the family members who were opposed to it began to argue that their loved ones had *not* died for freedom; rather, they had died because they were in the wrong place at the wrong time. One relative stated, "These people didn't die for freedom—they were murdered," and Charles Wolf, whose wife died at the World Trade Center, said, "It's a hook to turn 9/11 people who went to work that day into part of this bigger idea for freedom. My wife was not a goddamn freedom fighter. All she was fighting for was a chance that we might move to a bigger apartment." [140]

FIGURE 104. Design for canceled Freedom Center, 2005. Courtesy of Lower Manhattan Development Corporation. Reproduced with permission.

In many ways, the battle over the Freedom Center clarified the mission of the Memorial Museum, which is to be housed above and below ground and will be integrated with the memorial. The museum, which is slated to open in 2010, will house many artifacts, potentially including the last steel beam taken from Ground Zero, from many collections, including those currently housed at Hangar 17 at JFK Airport by the Port Authority. Other potential objects include tableware from the Windows on the World restaurant, parts of the airplanes, a cell phone used by Mayor Giuliani, remnants of the bronze Rodin sculptures from the Cantor Fitzgerald offices, the 9/11 quilt, and fire-fighter gear.[141] Because the museum is under the control of the private Memorial Foundation, it will have to present a legal petition to acquire these artifacts to the Port Authority, which has legal ownership of them. Finding the right tone for the museum is a challenge, as the example of Oklahoma City has shown, since the site is already fraught with so many agendas. Alice Greenwald, director of the museum, characterizes its key messages as chronicling the events of 9/11, emphasizing that 9/11 happened to everyone and that everyone has a 9/11 story, that it was an event of loss—loss of life,

FIGURE 105. Memorial Hall, 2006. Rendering by Davis Brody Bond, LLC. Courtesy of Lower Manhattan Development Corporation. Reproduced with permission.

loss of community life, loss of loved ones, a spiritual loss, the loss of buildings, and the loss of a sense of invulnerability in the United States—that it is fundamentally a global event and that it brought out the full range, the best and the worst, of humanity. It's crucial, she notes, that the museum is not disembodied from the place where it resides. The lesson from the Freedom Center controversy, says Greenwald, is that the museum has to establish its credibility as a memorial that can interpret 9/11 before it can begin to talk about other events. "It is not exceptional, in order to say what we can learn from it we will have to extrapolate to other events."[142] It will be key to its experience that the museum will have a room (under the supervision of the medical examiner's office) that will house unidentified remains, and that it will have a separate room for families. Visitors will not be able to enter the room holding remains, but they will know it's there, like the remains in the tombs of unknown soldiers. The museum will also, inevitably, have a gift shop, since retail has become an integral part of the memorial and museum experience, driven in part by economic necessity.

The museum is not scheduled to be opened until 2010, but there are several interpretive sites that have emerged in the interim. The most ambitious

CHAPTER 5

FIGURE 106. Design for Memorial Museum, 2006. Rendering by Davis Brody Bond, LLC. Courtesy of Lower Manhattan Development Corporation. Reproduced with permission.

of these is the Tribute Center, a visitors center next door to the firehouse that now houses the firefighter memorial, opened in September 2006, and that stands in for the still-to-be-designed museum. Created by the September 11th Families Association, with funding from the LMDC and the Port Authority, the center defines itself as an "interim destination" for people searching for something meaningful at the site. The Tribute Center has several galleries, including one depicting daily life in the World Trade Center and one that is a tribute to those lost. Family members were asked to send the center something to remember their loved ones by. Interestingly, while this produced some expected objects (firefighter jackets, mangled artifacts from the site, ID cards, posters of the missing), it also contains objects that are biting, including a death certificate, dated October 2001, for Scott Johnson, whose body was not found, with the cause of death listed on the official form as "homicide." Along with the firefighter memorial, the Tribute Center participates in a kind of alternative interpretive context, one that is dictated by victims' surrogates (firefighters and families) on their own terms.

The Tribute Center also runs twice-daily tours of the site by volunteers who have some connection to the events of 9/11, taking visitors around the

FIGURE 107. Tribute Center coffee mug.

periphery of Ground Zero as guides recount the events of that day. Ground
Zero is thus the site of a constant replaying of the stories of 9/11. This is one
of the ways that grief is played out: through a retelling and replaying. Here,
as in the architectural designs that remake the towers over and over, as in
the overinvestment in the footprints, as in the fears that the site will lose its
sense of sacredness, we see enactments of grief in its many forms.

It is most likely that the World Trade Center Memorial Museum will es-
chew the kind of direct reenactment that exists at the Oklahoma City National Memorial, where visitors are subjected to a replay via audiotape of the
bombing. Yet, the dominance of the museum over the memorial at Ground
Zero makes clear that telling and retelling the story will be the primary
mode there. As I have noted, reenactment has been a dominant form of
remembrance for 9/11, often as a kind of compulsive repetition. As with the
numerous reenactments of the Oklahoma City photograph of the firefighter
holding Baylee Almon, the reenactments of 9/11 have often taken the form
of redemptive rescripting, though with fewer of the religious overtones. As

time passes, the range of tones encompassed by these reenactments will continue to shift.

It may be that the space of Ground Zero cannot yet be reconceived in terms that are not about reenacting 9/11, nor could be for a long time; that the sense of loss in this place, where those who died were never found, constitutes a particular kind of tarrying with grief. Yet the memorial design in its final eviscerated state seems likely to stand as testimony to the fact that the process of memorialization was rushed and without vision. As Nicolai Ouroussoff writes, "At ground zero, the gush of information and emotion comes dangerously close to kitsch. It raises the question of whether a worthwhile memorial, or urban reconstruction, can be created within such a short time frame."[143] In many ways the rebuilding of Ground Zero has produced a set of patriotic and, ultimately, provincial discourses, that will define lower Manhattan as a place that looks backward, toward its moment of trauma. Ultimately, the exceptionalist narratives that have come to dominate 9/11 and Ground Zero have meant that the city is being rebuilt through the demands of simplistic symbolism and security design, and that the vast energy of the architectural community, which may result in a few interesting skyscrapers, will largely be absent at the memorial and museum. Finally, it seems that security will be the aesthetic most easy to read at the rebuilt site. As Goldberger writes, "It is a remarkable message to send the world—yes, we rebuild, but we do it by barricading ourselves behind bollards and solid concrete walls and if that is not enough, then we make sure that any culture we show the public here is fully prechecked for controversy. It's a dismal vision of what freedom means. . . . Then again, it isn't much of a vision of what architecture means, either."[144]

CULTURAL MEMORY AND CULTURAL LABOR

Reenactment does not have to take the form of kitsch or simply reiterate codes of patriotism. Strategies of remaking and reenacting can also be used to recode and renarrate history within new frameworks, ones that incorporate irony and political critique. While the repetition of traumatic images can be seen as a kind of stasis, in which the image of trauma is repeated in an increasingly kitsch form of politics and so-called universal emotions are packaged and sold, other forms of repetition can jolt. In an ad campaign produced by Médicos del Mundo, a European nonprofit, the image of the top of the north tower starting to collapse, its antenna tilting to the side as the building begins to pancake downward, is repeated again and again, intercut with the days of the week: lunes, mardes, and so on. After repeating several times, the text reads (in Spanish), "In some countries, every day is September 11. In Subsaharan Africa more than 3000 people die daily from lack of medical attention." The repetition of the image in this ad is effectively harrowing. There is a distant roar and human voices screaming in horror in the background, and the immensity of the collapse is disturbing. Yet the text effectively argues against the exceptionalism produced by the spectacle of the image. It is a reminder, rhetorically pungent, of the ways that some human lives count more than others and the role that spectacle plays in that equation.

Marianne Hirsch writes that while the repetition of certain images can constitute a kind of traumatic fixation, the redeployment of images in new contexts can facilitate a working through of trauma: "It is only when they are redeployed, in new texts and new contexts, that they regain a capacity to enable a postmemorial working through."[145] In these ways, they can facilitate a particular kind of cultural labor.

This labor, and this redeployment in new texts and contexts, in Hirsch's terms, can be seen in the work of the comic book artist Art Spiegelman, who lives in lower Manhattan and who spent three years after 9/11 producing a series of full-page, broadsheet-size, color comics about his traumatic experience that day. Spiegelman's comics were first serialized in a number of alternative publications, including many non-U.S. magazines, such as *Die Zeit*, the *Forward*, *Courrier International*, the *London Review of Books*, *Internazionale*, the *LA Weekly*, the *Chicago Weekly*, and *World War Three Illustrated*, when they were considered to be too controversial by editors of mainstream publications in the censorious cultural context immediately after 9/11. He notes that the climate changed considerably by the time the series was done, when the *New York Times*, which had previously rejected the series, as did the *New Yorker* and the *New York Review of Books*, ran a feature on him in fall 2003 and included a panel it had refused to publish two years before.[146]

Spiegelman's tortured work evokes the compulsion to reenact and the confusion of how to think about 9/11 in the context of a U.S.-led war in Iraq. His character states, "Doomed to drag this damned albatross around my neck and compulsively retell the calamities of Sept. 11 to anyone who'll still listen" as the eagle he is dragging around squawks, "Everything's changed! Awk!" In its adept mix of past and present, including the transformation of Spiegelman and his wife into cartoon characters inspired by historical comic figures with the burning towers stuck on their heads, *In the Shadow of*

FIGURE 108. From *In the Shadow of No Towers* by Art Spiegelman. © 2004 by Art Spiegelman. Used by permission of Pantheon Books, a division of Random House, Inc. Reprinted with permission of the Wylie Agency, Inc.

No Towers is a working-through of Spiegelman's own damaged psyche, his need to relive and repeat the images and feelings of that day. He reenacts what he saw that day, what he saw on television, and what he didn't see: "He is haunted by the images he didn't witness . . . images of people tumbling to the streets below . . . especially one man (according to a neighbor) who executed a graceful Olympic dive as his last living act." He struggles with his inability to get past this repetition: "Many months have passed. It's time to move on. . . . I guess I'm finally up to about September 20 . . . but I'd feel like such a jerk if a new disaster strikes while I'm still chipping away at the last one."

One of the powerful effects of Spiegelman's book is its portrayal of the dilemma of the subject who is stuck in the moment of trauma yet who wants to resist the way that stasis is exploited politically. He depicts himself with both Osama bin Laden and President Bush towering over his desk, "equally terrorized by al-Qaeda and by his own government." His book integrates his own mourning—even his newly found affection for "the rascals" (the missing towers)—with his own conflicted recognition of the ironies of post-9/11 life. In a segment entitled "An Upside Down World," a cast of animal characters follows a cartoonish Bush upside down across the top of the frame,

FIGURE 109. From *In the Shadow of No Towers* by Art Spiegelman. © 2004 by Art Spiegelman. Used by permission of Pantheon Books, a division of Random House, Inc. Reprinted with permission of the Wylie Agency, Inc.

yelling "Redemption! Pre-emption!" Spiegelman's character says, "Despair slows me down, so I worry whether NYC or I will still be around to see if my page was well-printed." The image of the falling towers embedded in his mind is repeated from page to page, until it becomes the subject of his own nostalgia: "He's starting to get nostalgic about his near-death experience back in September 01. . . . But why did those provincial American flags have to sprout out of the embers of Ground Zero? Why not a Globe?" These evocations of involuntary memory are juxtaposed with Spiegelman's anger at the ways the Bush administration deployed a rhetoric of 9/11 to marshal support first for the war in Afghanistan and then war in Iraq.

Spiegelman's large panels produce a layered set of narratives within each large page. In panel 2, for instance, the two shadows of the towers peek through underneath the panels, and the style of various image elements evokes early comics, photographs, and newsprint. As his identity shifts, Spiegelman represents himself as an early cartoon figure (with a burning tower on his head) and as a mouse, as he did in his well-known work, *Maus*. The motif of the burning towers repeats from page to page, growing more impressionistic each time. In the last panel, the burning towers are beginning to fade ("The towers have come to loom far larger than life . . . but they

FIGURE 110. From *In the Shadow of No Towers* by Art Spiegelman. © 2004 by Art Spiegelman. Used by permission of Pantheon Books, a division of Random House, Inc. Reprinted with permission of the Wylie Agency, Inc.

seem to get smaller every day. . . . Happy Anniversary"), as if their memory were less vibrant.

The book reflects on the nonexceptionalism of the destruction of 9/11 by situating Spiegelman's renditions of his experience of trauma that day amid a group of early twentieth-century comics, such as the Katzenjammer Kids, the Kinder Kids, Krazy Kat, and Little Nemo. Integrating the style of these early comics into his own pages, and then following his own images with reproductions of the early comics, he points to the fact that the destruction of the city has been a long-standing cultural theme. Indeed, as the work of Max Page and others has pointed out, the history of the imaginary destruction of New York City is a long one, in which the urban landscape itself seems to acquire meaning, if not an affirmation of its importance, through its imagined demise.[147] In *In the Shadow of No Towers*, haunted as it is by the destruction of the twin towers, this is most poignantly rendered in Winsor McCay's 1907 "Little Nemo in Slumberland," in which the young boy Nemo travels in his nighttime dreams through the nocturnal landscape of lower Manhattan with his companions. Several stories high, Nemo crawls the sides of skyscrapers and clings to the tops of buildings. He is lost, though he wonders why none of the diminutive people on the street helps them find their way: "These people ought to know who we are and tell that we are here." As his companion Flip runs across the skyline to greet them, the buildings crash and fall under his feet. It is a compelling artifact, evocative and mysterious yet also casual in its depiction of the violence of the crumbling urban landscape.

In the Shadow of No Towers demonstrates a kind of reworking and wrestling with memory that can take place within compulsive repetition: Spiegelman repeats and repeats the image until it is subsumed within other images and, importantly, ironized and contextualized. Making comics is labor-intensive, and in that labor is a certain reconfiguration of the sense of trauma. Spiegelman wrestles control of the image's power by remaking it over and over again. Like the artists of Oklahoma City who remade Baylee Almon's image, he recodes the image in order to mediate its power over him. Yet unlike those artists, he produces not an image of reassuring religious redemption but a complex demand to historically contextualize the discourses of 9/11 and an ironic commentary on how distorted the remembrance of 9/11 has become.

Repetition and reenactment can work to foster certain kinds of banality; after one sits through the Oklahoma City reenactment a few times, for instance, it loses its shock impact, and, by extension, the bombing comes to seem mundane. This quality of repetition can be seen as an achievement of boredom. Thus, it could be argued that kitschy souvenirs and the experience of reenactments, whether in souvenirs, photographic remakes, or architecture, can provide comfort in their familiarity, comfort that ultimately produces banality and perhaps the bored need to move on. Hal Foster writes that Andy Warhol deployed repetition in his work as a means to work toward a deadening affect. He quotes Warhol as stating, "When you see a gruesome picture over and over again, it doesn't really have any effect," what Foster terms "both a draining of significance and a defending against affect." Foster argues that Warhol's repetitions of violent images (a burning car, an accident, an execution) in his *Death in America* series of the early 1960s actually produce traumatic effects while fending them off: "Somehow in these repetitions . . . several contradictory things occur at the same time: a warding away of traumatic significance *and* an opening out to it, a defending against traumatic affect *and* a producing of it."[148] This points to the contradictory nature of repetitions, how they produce both a heightening and a flattening of emotion, a catharsis and a mundane sense of something familiar.

Which returns me to my snow globes. For each, the intended gesture is to give the globe a shake, to temporarily fill it with a kind of metaphoric dust, and then to let it settle back down. Each demands a constant animation, a repetition of the shaking of the globe world. Yet the point is that it returns to its original state, that the dynamism of the shaken globe settles down into calmness. This is the desire embedded in the snow globe, that it is a miniature world in which the chaos of being shaken up will predictably settle down. This is also the promise of the kitsch object: that the good feelings that come from acknowledging the pain and grief will make everything better, that innocence can be regained. Whether this takes place in the intended effect of reenacting 9/11 through architecture or in the purchase and display of a snow globe souvenir as a means of feeling connected to the events of the Oklahoma City bombing or the events of 9/11, what matters is what such gestures leave out. The past remains in the present, it is integrated into our lives, we live with it every day. How we choose to make sense of that integration makes all the difference.

CONCLUSION

Six months after 9/11, Afghan war rugs that depicted the events of 9/11 began to appear on the streets of New York City. Emerging from a tradition of integrating war themes into traditional Afghan weaving styles, which began in the 1980s during the Soviet Union's occupation of Afghanistan, the 9/11 war rugs are produced by rug makers who often spend six weeks to make one rug. Many of them depict the twin towers on fire, with the planes approaching, and a combination of the U.S. and Afghan flags. Like the snow globes with which I began this book, these rugs combine several time frames simultaneously. The towers are already in flames to signal the moment of catastrophe, yet the airplanes are still approaching, to explain how it happened. Some rugs include a U.S. aircraft carrier and a map of Afghanistan, to make connections between the war in Afghanistan and the events of 9/11 that put it into motion. Others include helicopters, F-16 planes, U.S. tanks, and missiles. The direct political messages of these rugs are often quite ambiguous. Most have misspelled words, and most signal an allegiance between the people of the United States and the people of Afghanistan, yet others appear to depict ambiguous meanings of the twin towers burning. On one rug, the words "twin terrors" could mean many things: that the towers became twin sites of terrorism; that once hit, the

FIGURE 111. Afghan war rug of 9/11. Courtesy of Kevin Sudeith, warrug.com.

towers became terrifying; or that the towers were themselves, already, terrors. In the translation, of course, many nuances can be lost or inserted after the fact.

Most of the Afghan rug makers do not make war rugs; only about 1 percent of the rugs made there have war themes. Whereas during the Soviet conflict, rugs were often used to tell stories of conflict that the weavers had themselves experienced, the 9/11 rugs are much less personal in their intent. These rugs are at once tourist art and forums for history telling. They are produced for a new, global market, and production increased when the market demand for them grew. They are often made by poor rural craftspeople who are not interested in politics so much as they are interested in making a living. Their primary meaning is thus not as political statements but as consumer objects produced for a global market.

FIGURE 112. Rug in shop in Kandahar, Afghanistan, August 6, 2002, made by a Herat carpet weaver who visited New York after 9/11. AP Photo/Tomas van Houtryve.

When the rugs first began to appear for sale on the streets in early 2003 in New York, they produced outrage and disgust. It was too close to the sense of horror of that day; the rugs were seen to be too kitschy and too strange, and many of their more ambiguous meanings were interpreted as rejoicing in the towers' destruction.[1] Their meanings were too easily read as anti-American at a time when American culture was intensely censorious. Since that time, Afghan weavers and the rug sellers have found a market for the rugs not only for export to the United States, but with American soldiers stationed in Afghanistan. Indeed, some soldiers have become buyers for U.S. dealers, essentially acting as middle men between them and local weavers.[2] One weaver who was interviewed for an exhibition of war weavings stated that while many of her aunts weave rugs that express their own memories of war, she weaves them "because they will sell," after her husband discovered that they would get higher prices at the marketplace. "We sold the rugs in the bazaar to the people, commanders, for example, who were coming from foreign countries at that time."[3] The rugs sell for anywhere from $150 to $9,000, depending on their size and intricacy, and they have now acquired collectable status, selling on eBay, at flea markets, and in art galleries. Kevin Sudeith, who sells the war rugs, had trouble initially selling the rugs in New York, but he states, "After 9/11, people's interest in war rugs went up dramatically. People suddenly knew a lot more about Afghanistan and they wanted the rugs as a way to remember 9/11. Many people buy two at a time—one to use and the other to show to their children, as a way to talk about the event, much like a document."[4]

With their fetishizing of military hardware (easily adaptable to warp and weft), these rugs depict the relentless, ongoing presence of war in this conflict-ridden part of the world. Yet the 9/11 rugs also attempt to make connections between the destruction of the twin towers and the U.S. war against the Taliban that followed. They situate the destruction of the towers in relation to longer histories of global conflict. In rudimentary ways, with sometimes crude iconography, they can be seen as objects that embody both cosmopolitanism and kitsch. In the world imagined in these rugs, one defined by global conflict and produced for a global economy of tourism, kitsch, and war, the world is connected by the circulation of objects through formal and informal networks. Thus, the Afghan war rugs bear a relationship to the flags sent by the Oklahoma City National Memorial to soldiers in Afghanistan and to the souvenirs that circulate at Ground Zero that were made in China. To connect these events as part of a broader context of terrorism is to see that terrorism is part of a much longer and tragic history of human conflict that has its roots in colonialism, Western imperialism, and tribal conflict. It is to see how violence grows out of disempowerment.

It has been my intent in this book to examine the ways that American culture processes, makes sense of, and smoothes over loss, and the consequences of what I see as the U.S. tourist relationship to history and global conflict. While consumerism is a key aspect of this tourist relationship, it is not simply a problem that needs to be eliminated or rectified (nor could it be), so much as a process that needs to be examined and understood. Consumerism in today's global economic context is, as the example of the Afghan war rugs makes clear, a varied and complex practice that can promote and define diverse kinds of engagements with the world. Yet it has been and remains a fundamental aspect of consumerism that it makes promises about states of being (happiness, fulfillment, safety, preparedness) that it cannot keep. It is possible to participate in acts of consumerism while knowing that these promises are false, to participate in what one could call ironic, self-reflexive consumerism. We buy the duct tape even though we know it won't protect us, and we buy the teddy bear even though we know it cannot take away the pain. Perhaps ironic consumerism acknowledges that the consumption of comfort culture can effectively promise comfort but will never achieve more than a superficial veneer over the pervasive sense of loss brought on not simply by the ongoing cycle of violence—from Kabul to New York to London, from Waco to Oklahoma City to Falluja, from Terre Haute to Baghdad, from Madrid to Beirut—but also in the ongoing struggles of those people, so evocatively depicted in the attempts to proclaim citizenship in the Oklahoma City Memorial Center, just trying to get through the day, to provide for their families and to make a small bit of meaning somewhere, somehow.

The production of innocence (and its manifestation in the marketing of comfort culture) and the circulation of irony work in tension together. What does irony accomplish? If, as I have posited throughout this book, irony can be a counterpart to kitsch, then what does it offer that the prescribed and limited forms of kitsch cannot? It is possible that irony can offer a pose from which to understand the arbitrariness of daily life, the unpredictability of tragedy, and the meaninglessness of so much loss. It allows us to see that things are not what they seem to be. In order to see them as they are, we must look so much harder.

Yet, I write this book with a sense of urgency, in which such an ironic pose seems so inadequate. As the global conflict in the post-9/11 years continues to escalate, the incoherence of American public discourse grows. As the United States continues to perpetrate increasingly brutal, destructive, and misguided foreign policies, the American urge to seek comfort in kitsch artifacts and consumer products that promise safety and to acquiesce to brutal domestic policies remains unexamined. These contradictions converge in the complex politics of memory and affect—where a comfort culture sells itself as the answer to loss, as the correct set of emotional registers for those who are grieving. All will be okay, it promises; this will make you feel better. We need to examine this promise of comfort in order to see past its empty promises.

The shadow city to the contexts I have discussed in this book, to Okla-

FIGURE 113. Afghan war rug of Iraq. Courtesy of Kevin Sudeith, warrug.com.

homa City and New York and Washington, D.C., is of course Baghdad. The Afghan rug weavers wasted no time in adding an Iraqi war rug to their set of template designs. Here we see Iraq as a tumble of war equipment: helicopters, bombs, grenades, and tanks. What's missing, because they are so difficult to weave effectively, are the people. The tens of thousands of Iraqis who attempt to survive day to day in the horror of escalating war, and the tens of thousands who have lost their lives because another nation managed to sell its false promises to a cowed public (and set of politicians) because they themselves felt like victims and were scared. This is the cost of the selling of innocence and comfort, of the capacity of the aggressors to see themselves as threatened and victimized. These are the stakes, finally, in why we must look at the practices of remembrance, the consequences of the equation of consumerism with citizenship, the political acquiescence that is enabled by kitsch objects of comfort, and the constant and consistent erasure of the vast majority of U.S. citizens and residents from public discourses. American culture clings tenaciously to its tourism of history, to its belief that the world and its ills are somehow elsewhere. To see these connections is thus to demand that Americans bring the world into focus. These are the stakes in seeing those global connections, connections that are ironically demonstrated to us in the smallest and seemingly least significant of consumer objects: the snow globe made in China and sold at Ground Zero, the teddy bear made in Korea that is left at the fence at the Oklahoma City National Memorial and then sent to refugee Iraqi children in Jordan, the postcard of the twin towers that is stuck on a fence to reinsert them into the skyline, the rug made by a weaver in Afghanistan that depicts the war in Iraq that is sold to a U.S. soldier who simply hopes to go home.

NOTES

INTRODUCTION

1. Erica Rand discusses an Ellis Island snow globe in her book *The Ellis Island Snow Globe*. For Rand, the Ellis Island snow globe is emblematic of the mix of consumer culture, nation, sexuality, and multiculturalism. She sees it as the epitome of the simplifying aspects of souvenir culture of national history. She reports that she joked to her date, "Honey, when we get there, I want you to buy me an Ellis Island snow globe," to which she replied, "That would be like having snow globes at a concentration camp" (2). Yet when they arrive, they see that indeed the gift shop does have snow globes, erasers, and backscratchers.

2. I am indebted to Jani Scandura for first pointing this out to me at an American Studies Association panel on the topic of kitsch.

3. Olalquiaga, *The Artificial Kingdom*, 63–65.

4. I am grateful to Barbara Rose Haum for pointing out this quality of snow globes to me.

5. Glassner, *The Culture of Fear*.

6. Daniel Harris, *Cute, Quaint, Hungry and Romantic*, 10. Harris sees these teddy bears as part of a culture of "cute sex."

7. I learned this from one of the Salvation Army volunteers who is working as a tour guide for the Tribute Center at Ground Zero.

8. E-mail correspondence with Helen Stiefmiller, collections manager, Oklahoma City National Memorial archive, November 7, 2006.

9. See Kaplan, "Left Alone with America," 11–13.

10. On new ways of understanding tourism, see Urry, *The Tourist Gaze*; Kirschenblatt-Gimblett, *Destination Culture*; Desmond, *Staging Tourism*; Strain, *Public Places*; Crouch and Lübbren, *Visual Culture*; and Lasansky and McLaren, *Architecture and Tourism*.

11. MacCannell, *The Tourist*, 1, 8.

12. See Kirschenblatt-Gimblett, *Destination Culture*; and Desmond, *Staging Tourism*.

13. MacCannell, *The Tourist*, 10.

14. See Lennon and Foley, *Dark Tourism*; and Lippard, "The Fall," 72.

15. See Couldry, *Media Rituals*.

16. See Weeks, *Gettysburg*. See also Shaffer, *See America First*.

17. See Breen, *The Marketplace of Revolution*.

18. Lears, "From Salvation to Self-Realization."

19. Cohen, *A Consumers' Republic*.

20. Billig, *Banal Nationalism*, chapter 3.

21. Noble, *The End of American History*. See also Lipsitz, *American Studies*, chapter 2.

22. Noble, *Death of a Nation*, 296.

23. See Calinescu, "Kitsch and Modernity," 234.

24. See McDonald, "Masscult and Midcult."

25. Broch, "Notes on the Problem of Kitsch," 49.

26. Calinescu, "Kitsch and Modernity," 243.

27. Ibid., 229, 237.

28. Greenberg, "Avant-Garde and Kitsch," 12.

29. Calinescu, "Kitsch and Modernity," 258.

30. Olalquiaga, *The Artificial Kingdom*, 291–92.

31. Clifford, *The Predicament of Culture*, 224.

32. Giesz, "Kitsch-man as Tourist," 167, 169.

33. Daniel Harris, "Kiddie Kitsch."

34. Greenberg, "Avant-Garde and Kitsch," 20.

35. Kundera, *The Unbearable Lightness of Being*, 248–51.

36. Daniel Harris, "Making Kitsch from AIDS," 55.

37. Ehrenreich, "Welcome to Cancerland," 46–47, 50.

38. Rebecca Traister, "Breast Cancer Barbie," *Salon.com*, October 3, 2006.

39. Foster, "Yellow Ribbons," 29.

40. Kundera, *The Unbearable Lightness of Being*, 251.

41. Berlant, "The Subject of True Feeling," 53.

42. Freud, "Remembering, Repeating."

43. This is the key aspect of the trauma/dissociation model, which was developed by the early psychoanalyst Pierre Janet and is ascribed to by contemporary psychiatrists such as Judith Herman, in which traumatic memory is depicted as prenarrative. This prenarrative reenactment is described in Janet's well-known case of Irene, a young woman who was disassociated from her mother's death and compulsively reenacted her actions on the night her mother died. Janet helped this woman to narrate the story of this night. This case is described in van der Kolk and van der Hart, "The Intrusive Past."

44. Brison, *Aftermath*, 54.

45. Butler, *Precarious Life*, 30.

46. See LeDuff, *Work and Other Sins*, 298. LeDuff's story about Aidan Fontana, whose father, Dave Fontana, was a firefighter killed at the World Trade Center, and whose mother, Marian, has become a well-known advocate for the families, was first run in the *New York Times*.

47. Kaplan, *The Anarchy of Empire*, 16.

CHAPTER 1: CONSUMING FEAR AND SELLING SECURITY

1. Lori Wagner, quoted in Ginia Bellafante, "Sell That Dress: Back to Basics in Spring Advertising," *New York Times*, February 5, 2002, B8.
2. Stamelman, "September 11," 18.
3. Campbell, *Writing Security*, 3.
4. Williams, *Empire*, 113.
5. Cohen, *A Consumers' Republic*, 7, 401–10.
6. Morley, *Home Territories*, 3.
7. See Dyer, *Harvest of Rage*.
8. The SPLC has numerous informative intelligence reports on its website: http://www.splcenter.org. See also Steve Johnson, "10 Years after Terror, Radical Right Still a Threat," MSNBC, April 18, 2005, http://www.msnbc.msn.com/id/7408353.
9. Paranoia can also be understood as a kind of knowing. There has been much recent analysis of the degree to which Freud's theory is itself one of paranoia, that the practice of psychoanalysis in its search for overreaching narratives and connection is a paranoid theory. See Farrell, *Freud's Paranoid Quest*. On the question of what it means to take the position of paranoid knowing, Eve Sedgwick has written most persuasively; see "Paranoid Reading," 4.
10. Hofstadter, *The Paranoid Style*, 29. For an interesting analysis of Hofstadter's theories and their impact, see Fenster, *Conspiracy Theories*, chapter 1.
11. For discussion of cultural paranoia as a methodology for examining the interconnectedness of political and epistemological elements, see O'Donnell, "Engendering Paranoia," and *Latent Destinies*.
12. See P. Knight, *Conspiracy Culture*.
13. Gallop Poll Monthly, referenced in Linenthal, *The Unfinished Bombing*, 79.
14. For discussion of the conspiracy theories around 9/11, see Murphy, "The Seekers"; Will Sullivan, "Viewing 9/11 from a Grassy Knoll," *U.S. News and World Report*, September 11, 2006, 39–40; and Sales, "Click Here for Conspiracy."
15. Berlant, "The Theory of Infantile Citizenship," 27–28.
16. Hofstadter, *The Paranoid Style*, 3.
17. See *Special Report: Paranoia as Patriotism: Far-Right Influences on the Militia Movement* (Anti-Defamation League, 1996); and Dees, *The Gathering Storm*.
18. Dyer, *Harvest of Rage*, 174.
19. Terry Nichols, quoted in ibid., 220. The Michigan militia is one of the largest, with six thousand members at its peak. See the "False Patriots Timeline" on the SPLC website, http://www.splcenter.org.
20. "False Patriots Timeline."
21. "Patriots for Profit," Southern Poverty Law Center Intelligence Report, spring 1999, http://splcenter.org.
22. Mike Tharp and William J. Holstein, "Mainstreaming the Militia," *U.S. News and World Report* 122.15 (April 21, 1997): 24.
23. Freud, "On Narcissism," 95.
24. Michel and Herbeck, *American Terrorist*, 133.

25. Glassner, *The Culture of Fear*.

26. U.S. Department of Justice, Bureau of Justice Statistics, "Prison and Jail Inmates at Midyear 2003" (May 2004), NCJ 203947; see http://www.ojp.usdoj.gov. See also "The Sentencing Project," http://www.sentencingproject.org; M. Brown, "'Setting the Conditions.'"

27. Hallinan, *Going up the River*. See also Peter T. Kilborn, "Rural Towns Turn to Prisons to Reignite Their Economies," *New York Times*, August 1, 2001, A1.

28. Hallinan, *Going up the River*.

29. Gilmore, *Golden Gulag*, 23.

30. Nicholas Kulish, "Crime Pays: Since Census Counts Convicts, Some Towns Can't Get Enough," *Wall Street Journal*, August 9, 2001, A1, A6.

31. M. Brown, "'Setting the Conditions,'" 987, 989.

32. Lockard, "Social Fear."

33. Heller, "Introduction: Consuming 9/11," in *The Selling of 9/11*, 3.

34. Edward Rothstein, "Attacks on U.S. Challenge Postmodern True Believers," *New York Times*, September 22, 2001. See also Stanley Kurtz, "Postmodernism Kills," *National Review*, August 12, 2002, http://www.nationalreview.com.

35. Wayne Friedman and Richard Linnett, "Commercial-Free TV: Cost $400 Mil," *Advertising Age* 72.38 (2001): 3. They reported $378 million in losses, while the *Wall Street Journal* estimated $320 million. Venessa O'Connell, "TV Networks Cut $320 Million of Ads in Crisis," *Wall Street Journal*, September 19, 2001, B5.

36. Spigel, "Entertainment Wars," 236–37.

37. Scanlon, "'Your Flag Decal,'" 176.

38. Ibid., 177.

39. S. Willis, *Portents of the Real*, 20.

40. Spiegelman, *In the Shadow of No Towers*, 7.

41. Gitlin, *The Intellectuals*, 129.

42. Scanlon, "'Your Flag Decal,'" 177.

43. Davis, "The Flames of New York," 11. This essay was originally published in *New Left Review* 12 (November/December 2001).

44. Leslie Kaufman, "Consumer Spending Returning to Normal," *New York Times*, September 19, 2001, C1.

45. James Gerstenzang, "Response to Terror: Bush Works to Get a Point Across: Time for Life to Return to Normal," *Los Angeles Times*, September 29, 2001, A3.

46. At various times of heightened security, such as the period before the beginning of the Iraq War and at times of security alert, there is a focus on Disneyland as a potential target. See Connie Skipitares, "California Theme Parks Tighten Security," *Knight Ridder Business News*, March 27, 2003, 1.

47. John Lancaster, "The Homeland Shopping Network," *Washington Post*, November 1, 2001, C1.

48. Louis Uchitelle, "Why Americans Must Keep Spending," *New York Times*, December 1, 2003, C1. Uchitelle states that in 2003, with consumer debt at a record level of almost $8 trillion, government outlays were $2.1 trillion and business investment $1.2 trillion, whereas consumer spending was $7.6 trillion.

49. Gerstenzang, "Response to Terror."

50. Stefano Hatfield, "New Boundaries for Advertisers," *Guardian*, September 19, 2001, http://www.guardian.co.uk.

51. "Judging the Mood of the Nation," *NewsHour with Jim Lehrer*, October 24, 2001.

52. Judann Pollack et al., "Marketing Put on Hold," *Advertising Age* 72.38 (September 17, 2001): 1.

53. Frascina, "*The New York Times*," 100.

54. Becky Ebenkamp and Andrew Greenfield, "Seeking Situation 'Normal,'" *Brandweek*, 42.36 (October 1, 2001): 16–17.

55. Noel C. Paul, "Who Is the New American Consumer?," *Christian Science Monitor*, October 22, 2001.

56. Greg Johnson and Marla Dickerson, "Running Ads Up the Flagpole," *Los Angeles Times*, October 18, 2001, A1.

57. Bob Garfield, "The Bad, the Worse, the Ugly," *Advertising Age* 72.52 (2001): 14. See also Bob Garfield, "Patriot Games," *Advertising Age* 72.42 (2001): 1.

58. Heller, "Introduction," 12.

59. David Barstow and Diana B. Henriques, "9/11 Tie-Ins Blur Lines of Charity and Profit," *New York Times*, February 2, 2002, A1.

60. Katherine Kinnick, "How Corporate America Grieves: Responses to September 11 in Public Relations Advertising," *Public Relations Review* 29.4 (2003): 443–59.

61. Associated Press, "Saudi Arabia Launches P.R. Campaign in U.S.," May 1, 2002 (on FoxNews.com website).

62. "Marketing Mood," *NewsHour with Jim Lehrer,* December 27, 2001, http://www.pbs.org.

63. Thanks to Erika Doss for making this point to me.

64. Aaron Shuman and Jonathan Sterne, "These Colors Don't Run: Things They Roll Over, and Some Issues That Stick," *Bad Subjects* 59 (February 2002), http://bad.eserver.org.

65. Dan Eggen and Mary Beth Sheridan, "Anti-Terror Funding Cut in D.C. and New York," *Washington Post*, June 1, 2006, A1.

66. See Finnegan, "The Terrorism Beat," 58.

67. Kaplan, "Homeland Insecurities," 59.

68. Kaplan, "Violent Belongings," 9.

69. See William Safire, "Why a Duck? Old Taping System Makes the Headlines," *New York Times Magazine*, March 2, 2003, 24.

70. Robertson, "High Anxiety," 18.

71. Maureen Dowd, "Ready or Not . . . ," *New York Times*, February 23, 2003, sect. 4, p. 11.

72. Lynette Clemetson, "Reshaping Message on Terror, Ridge Urges Calm with Caution," *New York Times*, February 20, 2003, A1.

73. Sarah Sue Ingram, "Silver Symbol of Troubled Times," *Los Angeles Times*, February 17, 2001, E14.

74. Aaron Zitner, "Ridge Revisits Terrorism Preparedness," *Los Angeles Times*, February 15, 2003, A24.

75. Gary Strauss, "Duct Tape Makers Swing into High Gear," *USA Today*, February 14, 2003, B1.

76. Andrejevic, "Interactive (In)Security," 447.

77. Scarry, *Who Defended the Country?*, 27.

78. Hay, "Designing Homes," 370.

79. Kenneth Chang and Judith Miller, "Duct Tape and Plastic Sheeting Can Offer Solace, If Not Real Security," *New York Times*, February 13, 2003, A21.

80. Hay and Andrejevic, "Introduction," 343; and Naomi Klein, "Pay to Be Saved: A Future of Disaster Apartheid," *ZNet Commentary*, August 29, 2006. See also the special issue "Homeland Securities," of *Radical History Review* 93 (fall 2005), edited by Philip, Reilly, and Serlin.

81. See http://www.saferamerica.com.

82. Heather Sinclair, "Personal Parachutes: The Ethics of Safety," October 19, 2001, http://www.dropzone.com.

83. Davis, "Fortress L.A.," in *City of Quartz*, 224. See also Ellin, *Architecture of Fear*.

84. Low, "The Memorialization of 9/11," 328. See also Blair Kamin, "Land of the Sort of Free," *Chicago Tribune*, October 29, 2001.

85. Mark Maremont, "Disguising Security as Something Artful," *Wall Street Journal*, June 24, 2004, A1.

86. Catesby Leigh, "A Monumental Task of Security and Aesthetics," *Wall Street Journal*, June 30, 2005, D8.

87. Maremont, "Disguising Security as Something Artful."

88. Manjoo, "Cityscape of Fear."

89. Ibid.

90. Antonelli, *Safe*.

91. See Megyeri's website, http://www.sweetdreamsecurity.com.

92. Antonelli, *Safe*, 100. See also Julie V. Iovine, "Which Way Design?," *New York Times*, April 21, 2005.

93. Telephone conversation with Matthew Megyeri, September 20, 2006.

94. Antonelli, *Safe*, 72–73, 84.

95. Hideki Yamamoto, "Final Home 44-Pocket Parka" and "Final Home Bear," in Antonelli, *Safe*, 70.

96. Jim Bulin, quoted in Bradsher, *High and Mighty*, 106.

97. Amy Chozick, "Military Fatigue: Iraq Vets Find Work Shaping Up Urbanites," *Wall Street Journal*, October 15–16, 2005, A1, A8.

98. Bradsher, *High and Mighty*, xviii. See also Lauer, "Driven to Extremes."

99. Bradsher, *High and Mighty*, 96. See also Rapaille, *The Culture Code*.

100. Mirzoeff, *Watching Babylon*, 36.

101. Gladwell, "Big and Bad," 31. See also Lauer, "Driven to Extremes."

102. Keith Bradsher, "G.M. Has High Hopes for Vehicle Truly Meant for Road Warriors," *New York Times*, August 6, 2000, 1.

103. Tim Goodman, "Candidates' Debate—All Sizzle, No Steak," *San Francisco Chronicle*, September 25, 2003, A15.

104. Brian O'Reilly, "What in the World Is That Thing?," *Fortune*, October 2, 1995, 146.

105. See Michael Hirsch, Barry, and Dehghanpisheh, "Hillbilly Armor," 24; and Scott Shane, "Hillbilly Armor," *New York Times*, December 26, 2004, sec. 4, p. 4.

106. Danny Hakim, "In Their Hummers, Right beside Uncle Sam," *New York Times*, April 5, 2003, C1.

107. See http://www.hummer.com.

108. Campbell, "The Biopolitics of Security," 967.

109. S. Willis, *Portents of the Real*, 129.

110. Sedgwick, "Paranoid Reading," 24.

CHAPTER 2: CITIZENS AND SURVIVORS

1. Interview with Heidi Vaughn, curator of the archive, Oklahoma City National Memorial, October 17, 2005. The program also sent one thousand stuffed animals to Ukraine in 2006, and to Israel and Lebanon in 2006. E-mail correspondence with Helen Stiefmiller, collections manager, November 3, 2006.

2. Linenthal, *The Unfinished Bombing*, 2.

3. The story of the photograph is told in detail in ibid., chapter 4.

4. There was some debate in news rooms about whether the image should be published at all. See Strupp, "The Photo Felt around the World," 12.

5. Linenthal, *The Unfinished Bombing*, 150–51.

6. Ibid.

7. Ibid., 152.

8. Astor, "National Furor," 33.

9. See C. Willis, "Tempered by Flame."

10. For a detailed history of the negotiations that produced the memorial, see Linenthal, *The Unfinished Bombing*, chapter 4.

11. Rimer, "Victims Not of One Voice," A1.

12. See Linenthal, *The Unfinished Bombing*, 71; and David W. Smith et al., "Population Effects of the Bombing."

13. Linenthal, *The Unfinished Bombing*, 4.

14. Ibid., 121.

15. Ibid., 141–45.

16. Butzer, "Deciding What Our Loss Means."

17. Linenthal describes these proposals in depth in chapter 4 of *The Unfinished Bombing*.

18. Ibid., 160–62.

19. See ibid., 175–86; and Alexei Barrionuevo, "How Oklahoma City Remembers," *Wall Street Journal*, November 13, 2001, B1.

20. Linenthal, *The Unfinished Bombing*, 191–92.

21. Ibid., 187.

22. Spreiregen, "Oklahoma Memorial."

23. Goldberger, "Requiem."

24. For discussion of some of the other final designs, see Collyer, "The Search for an Appropriate Symbol." The evaluation panel that chose the five finalists consisted of family member Toby Thompson; survivors Richard Williams and Polly Nichols; Robert Campbell, architecture critic for the *Boston Globe*; Richard Haag, founder

of the Department of Landscape Architecture at the University of Washington; Bill Moggridge, senior fellow of the Royal College of Art in London; Michaele Pride-Wells, assistant professor of urban design at the University of Kentucky; Adele Naude Santos, founding dean of the School of Architecture of the University of California, San Diego; and Native American artist Jaune Quick-To-See Smith. The Selection Committee that chose the final design consisted of Laurie Beckelman, vice president of World Monuments Fund; landscape architect Ignacio Bunster-Ossa; Luke Corbett, CEO of Kerr-McGee Corporation; San Francisco artist Douglas Hollis; Lars Lerup, dean of Rice University School of Architecture; David Lopez, president of Oklahoma Southwestern Bell; Mayor Ronald Norick; family members John Cole, Jeannine Gist, Cheryl Scroggins, Philip Thompson, and Bud Welch; and survivors Tom Hall, Paul Heath, and Calvin Moser. Don Stastny and Paul Morris from Portland, Oregon served as competition advisors, along with Helene Fried, a public art consultant from San Francisco.

25. Linenthal, *The Unfinished Bombing*, 217.

26. Ibid., 221–24.

27. Ibid., 197–204.

28. Linenthal quoted in Brandon Beard, "Elusive Ending: Will Oklahomans Ever Find Closure for the Federal Building Bombing?," *Oklahoma Gazette*, April, 19, 2001, 16.

29. Warner, "The Mass Public," 248.

30. Linenthal, *The Unfinished Bombing*, 221.

31. Interview with Jane Thomas, collections and archive manager, Oklahoma City National Memorial, April 18, 2001.

32. Ibid.

33. Interview with Heidi Vaughn; e-mail correspondence with Helen Stiefmiller.

34. For an in-depth discussion of the Vietnam Veterans Memorial, see Sturken, *Tangled Memories*, chapter 2. See also Haas, *Carried to the Wall*.

35. Interview with Heidi Vaughn.

36. Interview with Kari Watkins, Oklahoma City National Memorial, October 17, 2005.

37. Griswold, "The Vietnam Veterans Memorial," 689.

38. An explanation of the Institute's work is on its website: http://www.mipt.org.

39. The other agencies were divisions of the U.S. Army Recruiting Battalion, the Defense Investigative Service, the U.S. Postal Service, the U.S. Marine Corps Recruiting Command, the Federal Employees Credit Union, the Oklahoma Department of Rehabilitative Services, the General Services Administration, the U.S. Customs Service, the Department of Transportation Federal Highway Administration, and the Veterans Administration.

40. For discussion of the AIDS memorial quilt, see Sturken, *Tangled Memories*, chapter 6.

41. The stories of many survivors and family members are told in M. Knight, *Forever Changed*.

42. Doss, "Death, Art, and Memory in the Public Sphere," 80.

43. Sam Walker, "Out of Its Darkest Moment, a Blueprint for Renewal," *Christian Science Monitor*, April 19, 1996.

44. Ryan Chittum, "Oklahoma City's Revival," *Wall Street Journal*, April 13, 2005, B1. Chittum notes that the city still has one-third vacancies in downtown office space.

45. Interview with Hans Butzer, Oklahoma City, October 17, 2005.

46. Interview with Kari Watkins.

47. *Oklahoma City National Memorial Market Research Project* (April 1, 2002–March 31, 2003), Randall Travel Marketing, May 14, 2003; and *Oklahoma City National Memorial Image Study*, Randall Travel Marketing, October 2004. See also Alexander Holmes, "An Estimate of the Economic Impact of the Oklahoma City National Memorial on the State of Oklahoma," University of Oklahoma.

48. Interview with Kari Watkins.

49. Cal Hobson, quoted in Beard, "Elusive Ending," 20.

50. Richard Mize, "Murrah Memorial to Play a Big Role in City Conference," *Knight Ridder Tribune Business News*, April 20, 2006, 1.

51. Jim Yardley, "Uneasily, Oklahoma City Welcomes Tourists," *New York Times*, June 11, 2001, A1.

52. Ibid.

53. These figures are from the brochure, *Securing the Future of the Oklahoma National Memorial and Museum*, produced for the Second Decade Campaign.

54. Linenthal, *Unfinished Bombing*, 128.

55. Ibid., 127.

56. The shop at the Holocaust Museum sells magnets and key chains with images of the museum building and posters related to the political issues raised by the Holocaust. The rest of its merchandise is books.

57. Interview with Heidi Vaughn.

58. According to Watkins, the Memorial Foundation had an intergovernmental letter from various levels of political government that stated that there would be no political involvement in the memorial process. Interview with Kari Watkins.

59. Ibid.

CHAPTER 3: THE SPECTACLE OF DEATH

1. See Rick Bragg, "McVeigh Dies for Oklahoma City Blast," *New York Times*, June 12, 2001, A1, A19; Anthony Lloyd, "Final Moments of a Calm Affable Killer," *The Times* (London), June 12, 2001, 5.

2. Linenthal, *The Unfinished Bombing*, 100.

3. See Megan K. Stack, "For Oklahoma City, a Wound Too Deep for 'Closure,'" *Los Angeles Times*, June 6, 2001, A14.

4. Michel and Herbeck, *American Terrorist*, 257.

5. Gabler, *Life*, 181–82.

6. Michel and Herbeck, *American Terrorist*, 377.

7. Bacharach, "The Prison Letters."

8. Michel and Herbeck, *American Terrorist*, 361.

9. Ibid., 400.

10. Susan Saulny, "McVeigh Says He Considered Killing Reno," *New York Times*, April 27, 2001, A10.

11. Richard Serrano, "Writings of a Home-Grown Terrorist," *Los Angeles Times*, June 10, 2001, A25.

12. Associated Press, "Vidal Is to Witness McVeigh Execution," *New York Times*, May 7, 2001, A12.

13. McVeigh stated to Michael and Herbeck, "If it was known that there was an entire day-care center, it might have given me pause to switch targets. That's a large amount of collateral damage" (*American Terrorist*, 188). However, he also made contradictory remarks that would indicate that he had been aware of the day care center and had thoroughly cased the building beforehand.

14. Richard Serrano, "McVeigh Called Model Prisoner," *Los Angeles Times*, October 18, 2001, A28.

15. See Lesser, *Pictures at an Execution*, and Austin Sarat's critique of it in his book *When the State Kills*, chapter 7.

16. See, for instance, Renée Montagne, "There Was a Reason They Outlawed Public Executions," *New York Times*, May 6, 2001.

17. McVeigh's defense cost $13.8 million, not including the legal costs of his appeals, according to a report issued by a federal judge in Denver. Kevin Johnson, "McVeigh's Defense Costs Taxpayers $13.8 million," *USA Today*, July 3, 2001, 3A.

18. See Dyer, *Harvest of Rage*.

19. Rimer, "A City Consumed in Plans for McVeigh's Execution," *New York Times*, April 19, 2001, A1.

20. "World-Wide," *Wall Street Journal*, June 7, 2001, A1.

21. "Venders Selling Execution Souvenir T-Shirts," CourtTV.com, April 23, 2001, http://www.courttv.com.

22. Rimer, "A City Consumed," A1.

23. Quoted in Roger Simon, "Death Watch," *U.S. News and World Report*, May 14, 2001, http//www.usnewsclassroom.com.

24. Jo Slater, "Indiana Execution Site Is Facing More Strain," *New York Times*, May 12, 2001, A10; Eric Slater, "For Terre Haute, a Month's Reprieve," *Los Angeles Times*, May 12, 2001, A16.

25. Sarat, *When the State Kills*, 18.

26. Robert Verkaik, "The American Way of Death," *Independent*, June 12, 2001, 10.

27. Foucault, *Discipline and Punish*, 57–58.

28. Lokaneeta, "Revenge and the Spectacular Execution," 210.

29. Sarat, *When the State Kills*, 189.

30. Ibid, 73.

31. In his book *When the State Kills*, Austin Sarat published the photographs of the execution of Allen Lee Davis, which were evidence in a trial about the constitutionality of execution by electrocution in Florida.

32. Denise Grady, "Doctors See Way to Cut Risks of Suffering in Lethal Injection," *New York Times*, June 23, 2006, A1.

33. Michel and Herbeck, *American Terrorist*, 314–15.

34. Sarat, *When the State Kills*, 64; "Those Left Grief-Stricken by Bombing Cry for Vengeance," *St. Louis Post-Dispatch* (June 4, 1997), A1.

35. Sarat, *When the State Kills*, 42, 35.

36. Minow, "Surviving Victim Talk," 1416.

37. Richard A. Serrano, "The Slow Rot at Supermax," *Los Angeles Times*, May 5, 2006, A1.

38. Jerry Markon, "Moussaoui Trial to Bring Attacks Back for Jury," *Washington Post*, April 6, 2006, A12.

39. Rogers, "Closing the Book."

40. Megan K. Stack, "An Execution Backlash in an Unlikely Place," *Los Angeles Times*, June 9, 2001, A1, A17.

41. Interview with Kari Watkins.

42. See Rimer, "Victims Not of One Voice," A16; and Goodell, "Letting Go of McVeigh."

43. Stack, "An Execution Backlash," A17.

44. Renny Cushing and Bud Welch, "Not in Our Name: Homicide Survivors Speak Out against the Death Penalty," presentation at Harvard University, March 16, 1999, http://www.mvfr.org.

45. Caryn James, "The Oklahoma Bomber's Final Hours Are Hardly Television News's Finest," *New York Times*, June 12, 2001, A19.

46. Frank Rich, "Death with Commercials," *New York Times*, June 23, 2001, A25.

47. "NB," *Times Literary Supplement*, June 15, 2001, 18.

48. J. William Gibson, "The Blast That Finished Off Militia Culture," *Los Angeles Times*, May 13, 2001, M2; Southern Poverty Law Center Intelligence Report, http://www.splcenter.org.

49. See the intelligence reports on the SPLC website: http://www.splcenter.org; and Steve Johnson, "10 Years after Terror."

50. The term "others unknown," which was used by defense lawyers in the trial, was also the title of a book by Stephen Jones, McVeigh's initial defense lawyer. Conspiracies about Oklahoma City have also included speculation about possible connections to bin Laden's al Qaeda network, in particular because of trips made by McVeigh and Nichols to the Philippines (Nichols's wife, Marife, is Filipino). Jim Crogan, "Heartland Conspiracy," *LA Weekly*, September 28–October 4, 2001, 23.

51. Kevin Johnson, "Oklahomans' Feelings Are Mixed on Nichols' Trial," *USA Today*, May 10, 2004, A3.

52. Lianne Hart and Scott Gold, "Nichols Guilty in Oklahoma Trial," *Los Angeles Times*, May 27, 2004, A14.

53. Associated Press, "Apologetic Nichols Is Sentenced to Life for Oklahoma Bombing," *New York Times*, August 10, 2004, A19.

54. Richard Willing, "Nichols Says He's Sorry," *USA Today*, August 10, 2004, A1.

55. John Kifner, "In Oklahoma, a Week of Remembrance," *New York Times*, April 18, 2005, A14.

56. Howard Witt, "Torment Lingers in OK City," *Chicago Tribune*, April 17, 2005, 20.

57. Alexei Barrionuevo, "Trauma Haunts Oklahoma City Rescuers Still," *Wall Street Journal*, September 26, 2001, B1; Howard Witt, "Tragedy Haunts the Heroes," *Chicago Tribune*, April 18, 2005, 1.

58. Charisse Jones, "Still Afraid to Go Back to Work," *USA Today*, April 19, 2005, A1.

59. Kelly Crow, "On a Site of Terror and Death, Survivors Find a Role," *New York Times*, May 2, 2001, 6.

60. Linenthal, *The Unfinished Bombing*, 163.

61. E-mail correspondence with Helen Siefmiller.

62. Witt, "Torment Lingers."

63. Interview with Kari Watkins.

CHAPTER 4: TOURISM AND "SACRED GROUND"

1. The name Fresh Kills, which has the potential to sound morbid in this context, is actually derived from the Dutch language, in which *kills* means streams. There are many names in New York that come from its early Dutch settlers.

2. Amy Waldman, "Mementos: With Solemn Detail, Dust of Ground Zero Is Put in Urns," *New York Times*, October 15, 2001, B11.

3. The death of NYPD detective James Zadroga, at the age of thirty-four, received the most attention. Emergency Medical Technicians Timothy Keller, forty-one, and Felix Hernandez, thirty-one, also died from lung-related diseases after fighting for workers' compensation. In addition, the family of Felicia Dunn-Jones, a civil rights lawyer who worked one block from the World Trade Center and who died five months after the attacks, was awarded compensation by the Sept. 11 Victim Compensation Fund. Erika Martinez, "Hidden Victims of WTC," *New York Post*, January 17, 2006, 15; Anthony DePalma, "Debate Revives as 9/11 Dust Is Called Fatal," *New York Times*, April 14, 2006, B1; Anthony DePalma, "Medical Views of 9/11 Dust Show Big Gaps," *New York Times*, October 24, 2006, A1, B4. See also Ridgely Ochs, "Their '9/11 Plague': Almost 5 years after the Terror Attacks, New, Critical Cases Are Surfacing," *Knight Ridder Tribune Business News*, June 1, 2006, 1; Kristen Lombardi, "Death by Dust."

4. According to Michael Tomasky, the first use of the term in print was by the Associated Press reporter Larry McShane on the evening of September 11: "Shortly after 7 PM, crews began heading into ground zero of the terrorist attack to search for survivors and recover bodies." Tomasky, "Battleground Zero," 18.

5. Sorkin, *Starting from Zero*.

6. Kaplan, "Homeland Insecurities," 56.

7. Seth Schiesel and Saul Hansell, "A Flood of Anxious Phone Calls Clog Lines, and TV Channels Go Off the Air," *New York Times*, September 12, 2001, A8. When the World Trade Center was built, the broadcasting masts were moved there from the Empire State Building when there were concerns about the buildings blocking broadcast signals. See Gillespie, *Twin Towers*, 139.

8. In the mid-1980s, I took a video camera up on the observation deck of the World Trade Center. The power of the antenna (which was on the other tower) was such

that it completely distorted the video and audio signals when one stood at that end of the deck.

9. Lowood, "Death in the City." According to Lowood, Microsoft delayed the release of the 2002 version of the game in order to change the New York skyline and offered users a software patch to erase the offending comments. After September 11, reporters used the 2000 version of the game to learn to fly jetliners into the twin towers, and after the release of the 2002 version, players created their own patch to reinsert the "towers back *into* the default scenery."

10. Žižek, *Welcome to the Desert of the Real!*, 11.

11. Retort, *Afflicted Powers*, 34.

12. Stallabrass, "Spectacle and Terror," 92.

13. See Peterson, "Walking in Sin City," 123.

14. Miller, "Reporting the Disaster," 46. See also Simpson, *9/11*, 36–43.

15. *9/11*, DVD, directed by Jules Naudet, Gédéon Naudet, and James Hanlon (2002, Paramount Pictures).

16. Michael Kimmelman, "Art in Ashes, Drama in Dust," *New York Times*, August 19, 2002, B1; Randal Archibold, "Preserving a Tea Set That Captured the Moment," *New York Times*, September 6, 2002, A21; Christy Ferer, "Unforgotten Soldiers," *New York Times*, October 25, 2001, A21; Dan Barry, "From a World Lost, Ephemeral Notes Bear Witness to the Unspeakable," *New York Times*, September 25, 2001, B9.

17. Yaeger, "Rubble as Archive," 187.

18. See Douglas, *Purity and Danger.*

19. See Mark Schools, "A Landfill That Tells Eight Million Stories Now Has One More," *Wall Street Journal*, September 28, 2001, A1; and Anthony DePalma, "Plans for Fresh Kills Trouble 9/11 Families Who Sense Loved Ones in the Dust," *New York Times*, June 14, 2004, B1.

20. Steedman, *Dust*, 164.

21. Luis Perez, "70% Have WTC Lung Ailments," *Knight Ridder Tribune Business News*, September 6, 2006, 1. See also Ellen Barry, "Lost in the Dust of 9/11," *Los Angeles Times*, October 14, 2006, A1, about janitors who became ill after clearing dust from downtown office buildings; and William Keegan Jr., "Our Slow Death," *New York Times*, September 10, 2006, 14.

22. Glenn Collins, "A 9/11 Shrine, with the Tragic, Toxic Dust," *New York Times*, August 25, 2006, B1.

23. Langewiesche, *American Ground*, 11.

24. Ibid., 70.

25. See Charles V. Bagli, "At Ground Zero, Builder Is Barred But Not His Kin," *New York Times*, July 21, 2006, 1.

26. Kevin Bubriski produced a book of photographs of people looking at Ground Zero, titled *Pilgrimage.*

27. Dan Barry, "Where Twin Towers Stood, a Silent Goodbye," *New York Times*, May 31, 2002, A1, A22–A23.

28. Marianne Hirsch, "I Took Pictures," 73.

29. On the images of people falling from the towers, see Junod, "The Falling Man," 177.

30. See Sturken, *Tangled Memories*, chapters 2 and 6.

31. Lorie Novak, "Photographs," in Greenberg, *Trauma at Home*, 93.

32. See, for instance, the essay by Sella, "Missing."

33. See http://www.bronston.com. For a discussion of the mixed responses to the exhibit, see Kirshenblatt-Gimblett, "Kodak Moments," 30–31.

34. On the changes that 9/11 produced in photojournalism and newspaper layout of images, see Zelizer, "Photography, Journalism."

35. See Andén-Papadopoulus, "The Trauma of Representation."

36. Hirsch, "I Took Pictures," 69.

37. Quoted in Kirshenblatt-Gimblett, "Kodak Moments," 14.

38. See Andén-Papadopoulus, "The Trauma of Representation"; and Kirshenblatt-Gimblett, "Kodak Moments." George et al., *Here Is New York*, http://www.hereisnewyork.com. It was conceived and organized by Alice Rose George, Gilles Peress, Michal Shulan, and Charles Traub. Funds raised by selling copies of the images for $25 each were donated to the Children's Aid Society.

39. Andén-Papadopoulus, "The Trauma of Representation," 95.

40. Taylor, *The Archive and the Repertoire*, 256.

41. On debunking the firefighter image post-9/11, see C. Willis, "Tempered by Flame."

42. Jonathan Lemire, "'Bronzed' FDNY Photo Finds Home in Woodside," *Daily News*, September 11, 2003, 6.

43. Arthur Bovino, "Gifts Pour In, but Space for Them Grows Scarce," *New York Times*, July 24, 2002, B1.

44. See Zelizer, "Photography, Journalism," on the ways that journalism images repeat templates.

45. See Marling and Wetenhall, *Iwo Jima*.

46. See Hariman and Lucaites, "Performing Civic Identity."

47. The back story of the image is told in detail in Friend, *Watching the World Change*, 311–46. See in particular the discussion of the editorial response to the image on page 321.

48. Ibid., 319.

49. Irby, "One Man's Path."

50. Andén-Papadopoulus, "The Trauma of Representation."

51. Quoted in Friend, *Watching the World Change*, 329–30.

52. S. Willis, *Portents of the Real*, 15.

53. See Friend, *Watching the World Change*, 335–44; and Tony Germanotta, "Whatever Happened to . . . the Flag Erected by Firemen Sept. 11?," *Knight Ridder Tribune Business News*, September 11, 2006, 1.

54. Friend, *Watching the World Change*, 313–15; Kevin Flynn, "Firefighters Block a Plan for Statue in Their Honor," *New York Times*, January 18, 2002, A21.

55. Sturken, *Tangled Memories*, 56–57.

56. John Ydstie, host, Leon Wynter, reporter, story on the New York Fire Depart-

ment, *Weekend Edition Saturday*, National Public Radio, February 16, 2002. Many in the black community in New York blame former mayor Rudy Giuliani for the continued lack of integration in the Fire Department. See James C. McIntosh, "For Blacks, Giuliani Was Not the Hero, but the Zero, of Ground Zero, *New York Amsterdam News*, February 14, 2002, 13.

57. Meyerowitz, *Aftermath*, 16. Like Langewiesche, who gained access to the site through his connections (and the fact that one of the city employees in charge of the site knew his writing in *Atlantic Monthly*), Meyerowitz gained access because he knew someone with clout in the city government.

58. Ibid., 185.

59. Weschler, "Echoes at Ground Zero."

60. Quoted in Kenneth Baker, "Ground Zero Photos," *San Francisco Chronicle*, October 17, 2006, D1.

61. Kennedy, "Remembering September 11," 320.

62. The exhibition is available at http://www.911exhibit.state.gov.

63. Kennedy, "Remembering September 11," 325.

64. Ibid., 326.

65. Jennifer Steinhauer, "A Symbol of Faith Marks a City's Hallowed Ground," *New York Times*, October 5, 2001, B12.

66. Linenthal, *Sacred Ground*, 3.

67. Low, "The Memorialization of September 11," 326–39, 333.

68. Rosario, "Making Progress."

69. Foote, *Shadowed Ground*, 9.

70. In 2005, the *New York Times* published a chart that shows in grim detail the location of the remains. While the majority of remains were found in the area of the two towers, with more near the North Tower, the dots that represent remains are scattered throughout a very large area. See David W. Dunlap, "Marking Off Sacred Ground at the Trade Center Site," *New York Times*, October 6, 2005, B4.

71. Pataki's remark was apparently spontaneous enough to have taken by surprise others involved in the early stages of the rebuilding process. See Goldberger, *Up from Zero*, 212.

72. See ibid., 28. There are several excellent books on the history of the World Trade Center, including Darton, *Divided We Stand*; and Glanz and Lipton, *City in the Sky*.

73. De Certeau, "Walking in the City," 92.

74. Philip Nobel writes that a photograph circulated early on of construction equipment revealing the towers' perimeter columns at the bottom of the excavated site: *Sixteen Acres*, 116.

75. See William Neuman, "9/11 Kin Plead: Put Sacred Ground First," *New York Post*, November 2, 2002, 14; Josh Getlin, "Ground Zero Now a Center of Disunity," *Los Angeles Times*, September 7, 2003, A1, A20.

76. See Nobel, *Sixteen Acres*, 246.

77. David W. Dunlap, "At 9/11 Memorial, Actual Sizes May Vary," *New York Times*, February 12, 2004, A31.

78. The Port Authority released a document in March 2005 stating that it would "preserve to the maximum extent feasible the bases of 84 columns from the north tower and 39 columns from the south tower, and install a glass wall that will afford views of column bases." Glenn Collins, "Port Authority Details Efforts to Save Trade Center Remnants," *New York Times*, March 23, 2005.

79. Nobel, *Sixteen Acres*, 116–17.

80. Philippe de Montebello, "The Iconic Power of an Artifact," *New York Times*, September 25, 2001, A29.

81. See Stuart D. Gosswein, "What About the Trade Center Facades?," letter to the arts editor, *Washington Post*, April 25, 2004, N2.

82. See Boehm, "Privatizing Public Memory."

83. Langewiesche, *American Ground*, 205.

84. Nobel, *Sixteen Acres*, 208.

85. On personal collections, see Felicia R. Lee, "Plucking 9/11 Objects from History's Dustbin," *New York Times*, May 30, 2005. See also Glenn Collins, "It's an Abundant Record, but How to House and Share It?," *New York Times*, May 30, 2006, B1. Personal collections often prompt concerns about ghoulishness. There is speculation that many amateur collectors will contribute their collections when an official memorial center is established.

86. Eric Lipton, "Surplus History from Ground Zero," *New York Times*, December 19, 2003, B1.

87. Rick Hampson, "Americans Rush to Build Memorials to 9/11," *USA Today*, May 22, 2003, A1.

88. David W. Dunlap, "Victims' Relatives May Claim Photographs from 9/11 Ruins," *New York Times*, January 8, 2005. A database for jewelry was also set up. It's interesting to note that stories such as this emphasized the victims' families, when in fact the majority of the photographs are likely to belong to people who survived 9/11.

89. Eric Lichtblau, "F.B.I. Agents Took Mementos from Rubble of Twin Towers," *New York Times*, February 26, 2004, B1; Dan Barry, "Ghoul Charges Add Insult to Tragedy," *New York Times*, February 28, 2004, B1.

90. Associated Press, "Rumsfeld Has 9/11 Debris," *Los Angeles Times*, March 14, 2004, A25.

91. The *Wall Street Journal* reporter Daniel Henninger wrote an essay for Memorial Day in May 2002 advocating that Fresh Kills be considered an American memorial: "Memorial Day Should Touch September 11," *Wall Street Journal*, May 24, 2002, A12.

92. Anthony DePalma, "Plans for Fresh Kills Trouble 9/11 Families Who Sense Loved Ones in the Dust," *New York Times*, June 14, 2004, B1.

93. Michelle O'Donnell, "9/11 Families to Sue City over Remains," *New York Times*, August 17, 2005, B3.

94. See Robert Lee Holtz, "Probing the DNA of Death," *Los Angeles Times*, October 9, 2002; Eric Lipton, "At the Limits of Science, 9/11 ID Effort Comes to End," *New York Times*, April 3, 2005.

95. See David W. Dunlap, "Remains Found on Skyscraper Near Ground Zero Are

Human," *New York Times*, October 28, 2005, B5; and Martha T. Moore, "Remains Bring Hope, Frustration for 9/11 Families," *USA Today*, April 20, 2006, A4.

96. "Sen. Schumer, 9–11 Families Call for Expert Army Unit to Search for, Identify Bone, Other Human Remains at Ground Zero," *U.S. Fed News Service*, Washington, D.C., April 23, 2006.

97. Moore, "Remains Bring Hope," A4.

98. David W. Dunlap, "Officials Try to Identify Sites Where Body Parts Still Lie," *New York Times*, October 25, 2006, B3.

99. Penley, *NASA/Trek*, 59–60.

100. Martha T. Moore, "NYC's Work to ID 9/11 Victims Ends—For Now," *USA Today*, February 24, 3005, A1.

101. Gail Collins, "New York Notes: 8 Million Survivors in Need of Affection," *New York Times*, September 17, 2001, A14.

102. See Janet Wilson, "'Sacred Ground' in N.Y.," *Los Angeles Times*, November 29, 2001, A1, A19; and Susan Saulny, "Pilgrimage to New York City: Paying Respects and Spending Little," *New York Times*, December 29, 2001, B1.

103. See John Leland, "Letting the View Speak for Itself," *New York Times*, January 3, 2002, B14. Some observers commented that the ramp bore a resemblance to the Vietnam Veterans Memorial in its form.

104. S. Irene Virbila, "Ground Zero: Downtown Restaurants Have Reopened, Stirring Up Hope," *Los Angeles Times*, March 17, 2002, L1, L11.

105. Steve Cuozzo and Gillian Harris, "Room to Reflect: Hotel's Ground Zero Views Are Drawing Guests," *New York Post*, July 7, 2003, 11.

106. *Los Angeles Times*, "After the Attack: The New Yorkers: Big Apple Pride Is in Fashion," September 19, 2001, A21.

107. Broderick and Gibson, "Mourning, Monomyth," 201.

108. Michael Luo, "Inside Ground Zero, a Stream of Commuters, and of Tears," *New York Times*, November 25, 2003, A23.

109. Lynette Holloway, "Wholesalers, in Rush to Market, Got Sept. 11 Souvenirs on Street," *New York Times*, December 8, 2001, D1.

110. Hurley and Trimarco, "Morality and Merchandise," 61–64.

111. Ibid., 71.

112. Reuters, "NYC Warns eBay about 9/11 Item Sales," February 21, 2002. See also Broderick and Gibson, "Mourning, Monomyth," 202.

113. B. Brown, "American Kitsch."

114. Havrilesky, "The Selling of 9/11."

115. Daniel Harris, "The Kitschification of Sept. 11."

CHAPTER 5: ARCHITECTURES OF GRIEF

1. Stephens, *Imagining Ground Zero*, 129.

2. Muschamp, "Don't Rebuild," 53.

3. Peter Eisenman, on *The Charlie Rose Show*, PBS, September 13, 2002.

4. Stephens, *Imagining Ground Zero*, 107.

5. Giovannini, "Rising to Greatness." These are also reprinted in Stephens, *Imagining Ground Zero*.

6. See Blair Kamin, "Racing to the Sky," *Chicago Tribune*, September 10, 2006, 5.

7. Sella, "Missing," 50; A. Wallace, "Missing Twins," 17.

8. Goldberger, *Up from Zero*, 34.

9. Martin Miller, "A Skyline That Won't Go Away," *Los Angeles Times*, December 18, 2001, E1.

10. In the following months, Gristede's Supermarkets decided to leave the towers on their shopping bags, with memorial text: "Always on Our Minds. Forever in Our Hearts. Never Forget What They Did." See David W. Dunlap, "Lost from Skyline, but Not from the Landscape," *New York Times*, September 9, 2004, A32. The phrase on the Gristede's bags is a bit confusing. If the first two phrases seem to refer to those who lost their lives, "always on our minds," the "they" of the third phrase, "never forget what they did," is not entirely clear.

11. Taylor, *The Archive and the Repertoire*, 247.

12. Paul Myoda and Julian LaVerdiere, "Filling the Void," *New York Times Magazine*, September 23, 2001, 80.

13. *New Yorker*, September 24, 2001.

14. Ockman and Frausto, *Architourism*, 80.

15. Tomkins, "After the Towers."

16. *New York Post*, "Half of New York Want the Twin Towers Rebuilt: Our City Poll," July 14, 2002, 1; Edward Wyatt, "At Hearing, New Yorkers' Verdict Is Clear: Rebuild the Twin Towers," *New York Times*, May 26, 2002, 25.

17. Edward Wyatt, "Longing for a Sept. 10 Skyline," *New York Times*, November 2, 2002, B1, B4.

18. Hugo Lindgren, "Keep Your New Towers: They Want *the* Towers," *New York Times*, August 31, 2003, Arts Section, 23.

19. See http://www.teamtwintowers.org.

20. One exception is Joan Ockman's edited book, *Out of Ground Zero*, which looks at other cities that have undergone large-scale renewal, such as Lisbon, Chicago, Hiroshima, Berlin, and Jerusalem, in comparison to New York. In addition, in September 2005 and 2006, the Lower Manhattan Cultural Council organized international summits, "What Comes After: Cities, Art and Recovery," which included many participants from around the world and was clearly an attempt to work against the exceptionalist framework of 9/11 and Ground Zero.

21. *New York Times Magazine*, "To Rebuild or Not: Architects Respond," September 23, 2001, 81.

22. See Darton, *Divided We Stand*; Glanz and Lipton, *City in the Sky*; Mosco, *The Digital Sublime*, chapter 6; and M. Wallace, *A New Deal for New York*. Mosco and Wallace, among others, suggest that the destruction of Radio Row is responsible for the fact that the emergence of the personal computer industry began in California, in Silicon Valley, rather than in New York.

23. It was not until the late 1990s that the complex began to turn a profit. See Goldberger, *Up from Zero*, 38.

24. Ibid., 25, 57.

25. Huxtable, "The New York Process."

26. Sorkin and Zukin, *After the World Trade Center.*

27. Sorkin, *Starting from Zero*, 12.

28. Sarah Boxer, "Debating Ground Zero Architecture and the Value of the Void," *New York Times*, September 30, 2002, B1.

29. Steve Cuozzo, "The Wrong Stuff—Keep World Architects Away from Ground Zero," *New York Post*, May 28, 2002, 27. Cuozzo and other tabloid writers usually ended up advocating that the real estate developers should just be left alone to build their buildings without high-profile architects meddling. See Goldberger, *Up from Zero*, 137.

30. Protetch, *A New World Trade Center.*

31. Nobel, *Sixteen Acres*, 82.

32. Protetch, *The New World Trade Center*, 25. See also Stephens, *Imaging Ground Zero*, 132–85.

33. Most of the proposals are included in Stephens, *Imagining Ground Zero*. See also Gullbring et al., "New York Naked City."

34. Nobel, *Sixteen Acres*, 71.

35. Muschamp, "Don't Rebuild," 46–58; Giovannini, "Rising to Greatness." See also Stephens, *Imagining Ground Zero.*

36. Philip Nobel makes the case that the initial design campaign was hastily put together because it was rushed by the political interests swarming around the site, in particular the fall campaign for the governor's race in New York, in which Pataki was running against Andrew Cuomo. Cuomo made a campaign issue of the slow process, which prompted Pataki to create a series of unreasonable deadlines motivated by politics. "By spurring action when and how he did," Nobel writes, "Andrew Cuomo is among the foremost architects of the next World Trade Center," though he does not mean this as a compliment. Nobel, *Sixteen Acres*, 109.

37. Ada Louise Huxtable, "Another World Trade Center Horror," *Wall Street Journal*, July 25, 2002, B13. Certain officials in the city had attempted several times to get more control of the site by swapping the ownership of the land with the land under the two New York airports, and several attempts to buy out Silverstein had been circulated, but none had enough political support to work.

38. Nobel's *Sixteen Acres* and Goldberg's *Up from Zero* both tell the story of this competition in great detail. In addition, Libeskind chronicles his version of it in his book *Breaking Ground.*

39. Goldberger, *Up from Zero*, 160.

40. Protetch, *A New World Trade Center*, 23, 27.

41. Ibid., 61.

42. See Sorkin, *Starting from Zero*, 38–51; and "Why Not a Park? Four Landscape-Architecture Firms Reimagine Ground Zero," *New York Times Magazine*, May 16, 2004, 55–63. Any proposals that advocated against rebuilding office space on the site were in themselves radical critiques of the way that commercial interests have dominated the discussion of how to rebuild.

43. Goldberger, *Up from Zero*, 10; the plan is outlined in Stephens, *Imagining Ground Zero*, 78–81.

44. Stephens, *Imagining Ground Zero*, 82–85.

45. Ibid., 66.

46. Goldberger, *Up from Zero*, 155.

47. Quoted in Pearman, "The Battle for Ground Zero."

48. On the image of people falling from the towers, see Junod, "The Falling Man"; and Lurie, "Falling Persons."

49. Deyan Sudjic, "Towering Ambition," *Guardian*, March 2, 2003.

50. Interestingly, Libeskind attributes Pataki's choice of his design in part to the bonding the two men felt as fellow immigrants. Libeskind, *Breaking Ground*, 187.

51. Martin C. Pedersen, "The Danny Libeskind Show," *Metropolis*, March 1, 2004. Both *Slate* and the *New Republic* have harped on Libeskind's self-promotion: Christopher Hawthorn, "Living with Our Mistake," *Slate.com*, February 25, 3002; Franklin, "Mr. Memory."

52. Libeskind, *Breaking Ground*, 13, 49–50.

53. Lutyens, "Ground Hero." See also Jones, "The Sociology of Architecture."

54. Quoted in Goldberger, *Up from Zero*, 120.

55. Isenberg, "Reading 'between the Lines,'" 171. For a more positive evaluation of the museum, see Young, "Daniel Libeskind's Jewish Museum in Berlin," in *At Memory's Edge*, 152–83. See also Huyssen, "The Voids of Berlin," in *Present Pasts*, 49–71.

56. Filler, "Into the Void," 28.

57. Daniel Libeskind, from a symposium on "Monument and Memory" held September 2002 at the New-York Historical Society, quoted in Goldberger, *Up from Zero*, 120.

58. See Ruth Franklin's scathing review of Libeskind's book *Breaking Ground*: "Mr. Memory," 29.

59. Libeskind, *Breaking Ground*, 12.

60. Muschamp, "Balancing Reason and Emotion."

61. See Goldberger, *Up from Zero*, 117–18.

62. Libeskind, *Breaking Ground*, 43. See also Simpson, *9/11*, 70.

63. Foster, "In New York." Similar critiques of Libeskind's Jewish Museum have referred to it as having a "Disneyland aesthetic": Julius Schoeps, quoted in Isenberg, "Reading 'Between the Lines,'" 172.

64. Pogrebin, "Architecture."

65. Nobel, *Sixteen Acres*, 198.

66. Santiago Calatrava, quoted in David W. Dunlap, "Architect Finds Spot for Flag Found in Ruins of 9/11 Site," *New York Times*, July 29, 2005, B8.

67. Stephens, *Imagining Ground Zero*, 50.

68. Debra Burlingame, "Ground Zero," *Wall Street Journal*, June 6, 2006, A14.

69. Noble, *Sixteen Acres*; Goldberger, *Up from Zero*. The documentary film *Sacred Ground* aired on PBS in September 2004.

70. Steve Cuozzo, "Urban Planning by Atta: Downtown Defeatists Would Let Hijackers Kill the World's Financial Capital," *New York Post*, April 19, 2002, 27. Atta is Mohammed Atta, the apparent leader of the group who hijacked the airplanes on September 11.

71. Sontag, "The Hole in the City's Heart," 1.

72. Paul Goldberger has argued that the area should be rebuilt with multiuse buildings, including residential housing: "A New Beginning."

73. David W. Dunlap and Glenn Collins, "Redesign Puts Freedom Tower on a Fortified Base," *New York Times*, June 29, 2005, A1, B2.

74. Ouroussoff, "A Tower of Impregnability."

75. Alex Frangos, "Federal Offices to Be Anchor in Trade Center," *Wall Street Journal*, June 30, 2006, A2.

76. Michael Powell, "Towering Rents at Ground Zero," *Washington Post*, September 24, 2006, A2. See also Alex Frangos, "Agencies May Overpay for Freedom Tower Space," *Wall Street Journal*, September 20, 2006, A22; and Sewell Chan, "Plan to Fill Freedom Tower Stirs a Debate," *New York Times*, September 20, 2006, B3.

77. Patrick McGeehan, "Employees Say No to Working in Freedom Tower," *New York Times*, September 19, 2006, B1.

78. Michael Goodwin, "Lose the Freedom Tower," *Daily News*, March 26, 2006, 37.

79. Heilemann, "Poker at Ground Zero," 22.

80. David W. Dunlap and Glenn Collins, "In Revised Design, Freedom Tower Sheds Its Look of Bulky Armor," *New York Times*, June 29, 2006, B1.

81. This campaign is featured in the PBS documentary *America Rebuilds II: Return to Ground Zero*, which aired in September 2006. See also Stuart Elliot, "Marketers Must Walk Fine Line in Appeals That Recall Sept. 11," *New York Times*, September 11, 2006, C8.

82. Manjoo, "Cityscape of Fear."

83. Ouroussoff, "At Ground Zero," E1.

84. Huxtable, "The Disaster."

85. Alex Frangos, "Officials Focus on Retail Plans at Ground Zero," *Wall Street Journal*, June 29, 2005, A5.

86. Charles Wolf, quoted in David W. Dunlap, "Focus Shifts to Retail Plans at Ground Zero," *New York Times*, September 30, 2005, B1.

87. Goldberger, *Up from Zero*, 65. On the distinctions between the two memorial processes, see also Linenthal, "'The Predicament of Aftermath.'"

88. Quoted in Catherine Fox, "Path to 9/11 Memorial Marked by Arguments," *Atlanta Journal-Constitution*, September 10, 2006, G3.

89. Sanders, "Honoring the Dead."

90. The PBS documentary *America Rebuilds*, which aired in September 2002, tells the story of the negotiations between the 9/11 families and the residents about where the sphere should be placed.

91. Jimmy Breslin, "A Grim Walking Tour of City's Misery Mile," *Newsday*, July 18, 2002, A4. See also Julie V. Iovine, "Memorials Proliferate in Crowded Downtown," *New York Times*, March 13, 2003.

92. Zuber, "Flanerie at Ground Zero," 287–88.

93. Alex Frangos, "Three Years On, Sept. 11 Families Find Solace in Memorials," *Wall Street Journal*, September 10, 2004, B1.

94. Timothy Dwyer, "9/11 Pentagon Memorial to Reflect Pangs of Loss, Recollections of Joy," *Washington Post*, June 16, 2006, B1.

95. Christopher Hawthorne, "Reading Symbolism in the Sept. 11 Era," *Los Angeles Times*, October 5, 2005; Catesby Leigh, "Monumental Loss," *Weekly Standard*, May 29, 2006, 33. On the Columbine memorial, see Kevin Simpson, "From Heartbreaking to Groundbreaking," *Denver Post*, June 15, 2006, A1; and Kirk Johnson and Katie Kelly, "A Memorial at Last for Columbine Killings," *New York Times*, June 17, 2006, A10.

96. See Frankel, "The Architecture of Loss"; Lerner, "9/11 Memorials"; Frangos, "Three Years On"; Sarah Boxer, "New Jersey Selects Its Sept. 11 Memorial," *New York Times*, July 1, 2003, B3; Philip Nobel, "Soaring Modesty," *Metropolismag.com*, August 1, 2004.

97. David W. Dunlap, "A Hands-on Tribute to 9/11 Firefighters, in Stark Relief," *New York Times*, June 11, 2006, sec. 1, 39.

98. Quoted in Goldberger, *Up from Zero*, 215.

99. *New York Times*, "Giuliani Talks of a City's Spirit, and a Grand Monument to Those Who Died," December 28, 2001, D6.

100. Kimmelman, "Ground Zero's Only Hope." His article was reportedly considered to be "smug cultural superiority" by some jurors. See Michael Kimmelman, "Ground Zero Finally Grows Up," *New York Times*, February 1, sec. 1, p. 1.

101. Paul Goldberger discusses in detail the influence that Lin had on the jury in *Up from Zero*, 227–28.

102. Other jury members were Paula Grant Berry, a businesswoman and widow of victim David Berry; Susan Freedman, president of the Public Art Fund; Patricia Harris, deputy mayor of New York; Michael McKeon, former director of communications for Governor George Pataki; Julie Menin, an attorney and resident of lower Manhattan who is a founder of Wall Street Rising; the architect Enrique Norten; the artist Martin Puryear; Nancy Rosen, a curator of public art; Lowery Stokes Sims, director of the Studio Museum in Harlem; Michael Van Valkenburgh; James E. Young, professor and chair of the Department of Judaic and New Eastern Studies at the University of Massachusetts, Amherst, and a specialist in Holocaust memorials; with David Rockefeller as an honorary member and Vartan Gregorian, president of the Carnegie Corporation and former president of Brown University, as the chair.

103. See Sturken, *Tangled Memories*, chapter 2.

104. Catesby Leigh, "9/11 Memorial Needs an Heroic Touch," *Los Angeles Times*, December 9, 2003, B13.

105. Dennis Smith, "Memorials without a Memory," *New York Times*, November 26, 2003, A29. See also Dennis Smith, *Report from Ground Zero*.

106. Glenn Collins and David W. Dunlap, "Unveiling of the Trade Center Memorial Reveals an Abundance of New Details," *New York Times*, January 15, 2004, A26. The website of all the designs is http://www.wtcsitememorial.org.

107. David W. Dunlap, "5,201 Ideas for 9/11 Memorial, from the Sublime to the Less So," *New York Times*, February 20, 2004, A1.

108. From the design description, http://www.wtcsitememorial.org.

109. Glenn Collins and David W. Dunlap, "The 9/11 Memorial: How Pluribus Became

Unum," *New York Times*, January 19, 2004, A1, A18; David W. Dunlap, "Ground Zero Memorial Cost Estimated at $490 Million," *New York Times*, November 23, 2005, B3. Full descriptions and images of the memorial are on the LMDC website: http://www.renewnyc.com.

110. Stephens, *Imagining Ground Zero*, 38.

111. Steve Cuozzo, "Kill It Now, Mike," *New York Post*, August 22, 2006.

112. The art historian Wouter Weijers notes that it is a misnomer to label the design minimalist, since the artists who pioneered minimalism in the 1960s, such as Donald Judd and Robert Morris, aimed primarily to "attack widely recognized, respected and expected artistic goals such as the creation of transcendent beauty, the expression of complex inner feelings or the unique interpretation of the world by the artist": "Minimalism, Memory."

113. Joan Molinaro, letter to the editor, *New York Times*, January 20, 2004, A18.

114. Monica Gabrielle, "For Those Lost on That Terrible Day," letter to the editor, *New York Times*, January 8, 2004, A32.

115. Young, "The Memorial Process," 161.

116. Ouroussoff, "For the Ground Zero Memorial."

117. Philip Nobel writes in gossipy fashion that Maya Lin told friends that she intended to use the jury as a means to roll back Libeskind's influence on the memorial (*Sixteen Acres*, 242), and Libeskind himself noted that the memorial jury strangely never had the designers meet with him or the other planners involved in the space, as if they were designing in a vacuum (Goldberger, *Up from Zero*, 229–30).

118. Hagan, "The Breaking of Michael Arad," 24. Nevertheless, Libeskind insists in his book that the memorial was not in conflict with his plan but was accommodated into it: *Breaking Ground*, 271.

119. Hagan, "The Breaking of Michael Arad," 20–27, 100–101.

120. Amy Westfeldt, "Official: Smart Cameras, Armed Guards to Protect WTC Site," Associated Press, February 25, 2006.

121. Ellen Barry, "Trying to Fill a Void Left by 9/11," *Los Angeles Times*, March 25, 2006, A1. Goetz, who famously shot four would-be muggers on the subway in 1987, apparently now runs a company called Vigilante Electronics.

122. See *America Rebuilds II*.

123. Kolker, "The Grief Police."

124. Samuel Maull, "9/11 Families File Lawsuit to Stop WTC Ground Zero Memorial," Associated Press, March 11, 2006.

125. Paul D. Colford, "9/11 Kin Ripped on Lawsuit," *Daily News*, April 27, 2006, 6.

126. Young and Van Valkenburgh, "A Last Chance for Ground Zero."

127. Charles V. Bagli and David W. Dunlap, "Memorial's Cost at Ground Zero Nears $1 Billion," *New York Times*, May 5, 2006, A1.

128. *New York Times*, "A Memorial Amiss," May 6, 2006, A14.

129. David W. Dunlap and Charles V. Bagli, "A New Look at Memorial Lowers Cost," *New York Times*, June 21, 2006, B1.

130. Ouroussoff, "The Ground Zero Memorial."

131. Elliot, "Markets Must Walk Fine Line," C8.

132. For an in-depth discussion of the names at the Vietnam Veterans Memorial, see Sturken, *Tangled Memories*, chapter 2.

133. David W. Dunlap, "9/11 Memorial Faces Setback over Names," *New York Times*, June 27, 2006, B1; David W. Dunlap, "Plan is Changed for Arranging Names on Trade Center Memorial," *New York Times*, December 14, 2006, B3.

134. Andrea Peyser, "Public Weary of Kin Who Can't Let Go," *New York Post*, October 18, 2005, 24.

135. David W. Dunlap, "Security Concerns Raised about Memorial at Ground Zero," *New York Times*, April 21, 2006, B1.

136. Burlingame, "The Great Ground Zero Heist."

137. *New York Times*, "Keeping Ground Zero Free," July 12, 2005.

138. *New York Post*, "The Freedom Center: Good Riddance," September 29, 2005, 32; Tom Topousis, "Freedom Center Is Zeroed Out," *New York Post*, September 29, 2005, 7; *New York Post*, "Zero Hour for Ground Zero," September 23, 2005, 38.

139. David W. Dunlap, "Varying Boundaries of Hallowed Ground," *New York Times*, September 8, 2005, B4.

140. Matthew Schuerman, "Bloomberg Evades on Freedom Museum as Founders Lobby," *New York Observer*, October 3, 2005, 13; see also Andrea Peyser, "9/11-Center Plan Buries Dead under Heap of Nonsense," *New York Post*, September 23, 2005, 13.

141. David W. Dunlap, "Memorial Museum Will Depict Life at Trade Center," *New York Times*, August 29, 2005, B1; Tom Topousis, "9/11 Pieces of History—Museum Will Feature Mementos of Tragedy," *New York Post*, October 14, 2005, 4; David W. Dunlap, "Oh, the Stories These Mute Pieces Could Tell," *New York Times*, March 31, 2004, G1.

142. Interview with Alice Greenwald, November 13, 2006.

143. Ouroussoff, "For the Ground Zero Memorial."

144. Goldberger, "Dashed Hopes."

145. Marianne Hirsch, "Surviving Images," 238.

146. Spiegelman, "Introduction," *In the Shadow of No Towers*.

147. Page, *The Creative Destruction*.

148. Foster, *The Return of the Real*, 131, 132. See also Marianne Hirsch, "Surviving Images," 237–38.

CONCLUSION

1. Corey Kilgannon, "Rugs Depict Terror Attack, but New York Isn't Ready for 9/11 Kitsch," *New York Times*, December 15, 2003, B1.

2. Christopher Helman, "Collector's Guide: Carpet Bombing," *Forbes.com*, December 22, 2003, http://www.forbes.com.

3. Cooke, "Michgan and Merza Hozain, Hazare Weavers," in *Weavings of War*, 61.

4. Anglica Pence, "War's Warp and Weft," *San Francisco Chronicle*, May 12, 2004, 1. Sudeith's website is warrug.com.

BIBLIOGRAPHY

Andén-Papadopoulus, Kari. "The Trauma of Representation: Visual Culture, Photojournalism and the September 11 Terrorist Attack." *Nordicon Review* 24 (2003): 89–104. http://www.nordicom.gu.

Andrejevic, Mark. "Interactive (In)Security: The Participatory Promise of Ready. Gov." *Cultural Studies* 20.4–5 (2006): 441–58.

Anti-Defamation League. *Special Report: Paranoia as Patriotism: Far-Right Influences on the Militia Movement.* 1996.

Antonelli, Paola, ed. *Safe: Design Takes on Risk.* New York: Museum of Modern Art, 2005.

Astor, David. "National Furor over Editorial Cartoon," *Editor and Publisher* 130.27 (1997): 33.

Bacharach, Phil. "The Prison Letters of Timothy McVeigh." *Esquire*, May 2001, 130–35.

Baravalle, Georgio, and Cari Modine, eds. *Newyorkseptembereleventwothousandone.* Millbrook, N.Y.: de.MO, 2001.

Berlant, Lauren. "The Subject of True Feeling: Pain, Privacy, and Politics." In *Cultural Pluralism, Identity Politics and the Law*, edited by Austin Sarat and Thomas R. Kearns. Ann Arbor: University of Michigan Press, 1999, 49–84.

———. "The Theory of Infantile Citizenship." In *The Queen of America Goes to Washington City.* Durham: Duke University Press, 1997, 25–53.

Billig, Michael. *Banal Nationalism.* Thousand Oaks, Calif.: Sage, 1995.

Boehm, Scott. "Privatizing Public Memory: The Price of Patriotic Philanthropy and the Post-9/11 Politics of Display." *American Quarterly* 58.4 (2006): 1147–66.

Bradsher, Keith. *High and Mighty: The Dangerous Rise of the SUV.* New York: Public Affairs, 2002.

Breen, T. H. *The Marketplace of Revolution: How Consumer Politics Shaped American Independence.* New York: Oxford University Press, 2004.

Brison, Susan J. *Aftermath: Violence and the Remaking of a Self.* Princeton: Princeton University Press, 2002.

Broch, Hermann. "Notes on the Problem of Kitsch." In *Kitsch: The World of Bad Taste*, edited by Gilles Dorfles. New York: Bell, 1968, 49–67.

Broderick, Mick, and Mark Gibson. "Mourning, Monomyth and Memorabilia: Consumer Logics of Collecting 9/11." In *The Selling of 9/11: How a National Tragedy Became a Commodity*, edited by Dana Heller. New York: Palgrave Macmillan, 2005, 200–220.

Brown, Bill. "American Kitsch: The Souvenir." Paper presented at the American Studies Association annual meeting, Atlanta, November 2004.

———. *A Sense of Things: The Object Matter of American Literature*. Chicago: University of Chicago Press, 2003.

Brown, Michelle. "'Setting the Conditions' for Abu Ghraib: The Prison Nation Abroad." *American Quarterly* 57.3 (2005): 973–97.

Bubriski, Kevin. *Pilgrimage: Looking at Ground Zero*. New York: Powerhouse Books, 2002.

Burlingame, Debra. "The Great Ground Zero Heist." *Wall Street Journal*, June 7, 2005, A14.

Burton-Rose, Daniel, Dan Pens, and Paul Wright, eds. *The Celling of America: An Inside Look at the U.S. Prison Industry*. Monroe, Maine: Common Courage Press, 1998.

Butler, Judith. *Precarious Life: The Powers of Mourning and Violence*. London: Verso, 2003.

Butzer, Hans. "Deciding What Our Loss Means." *New York Times*, October 10, 2001, A19.

Calhoun, Craig, Paul Price, and Ashley Timmer, eds. *Understanding September 11*. New York: New Press, 2002.

Calinescu, Matei. "Kitsch and Modernity." In *Five Faces of Modernity*. Durham: Duke University Press, 1987, 225–62.

Campbell, David. "The Biopolitics of Security: Oil, Empire, and the Sports Utility Vehicle." *American Quarterly* 57.3 (2005): 943–72.

———. *Writing Security: United States Foreign Policy and the Politics of Identity*. 1992. Rev. ed. Minneapolis: University of Minnesota Press, 1998.

Caputi, Jane, and James F. Tracy, eds. "Theme Issue: Responses to 9/11." Special issue of *Journal of American Culture*. 28.1 (2005).

Clark, Laurie Beth. "Placed and Displaced: Trauma Memorials." In *Performance and Place*, edited by Leslie Hill and Helen Paris. New York: Palgrave Macmillan, 2006, 129–38.

Clifford, James. *The Predicament of Culture: Twentieth-Century Literature, Ethnography, and Art*. Cambridge, Mass.: Harvard University Press, 1988.

Cohen, Lizabeth. *A Consumers' Republic: The Politics of Mass Consumption in Postwar America*. New York: Vintage, 2003.

Collyer, Stanley. "The Search for an Appropriate Symbol: The Oklahoma City Memorial Competition." *Competitions* 7.3 (1997): 4–15.

Cooke, Ariel Zeitlin, and Marsha MacDowell, eds. *Weavings of War: Fabrics of Memory*. East Lansing: Michigan State University Museum, 2005.

Couldry, Nick. *Media Rituals: A Critical Approach*. New York: Routledge, 2003.

Crouch, David, and Nina Lübbren, eds. *Visual Culture and Tourism*. New York: Berg, 2003.

Darton, Eric. *Divided We Stand: A Biography of New York's World Trade Center.* New York: Basic Books, 1999.

Davis, Mike. *City of Quartz: Excavating the Future in Los Angeles.* London: Verso, 1990.

———. "The Flames of New York." In *Dead Cities and Other Tales.* New York: New Press, 2002, 1–20.

de Certeau, Michel. "Walking in the City." In *The Practice of Everyday Life.* Translated by Steven Rendall. Berkeley: University of California Press, 1984, 91–110.

Dees, Morris, ed. *The Gathering Storm: America's Militia Threat.* New York: HarperCollins, 1996.

Desmond, Jane. *Staging Tourism: Bodies on Display from Waikiki to Sea World.* Chicago: University of Chicago Press, 1999.

Dorfles, Gilles, ed. *Kitsch: The World of Bad Taste.* New York: Bell, 1968.

Doss, Erika. "Death, Art and Memory in the Public Sphere: The Visual and Material Culture of Grief in America." *Mortality* 7.1 (2002): 63–82.

Douglas, Mary. *Purity and Danger: An Analysis of Concepts of Pollution and Taboo.* 1966. New York: Routledge, 1980.

Dudziak, Mary L., ed. *September 11 in History: A Watershed Moment?* Durham: Duke University Press, 2003.

Dyer, Joel. *Harvest of Rage: Why Oklahoma City Is Only the Beginning.* New York: Westview, 1997.

Easterling, Keller. *Enduring Innocence: Global Architecture and Its Political Masquerades.* Cambridge, Mass.: MIT Press, 2005.

Ehrenreich, Barbara. "Welcome to Cancerland: A Mammogram Leads to a Cult of Pink Kitsch." *Harper's,* November 2001, 43–53.

Ellin, Nan, ed. *Architecture of Fear.* New York: Princeton Architectural Press, 1997.

Espiritu, Karen. "'Putting Grief into Boxes': Trauma and the Crisis of Democracy in Art Spiegelman's *In the Shadow of No Towers.*" *Review of Education, Pedagogy, and Cultural Studies* 28 (2006): 179–201.

Farrell, John. *Freud's Paranoid Quest: Psychoanalysis and Modern Suspicion.* New York: New York University Press, 1996.

Feldman, Allen. "Ground Zero Point One: On the Cinematics of History." In *The World Trade Center and Global Crisis,* edited by Bruce Kapferer. New York: Berghahn Books, 2004, 26–36.

Fenster, Mark. *Conspiracy Theories: Secrecy and Power in American Culture.* Minneapolis: University of Minnesota Press, 1999.

Filler, Martin. "Back to Babel." *New Republic,* February 2, 2003, 23.

———. "Filling the Hole." *New York Review of Books,* February 24, 2005, 6–11.

———. "Into the Void." *New Republic,* October 1, 2001, 26–31.

Finnegan, William. "The Terrorism Beat: A Reporter at Large." *New Yorker,* July 25, 2005, 58–70.

Foote, Kenneth E. *Shadowed Ground: America's Landscapes of Violence and Tragedy.* 1997. Revised and updated. Austin: University of Texas Press, 2003.

Foster, Hal. "In New York." *London Review of Books,* March 20, 2003, 17.

———. *The Return of the Real: The Avant-Garde at the End of the Century.* Cambridge, Mass.: MIT Press, 1996.

———. "Yellow Ribbons: Kitsch in Bush's America." *London Review of Books,* July 7, 2005, 29–31.

Foucault, Michel. *Discipline and Punish: The Birth of the Prison.* 1975. New York: Vintage, 1979.

Frankel, Glenn. "The Architecture of Loss." *Washington Post Magazine,* September 10, 2006, 12–33.

Franklin, Ruth. "Mr. Memory." *New Republic,* February 7, 2005, 28–33.

Frascina, Francis. "*The New York Times,* Norman Rockwell and the New Patriotism." *Journal of Visual Culture* 2.1 (2003): 99–130.

Freud, Sigmund. "On Narcissism: An Introduction." 1914. In *The Standard Edition of the Complete Psychological Works of Sigmund Freud*, vol. 14. Translated by James Strachey. London: Hogarth, 1957, 67–104.

———. "Psycho-Analytic Notes on an Autobiographical Account of a Case of Paranoia." 1911. In *The Standard Edition of the Complete Psychological Works of Sigmund Freud*, vol. 12. Translated by James Strachey. London: Hogarth, 1958, 3–82.

———. "Remembering, Repeating and Working-Through." 1914. In *The Standard Edition of the Complete Psychological Works of Sigmund Freud*, vol. 12. Translated by James Strachey. London: Hogarth, 1958, 145–56.

Friend, David. *Watching the World Change: The Stories behind the Images of 9/11.* New York: Farrar, Strauss and Giroux, 2006.

Gabler, Neal. *Life: The Movie. How Entertainment Conquered Reality.* New York: Vintage, 2000.

George, Alice Rose, Gilles Peress, Michal Shulan, and Charles Traub, eds. *Here Is New York: A Democracy of Photographs.* New York: Scalo, 2002.

Giesz, Ludwig. "Kitsch-man as Tourist." In *Kitsch: The World of Bad Taste*, edited by Gilles Dorfles. New York: Bell Publishing, 1968, 156–74.

Gillespie, Angus Kress. *Twin Towers: The Life of New York City's World Trade Center.* 1999. New York: New American Library, 2002.

Gilmore, Ruth Wilson. *Golden Gulag: Prisons, Surplus, Crisis, and Opposition in Globalizing California.* Berkeley: University of California Press, 2007.

Giovannini, Joseph. "Rising to Greatness." *New York,* September 16, 2002, 46.

Gitlin, Todd. *The Intellectuals and the Flag.* New York: Columbia University Press, 2006.

Gladwell, Malcolm. "Big and Bad: How the S.U.V. Ran Over Automotive Safety." *New Yorker,* January 12, 2004, 28–33.

Glanz, James, and Eric Lipton. *City in the Sky: The Rise and Fall of the World Trade Center.* New York: Times Books, 2003.

Glassner, Barry. *The Culture of Fear: Why Americans Are Afraid of the Wrong Things.* New York: Basic Books, 1999.

Goldberger, Paul. "Dashed Hopes for a Charged Site: What Went Wrong at Ground Zero." *Architectural Record* 193.9 (2005): 61.

———. "A New Beginning." *New Yorker,* May 30, 2005, 54–57.

————. "Requiem: Memorializing Terrorism's Victims in Oklahoma." *New Yorker*, January 14, 2002, 90.

————. *Up from Zero: Politics, Architecture, and the Rebuilding of New York*. New York: Random House, 2004.

Goodell, Jeff. "Letting Go of McVeigh." *New York Times Magazine*, May 13, 2001, 40–44.

Greenberg, Clement. "Avant-Garde and Kitsch." 1939. In *Clement Greenberg: The Collected Essays and Criticism*, vol. 1: *Perceptions and Judgments, 1939–1944*, edited by John O'Brian. Chicago: University of Chicago Press, 1986, 5–22.

Griswold, Charles. "The Vietnam Veterans Memorial and the Washington Mall: Philosophical Thoughts on Political Iconography." *Critical Inquiry* 12 (summer 1986): 688–719.

Gullbring, Leo, Maria Hellström, and Jennifer Magnolfi, eds. "New York Naked City: Spatial Realities after 9/11." Special Issue of *Area: Magazine of Landscape Architecture and Urban Planning* 1–2 (2003).

Haas, Kristin. *Carried to the Wall: American Memory and the Vietnam Veterans Memorial*. Berkeley: University of California Press, 1998.

Hagan, Joe. "The Breaking of Michael Arad." *New York*, May 22, 2006, 20–27, 100–102.

Hallinan, Joseph T. *Going up the River: Travels in a Prison Nation*. New York: Random House, 2001.

Hariman, Robert, and John Louis Lucaites. "Performing Civic Identity: The Iconic Photograph of the Flag Raising on Iwo Jima." *Quarterly Journal of Speech* 88.4 (2002): 363–92.

Harris, Daniel. "Kiddie Kitsch and the Twice-Removed Aesthetic." Paper presented at the Society for Cinema Studies conference, New York, 1995.

————. *Cute, Quaint, Hungry and Romantic: The Aesthetics of Consumerism*. Cambridge, Mass.: Da Capo Press, 2001.

————. "The Kitschification of Sept. 11." *Salon.com*, January 25, 2002. http://www.salon.com.

————. "Making Kitsch from AIDS." *Harper's*, June 1994, 55–61.

Hauerwas, Stanley, and Frank Lentricchia, eds. *Dissent from the Homeland: Essays after September 11*. Durham: Duke University Press, 2003.

Havrilesky, Heather. "The Selling of 9/11," *Salon.com*, September 7, 2002. http://archive.salon.com.

Hay, James. "Designing Homes to Be the First Line of Defense: Safe Households, Mobilization, and the New Mobile Privatization." *Cultural Studies* 20.4–5 (2006): 349–77.

Hay, James, and Mark Andrejevic. "Introduction: Toward an Analytic of Governmental Experiments in These Times: Homeland Security as the New Social Security." *Cultural Studies* 20.4–5 (2006): 331–48.

Heilemann, John. "Poker at Ground Zero." *New York*, March 27, 2006, 22–24.

Hein, Laura, and Daizaburo Yui, eds. *Crossed Memories: Perspectives on 9/11 and American Power*. Tokyo: Center for Pacific and American Studies, 2003.

Heller, Dana, ed. *The Selling of 9/11: How a National Tragedy Became a Commodity*. New York: Palgrave Macmillan, 2005.

Hirsch, Marianne. "I Took Pictures: September 2001 and Beyond." In *Trauma at Home: After 9/11*, edited by Judith Greenberg. Lincoln: University of Nebraska Press, 2003, 69–86.

———. "Surviving Images: Holocaust Photographs and the Work of Postmemory." In *Visual Culture and the Holocaust*, edited by Barbie Zelizer. New Brunswick, N.J.: Rutgers University Press, 2001, 215–46.

Hirsch, Michael, John Barry, and Babak Dehghanpisheh. "Hillbilly Armor." *Newsweek*, December 20, 2004, 24–30.

Hofstadter, Richard. *The Paranoid Style in American Politics and Other Essays*. New York: Vintage, 1967.

Hurley, Molly, and James Trimarco. "Morality and Merchandise: Vendors, Visitors and Police at New York City's Ground Zero." *Critique of Anthropology* 24.1 (2004): 51–78.

Huxtable, Ada Louise. "Another World Trade Center Horror." *Wall Street Journal*, July 25, 2002, B13.

———. "The Disaster That Has Followed the Tragedy." *Wall Street Journal*, September 28, 2006, D8.

———. "The New York Process: Don't Expect Anything Uplifting from the Pols and Realtors Now Pondering the WTC Site." *Wall Street Journal*, September 17, 2001, A20.

Huyssen, Andreas. *Present Pasts: Urban Palimpsests and the Politics of Memory*. Stanford: Stanford University Press, 2003.

Irby, Kenney. "One Man's Path to Historic Photo: Persistence and a Lift on a Tug," *Poynter.org*, October 17, 2001. http://www.poynter.org.

Isenberg, Noah. "Reading 'Between the Lines': Daniel Libeskind's Berlin Jewish Museum and the Shattered Symbiosis." In *Unlikely History: The Changing German-Jewish Symbiosis, 1945–2000*, edited by Leslie Morris and Jack Zipes. New York: Palgrave, 2002, 155–79.

Jones, Paul R. "The Sociology of Architecture and the Politics of Building: The Discursive Construction of Ground Zero." *Sociology* 40.3 (2006): 549–65.

Jorgensen-Earp, Cheryl R., and Lori A. Lanzilotti. "Public Memory and Private Grief: The Construction of Shrines at the Sites of Public Tragedy." *Quarterly Journal of Speech* 84 (1998): 150–70.

Junod, Tom. "The Falling Man." *Esquire*, September 2003, 177–82.

Kapferer, Bruce, ed. *The World Trade Center and Global Crisis*. New York: Berghahn Books, 2004.

Kaplan, Amy. *The Anarchy of Empire in the Making of U.S. Culture*. Cambridge, Mass.: Harvard University Press, 2002.

———. "Homeland Insecurities: Transformations of Language and Space." In *September 11 in History: A Watershed Moment?*, edited by Mary L. Dudziak. Durham: Duke University Press, 2003, 55–69

————. "Left Alone with America: The Absence of Empire in the Study of American Culture." In *Cultures of United States Imperialism*, edited by Amy Kaplan and Donald Pease. Durham: Duke University Press, 1993, 3–21.

————. "Violent Belongings and the Question of Empire Today: Presidential Address to the American Studies Association." *American Quarterly* 56.1 (2004): 1–18.

Kennedy, Liam. "Remembering September 11: Photography as Cultural Diplomacy." *International Affairs* 79.2 (2003): 315–26.

Kimmelman, Michael. "Ground Zero's Only Hope: Elitism." *New York Times*, December 7, 2003, sec. 2, p. 1.

Kirschenblatt-Gimblett, Barbara. *Destination Culture: Tourism, Museums, and Heritage*. Berkeley: University of California Press, 1998.

————. "Kodak Moments, Flashbulb Memories: Reflections on 9/11." *Drama Review* 47.1 (2003): 11–48.

Knight, Marsha. *Forever Changed: Remembering Oklahoma City, April 19, 1995*. Amherst, N.Y.: Prometheus Books, 1998.

Knight, Peter. *Conspiracy Culture: From Kennedy to the X Files*. New York: Routledge, 2000.

Kolker, Robert. "The Grief Police." *New York*, November 28, 2005, 46–55.

Kuipers, Giselinde. "Media Culture and Internet Disaster Jokes." *European Journal of Cultural Studies* 5.4 (2002): 450–70.

Kundera, Milan. *The Unbearable Lightness of Being*. 1984. Translated by Michael Henry Heim. New York: Harper and Row, 1984.

Langewiesche, William. *American Ground: Unbuilding the World Trade Center*. New York: North Point Press, 2002.

Lasansky, D. Medina, and Brian McLaren, eds. *Architecture and Tourism: Perception, Performance and Place*. New York: Berg, 2004.

Lauer, Josh. "Driven to Extremes: Fear of Crime and the Rise of the Sport Utility Vehicle in the United States." *Crime Media Culture* 1.2 (2005): 149–68.

Lears, T. J. Jackson. "From Salvation to Self-Realization: Advertising and the Therapeutic Roots of the Consumer Culture, 1880–1930." In *The Culture of Consumption: Critical Essays in American History, 1880–1980*, edited by Richard Wrightman Fox and T. J. Jackson Lears. New York: Pantheon, 1983, 3–38.

LeDuff, Charles. *Work and Other Sins: Life in New York City and Thereabouts*. New York: Penguin, 2004.

Lennon, John, and Malcolm Foley. *Dark Tourism: The Attraction of Death and Disaster*. New York: Continuum, 2000.

Lerner, Kevin. "9/11 Memorials, Not Just in Manhattan." *Architectural Record* 192.6 (2004): 48.

Lesser, Wendy. *Pictures at an Execution: An Inquiry into the Subject of Murder*. Cambridge, Mass.: Harvard University Press, 1993.

Libeskind, Daniel. *Breaking Ground: Adventures in Life and Architecture*. New York: Riverhead Books, 2004.

————. *Jewish Museum Berlin*. Berlin: G and B Arts International, 1999.

————. *The Space of Encounter.* New York: Universe, 2000.

Lifton, Robert Jay, and Greg Mitchell. *Who Owns Death? Capital Punishment, the American Conscience, and the End of Executions.* New York: William Morrow/HaperCollins, 2000.

Linenthal, Edward T. "'The Predicament of Aftermath': Oklahoma City and September 11." In *The Resilient City: How Modern Cities Recover from Disaster,* edited by Lawrence J. Vale and Thomas J. Campanella. New York: Oxford University Press, 2005, 55–74.

————. *Sacred Ground: Americans and Their Battlefields.* Urbana: University of Illinois Press, 1991.

————. *The Unfinished Bombing: Oklahoma City in American Memory.* New York: Oxford University Press, 2001.

Lippard, Lucy R. "The Fall." In *Architourism: Authentic Escapist Exotic Spectacular,* edited by Joan Ockman and Salomon Frausto. Munich: Prestel Verlag, 2005, 68–79.

Lipsitz, George. *American Studies in a Moment of Danger.* Minneapolis: University of Minnesota Press, 2001.

Lockard, Joe. "Social Fear and the Commodification of Terrorism." *Bad Subjects* 59 (February 2002), http://bad.eserver.org.

Lokaneeta, Jinee. "Revenge and the Spectacular Execution: The Timothy McVeigh Case." In *Studies in Law, Politics, and Society,* edited by Austin Sarat and Patricia Ewick. Amsterdam: Elsevier, 2004, 201–20.

Lombardi, Kristen. "Death by Dust." *Village Voice* (November 29–December 5, 2006), 14–30.

Low, Setha M. "The Memorialization of September 11: Dominant and Local Discourses on the Rebuilding of the World Trade Center Site." *American Ethnologist* 31.3 (2004): 326–39.

Lowood, Henry. "Death in the City: Computer Games and the Urban Battlefield." Paper presented at the Urban Trauma and the Metropolitan Imagination conference, Stanford University, May 6, 2005.

Lurie, Susan. "Falling Persons and National Embodiment: The Reconstruction of Safe Spectatorship in the Photographic Record of 9/11." In *Terror, Culture, Politics: Rethinking 9/11,* edited by Daniel J. Sherman and Terry Nardin. Bloomington: Indiana University Press, 2006, 44–68.

Lutyens, Dominic. "Ground Hero." *The Observer,* June 22, 2003.

MacCannell, Dean. *The Tourist: A New Theory of the Leisure Class.* 1976. Berkeley: University of California Press, 1999.

Manjoo, Farhad. "Cityscape of Fear." *Salon.com,* August 22, 2006. http://www.salon.com.

Marling, Karal Ann, and John Wetenhall. *Iwo Jima: Monuments, Memories, and the American Hero.* Cambridge, Mass.: Harvard University Press, 1991.

McDonald, Dwight. "Masscult and Midcult." In *Against the American Grain.* New York: Random House, 1952, 3–75.

Melley, Timothy. *Empire of Conspiracy: The Culture of Paranoia in Postwar America.* Ithaca, N.Y.: Cornell University Press, 2000.

Meyerowitz, Joel. *Aftermath: World Trade Center Archive*. New York: Phaidon, 2006.

Michel, Lou, and Dan Herbeck. *American Terrorist: Timothy McVeigh and the Oklahoma City Bombing*. New York: Reganbooks, 2001.

Miller, Nancy K. "Reporting the Disaster." In *Trauma at Home: After 9/11*, edited by Judith Greenberg. Lincoln: University of Nebraska Press, 2003, 39–47.

Minow, Martha. "Surviving Victim Talk." *UCLA Law Review* 40 (1993): 1411–45.

Mirzoeff, Nicholas. *Watching Babylon: The War in Iraq and Global Visual Culture*. New York: Routledge, 2005.

Mollenkopf, John, ed. *Contentious City: The Politics of Recovery in New York City*. New York: Russell Sage Foundation, 2005.

Morley, David. *Home Territories: Media, Mobility, Identity*. New York: Routledge, 2000.

Mosco, Vincent. *The Digital Sublime: Myth, Power, and Cyberspace*. Cambridge, Mass.: MIT Press, 2004.

Murphy, Jarrett. "The Seekers: The Birth and Life of the '9-11 Truth' Movement." *Village Voice*, February 22–28, 2006, 23–28.

Muschamp, Herbert. "Balancing Reason and Emotion in Twin Towers Void." *New York Times*, February 6, 2003, E1.

———. "Don't Rebuild, Reimagine." *New York Times Magazine*, September 8, 2002, 46–58.

New York New Visions. "Principles for the Rebuilding of Lower Manhattan." Policy paper. February 2002.

New York Times Magazine. "To Rebuild or Not: Architects Respond." September 23, 2001, 81.

Nobel, Philip. *Sixteen Acres: Architecture and the Outrageous Struggle for the Future of Ground Zero*. New York: Metropolitan Books, 2005.

Noble, David W. *Death of a Nation: American Culture and the End of Exceptionalism*. Minneapolis: University of Minnesota Press, 2002.

———. *The End of American History: Democracy, Capitalism, and the Metaphor of Two Worlds in Anglo-American Historical Writing, 1880–1980*. Minneapolis: University of Minnesota Press, 1985.

Ockman, Joan, ed. *Out of Ground Zero: Case Studies in Urban Reinvention*. Munich: Prestel Verlag, 2002.

Ockman, Joan, and Salomon Frausto, eds. *Architourism: Authentic Escapist Exotic Spectacular*. Munich: Prestel Verlag, 2005.

O'Donnell, Patrick. "Engendering Paranoia in Contemporary Narrative." In *National Identities and Post-Americanist Narratives*, edited by Donald Pease. Durham: Duke University Press, 1994, 181–204.

———. *Latent Destinies: Cultural Paranoia and Contemporary U.S. Narrative*. Durham: Duke University Press, 2000.

Olalquiaga, Celeste. *The Artificial Kingdom: A Treasury of the Kitsch Experience*. New York: Pantheon, 1998.

Ouroussoff, Nicolai. "At Ground Zero, Towers for Forgetting." *New York Times*, September 11, 2006, E1, E7.

———. "For the Ground Zero Memorial, Death by Committee." *New York Times*, June 19, 2005, sec. 2, p. 1.

———. "The Ground Zero Memorial, Revised but Not Improved," *New York Times*, June 22, 2006, E5.

———. "A Tower of Impregnability, the Sort Politicians Love." *New York Times*, June 30, 2005, B1–B2.

Page, Max. *The Creative Destruction of Manhattan, 1900–1940*. Chicago: University of Chicago, 1999.

Pearman, Hugh. "The Battle for Ground Zero." *Gabion: Retained Writing on Architecture*, http://www.hughpearman.com.

Penley, Constance. *NASA/Trek: Popular Science and Sex in America*. London: Verso, 1997.

Peterson, Michael. "Walking in Sin City." In *Performance and Place*, edited by Leslie Hill and Helen Paris. New York: Palgrave Macmillan, 2006, 113–28.

Philip, Kavita, Eliza Jane Reilly, and David Serlin, eds. "Homeland Securities." Special issue of *Radical History Review* 93 (fall 2005).

Pogrebin, Robin. "Architecture: The Incredible Shrinking Daniel Libeskind." *New York Times*, June 20, 2004, sec. 2, p. 1.

Protetch, Max. *A New World Trade Center: Design Proposals from Leading Architects Worldwide*. New York: ReganBooks, 2002.

Rand, Erica. *The Ellis Island Snow Globe*. Durham: Duke University Press, 2005.

Rapaille, Clotaire. *The Culture Code*. New York: Broadway Books, 2006.

Retort (Ian Boal, T. J. Clark, Joseph Matthews, and Michael Watts). *Afflicted Powers: Capital and Spectacle in a New Age of War*. London: Verso, 2005.

Rich, Frank. "It's Closure Mongering Time." *New York Times*, April 28, 2001, A23.

Richards, Eugene, and Janine Altongy. *Stepping through the Ashes*. New York: Aperture, 2002.

Riley, Terrence. "What to Build." *New York Times Magazine*, November 11, 2001, 92–96.

Rimer, Sara. "Victims Not of One Voice on Execution of McVeigh." *New York Times*, April 25, 2001, A1, A16.

Robertson, Lori. "High Anxiety." *American Journalism Review* 25.3 (2003): 18–21.

Rogers, Patrick. "Closing the Book." *People*, June 25, 2001, 55–59.

Rosario, Kevin. "Making Progress: Disaster Narratives and the Art of Optimism in Modern America." In *The Resilient City: How Modern Cities Recover from Disaster*, edited by Lawrence J. Vale and Thomas J. Campanella. New York: Oxford University Press, 2005, 27–54.

Sales, Nancy Jo. "Click Here for Conspiracy." *Vanity Fair* (August 2006): 112–18.

Sanders, James. *Celluloid Skyline: New York and the Movies*. New York: Knopf, 2001.

———. "Honoring the Dead in the City That Never Weeps." *New York Times*, August 31, 2003, sec. 2, p. 19.

Sarat, Austin, ed. *The Killing State: Capital Punishment in Law, Politics, and Culture*. New York: Oxford University Press, 1999.

———. *When the State Kills: Capital Punishment and the American Condition*. Princeton: Princeton University Press, 2001.

Savage, Kirk. "Trauma, Healing, and the Therapeutic Monument." In *Terror, Culture, Politics: Rethinking 9/11*, edited by Daniel J. Sherman and Terry Nardin. Bloomington: Indiana University Press, 2006, 103–20.

Scanlon, Jennifer. "'Your Flag Decal Won't Get You into Heaven Anymore': U.S. Consumers, Wal-Mart, and the Commodification of Patriotism." In *The Selling of 9/11: How a National Tragedy Became a Commodity*, edited by Dana Heller. New York: Palgrave Macmillan, 2005, 174–99.

Scarry, Elaine. *Who Defended the Country?* Boston: Beacon, 2003.

Sedgwick, Eve Kosofsky. "Paranoid Reading and Reparative Reading; Or, You're so Paranoid, You Probably Think This Introduction Is about You." In *Novel Gazing: Queer Readings in Fiction*, edited by Eve Kosofsky Sedgwick. Durham: Duke University Press, 1997, 1–37.

Sella, Marshall. "Missing: How a Grief Ritual Is Born." *New York Times Magazine*, October 7, 2001, 48–51.

Shaffer, Marguerite S. *See America First: Tourism and National Identity, 1880–1940*. Washington, D.C.: Smithsonian Institution Press, 2001.

Sheehy, Gail. *Middletown, America: One Town's Passage from Trauma to Hope*. New York: Random House, 2003.

Sherman, Daniel J. "Naming and the Violence of Place." In *Terror, Culture, Politics: Rethinking 9/11*, edited by Daniel J. Sherman and Terry Nardin. Bloomington: Indiana University Press, 2006, 121–45.

Sherman, Daniel J., and Terry Nardin, eds. *Terror, Culture, Politics: Rethinking 9/11*. Bloomington: Indiana University Press, 2006, 121–45.

Simpson, David. *9/11: The Culture of Commemoration*. Chicago: University of Chicago Press, 2006.

Smith, David W., Elaine H. Christiansen, Robert Vincent, and Neil E. Hann. "Population Effects of the Bombing of Oklahoma City." *Journal: Oklahoma State Medical Association* (April 1999).

Smith, Dennis. *Report from Ground Zero: The Story of the Rescue Efforts at the World Trade Center*. New York: Viking Press, 2002.

Smith, Terry. *The Architecture of Aftermath*. Chicago: University of Chicago Press, 2006.

Sontag, Deborah. "The Hole in the City's Heart." *New York Times*, special section: "Broken Ground," September 11, 2006, 1–10.

Sorkin, Michael. *Starting from Zero: Reconstructing Downtown New York*. New York: Routledge, 2003.

Sorkin, Michael, and Sharon Zukin, eds. *After the World Trade Center: Rethinking New York City*. New York: Routledge, 2002.

Spiegelman, Art. *In the Shadow of No Towers*. New York: Pantheon, 2004.

Spigel, Lynn. "Entertainment Wars: Television Culture after 9/11." *American Quarterly* 56.2 (2004): 235–70.

Spreiregen, Paul. "Oklahoma Memorial: A Path Fraught with Pitfalls?" *Competitions* 6.1 (1996): 2.

Stallabrass, Julian. "Spectacle and Terror." *New Left Review* 37 (January/February 2006): 87–106.

Stamelman, Richard. "September 11: Between Memory and History." In *Trauma at Home: After 9/11*, edited by Judith Greenberg. Lincoln: University of Nebraska Press, 2003, 11–20.

Steedman, Carolyn. *Dust: The Archive and Cultural History*. New Brunswick, N.J.: Rutgers University Press, 2002.

Stephens, Suzanne. *Imagining Ground Zero: Official and Unofficial Proposals for the World Trade Center Site*. New York: Rizzoli, 2004.

Stewart, Susan. *On Longing: Narratives of the Miniature, the Gigantic, the Souvenir, the Collection*. Durham: Duke University Press, 1993.

Strain, Ellen. *Public Places, Private Journeys: Ethnography, Entertainment, and the Tourist Gaze*. New Brunswick, N.J.: Rutgers University Press, 2003.

Strupp, Joe. "The Photo Felt around the World." *Editor and Publisher*, May 13, 1995, 12–15.

Sturken, Marita. *Tangled Memories: The Vietnam War, the AIDS Epidemic, and the Politics of Remembering*. Berkeley: University of California Press, 1997.

Taylor, Diana. *The Archive and the Repertoire: Performing Cultural Memory in the Americas*. Durham: Duke University Press, 2003.

Tomasky, Michael. "Battleground Zero." *New York Review of Books*, May 1, 2003, 18–22.

Tomkins, Calvin. "After the Towers." *New Yorker*, July 15, 2002, 59–67.

Trimarco, James, and Molly Hurley Depret. "Wounded Nation, Broken Time." In *The Selling of 9/11: How a National Tragedy Became a Commodity*, edited by Dana Heller. New York: Palgrave Macmillan, 2005, 27–53.

Urry, John. *The Tourist Gaze*. Thousand Oaks, Calif.: Sage, 2002.

Vale, Lawrence J., and Thomas J. Campanella, eds. *The Resilient City: How Modern Cities Recover from Disaster*. New York: Oxford University Press, 2005.

van der Kolk, Bessel, and Onno van der Hart. "The Intrusive Past: The Flexibility of Memory and the Engraving of Trauma." In *Trauma: Explorations in Memory*, edited by Cathy Caruth. Baltimore: Johns Hopkins University Press, 1995, 158–82.

Vidal, Gore. "The Meaning of Timothy McVeigh." *Vanity Fair*, September 2001, 347–53, 409–15.

Walker, Rob. "Building Value." *New York Times Magazine*, May 21, 2006, 50.

Wallace, Aurora. "Missing Twins." *Philosophy and Geography* 5.1 (2002): 13–17.

Wallace, Mike. *A New Deal for New York*. New York: Bell and Weiland, 2002.

Warner, Michael. "The Mass Public and the Mass Subject." In *The Phantom Public Sphere*, edited by Bruce Robbins. Minneapolis: University of Minnesota Press, 1993, 234–56.

Weeks, Jim. *Gettysburg: Memory, Market, and an American Shrine*. Princeton: Princeton University Press, 2003.

Weijers, Wouter. "Minimalism, Memory and the Reflection of Absence." Paper presented at the Technologies of Memory in the Arts conference, Radboud University, Nijmegen, Netherlands, May 2006.

Weschler, Lawrence. "Echoes at Ground Zero: A Conversation with Joel Meyerowitz." In Weschler, *Everything That Rises: A Book of Convergences*. San Francisco: McSweeney's Books, 2006, 5–22.

Williams, William Appleman. *Empire as a Way of Life.* 1980. Brooklyn: Ig, 2007.

Willis, Cynthia. "Tempered by Flame: Heroism, Nationalism, and the New York Firefighter on 9/11 and Beyond." Ph.D. dissertation, University of Southern California, 2006.

Willis, Susan. *Portents of the Real: A Primer for Post-9/11 America.* London: Verso, 2005.

Wills, Gary. "The Dramaturgy of Death." *New York Review of Books,* June 21, 2001, 6–10.

Yaeger, Patricia. "Rubble as Archive, or 9/11 as Dust, Debris, and Bodily Vanishing." In *Trauma at Home: After 9/11,* edited by Judith Greenberg. Lincoln: University of Nebraska Press, 2003, 187–94.

Young, James E. *At Memory's Edge: After-Images of the Holocaust in Contemporary Art and Architecture.* New Haven: Yale University Press, 2000.

———. "The Memorial Process: A Juror's Report from Ground Zero." In *Contentious City: The Politics of Recovery in New York City,* edited by John Mollenkopf. New York: Russell Sage Foundation, 2005, 140–62.

Young, James E., and Michael Van Valkenburgh. "A Last Chance for Ground Zero." *New York Times,* May 18, 2006, A29.

Zelizer, Barbie. "Photography, Journalism, and Trauma." In *Journalism after September 11,* edited by Barbie Zelizer and Stuart Allan. New York: Routledge, 2002, 48–68.

Zelizer, Barbie, and Stuart Allan, eds. *Journalism after September 11.* New York: Routledge, 2002.

Žižek, Slavoj. *Welcome to the Desert of the Real!* London: Verso, 2002.

Zuber, Devin. "Flanerie at Ground Zero: Aesthetic Countermemories in Lower Manhattan." *American Quarterly* 58.2 (2006): 269–99.

INDEX

Page numbers in italics indicate figures.

Architecture (*continued*)
reenactment in, 9, 26, 28, 219–222, 235, 239–42, 244, 247–48, 250–51; security in, 70, 80–82, 127–28, 252–56; skyscrapers in, 79–80, 229, 231–33, 242–43, 253–54, 268

Ashcroft, Attorney General John, 145, 150, 153–54, 208

Asymptote (Hani Rashad and Lise Anne Couture), 235, *235*, 240

Baay, William, 154
Bacharach, Phil, 144
Baghdad, 74, 291–92
Ban, Shigeru, 235–38, *237*, *239*
Benson, Steve, 103
Berg, Sven, 109
Berlant, Lauren, 25, 46
Beyer Blinder Belle, 238
Billig, Michael, 15
Bill of Rights, 145
Bin Laden, Osama, 159–60, 281, 305 n.50
Blanchard, Arlene, 154
Bono, 57
Booker, Casandra, 115, 124
Borg, Jennifer, 193
Borland, Ralph, 83
Boym, Constantin, 100, *100*
Bradley, Daina, 124, 154
Bradsher, Keith, 86–87
Brady, James, 44
Brady Bill, 44
Branch Davidians, 44, 95
Breast cancer culture, 23–24
Brillembourg, Carlos, 235, *237*, 240
Brison, Susan J., 27
Broch, Hermann, 19
Brown, Michelle, 50
Bulin, Jim, 85
Bureau of Alcohol, Tobacco, and Firearms (ATF), 123
Burlingame, Debra, 251, 274

Bush, George W., 15, 56, 58–59, *194*, 198, 281; as Governor of Texas, 147; presidential administration of, 17, 71, 73, 151, 159, 198, 253, 282

Butler, Judith, 30
Butzer, Hans, 109, 127–28, 259
Butzer, Torrey, 109, 127

Cable News Network (CNN), 128, 158, 174, 233, 236
Calatrava, Santiago, 250–51, *252*
Calinescu, Matei, 19
Campbell, David, 38–39, 89
Cantor Fitzgerald, 62–63, 183, 275
Carter, Una Jean, 101, *102*
Cheney, Vice-President Richard, 161
Childs, David, 252, 254–55
China: death penalty in, 151; as source of manufactured goods, 3, 54, 214, 290, 293
Christo and Jean-Claude, *The Gates*, 260
Citizenship: infantile, 46; paranoia and, 46–48; representations of, 103–4; *See also* Consumerism; Oklahoma City National Memorial
Clifford, James, 20
Clinton, Bill, *133*, 148, 150, 153, 161; presidential administration of, 42
Cohen, Lizabeth, 15, 39, 89
Cold war, 20, 22, 39–40, 42, 74
Cole, Kenneth, 35–38, *36*, *37*, 65, 66
Columbine shootings, 5, 16–17; memorial for, 260
Comfort culture, 5–9, 22–24, 26, 36–38, 51, 64, 70, 90, 92, 94, 131–33, 153, 218, 291
Compensation, victim, 28, 163–64, 306 n.3. *See also* 9/11; Oklahoma City bombing
Consumerism: citizenship/national identity and, 6, 14–15, 26, 34, 39–42, 59, 64–70, 72–92, 135, 292–93; debt and, 298 n.48; home and, 40–41, 70–79, 90;

as innocent, 18, 25, 38, 41–42, 135, 218; at McVeigh execution, 33, 140, 148–50, *149*; memory and, 12, 95, 130–36, 211–18; from military technology, 41, 72, 85, 87–92; post-9/11, 17–18, 41–42, 53–73, 76–79, 92; of security, 4–5, 38–42, 70–92; as therapeutic, 14, 30

Consumers' republic (Cohen), 15, 39, 89

Contini, Anita, 261

Couture, Lise Anne, 235

Coventry Cathedral, 205, 207

Culture of fear, 5, 7, 32, 42, 48–49, 51

Cuomo, Andrew, 313 n.36

Cuozzo, Steve, 313 n.29

Daily Oklahoman, 97–98, *97*, 145

Davis, Mike, 58, 80

Death penalty: debate about, 140, 146–47, 150–51, 153–54, 156–57; legislation, 28, 153; vengeance and, 154–55. *See also* Execution

de Certeau, Michel, 202

Deering, John, 189, *191*

Defense Department, 79, 209

de Montebello, Philippe, 205

Denes, Agnes, 260

Department of Agriculture, 123

Department of Health and Human Services, 123

Department of Homeland Security (DHS), 71–76, *76, 77*, 194; color-coded alert system of, 73, *74*, 76

Department of Housing and Urban Development, 162

Department of Labor, 123

de Weldon, Felix, 106

Diller, Elizabeth, 211, 231

Disneyland, 9, 58, 298, 314 n.63

Disney World, 58

DNA identification, 179, 209–10

Doonesbury, 211, *212*

Doss, Erika, 126

Douglas, Mary, 179

Dowd, Maureen, 73

Downtown Study Group, 220

Doyeto, Clif, 101, *101*

Drug Enforcement Agency (DEA), 113, 123

Duct tape, 4, 8, 72–73, 78, 87, 291

Dunlap, David, 274

Dunne, Anthony, 83

Earth Liberation Front, 89

Eastwood, Clint, 189

eBay, 212, 215, 290

Ehrenreich, Barbara, 24

Eisenman, Peter, 219–21, *220, 221*, 240, *241*

Empire State Building, 169, 171, 306 n.7

Execution: consumerism at, 33, 140, 148–50, *149*; debate about, 140, 146–47, 150–51, 153–54, 156–57, 304 n.31; methods of, 139–40, 152–53; spectacle of, 143, 146–50, 152–55; witnesses at, 152–54. *See also* Death penalty; McVeigh, Timothy

FDNY. *See* New York City Fire Department

Federal Bureau of Investigation (FBI), 123, 130, 142, 150, 158–59, 208

Federal Emergency Management Agency (FEMA), 71, 194

Federal Employees Credit Union, 123

Fields, Chris, 98–99, *98*, 103, 188

Filler, Martin, 247

Final Home 44-Pocket Parka and Bear, 83, 84, *86*

Firefighters, 29, 31, 63, 66, 98–103, 109, 181–83, 188–96, 192–96, 218, 261, 263, 267–68, 270–71, 277–78, 296 n. 46; memorial to, 261, *262*, 277. *See also* New York City Fire Department

Flags, U.S., 54–57, *55, 56*, 64, 94–95, 105, 251, 282, 287, 290; global production of, 4, 54–56, 214; at Ground Zero, 183, 188–90, 194–96; at Oklahoma City

destruction of, 283; memorials in, 259–60; Radio Row district in, 231, 312 n.22; security in, 71, 75, 80; skyline of, 224, 231, 252; street economy of, 214–15; tourism in, 57–58. *See also* Fresh Kills landfill; Ground Zero; World Trade Center

New York City Department of City Planning, 208

New York City Department of Design and Construction, 181–82

New York City Fire Department (FDNY), 7, 132, 163, 173, 188, 195, 213, 308–9 n.56; race and, 195–96, 309 n.56. *See also* Firefighters

New York City Police Department (NYPD), 163, 196, 254; police in, 163, 165, 181, 183, 186, 190, 211, 215, 306 n.3

New Yorker, 222, *224,* 227, *228, 229, 230,* 280

New-York Historical Society, 180, 207

New York magazine, 221, 236, 255, 267–68

New York New York Casino, 174

New York Post, 158, 174, 234, 252–53, 266, 272, 274, 313 n.29

New York State Museum, 207

New York Stock Exchange, 81, 178

New York Times, 180, 204, 211, 231, 234, 250, 252, 258, 268–69, 280, 296 n.46, 309 n.70; ads in, 60–61; advertising campaign of, 64; columnists, 73, 157; critics, 53, 248, 254, 263; design proposals in, 219–20, 236, 238, 240; "Portraits of Grief" in, 174–76; reporters, 59, 274

Nichols, Terry, 43, 47, 95, 116, 123, 144, 157, 160–61, 305 n.50

9/11, 4, 5, 7–8, 10, 24, 31, 46, 52, 78, 155–56; analogies of, to Pearl Harbor, 16, 64; artifacts of, 205–8, 212, 310 n.85, 310 n.88; compensation and, 28, 163–64, 271, 306 n.3; connection to Oklahoma City bombing, 4–5, 61–62, *62,* 94, 128, 162–64, 167, 188, 203,

239, 285; designation of survivors of, 30; exceptionalism of, 165, 167, 169, 186–87, 198, 218, 230, 263, 279–80, 283, 290, 312 n.20; families of the dead of, 203, 208, 263, 267–72, 274, 277, 312 n.20 315 n.90; kitsch and, 19–21, 25, 52, 207, 215, 217, 264, 279, 285–86; media coverage of, 168–69, 172, 174, 186, 211; memorialization of, 1–4, 30, 33, 60–62, 136, 164, 172–75, 205–12, 215, 217–18, 221, 225–27, 240–43, 258–73, 275–79, 315 n.90; memorialization in comparison to Oklahoma City, 61–62, 104, 107, 109, 136, 172, 207, 210, 215, 259; missing posters of, 183–86, *184, 185,* 188, 207; photographs of, 29, 33, 80, 169–73, 186–98; reenactment of, 26, 29, 31, 218–22, 239–42, 247–48, 250–51, 264, 278–85; spectacle of, 170–74, 186, 201; souvenirs of, 1–4, 21, 24, 212–18, *214, 216,* 218, 250, 290, 293; survivors of, 28, 166, 180, 208; vengeance for, 31, 192; victims of, 7, 156, 200, 226, 261, 264–65, 267, 269–71, 274, 277, 306 n.3; widows of, 48, 267. *See also* American society; Ground Zero; Pentagon; Shanksville, Pennsylvania; World Trade Center

9/11 (documentary), 175

Nobel, Philip, 250, 252, 309 n.74, 313 n.36, 317 n.117

Noble, David, 15–16, 18, 234

Novak, Lorie, *173,* 184–85, *184, 185*

NOX, 235, *236*

Ockman, Joan, 312 n.20

Oklahoma City, 1–2, 16–18, 93, 95, 98, 100, 103–9, 118–20, 126–34, 136, 139–40, 142, 144, 147–48, 150–51, 153–54, 156–57, 162–64, 275, 284, 291–92; comparison of, to New York City, 128, 164, 215, 238; new federal building in, 81, 127–28, 255; population of, 104;

Photographs: of disaster, 97–100, 103; of executions, 152, 304 n.31; found at Ground Zero, 208; iconic, 96–103, 188–95, 284; as memorials, 120, 124, 168–69, 172–75, 178, 183–88, 207; placed at memorials, 105, 113, 115, 116, 173–74; tourism and, 186, 212–13. *See also* Ground Zero

Popular culture, 18, 21, 26, 29

Port Authority of New York and New Jersey, 201, 206–7, 212, 230–33, 238, 250–51, 254–55, 267, 272, 275, 277, 310 n.78

Port Authority Trans-Hudson (PATH) trains, 202, 213, 250–51

Porter, Charles, IV, 98–99, *98*

Postindustrialization, 10, 43, 49–50, 214, 231–32

Postmodernism, 52–53

Powell, Secretary of State Colin, 66, 198

Preparedness, 47, 70–79, 90, 92; chic, 85. *See also* Security

Prisons, U.S., 32, 42, 49–51, 71, 92, 139–40, 144–45, 147–48, 161; supermax, 50–51, 144–45. *See also* Abu Ghraib; Death penalty; Execution

Protetch, Max. *See* Max Protetch Gallery

Purcell, Philip J., 61

Raby, Fiona, 83

Radko, Christopher, 215

Ramirez, Michael, 162, *163*

Rand, Erica, 295 n.1

Rapaille, G. Clotaire, 86–87

Rashad, Hani, 235

Reagan, Ronald, 44

Record, The (Bergen), 188, 193–94

Reeder, Frederick, 81, *82*

Reenactment/repetition: in architecture, 9, 218, 284; of iconic images, 96–103, 188–95, 284; of Iwo Jima, 188–95; of 9/11, 26, 29, 31, 218–22, 239–42, 247–48, 250–51, 264, 278–85; of

Oklahoma City, 29, 96–103, 119–21, 284; in popular culture, 29; in souvenirs, 9, 26, 28, 218, 284; trauma and, 26–32

Reflecting Absence. See World Trade Center memorial

Regenhard, Sally, 268

Reno, Attorney General Janet, 145, 150

Rich, Frank, 157

Ridge, Tom, 73, *74*

Right-wing militia groups, 5, 42–48, 51, 78, 123, 143, 158–61, 297 n.19

Rockefeller, David, 231, 316 n.102

Rockwell, Norman, 64

Rogers, Richard, 256, *257*

Roosevelt, Theodore, 6

Rosario, Kevin, 200

Ross Barney and Jankowski Architects, 127

Rothstein, Edward, 53

Rubins, Nancy, 227, *228*

Ruby Ridge, Idaho, 44, 157

Rukeyser, Louis, 224

Rumsfeld, Secretary of Defense Donald, 89, 208

Safe: Design Takes on Risk, 82–85

St. Paul's Chapel, 1, 173, 211

Salvation Army, 6

Sanders, James, 259

Sarat, Austin, 150, 154–55, 304 n.31

Saudi Arabia, 66, 151

Scanlon, Jennifer, 57

Scarry, Elaine, 78

Schwarzenegger, Arnold, 88

Scofidio, Ricardo, 211, 231

Second Amendment, 44

Secret Service, 123

Security, 4–5, 32, 51, 298 n.46; aesthetics of, 32, 72, 79–85, 272–73; alert system, 73, *74*, 76; architecture of, 70, 80–82, 127–28, 252–56; bollards, 4, 81–82, *82*, 128, 256, 279; consumerism of, 4–5,

Tsumura, Kosuke, 83, *86*
Tucker, Karla Faye, 147
Twin towers. *See* World Trade Center
Twin Towers Fund, 63

Uchitelle, Louis, 59
United Airlines: advertising, 64, 67, *68*;
    Flight 93 of, 78, 156, 167, 260, 271
United States. *See* American society
U.S. Holocaust Museum, 14, 104, 120,
    134, 303 n.56
USA PATRIOT Act, 48
USS *New York*, 206

Van Valkenburgh, Michael, 268, 316 n.102
Via Group, 255
Victims' Rights Clarification Act, 153
Victims' rights movement, 28, 153,
    155–56, 161
Vidal, Gore, 145–46
Vietnam, 211
Vietnam Veterans Memorial, 14, 104–5,
    111, 117, 133, 195, 263, 269, 271–72
Vietnam War, 13, 16, 106, 210
Vietnam Women's Memorial, 106
Viñoly, Rafael, 238, *239*

Waco, Texas, 44, 95, 157–59, 291
Walker, Peter, 265, 267
Wallace, Mike, 312 n.22
Wal-Mart, 54, 57–58, 258
Warhol, Andy, 284
Warner, Michael, 114
Washington, D.C., 46, 54, 71, 80–81,
    103–4, 111, 120, 195, 259, 292
Washington Monument, 111
Wasserman, Dan, 132, *134*
Watkins, Kari, 118, 122, 128, 130, 136–37,
    164, 303 n.58
Watts, Stan, 188
Weaver, Randy, 44
Weijers, Wouter, 317 n.112
Welch, Bud, 156–57, 159

Welch, Julie, 157
Weschler, Lawrence, 196
Wieseltier, Leon, 234
Williams, William Appleman, 38
Williamsburg, Virginia, 9
Willis, Susan, 54, 90
Windows on the World restaurant,
    245, 275
Winuk, Glenn, 261
Wolf, Charles, 274
World Financial Center, 238, 261
World Trade Center, 100, 109; absence
    of, 29, 33, 169–70, 221–30, 235–42;
    Building 7 of, 190, 255; design of,
    201–2, 222, 231–32; destruction of,
    2, 4, 60–62, 156, 167–68, 175–76,
    181, 183, 201, 204, 219–20, 287–90;
    footprints of, 199–205, 219, 263–65,
    273, 310 n.78; history of, 127, 201, 203,
    213, 231–32, 277, 306 n.7, 312 n.22;
    photographs of, 196, 212; reenactment
    of, 219–22, 224–31, *224–26, 228–30, 235,*
    236, *237,* 239–41, *239, 241,* 287–90, 293,
    312 n.10; souvenirs of, 1–4, 26, 212–15,
    216, 217; steel beams of, 182–83, 206–7,
    260; underground mall of, 202, 257. *See
    also* Ground Zero; 9/11; World Trade
    Center bombing; World Trade Center
    memorial
World Trade Center bombing (1993), 81,
    128, 232; memorial to, 259
World Trade Center memorial, 30, 201,
    210, 218, 256, 258–59, 261, 265–73, *265,*
    266, 270, 276, 279; comparison of, to the
    Oklahoma City National Memorial,
    210; cost of, 269; design of, 265–73,
    279, 317 n.112; design competition
    for, 261–65, 316 nn.100, 102; naming
    in, 265, 269–71; security at, 272–73.
    See also World Trade Center Memorial
    Museum
World Trade Center Memorial
    Foundation, 251, 267–68, 275

Marita Sturken is a professor in the Department of Media, Culture, and Communication at New York University. She is the author of *Tangled Memories: The Vietnam War, the AIDS Epidemic, and the Politics of Remembering* and the coauthor of *Practices of Looking: An Introduction to Visual Culture.*

Library of Congress Cataloging-in-Publication Data
Sturken, Marita
Tourists of history : memory, kitsch, and consumerism from Oklahoma City to
Ground Zero/Marita Sturken.
p. cm.
Includes bibliographical references and index.
ISBN 978-0-8223-4103-1 (cloth : alk. paper)
ISBN 978-0-8223-4122-2 (pbk. : alk. paper)
1. Collective memory—United States. 2. Psychic trauma—Social aspects—United
States. 3. Souvenirs (Keepsakes)—Social aspects—United States. 4. Consumption
(Economics)—Social aspects—United States. 5. National characteristics, American.
6. Popular culture—United States. 7. Oklahoma City Federal Building Bombing,
Oklahoma City, Okla., 1995. 8. September 11 Terrorist Attacks, 2001. I. Title.
E169.12.S8495 2007
973.93—dc22   2007018101